ATLA

CHINA

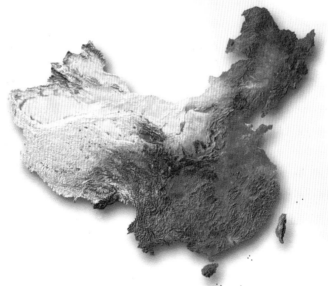

presented to :
Dave
By : zHucHAo.   Enjoy it 5
2009. 2. 9
祝你全家 健康、幸福、平安.
束超.

SINOMAPS PRESS

图书在版编目（CＩP）数据

中国地图册／中国地图出版社编著.—北京：中国地图

出版社，2007.11

ISBN 978－7－5031－4477－6

Ⅰ.中… Ⅱ.中… Ⅲ.地图集－中国 Ⅳ.K992

中国版本图书馆CIP数据核字（2007）第134961号

ATLAS OF CHINA

Published and distributed by SinoMaps Press
(3 Baizhifang Xijie, Beijing, 100054 China)
148×210   6 Printed sheets
1st Edition,3rd Impression April. 2008
ISBN 978-7-5031-4477-6/K • 2724   Impression 5001-15000
GS (2007)1297   Price: RMB 40.00

The national boundaries of China in this Atlas are drawn after the
1:4 000 000 Relief Map of the People's Republic of China,
published by SinoMaps Press in 1989

Printed in the People's Republic of China

CONTENTS

INTRODUCTORY MAPS

Administrative Divisions 6-7

Relief 8-9

Ethnic Groups 10-11

Population 12-13

Climate 14-15

Communications（Ⅰ） 16-17

Communications（Ⅱ） 18-19

Tourist Resources 20-21

PROVINCIAL MAPS

Beijing Municipality.. 22-23

Tianjin Municipality 24-25

Hebei Province 26-27

Shanxi Province 28-29

Nei Mongol (Inner Mongolia) Autonomous Region 30-31

Liaoning Province 32-33

Jilin Province 34-35

Heilongjiang Province 36-37

Shanghai Municipality 38-39

Jiangsu Province 40-41

Zhejiang Province 42-43

Anhui Province 44-45

Fujian Province 46-47

Jiangxi Province 48-49

Shandong Province 50-51

Henan Province 52-53

Hubei Province 54-55

Hunan Province 56-57

Guangdong Province 58-59

Guangxi Zhuang Autonomous Region 60-61

CONTENTS

LEGEND

Provincial Map

Settlement

⊛	**BEIJING**	Capital
◎	**Taiyuan**	Province-level administrative centre
◉	Baoding	Prefecture-level administrative centre
⊙	Mancheng Daxing Qu	County-level administrative centre (Major city outside China)
○	Shenxing	Town, village
◎	**SEOUL**	Foreign capital
	Jishou	Administrative centre of autonomous prefectures, prefectures and leagues

Communications

Under construction	Railway
Under construction	Expressway
	Main road
	Other road
✈	Airport
⚓	Port

Boundaries

Undefined	National boundary
	Boundary of province, autonomous region and municipality
	Boundary of special adminstrative region
	Regional boundary
+ + + + + + + + + + + +	Military demarcation line

Hydrography

	Coastline
	Perennial river, waterfall
	Underground river
	Seasonal river, dry river
	Reservoir, dam
	Lake
	Seasonal lake
	Canal
	Irrigation canal
● ♀ ⊚	Well, spring, hot spring

Topography & Others

	Desert
◌ ◌ ◔ ◌	Coral reefs
	Swamp, salt swamp
✵	Volcano
▲ Dahaituo Shan 2241	Peak and elevation (m)
✕	Pass
⌣⌣⌣⌣⌣	Great Wall
⊙	World Heritage
•	Important scenic area

City Map

	Street and block	★	Provincial government	◉	Stadium, gymnasium
	Park, green belt	★	Municipal government	■	Olympic venue
		⬓	Hotel	⟹	Bridge
Under construction	Expressway	⊖	Restaurant		Bus station
	Railway, station	⌂	School	✈	Airport
Under construction	Light Rail	◇	Hospital	▲	Peak
	Maglev	⊟	Bank	⚓	Port
Under construction	Subway	✉	Post office	⊙	World Heritage
	City wall	✹	Museum	•	Place of interest
	Cable car	⛨	Theatre	∘	Others

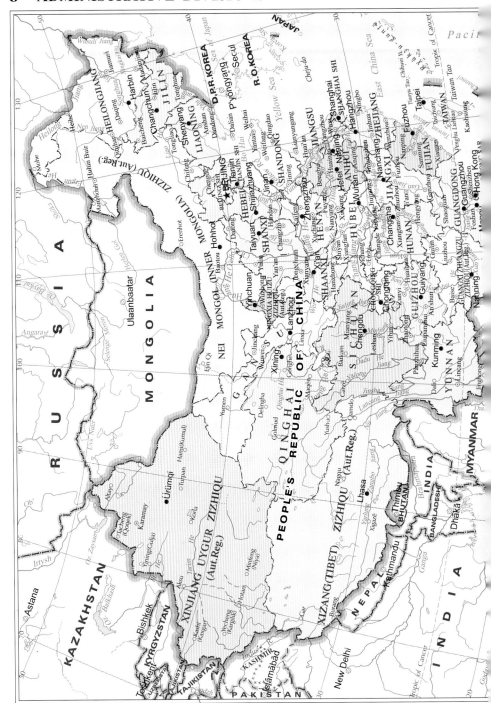

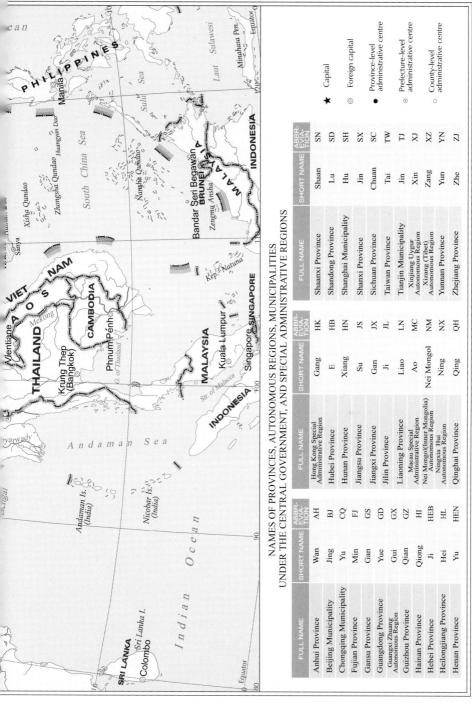

Capital
Foreign capital
Province-level administrative centre
Prefecture-level administrative centre
County-level administrative centre

NAMES OF PROVINCES, AUTONOMOUS REGIONS, MUNICIPALITIES UNDER THE CENTRAL GOVERNMENT, AND SPECIAL ADMINISTRATIVE REGIONS

FULL NAME	SHORT NAME	ABBREVIATION	FULL NAME	SHORT NAME	ABBREVIATION	FULL NAME	SHORT NAME	ABBREVIATION
Anhui Province	Wan	AH	Hong Kong Special Administrative Region	Gang	HK	Shaanxi Province	Shaan	SN
Beijing Municipality	Jing	BJ	Hubei Province	E	HB	Shandong Province	Lu	SD
Chongqing Municipality	Yu	CQ	Hunan Province	Xiang	HN	Shanghai Municipality	Hu	SH
Fujian Province	Min	FJ	Jiangsu Province	Su	JS	Shanxi Province	Jin	SX
Gansu Province	Gan	GS	Jiangxi Province	Gan	JX	Sichuan Province	Chuan	SC
Guangdong Province	Yue	GD	Jilin Province	Ji	JL	Taiwan Province	Tai	TW
Guangxi Zhuang Autonomous Region	Gui	GX	Liaoning Province	Liao	LN	Tianjin Municipality	Jin	TJ
Guizhou Province	Qian	GZ	Macau Special Administrative Region	Ao	MC	Xinjiang Uygur Autonomous Region	Xin	XJ
Hainan Province	Qiong	HI	Nei Mongol(Inner Mongolia) Autonomous Region	Nei Mongol	NM	Xizang (Tibet) Autonomous Region	Zang	XZ
Hebei Province	Ji	HEB	Ningxia Hui Autonomous Region	Ning	NX	Yunnan Province	Yun	YN
Heilongjiang Province	Hei	HL	Qinghai Province	Qing	QH	Zhejiang Province	Zhe	ZJ
Henan Province	Yu	HEN						

SCALE 1 : 29 000 000

0   290   580   870   1160km

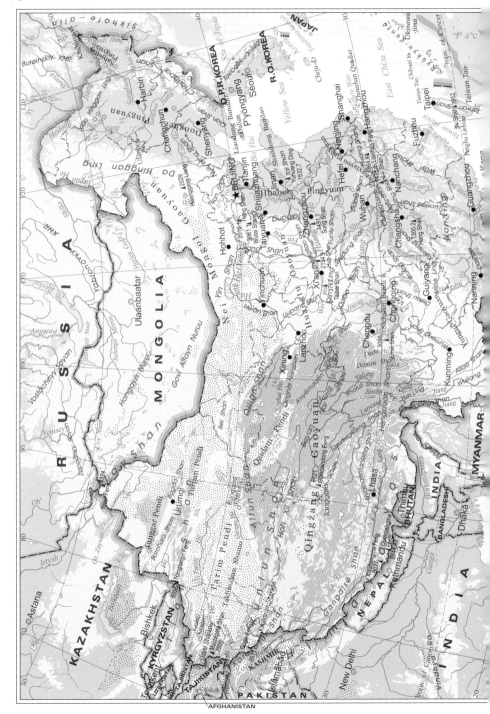

Map labels (selection): Ocean, Luzon, Mindanao, PHILIPPINES, Manila, Mindanao Pen., Equator, Huangyan Dao, Visayan Is., Laut Sulawesi, INDONESIA, Xisha Qundao, Zhongsha Qundao, South China Sea, Palawan, Sulu Sea, Nansha Qundao, Kalimantan, Bandar Seri Begawan, BRUNEI, MALAYSIA, Zengmu Ansha, Hainan Dao, Wuzhi Shan 1867, VIET NAM, LAOS, Vientiane, Mekong, THAILAND, CAMBODIA, Krung Thep (Bangkok), Phnum Pénh, Kep. Natuna, Kuala Lumpur, MALAYSIA, SINGAPORE, Singapore, Str. of Malacca, Malay Pen., Pulau Sumatera, INDONESIA, Andaman Sea, Mergui Arch., Andaman Is. (India), Nicobar Is. (India), Bay of Bengal, Indian Ocean, SRI LANKA, Sri Lanka I., Colombo, Equator

MAJOR MOUNTAINS

NAME	MAIN PEAK	ALTITUDE(m)
Himalayas	Qomolangma Feng	8 844.43
Karakorum Shan	Qogir Feng	8 611
Kunlun Shan	Kongur Shan	7 649
Daxue Shan	Gongga Shan	7 556
Hengduan Shan	Yulong Xueshan	5 596
Tian Shan	Tomür Feng	7 443
Nyainqêntanglha Shan	Nyainqêntanglha Feng	7 162
Gangdisê Shan	Loinbo Kangri	7 095
Tanggula Shan	Geladaindong Feng	6 621
Hoh Xil Shan	Kangzhag Ri	6 305
Qilian Shan	Qilian Shan	5 547
Bayan Har Shan	Nyainboyuzê Feng	5 369
Altay Shan	Youyi Feng	4 374

MAJOR MOUNTAINS

NAME	MAIN PEAK	ALTITUDE(m)
Taiwan Shan	Yu Shan	3 952
Qin Ling	Taibai Shan	3 767
Taihang Shan	Xiaowutai Shan	2 882
Yin Shan	Koh Baxig	2 364
Wuyi Shan	Huanggang Shan	2 157
Nan Ling	Mao'er Shan	2 141
Da Hinggan Ling	Huanggang Liang	2 029

MAJOR PLAINS

NAME	AREA (sq km)	ALTITUDE(m)
Dongbei Pingyuan	350 000	<200
Huabei Pingyuan	300 000	<100
Changjiang Zhongxiayou Pingyuan	200 000	<50
Zhujiang Sanjiaozhou Pingyuan	11 000	<20

MAJOR PLATEAUS

NAME	AREA(sq km)	ALTITUDE(m)
Qingzang Gaoyuan	2 500 000	3000~5000
Nei Mongol Gaoyuan	1 000 000	1000~1500
Yungui Gaoyuan	500 000	1000~2000
Huangtu Gaoyuan	500 000	800~2000

MAJOR BASINS

NAME	AREA(sq km)	ALTITUDE(m)
Tarim Pendi	560 000	778~1300
Junggar Pendi	380 000	500~1000
Qaidam Pendi	255 000	2600~3000
Sichuan Pendi	200 000	300~700

Height(m)

Icecap 5000 3000 0 200 500 3000 6000 3000 3000

SCALE 1 : 29 000 000   0   290   580   870   1160km

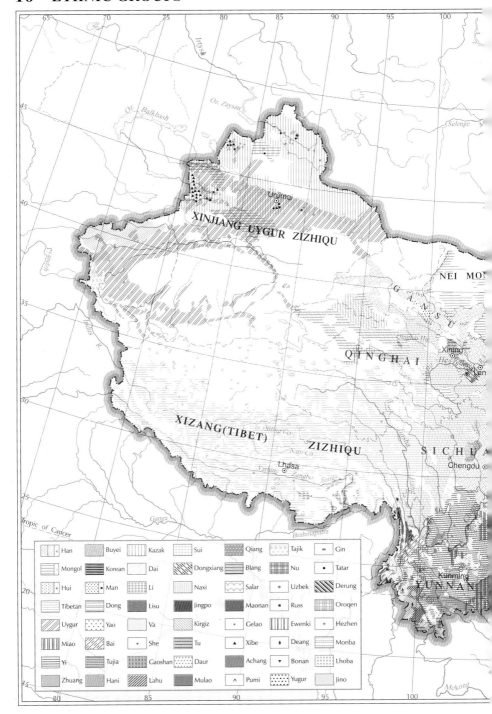

HEILONGJIANG

Harbin

Changchun

Shenyang

JILIN

LIAONING

INNER MONGOLIA) ZIZHIQU

Hohhot

BEIJING SHI
BEIJING

Tianjin TIANJIN SHI
Bo Hai

HEBEI

Taiyuan Shijiazhuang

SHANXI

Jinan

SHANDONG

Yellow Sea

SHAANXI Zhengzhou

Xi'an HENAN JIANGSU

ANHUI Nanjing

Hefei SHANGHAI SHI

Shanghai

HUBEI Hangzhou

Wuhan

ZHEJIANG

ongqing
GING

Nanchang

Changsha JIANGXI

HUNAN FUJIAN

Fuzhou

Taipei

TAIWAN Tropic of Cancer

GUANGXI ZHUANGZU GUANGDONG
ZIZHIQU
Guangzhou

Nanning Macau Hong Kong
MACAU SAR HONG KONG SAR

Beibu Gulf Haikou

HAINAN

South China Sea

Sea of Japan

Pacific Ocean

East China Sea

Nanning Guangzhou
GUANGXI ZHUANGZU Macau Hong Kong TAIWAN
ZIZHIQU MACAU SAR HONG KONG SAR
GUANGDONG

Haikou
HAINAN

South China Sea

SOUTH CHINA
SEA ISLANDS
1 : 44 000 000

SCALE 1 : 22 000 000

0   220   440   660   880km

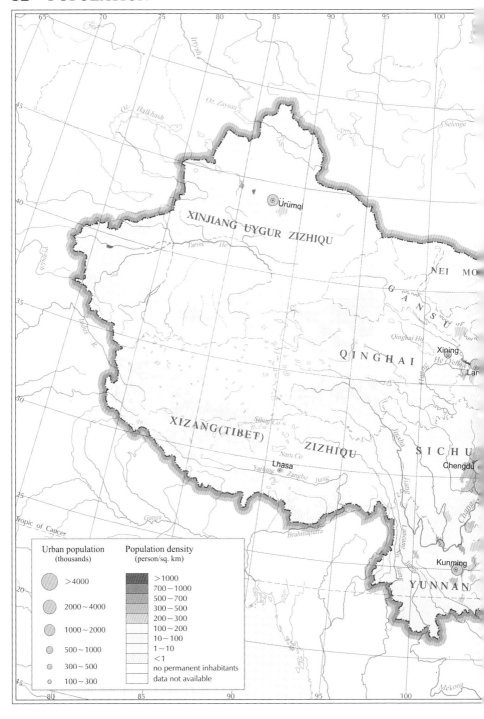

Urban population
(thousands)

- >4000
- 2000~4000
- 1000~2000
- 500~1000
- 300~500
- 100~300

Population density
(person/sq. km)

- >1000
- 700~1000
- 500~700
- 300~500
- 200~300
- 100~200
- 10~100
- 1~10
- <1
- no permanent inhabitants
- data not available

SCALE 1 : 22 000 000 0 220 440 660 880km

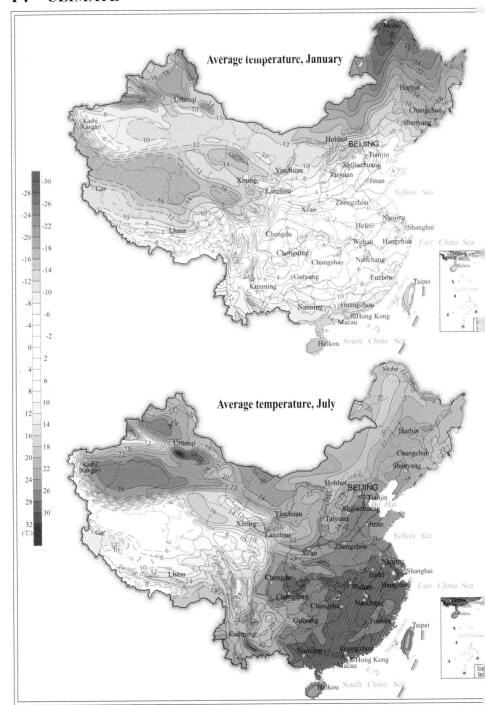

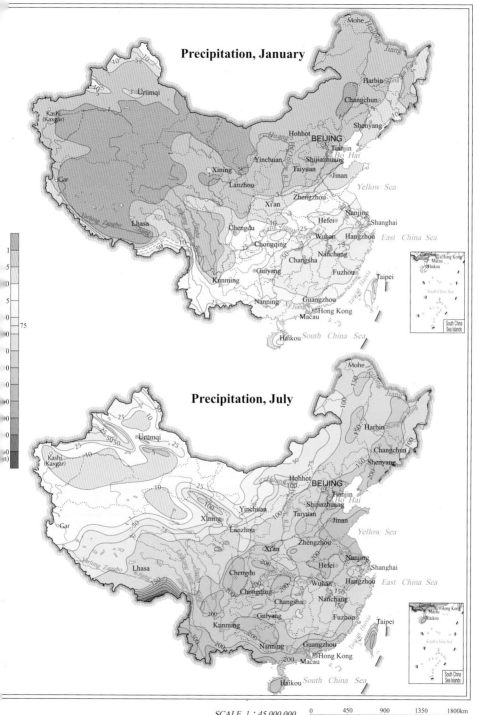

SCALE 1 : 45 000 000

0   450   900   1350   1800km

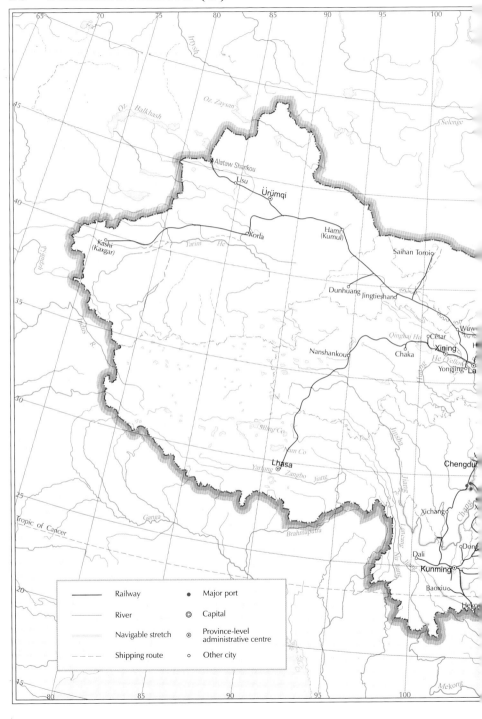

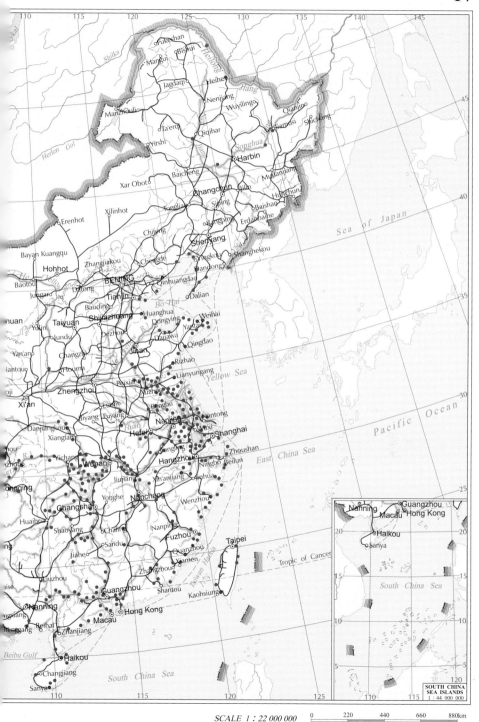

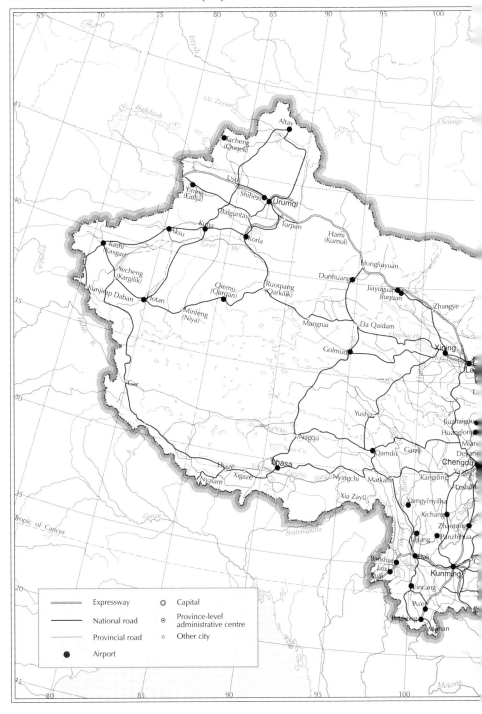

Expressway
National road
Provincial road
● Airport
◎ Capital
⊙ Province-level administrative centre
○ Other city

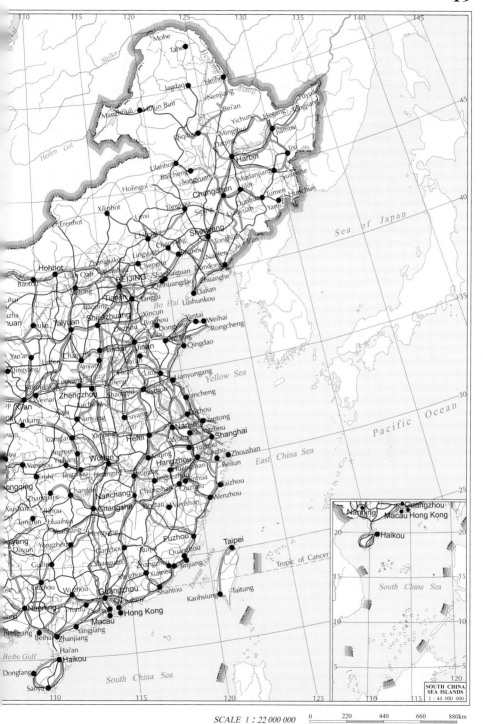

Mohe
Tahe
Jagdaqi
Heihe
Nenjiang
Bei'an
Yichun
Hegang
Fuyuan
Tongjiang
Manzhouli
Hulun Buir
Qiqihar
Mingshui
Daqing
Jiamusi
Harbin
Jixi
Ulanhot
Baicheng
Songyuan
Mudanjiang
Suifenhe
Holingol
Changchun
Jilin
Xilinhot
Tongliao
Siping
Dunhua
Tumen
Hunchun
Erenhot
Linxi
Shenyang
Tonghua
Yanji
Chifeng
Jinzhou
Dandong
Naifen
Zhangjiakou
Chengde
Hohhot
Ulan Qab
Shanhaiguan
Huanghe
Baotou
Datong
BEIJING
Qinhuangdao
Yulin
Taiyuan
Tianjin
Tanggu
Dalian
Shijiazhuang
Baoding
Xincun
Lüshunkou
Binzhou
Yantai
Weihai
Zibo
Dongying
Rongcheng
Yan'an
Handan
Jinan
Qingdao
Qingyang
Anyang
Heze
Linyi
Lianyungang
Zhengzhou
Xuchang
Yancheng
Xian
Weinan
Luoyang
Xiangyang
Nanyang
Fuyang
Nantong
Ankang
Xinyang
Hefei
Nanjing
Shanghai
Wanzhou
Yichang
Wuhan
Wuxi
Suzhou
Hangzhou
Ningbo
Zhoushan
Lishui
Jingzhou
Hengshui
Jiujiang
Beilun
Zhangjiajie
Changde
Nanchang
Quzhou
Taizhou
Xiushan
Jishou
Changsha
Xiangtan
Wenzhou
Tongren
Huaihua
Shaoyang
Hengyang
Fuzhou
Taipei
Duyun
Yongzhou
Ganzhou
Quanzhou
Guilin
Shaoguan
Zhangzhou
Xiamen
Jinjiang
Liuzhou
Wuzhou
Guangzhou
Shantou
Kaohsiung
Taitung
Nanning
Yulin
Macau
Hong Kong
Beihai
Zhanjiang
Yangjiang
Hai'an
Haikou
Dongfang
Sanya

Sea of Japan
Yellow Sea
East China Sea
Pacific Ocean
South China Sea
Bo Hai
Beibu Gulf
Tropic of Cancer

SOUTH CHINA
SEA ISLANDS
1 : 44 000 000
Nanning
Guangzhou
Macau Hong Kong
Haikou
South China Sea

SCALE 1 : 22 000 000

0   220   440   660   880km

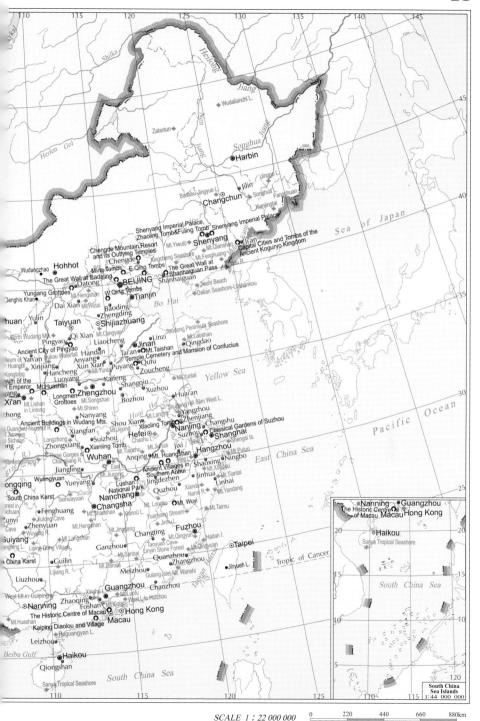

SCALE 1 : 22 000 000   0   220   440   660   880km

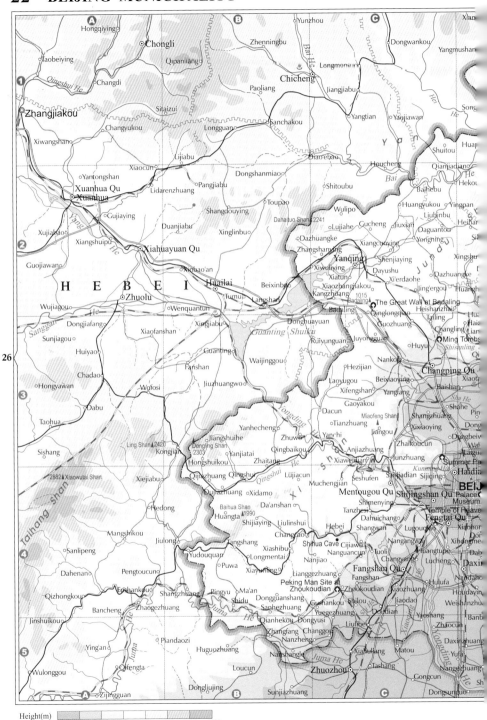

Height(m)

0 50 200 500 1000 1500 2000 3000

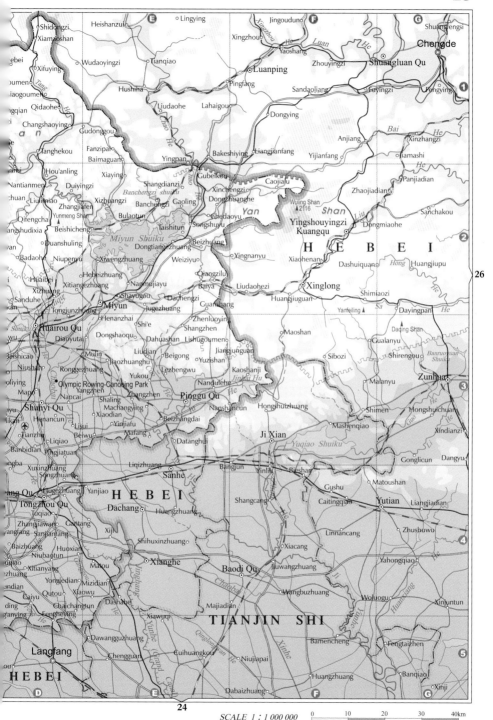

SCALE 1 : 1 000 000   0   10   20   30   40km

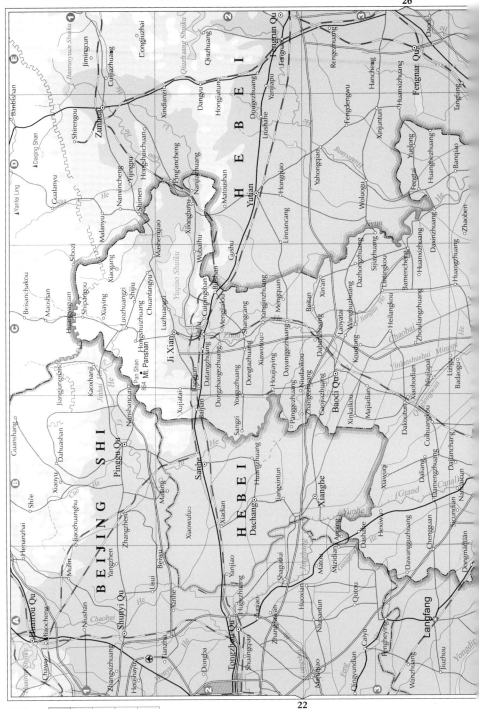

Height(m)

0   50   200   500   1000   1500

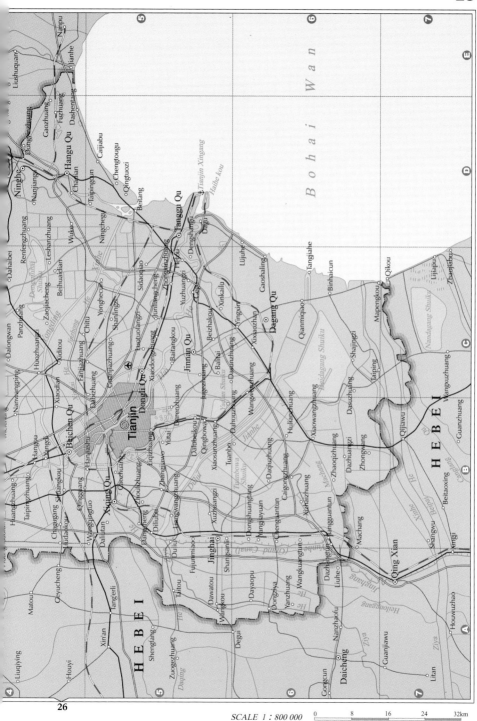

B o h a i   W a n

HEBEI

Tianjin

HEBEI

SCALE 1 : 800 000

| 0 | 8 | 16 | 24 | 32km |

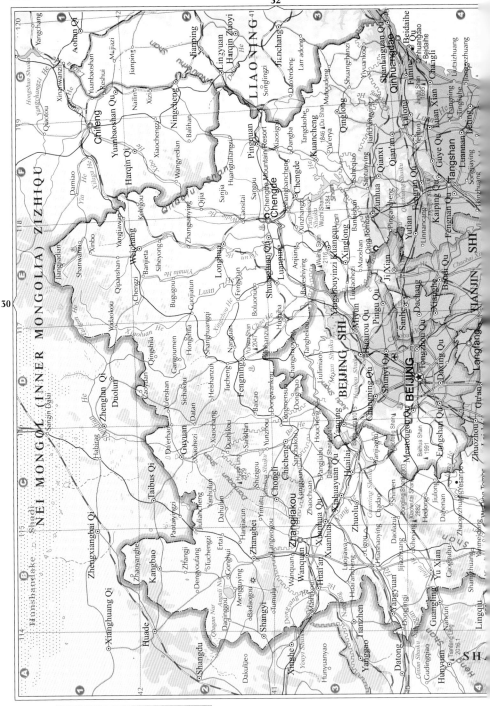

Height(m)

| 0 | 50 | 200 | 500 | 1000 | 1500 | 2000 | 3000 |

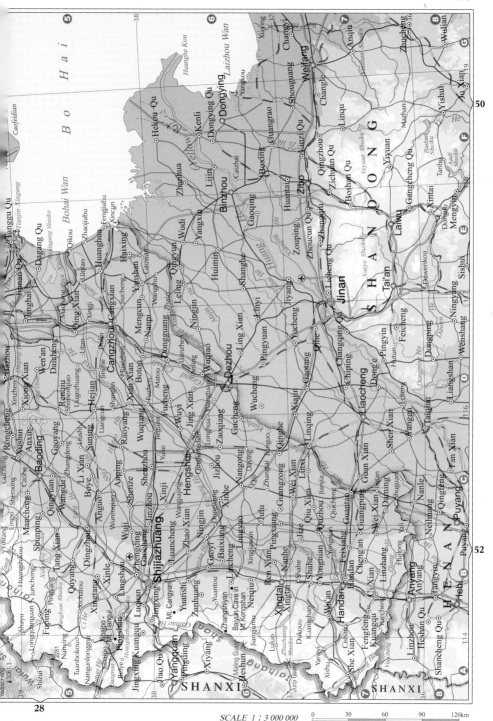

SCALE 1 : 3 000 000   0   30   60   90   120km

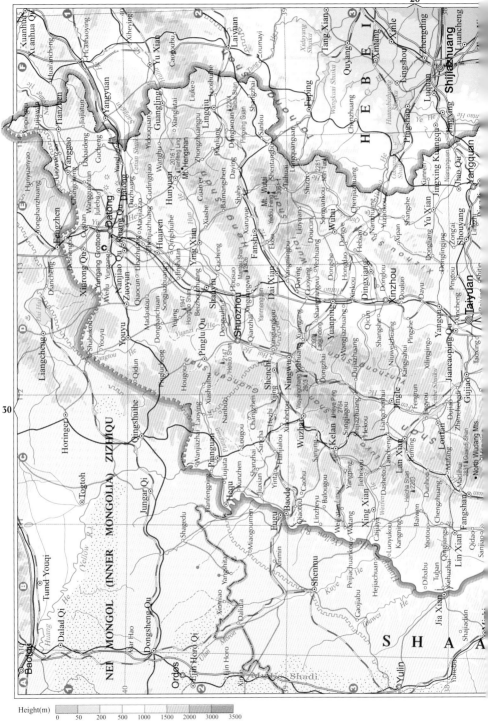

Height(m)

0   50   200   500   1000   1500   2000   3000   3500

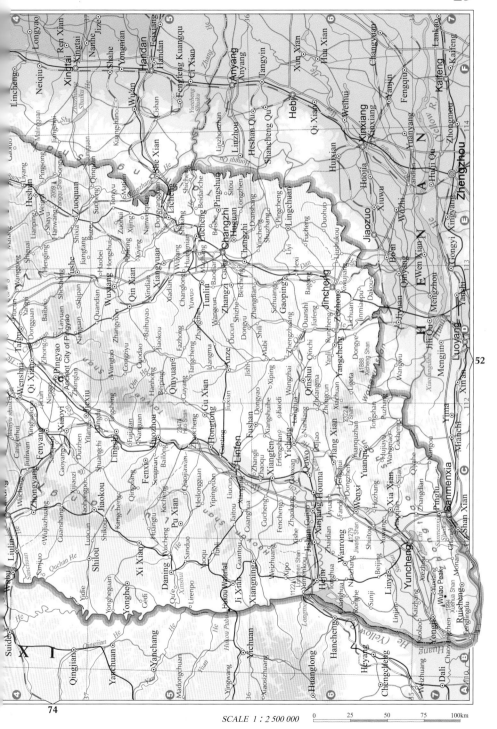

SCALE 1 : 2 500 000

0   25   50   75   100km

52

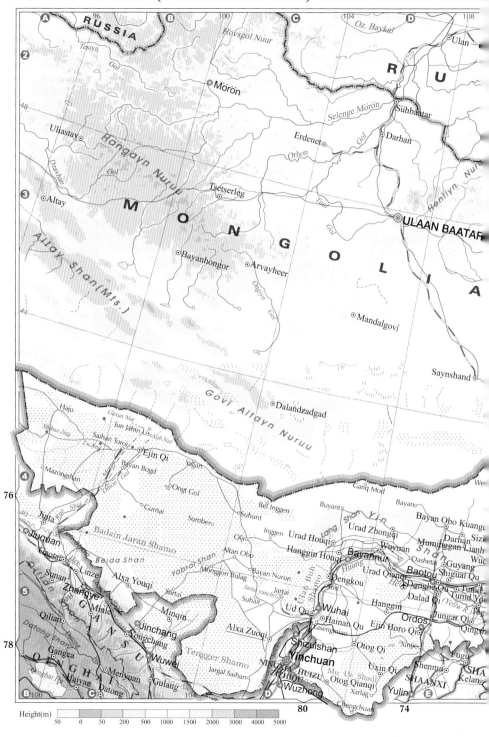

Height(m)

50 0 50 200 500 1000 1500 2000 3000 4000 5000

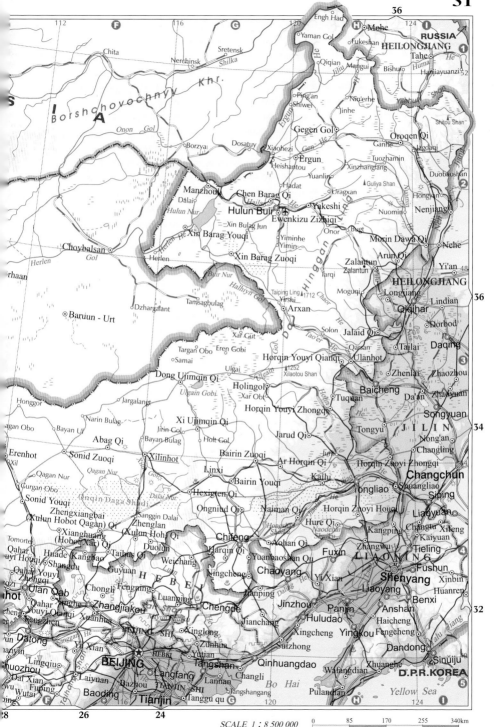

0   85   170   255   340km

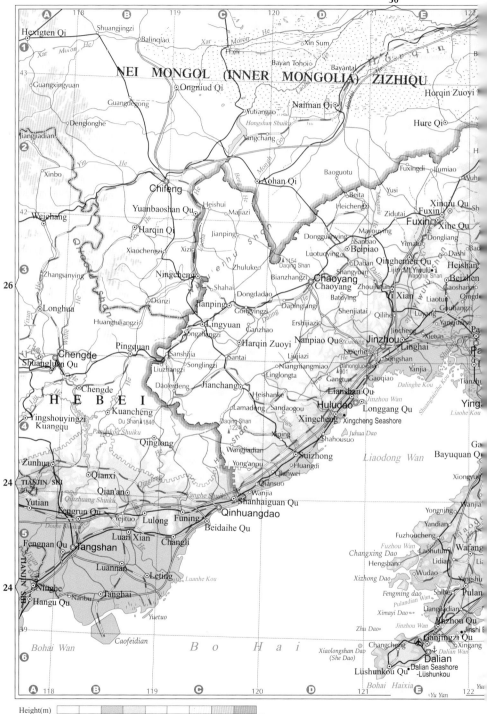

Height(m)
200 50 0 50 200 500 1000 1500 2000 3000

SCALE 1 : 3 000 000

0   30   60   90   120km

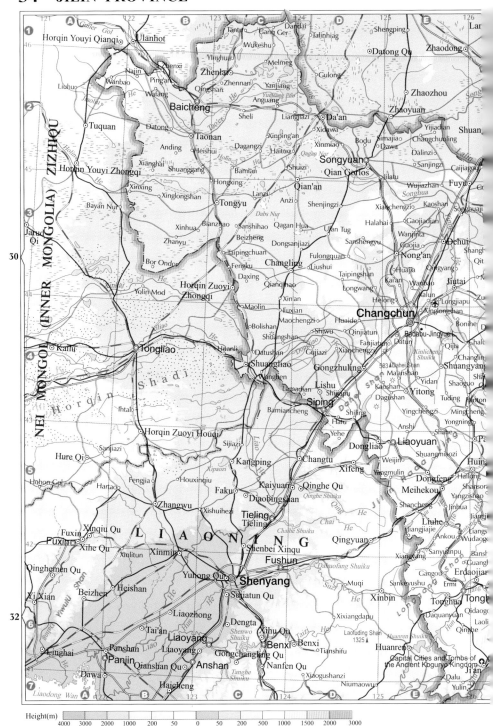

Height(m)
| 4000 | 3000 | 2000 | 1000 | 200 | 50 | 0 | 50 | 200 | 500 | 1000 | 1500 | 2000 | 3000 |

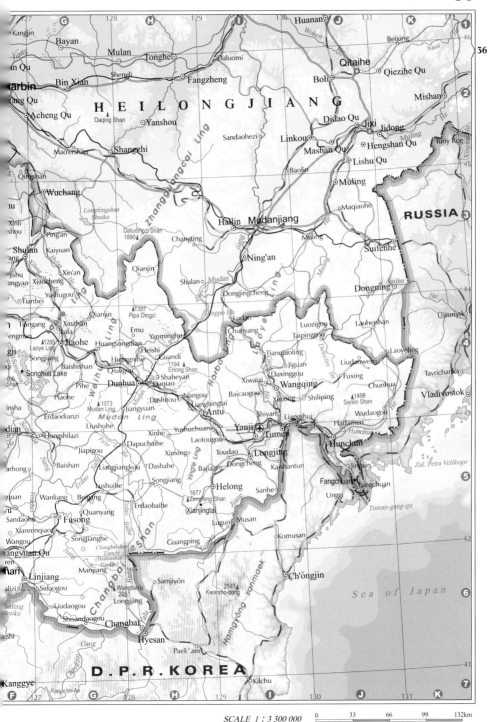

SCALE 1 : 3 300 000

0 33 66 99 132km

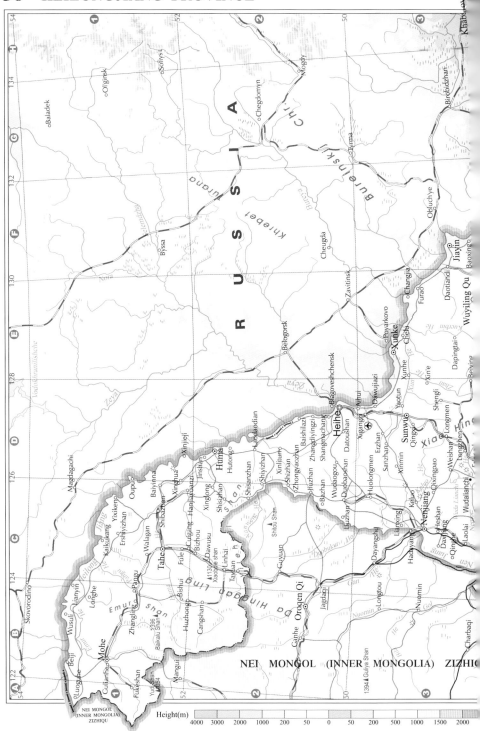

Height(m)

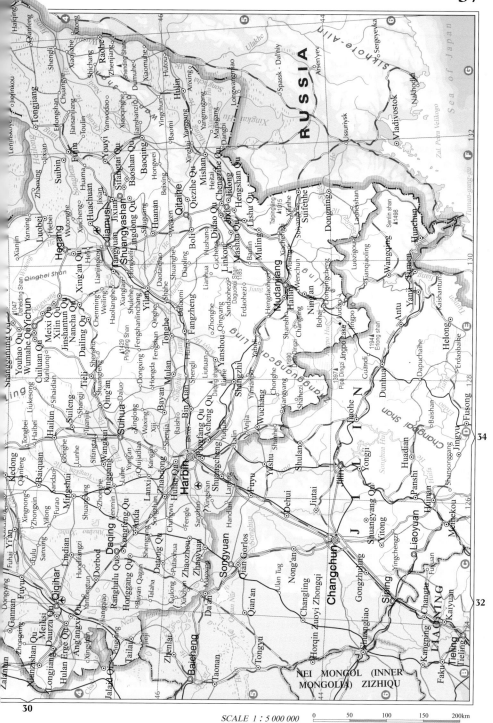

SCALE 1 : 5 000 000

0   50   100   150   200km

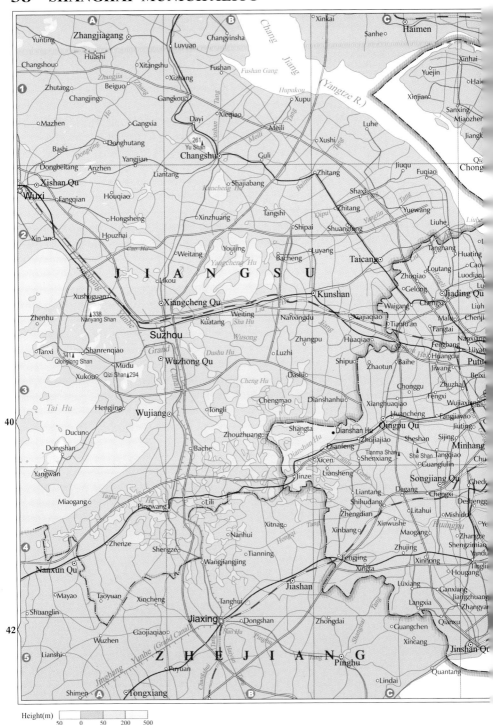

Height(m)

50 0 50 200 500

D · A · N · G · S · U

Jiulong
Xiangyang
Xingang
Beixin
Qidong
Xingken
Huifeng
Daxing
Hulping
Xinglong Sha
Dongfeng
Changjiang
Lianxinggang
Qianjin
Panlong
Xinmin
Maqiao
Hexing
Xinhe
Beibu
Dao
Zhuqiao
Nanbu
Xianghua
Niupeng
Baozhengang
Chenjia
Qingcao Sha
Shitou Sha
Panjiasha
Baoshan Qu
Panshi
Changxing Dao
Wusong Kou
Sanchagang
Fenghuang
Qianwei
Lingqiao
Majiagang
Fumin
Wusong
Gaoqiao
Hengsha Dao
Gaodong
Xinmin
Jiangwan
Donggou
Culu
Yuansha
Fengle
Yangpu Qu
ei Qu
Luhang
Heqing
anghai
Pudong Xinqu
Bailonggang
Airport
Zhangjiang
Cailu
u Qu
Beicai
Chuansha
Huangpu Jiang
Hengmian
Shizhen
uong
Sanlin
Zhoupu
Ljuzao
Pudong Airport
Waxie
Zhuqiao
aphang
Chenhang
Shenzhuang
Yancang
Chaoyang
Wujing
Xiasha
Nanhui Qu
Zhonggang
Hangtou
Luhui
Xuanqiao
Huanglu
inhang
Jinhuiqiao
Xinchang
Sanduno
Wanxiang
Tairi
Xinshi
Datuan
Qixian
Touqiao
Situan
Machang
Donghai
Qingcun
Fengcheng
Nisheng
Fengxian Qu
Tangwai
Wusi
Luchaogang
Guangming
Qianqiao
Liaoyuan
Zhelin
Fengxin
ojing
Donghai Bridge
Daji Shan
Jinji shan
Beidingxing
Shengsi
ui
Xiaoji Shan
Sijiao Shan
jin Shan
ajin Shan
Maji Shan
ajin Shan
Xiaoyang Shan
Xugong Dao
Shengsi Liedao
Hangzhou Wan

Yellow Sea

Changjiang

She Shan

Kou

East China Sea

Daji Yang

SCALE 1 : 800 000   0   8   16   24   32km

50

50

SHANDONG

Cao Xian · Shan Xian · Huankou · Longgu · Shunhe · Yangtun · Weishan · Shizhong Qu · Cangshan

Shunhe · Datun · Zaozhuang

Qingguji · Feng Xian · Pei Xian · S H A N D O N G

Maliangji · Huashan · Tai'erzhuang Qu · Tancheng · Shuangdian · Bai

Shangqiu · Songlou · Jing'an · Guanhu · Donghai

Shuiyang Qu · Yucheng · Dangshan · Zhengji · Jiawang Qu · Biapang · Ahu · Qingyi

H E N A N · Huangkou · Maocun · Xuzhou · Nianzhuang · Pizhou · Xinyi · Gaoliu · Miaotou

Wujiang · Xiayi · Xiao Xian · Tongshan · Shanji · Tushan · Wangzhuang · Yanji · Shuya

Cuoyang · Fangcun · Shuanggou · Gupi · Longjio · Zhangji

Huaibei · Duji Qu · Zaohe · Jingtou · Huji

Yongcheng · Suixi · Lieshan Qu · Wangji · Suqian · Suyu Qu · Wangji · Jia

Bozhou · Tiefosi · Yugou · Suining · Yanghe

Fuli · Daliji · Siyang

Yinji · Dazhuang · Guiren · Likou · Huaiy

Longshan · Suzhou · Jieji · Hua

Guoyang · Caoshi · Lingbi · Si Xian · Sihong · Peiwei · Hua

Niqiu · Zhaoji · Shangtang · Bancheng · Chenghe · Huangji · Ho

Zhangcun · He · Guzhen · Shuanggou · Laozishan · Ba

Taihe · Mengcheng · Xinmaqiao · Qianyao · Jiangba

Lixin · Wuhe · Baoji · Guanzhen · Weiqiao · Jinh

A N H U I · Gupei · Huayuanzui · Xuyi · Maba

Zhumadian · Huaiyuan · Bengbu · Linhuai · Heqiao · Tongeh

Fuyang · Guiji · Mingguang · Guiwu · Jiupu · Tianch

Funan · Fengtai · Zhanglou · Banta · Majio · Tianc

Yingshang · Bagongshan Qu · Huainan · Dingyuan · Chihe · Zhangbaling · Babai · Luhe

Qiaogou · Shou Xian · Xiejiaji Qu · Changfeng · Lai'an · Gua

Huoqiu · Zhengyang · Zhuxiang · Liangjiang · Chuzhou · Wuyi · Le

Gushi · Yangmiao · Gucheng · Quanjiao · Pukou Qu · Qixi

H E N A N · Changji · Zhongxing · Wushan · Wugang · Xingdian · Nanjing · Tom

Yeji · Yaoli · Erlangkou · Jiangning Qu · Chu

Lu'an · Guanting · Feidong · Tongjing · Moling

Jinzhai · Feixi · Zhegao · Hanshan · He Xian · Taowu · Guoz

Qingshan · Wuxian · Fengle · Zhongmiao · Ma'anshan

Daoshichong · Huoshan · Wuxian · Shengqiao · Chaohu · Dangtu · Lisl

Baima Jian ▲1774 · Xiaotian · Yuxikou · Wuwei · Erba · Wuhu · Gao

Tiantangzhai 1728 · Tongcheng · Wuhu

HUBEI · Laibang · Hetu · Yuexi · Hengbu · Tongling · Shizishan Qu · Nanling · Xuanch

Tongling

54

44

Height(m) 100 50 0 50 200 500 1000 1500 2000

Ping Dao
(Pingshan Dao)
Dashan Dao (Danian Shan)
Cheniu Shan
wang
35

E 120 F 121 G 122 H

inshan Kou
inshan Dao
n Qu
Dongxi Liandao
u Kou
↕

Mt. Yuntai

yungang
u Qu
ishan

Yanwei
Xuwei

1

n Qu Yangji
Chenjiagang
Touzeng

hangma
Dayou
Liutao
Batan
Biandanhe kou

Xiangshui
Yunti
Guoji
Liuduo

Guannan

Binhai
Linhai

Tangji
Tongyu

Wuxun
Qianqiu

Yangzhai
Tongyanggang
Haitong

ianshui
Chenji
Funing
Chenyang
Sheyang
Huangshagang

Banhu
Goudun
ZhongXingqiao

uzu
Donggou
Caoyankou

Yilin Jinayang
Huangjian

ou Qu
Shanggang
Sanqu

Jianhu
Xinxing
Sanlong

Yancheng
Xi'anfeng
Yandu Qu

Louwang
Shanghai Nongchang

Baoying
Dafeng

Dagang
Nanyang

Fanshui
Bei'anfeng
Shagou

Jieshou
Linze
Baiju
Xiaohai

Xinghua
Caoyan
Daqiao

Mapengwan
Shenzao

Hekou
Diduo
Dongtai
Caopie

Gaoyou
Laoge
Liangduo
Sancang

Cheluo
Zhouzhuang
Dainan
Jianggang

iaqiao
Xiaoji
Qintong
Fu'an

Dinggou
Tangyang

hao Hu
Baimi
Hai'an
Libao
Yangkou

Shaobo
Yiling
Huangang

Hill-Slim
Jiangyan
Dingsuo
Bencha

Lake
Jiangdu
Taizhou
Dongchen
Juzhen
Beikan

Yangzhou
Zhangdian
Rugao
Chahe
Rudong

Hanjiang Qu
Gaogang Qu
Banjin
Baipu
Datong

inshan Island
Yangzhong
Huangqiao
Shizhuang
Qi'an
Tongzhou
Sanyu

Zhenjiang
Taixing
Guangling
Pingchao
Tangzha
Sijia
Lüsigang

antu Qu
Picheng
Baqiao
Nantongang
Nantong
Yudong
Haifu

antu Qu
Xinfeng
Jingjiang
Baweigang
Jiangyin
Langshan
Sanyang

Danyang
Lucheng
Benniu
Zhangjiagang
Bejin

Erling
Changzhou
Zhouzhuang
Tangqiao
Haimen
Sanxing
Qidong

wang
Jintan
Qishuyan Qu
Beiguo
Xupu
Yinyang

Zhulin
Huishan Qu
Yu Shan
Xushi

Wujin Qu
Anzhen
Changshu
Fuqiao
Chongming Dao

Huangli
Luoshe
Zhitang
Liuhe

Bieqiao
Caoqiao
Xishan Qu
Chenjia

Liyang
Wuxi
Xin'an
Huangli
Taicang
Jiading Qu
Changxing Dao
She Shan

Chating
Xueyan
Taihu Lake
Zhengyi
Kunshan
Baoshan Qu
Hengsha Dao

Yixing
Heqiao
Maji Shan
Xushuguan
Xiangcheng Qu
Classical Gardens of Suzhou
Shanghai

ezhu
Daibu
Suzhou
Luzhi
SHANGHAI SHI
38

Zhangzhu
Piaomiao Feng
Wuzhong Qu
Jongli
Qingpu Qu

gxi
Xidongting Shan
Moli Feng
Wujiang
Zhouzhuang
Zhujiajiao
Minhang Qu
Nanhui Qu

liutoushan
Dongdongting Shan
Pingwang
Songjiang Qu
Fengxian Qu

Changxing
Shengze
East China Sea

ZHEJIANG
ZHEJIANG
ZHEJIANG
Daji Shan
ZHEJIANG

ngde
E 120 F Huzhou Jiashan G Donghai Bridge 122 H

31

Yellow Sea

Feihuanghe kou

Sheyanghe Kou

Xinyanggang Kou

Doulonggang Kou

Jiang (Yangtze)

Chuanyao Gang

Changjiang Kou

Wusong Kou

1
2
3
4
5

SCALE 1 : 2 500 000

0 25 50 75 100km

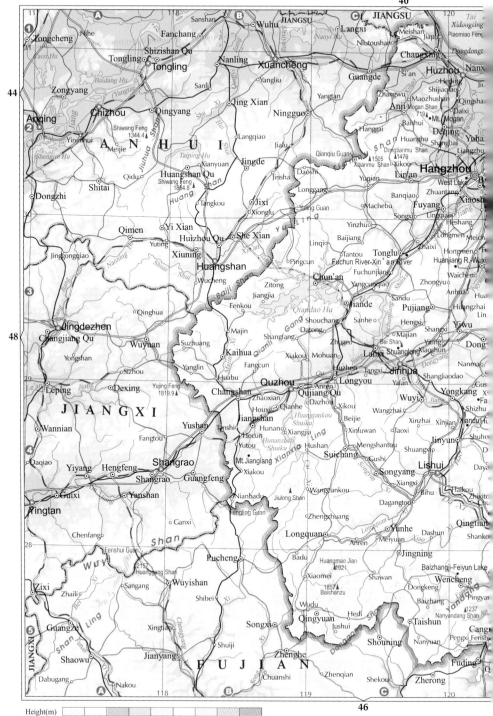

Height(m)

| 200 | 50 | 0 | 50 | 200 | 500 | 1000 | 1500 | 2000 | 2500 |

SCALE 1 : 2 500 000

| 0 | 25 | 50 | 75 | 100km |

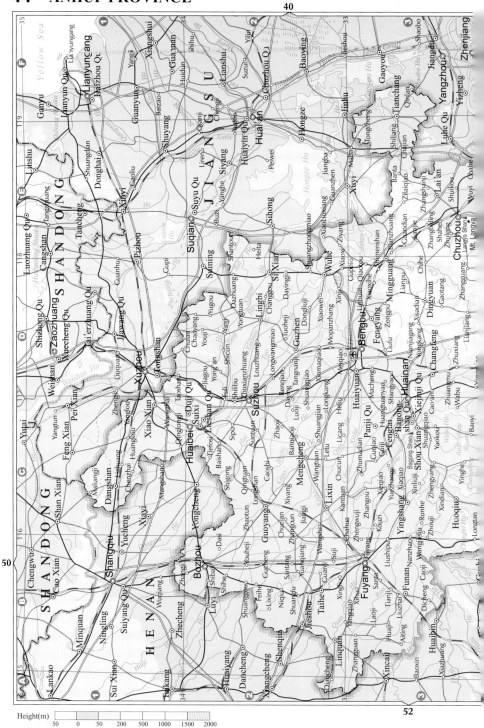

Height(m)
50 0 50 200 500 1000 1500 2000

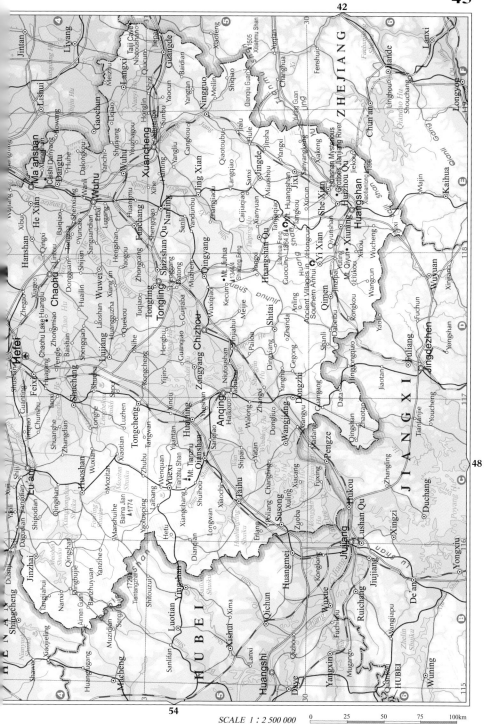

Taishan
Taishan Dayu Shan Liedao

Hengki
Huzher
Biliano
Fenshuiguan
Cangnan
Shacheng
Gang
Beichuang Dao
Sashuang Liedao
Tungtin
LieTiao

Pingyang
Shacheng
Sanxia Dayu Dao
Jianyun
Lishui
Taikou
Qingtian
Beishan
Pengxi
Fuding
Ballino
Mt. Taimu
Yacheng
Manshuang Dao
Xiapu
Changbiao Dao
Haiyang Dao
HsYin Tao
Matsu LieHtao

Wuyi
Songyang
Dagangtou
Yunhe
Jingning
Wencheng
Taishun
Zherong
Fu'an
Saikung
Zhangyan
Tieluan
Pukou
Beijiao
Guantou
Langqi
Matsu Tao
Tungtin
LieTiao

Taoxio
Z H E J I A N G
Lijiayang
Shouning
Nanyang
Shekou
Muyang
Qibu
Badu
Yangzhong
Heliang
Ningde
Luoyuan
Danyang
Baisha
Jiang

Yikou
Suichang
Longquan
Badu
Qingyuan
1921 Huangmao Jian 1657 Baishanzu
Chengyuan
Zhengjian
Zhouning
Yuhua Stream
Gantang
Heqiao
Bankengting
Luoqiao
Daping
Fuzhou

Changshan
Jiangshan
Hunanzhen Shuiku
Tiaoling Guan
Maoyangtou
Bucheng
Qianyang
Weitian
Tieshan
Chuanshi
Songxi
Zhenghe
Dongyou
1822 Ren Shan
Xiaoqiao
Yushan Pingnan
Dikou
Dixi
Fengdu
Degiao
Gutian
Xiongjiang
Huangtian
Eyang
Arenxi

Yushan
Fangtou
Guangfeng
Tongfang
Xianyang
Xikeng
Linjiang
Jiangxikou
Shibei
Hdlong
Dongping
Xijin
Shuiji
Dongyou
Nanya
Shan Ou
Renshou
Fangdao
Fangkou
Yangkou
Xiayang
Xiqin
Qingzhou
Nanping
Taiping
Xivang
Baizhong
Youxi
Tangchuan
Baiyan Shan

Shangrao
Yanshan
Huangang Shan
2157
Mt. Wuyi
Wuyishan
Wuyi
Shangmei
Chongyang
Xi
Xushio
Weimin
Pushang
Dagang
Wan'an
Shunchang
Yuhua Cave
Waiyang
Caoqiao
Caobsha
Sanming

Hengfeng
Tongfang
Tenshili Guan
Sangang
Huangkou
Jiaoxi
Masha
Bijia Shan 1162
Renshou
Zhukou
Xiamao
Bailian
Sha Xian
Yangxi
Gongchuan
Guangping

Zhongbu
Yiyang
Yanshan
Jiangkou
Shaikou
Wujiatang
Zhangguo
Dabugang
Xinqiao
Jiangle
Longxi Shan 1620
Huangtang
Shaxi
Mingxi
Ansha Shuiku
Yikou
Songkou

Wannian
Yuanfeng
Shangrao
Zhailil
Heshun
Jinkeng
Xiaohatang
Taining
Jinhu Lake
Longxi Shan
Gaiyang
Shaxi
Zhongsha
Ninghua

Yingtan
Jinxi
Zhaqian
Guangze
Shaowu
Dabugang
Jiangle
Huangtang
Caivang
Qinglui
Anle

Yugan
Huangjinbu
Yanshang
Daqiao
Tujiang
Jinxi
Daxu Shan 1107
Nancheng
Lichuan
Long'an
Hanming
Baish Feng 1858
Zhongsha
Songxi
Songkou

Nanchang
Ruhong
Sanyang
Jinxian
Dongxiang
Fuzhou
Dongshan
Huangshi
Nanfeng
Baishe
Guangchang
Lixin
Junkouo
Anyuan
Caotiano
Shishang
Ningdu
Shicheng
Longgang

J I A N G X I
Yihuang
Huangbei
Yihuang
Dagang
Chongren
Yihuang
Luokou
Chishang
Siqian
Caofang
Longgang

Height(m)
200 50 0 50 200 500 1000 1500 2000 3000

88

TAIWAN

Erlin
Taihsi
Chia-i
Chia-i
Putai
Tainan
Chialio
Tainan

Dongxiang Dao
Dongjing Dao

Penghu Shuitao

Haitan Island
Pingtan
Haitan Dao
Dalu
Caoyu

Penghu Liehtao
Penghu
Chipei Yu
Paisha Tao
Penghu Tao
Chiangchunao Yu
Chuangchuao Yu
Yaweng Tao
Hsichi Yu
Wangan Tao
(Pachao Tao)
Hui Yu
Yuweng Tao
Chinmei Yu
(Tai Yu)

Songxia
Tongtian
Caostan
Daitou
Narri Dao
Narri Qundao
Wenjia
Dinghai
Wizhu Yu
Lusi Yu
Meizhou Dao

Hangkou
Qiulu
Xinghua Wan
Shishang
Fengkou
Youxi

Shuikou
Youyang
Leifeng
Qiulu
Zhuangshan
Dongzhen Shuiku
Hanjiang Qu
Putian
Xiaoturogang
Xiaoturo
Xiangzhi
Shikou
Dehua
Duwei
Xianyou
Jinsha
Fengting
Meishan
Pingyuan
Licheng Qu
Quanzhou
Jinjiang
Shishi
Huian
Chongwu

Dongkiang Dao

Shuikou
Shiniu Shan
1781
Shanmei Shuiku
Yongchun
Shishan
Kuidou
Anxi
Nan'an
Chuanqiao
Jinjiang Qu
Xiang'an Qu
Weitou
Dongshi

Chinmen Tao

Xiayang
Penghu
Guandou
Xinwei
Luoyan
Yanyi
Tong'an Qu
Gaokeng
Xiamen
Chinmen

Chinmen Tao

Jiandou
Fude
Hutou
Longmen
Jinjiang Qu
Shuangyu Wan
Kuanao
Wutou Wan

Yidu
Xiandu
Xibei
Gao'an
Huichuan
Jiaomei
Longhai
Tongji Qu
Cuoke
Zhenhai
Fotan
Dongding Tao

Shipaio
Heping
Baisha
Yongfu
Longyan
Xinchi
Heshan
Dalongshan
Xinyang
Shiliu
Baishui
Nansheng
Changjiao
Zhangpu
Juzhen
Chihu
Qiu'ao
Nanding Tao

Cutian
Pengkou
Xikou
Caixi
Xinquan
Kanshi
Fushi
Chendong
Xiayang
Hushan
Anhou
Shilu
Huotian
Dongshan Dao
Xiongdi Yu

Nanjing
Pinghe
Shange
Yunxiao
Chencheng
Dongshan
Culeitou

Heitan
Mt Guanzhi
Tufang
Shifang
Shanghang
Dachi
Lanxi
Yongding
Meilin
Qiling
Quanbei
Changshan
Zhaoan
Nan'ao
Nan'ao Dao
Nanpeng Liedao

Xiaoxi
Xikou
Zhongshan
Yangshan
Jiaoling
Fenghuang
Gaobei
Sanrao
Raoping
Changhai Qu
Haojiang Qu
Shantou
Haimen Wan

Dongjia
Guangdong
Fenglang
Fengshun
Tonggu Zhang
1560
Chaozhou
Chaoan
Chaofu
Chaoyang Qu
Chaonan Qu
Puning
Huilai

Sidou
Zhuotian
Wuping
Meizhou
Mei Xian
Jieyang
Jiedong
Tropic of Cancer

South China Sea

Shenquan Gang

SCALE 1 : 2 500 000

0   25   50   75   100km

ANHUI

ZHEJIANG

HUBEI

HUNAN

FUJIAN

Nanchang

Jiujiang

Jingdezhen

Shangrao

Yingtan

Fuzhou

Ji'an

Yichun

Xinyu

Pingxiang

Huangshi

Height(m)

50	0	50	200	500	1000	1500	2000	3000

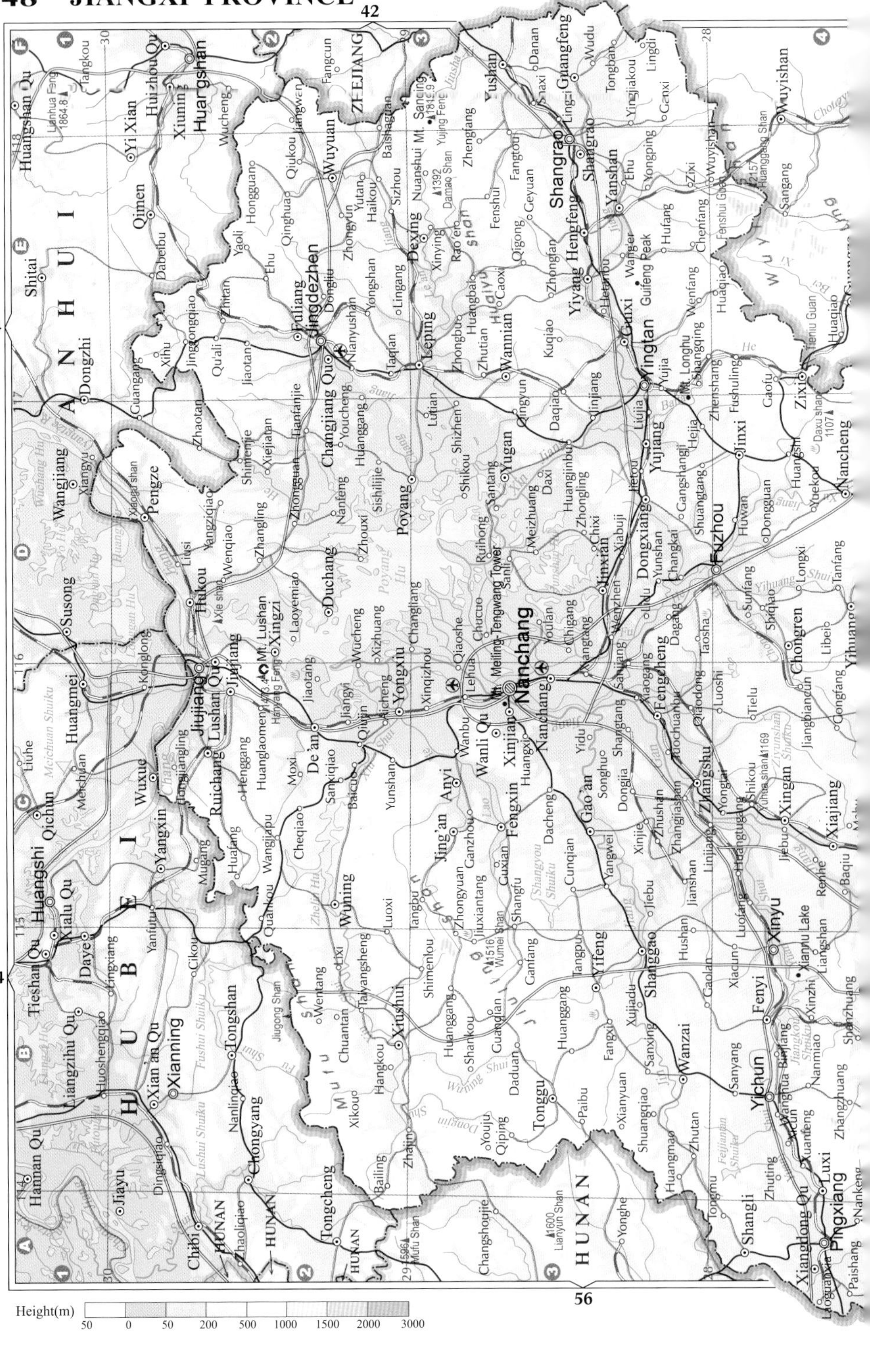

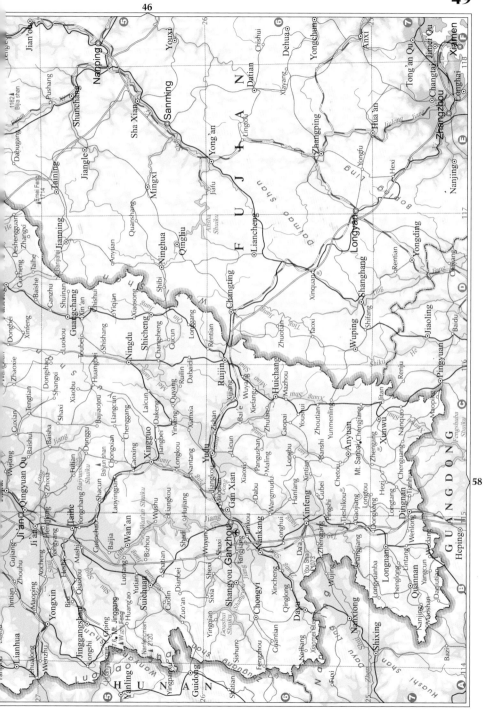

SCALE 1 : 2 500 000

| 0 | 25 | 50 | 75 | 100km |

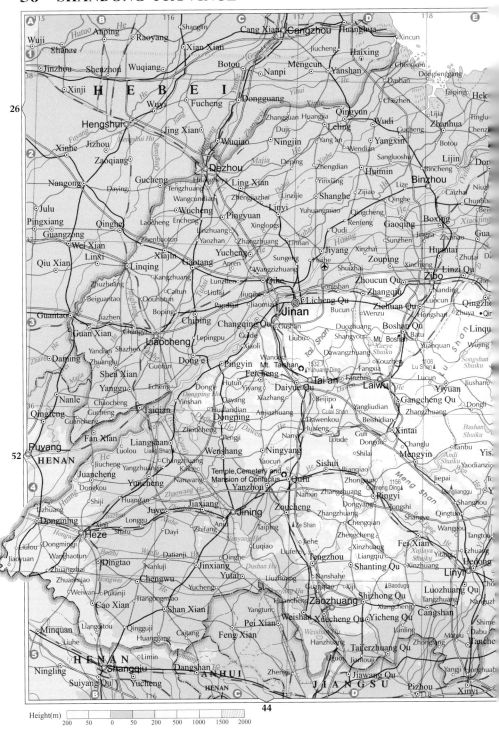

Height(m)

| 200 | 50 | 0 | 50 | 200 | 500 | 1000 | 1500 | 2000 |

Bohai Haixia

Yellow Sea

Bo Hai

Laizhou Wan

Shandong

Bandao Shan

Jiaodong Peninsula Seashore

Yellow Sea

Haizhou Wan

JIANGSU

SCALE 1 : 2 500 000

0   25   50   75   100km

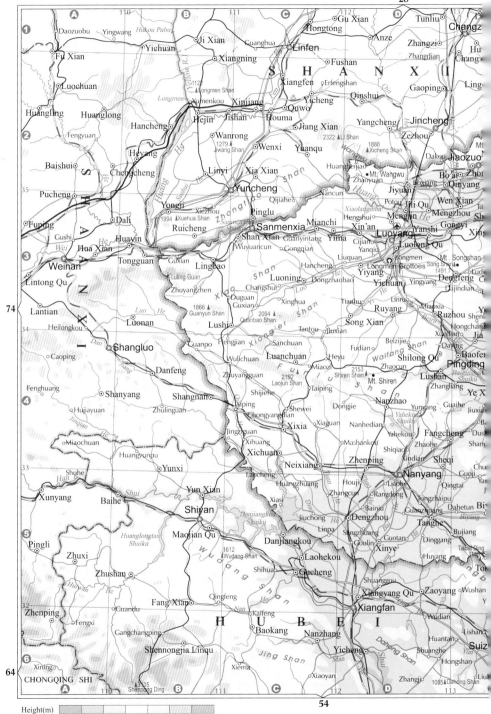

Height(m)
0   50   200   500   1000 1500 2000 3000

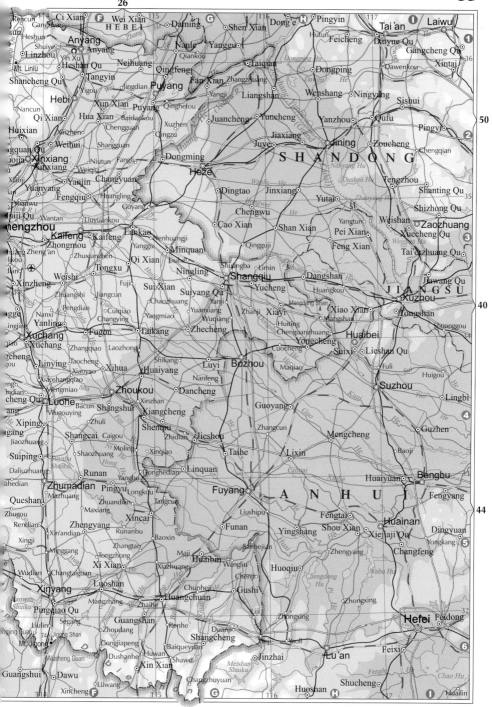

Renkun · Ci Xian · F · Wei Xian · 115 · Dong e · H · Pingyin · 117 · Tai'an · Laiwu · I
Gangcheng · HEBEI · Shen Xian · 116 · Hutun · Feicheng · Danyue Qu · Gangcheng Qu · 1
Heshun · Shuiye · Anyang · Anyang · Nanle · Yanggu · Qianlou · Taiqian · Dongping · Dawenkou · Xintai · 36
Linzhou · Yin Xu · Heshan Qu · Tangyin · Neihuang · Qingfeng · Fan Xian · Zhangzhuang · Dongping · Wenshang · Ningyang · Sishui
Mt.Linlü · Shancheng Qu · Jingdian · Puyang · Yangji · Liangshan · He · Qufu · Pingyi · 50
Nancun · Yigou · Xun Xian · Baidaokou · Qinghetou · Yuncheng · Yanzhou · Zoucheng · Chengqian · 2
Hebi · Qi Xian · Hua Xian · Chengguan · Xuzhen · Juancheng · SHANDONG · Jiaxiang · Jining · Zoucheng
Huixian · Weihui · Shangguan · Qingzu · Juye · Nahyang Hu · Tengzhou
guan Qu · Weiqiu · Dongming · Heze · Dingtao · Jinxiang · Dushan Hu · Shanting Qu · 35
jia · Xinxiang · Xinxiang · Changyuan · Niutun · Fangli · Wanfu · Yutai · Shizhong Qu · 3
Xiaoji · Yanjin · Huangling · Guyang · Chengwu · He · Yangtun · Weishan · Zaozhuang
Yuanyang · Fengqiu · Liuyuankou · Cao Xian · Shan Xian · Pei Xian · Xuecheng Qu
Yellow R · Wantan · Kaifeng · Kaifeng · Lankao · Nenhuangji · Qingguji · Feng Xian · Tai'erzhuang Qu
ngzhou · Zhongmou · Zheng'an · Zhuxianzhen · Yangji · Minquan · Limin · Huangkou · JIANGSU · 40
Xinzheng · Weishi · Tongxu · Qi Xian · Liuhe · Ningling · Shuangba · Dangshan · Xuzhou
Zhuangshi · Fuji · Sui Xian · Suiyang Qu · Shangqiu · Yucheng · Mangdang Shan · Xiao Xian · Tongshan
Pengdian · Jiangcun · Chaozhuang · Yuanxiang · Zhanji · Xiayi · Mangshan · Shuangguo
Yanling · Cuiqiao · Changying · Yangmiao · Wuqiang · Huiting · Chenguanzhuang · Yongcheng · Shixi · Lieshan Qu · Fuli
Xuchang · Xuchang · Fugou · Taikang · Zhecheng · Cuocheng · Maqiao · Huaibei · Huigou
Zhangqiao · Laozhong · Shiliang · Luyi · Bozhou · Suzhou · Lingbi · 4
Linying · Taocheng · Xihua · Huaiyang · Nanfeng · Guoyang · He · Guzhen
Xiaoshangqiao · Xinzhan · Zhangcun · Mengcheng
Mengmiao · Zhoukou · Dancheng · Baoji
Luohe · Bacun · Shangshui · Jiangcheng · Zhidian · Jieshou · Taihe · Lixin · Huaiyuan · Bengbu · 32
Xiping · Wugouying · Shenqiu · Xinqiao · ANHUI · Fengyang
Jiaozhuang · Zhuli · Molin · Shaozhuang · Huaiyuan
Suiping · Caigou · Donghedian · Linquan · Fuyang · Fengtai · Dingyuan
Daliuzhuang · Shuikou · Yangbu · Longkou · Liushipu · Shou Xian · Yongkang · 5
hedian · Runan · Pingyu · Tangcun · Funan · Yingshang · Xiejiaji Qu · Changfeng
Zhumadian · Mazhuang · Zhuandian · Liushipu · Fengtai · Zhengyang · Dingyuan
Queshan · Maxiang · Xincai · Baoxin · Sanhejian · Huaiyuan · Feidong
Zhugou · Rendian · Zhengyang · Runanbu · Maji · Wanglu · Huoqiu · Wabu Hu · Hefei · 6
Xingji · Xin'andian · Zhangtou · Xiazhuang · Chengjiao · Zhongxing
Xinyang · Minggang · Tongzhong · Xi Xian · Huaibin · Chunheji · Zhongxing · Feixi
Wudian · Changtaiguan · Luoshan · Zhaihe · Huangchuan · Renhe · Jinzhai · Lu'an · Feidong
Pingqiao Qu · Mangzhang · Guangshan · Zhoudang · Shangcheng · Meishan Shuiku · Fengle · Chao Hu
Liulin · Segang · Gongjiapeng · Baiqueyuan · Shawo · Huoshan · Shucheng · Huailin
Mt.Jigong · Dushanhe · Huwan · Changzhuyuan · H · 7 · I
Guangshui · Dawu · Lüwang · Xin Xian · Xincheng · F · 115 · G · 116 · Huoshan

SCALE 1 : 3 000 000

0   30   60   90   120km

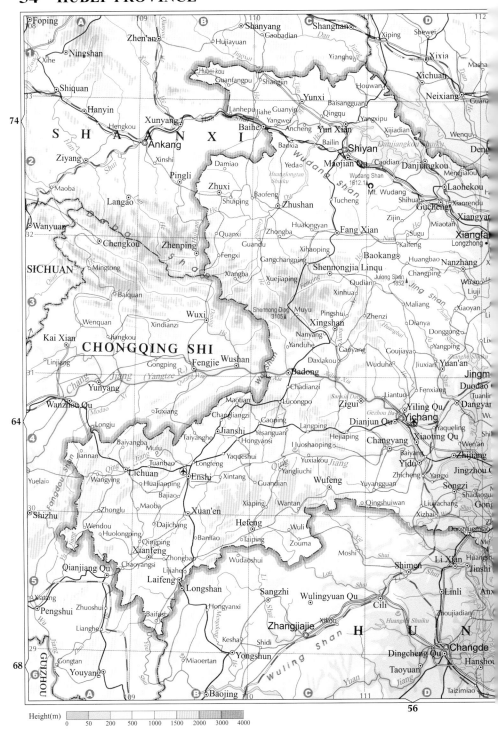

Height(m)

0   50   200   500   1000 1500 2000 3000 4000

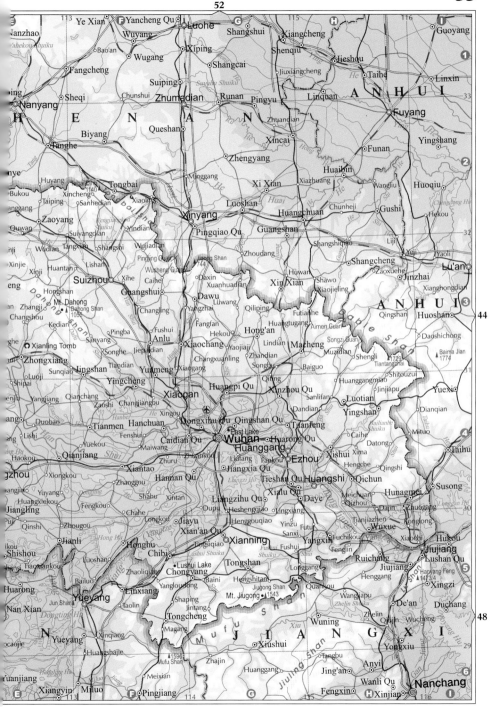

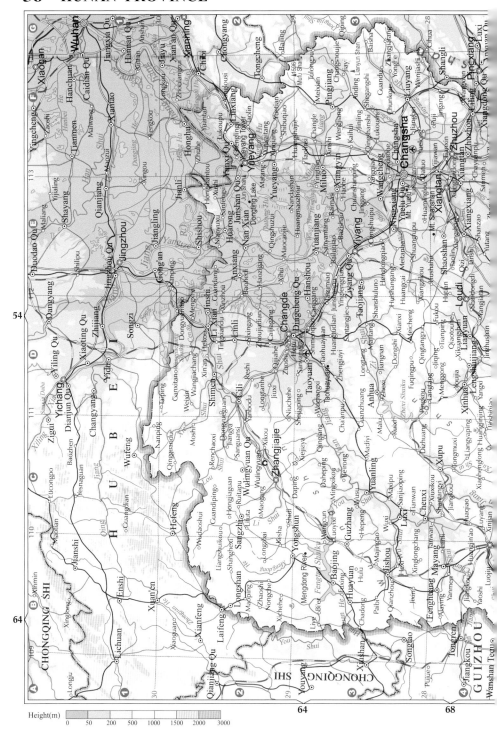

Height(m)

| 0 | 50 | 200 | 500 | 1000 | 1500 | 2000 | 3000 |

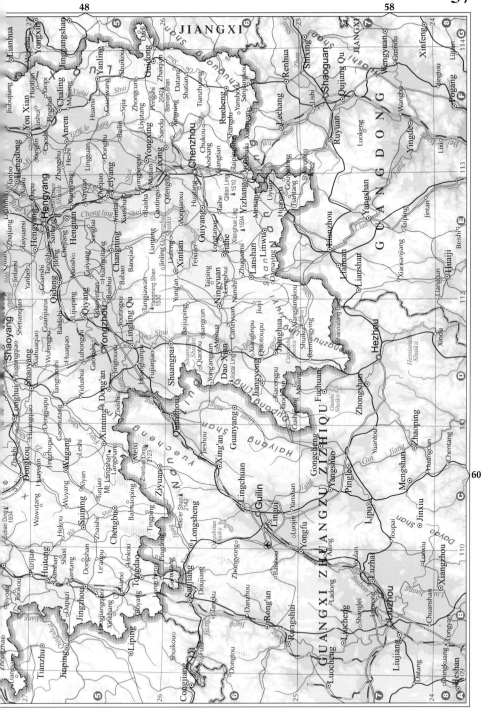

SCALE 1 : 3 000 000

0   30   60   90   120km

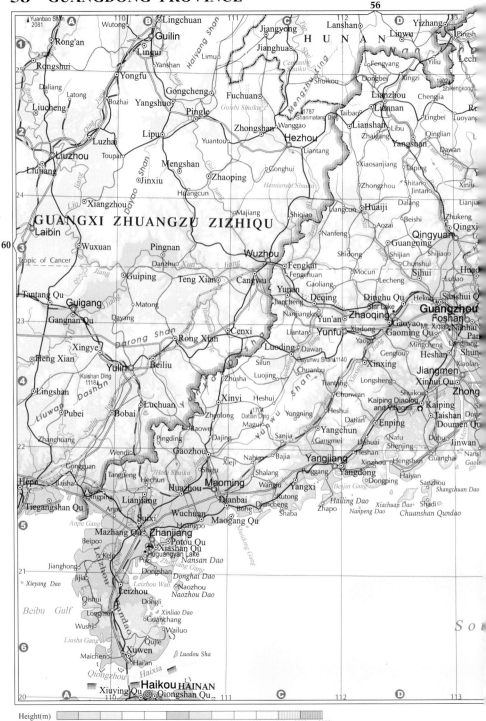

Height(m)

3000 2000 1000 200 50 0 50 200 500 1000 1500 2000 3000

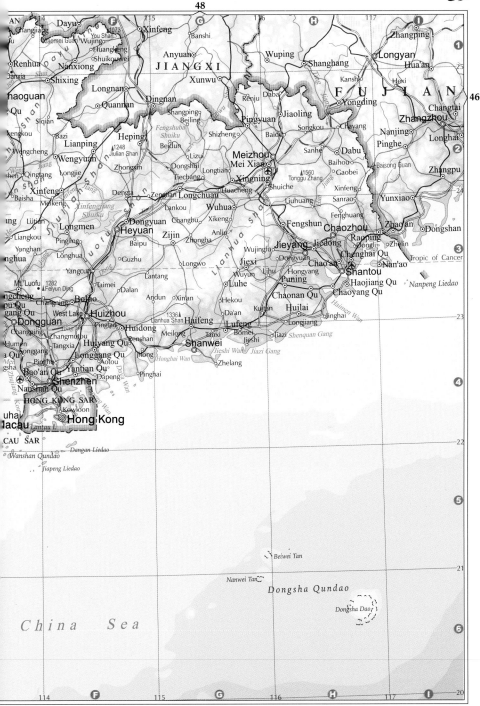

48

46

AN 114 Dayu ○ Xinfeng Banshi G H 117 I Zhangping 1
Changjiang △1073 You Shan
u Qiaomei Guan Wujing ○ Huangleng Anyuan ○ Wuping Shanghang Longyan Hua'an 25
○Renhua Shuikouwei Kanshi
anxia Nanxiong J I A N G X I Xunwu ○ Renju Daba Hexi
○Shixing Longnan ○ Pingyuan Jiaoling Yongding F U J I A N 46
haoguan ○Quannan Dingnan Shangping Songkou Chayang Zhangzhou
Qu Siqian Shizheng Baidu Nanjing Changtai
Kengkou Bazi Heping Beidun Sanhe Dabu Pinghe Longhai
Wengcheng Lianping Jiulian Shan Lizui Baihou Zhangpu
○Qingtang Longjie Zhongxin Dongshui Longtian Meizhou Baisong Guan
Xinfeng Dengta Zengtan Longchuan Huacheng Xinfeng
Baisha Mzikeng Lankou Changbu Xikeng Fenghuang Yunxiao 24
ng Lütian Longmen Heyuan Zijin Zhongba Anliu Fengshun Chaozhou Zhao'an Dongshan
Liangkou Pingling Baipu Wujingfu Jieyang Jiedong Raoping Zhelin
yonghan Longhua Guzhu Longwo Jiexi Dongyuan Chao'an Nan'ao
nghua Yangcun Lantang Lihu Hongyang Chenghai Qu Tropic of Cancer
Mt.Luofu 1282 Taimei Dalan Luhe Puning Shantou
 Feiyun Ding Andun Xin'an Hekou Chaonan Qu Haojiang Qu Nanpeng Liedao
ngcheng Boluo West Lake Huizhou Da'an Kuitan Huilai Chaoyang Qu
gang Qu Changping Lianhua Shan Haifeng Lufeng Longjiang Jinghai 23
Humen Zhangmutou Pingtan Meilong Tanxi Bomei Jieshi Shenquan Gang
a Qu Tangxia Huiyang Qu Renshen Shanwei Jishi Jiazi Gang
Mei Longgang Qu Hong Jieshi Wan Jiazi Gang
esha Bao'an Qu Yantian Qu Aotou Zhelang
uhai Nanshan Qu Dapeng Pinghai
Shenzhen Pinghai
HONG KONG SAR
acau Kowloon
CAU SAR Hong Kong 22
Wanshan Qundao Dangan Liedao
Jiapeng Liedao

Beiwei Tan 21

Nanwei Tan
Dongsha Qundao

Dongsha Dao

C h i n a S e a

114 F 115 G 116 H 117 I 20

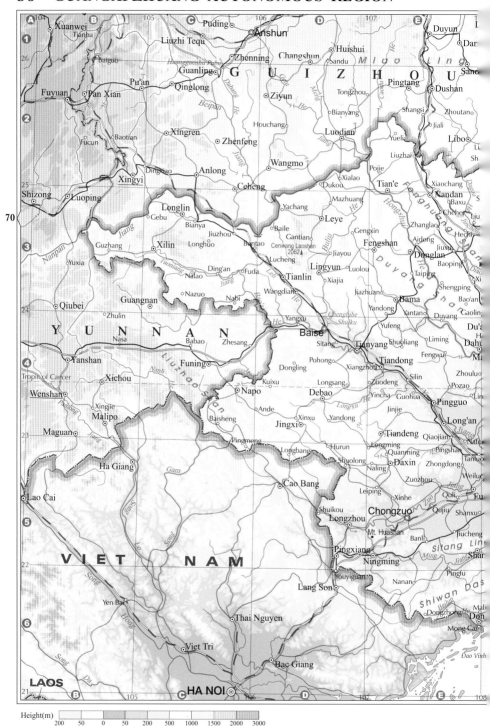

70

Height(m)
200 50 0 50 200 500 1000 1500 2000 3000

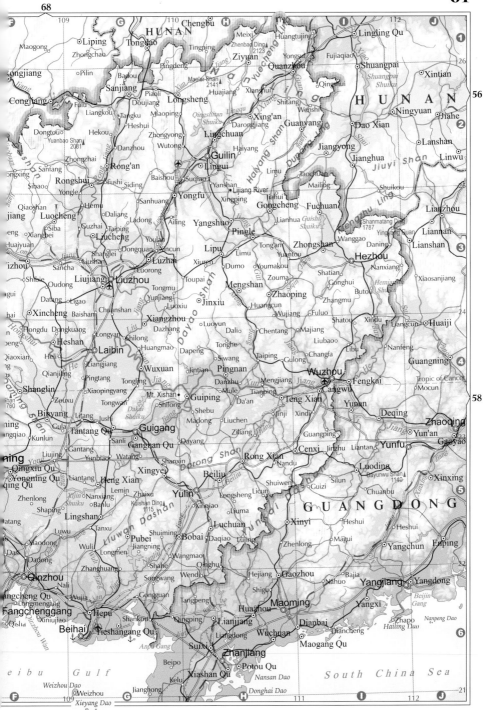

SCALE 1 : 3 300 000

0   33   66   99   132km

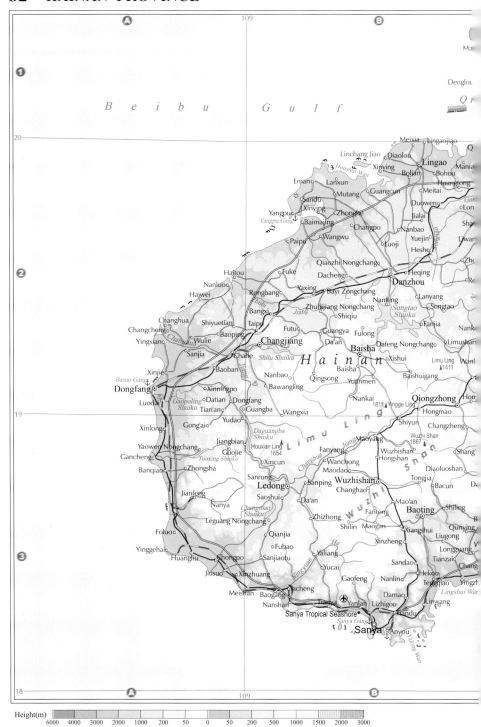

Height(m)

6000 4000 3000 2000 1000 200 50 0 50 200 500 1000 1500 2000 3000

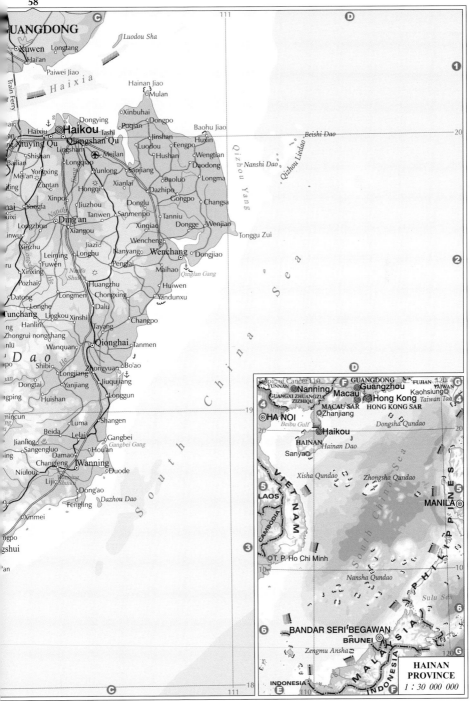

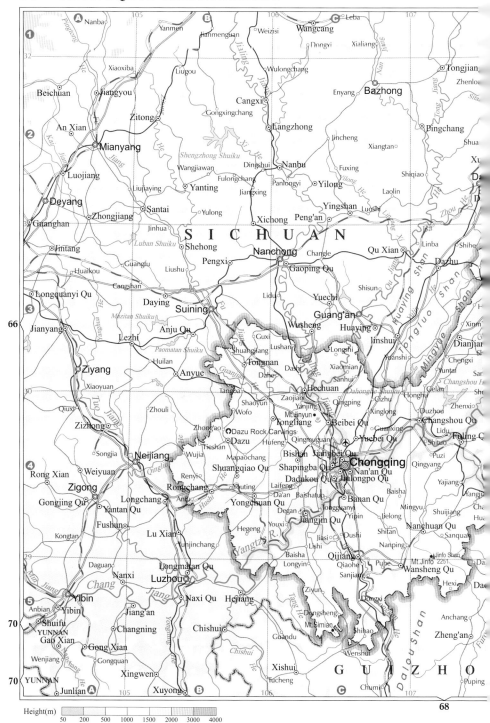

Nanba
Pingtong
Yanmen
Hanmenguan
Weizisi
Leba
Wangcang
Dongyi
Xialiang
Tongjian
Zhenlo
Xiaoxiba
Liugou
Wulongchang
Enyang
Bazhong
Beichuan
Jiangyou
Zitong
Cangxi
Gongxingchang
Langzhong
Jincheng
Xiangtan
Shua
An Xian
Mianyang
Nanbu
Fuxing
Shiqiao
Xu
Luojiang
Wangjiawan
Dingshui
Fulongchang
Panlongyi
Yilong
Laolin
Da
Yanting
Jiangxing
Yingshan
Luoshi
D
Deyang
Zhongjiang
Santai
Yulong
Xichong
Peng'an
Jinhua
Guanghan
S I C H U A N
Jintang
Luban Shuiku
Shehong
Nanchong
Changle
Qu Xian
Linba
Shihe
Guangfu
Pengxi
Gaoping Qu
Shisun
Dazhu
Huaikou
Liushu
Cangshan
Lidu
Yuechi
Longquanyi Qu
Daying
Suining
Wusheng
Guang'an
Mezitan Shuiku
Anju Qu
Guxi
Lushan
Longshi
Jinshui
Jianyang
Lezhi
Shuangjiang
Huailan
Tongnan
Dahe
Dashi
Xiaomian
Ydanshi
Dianjia
Ziyang
Anyue
Tangba
Sanhui
Hechuan
Chengxi
Sar
Xiaoyuan
Zhouli
Shaoyun
Zaojiao
Yanjing
Qingping
Cizhu
Honghu
Zhenxio
Qiuxi
Wofo
Mt.Jinyun
Xinglong
Duzhou
Changshou Qu
Zizhong
Zhongao
Dazu Rock Carvings
Tongliang
Beibei Qu
Guanxing
Lidu
Songjia
Dazu
Hufeng
Qingmuguan
Yuebei Qu
Shituo
Fuling C
Neijiang
Wujia
Tieshan
Bishan
Jiangbei Qu
Puzi
Rong Xian
Weiyuan
Mapaochang
Shuangqiao Qu
Shapingba Qu
Chongqing
Qingyang
Zigong
Renyi
Dadakou
Jiulongpo Qu
Nan'an Qu
Yajiang
Gongjing Qu
Rongchang
Yuting
Laifeng
Banan Qu
Baisha
Longchang
Anfu
Yongchuan Qu
Da'an
Baishatup
Yibin
Mingyu
Cha
Yantan Qu
Degan
Tongguanyi
Jielong
Shuijiang
Hua
Fushun
Youxi
Jiangjin Qu
Shitan
Nanchuan Qu
Kongtan
Lu Xian
Hegeng
Jiasi
Dushi
Nanping
Sanquan
Yunjinchang
Baisha
Lishi
Qijiang
Daguan
Longmatan Qu
Longyin
Qiaohe
Pube
Wansheng Qu
Da
Nanxi
Luzhou
Ziyun
Sanjiang
Hexi
Dac
Yibin
Naxi Qu
Hejiang
Dongxi
Anchang
Anbian
Yibin
Shuifu
Jiang'an
Chishui
Guandu
Mt.Simian
Shibao
Zheng'an
Gao Xian
Changning
Xishui
Wenshui
Gong Xian
Gongquan
Wenjiang
Xingwen
Tucheng
G U Z H O
Junlian
Xuyong
Chumi
Puping

Height(m)
50   200   500   1000   1500   2000   3000   4000

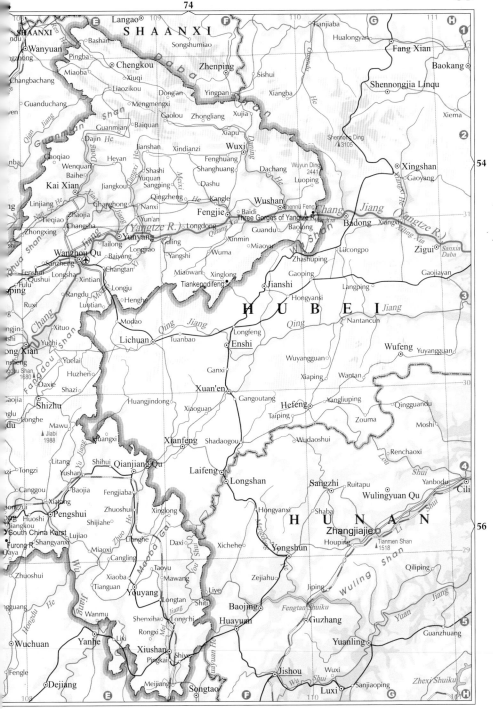

SCALE 1 : 2 500 000

0   25   50   75   100km

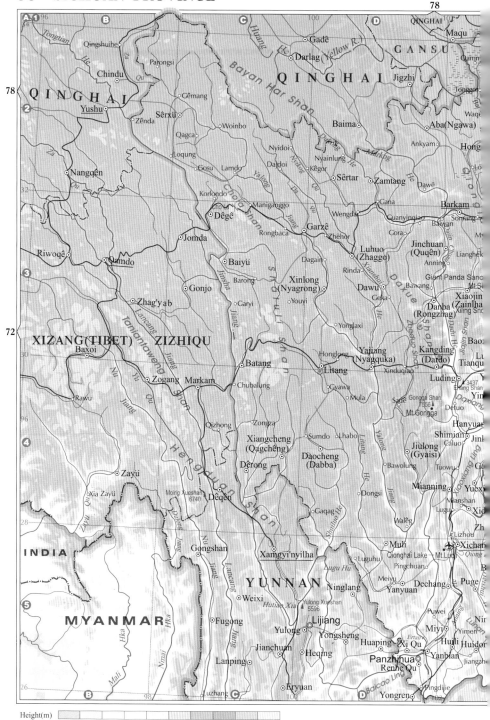

Height(m)
50 200 500 1000 1500 2000 3000 4000 5000 6000 7000

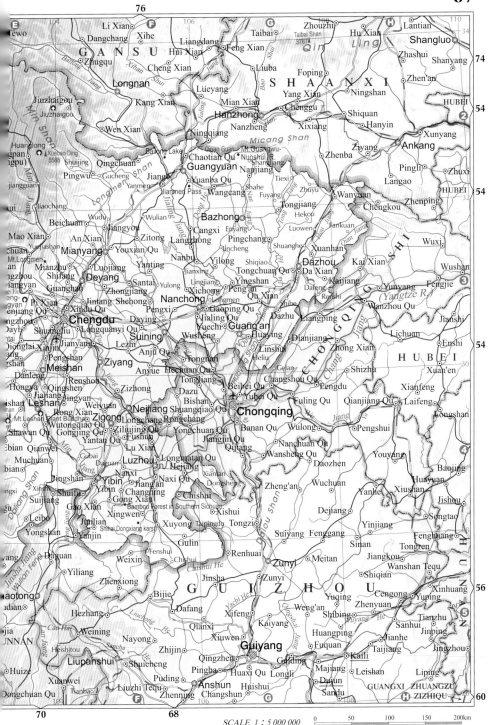

Tewo Li Xian Zhouzhi Hu Xian Lantian
Dangchang Xihe Taibai Ling Shangluo 34
Liangdang Feng Xian Taibai Shan Zhashui
GANSU Hui Xian 3767 Shanyang 74
Zhugqu Cheng Xian Liuba Qin Ling Zhen'an
Longnan Yihan Shui Foping SHAANXI Shiquan Xunyang HUBEI
Jiuzhaigou Kang Xian Lüeyang Yang Xian Ningshan Hanyin 54 2
Jiuzhaigou Wen Xian Mian Xian Chenggu Ankang
Huanglong Qingchuan Hanzhong Xixiang Ziyang Pingli Zhuxi
Pingwu Nanzheng Micang Shan Zhenba Langao HUBEI
Chaotian Qu Nanjiang Wanyuan Zhenping 54
Guangyuan Yuanba Qu Tongjiang Chengkou
Jiangmen Pass Wangcang Shahe Fuyang Zbuyu Wuxi
Bazhong Luowen Tiexi Hekou Fankuan
Beichuan Cangxi Pingchang Xuanhan Wushan
Mao Xian An Xian Zitong Langzhong Shuanghe Dazhou Kai Xian Fengjie 3
Mianyang Youxian Qu Nanbu Yilong Shiqiao Da Xian Kaijiang Yunyang (Yangtze R)
Mianzhu Luojiang Yanting Tongchuan Qu Yingshan Qu Xian Wanzhou Qu Jianshi
Guanghan Deyang Santai Yulong Xichong Pengan Longmen Renshi Lichuan
Pi Xian Zhongjiang Shehong Nanchong Gaoping Qu Dazhu Liangping Enshi 54
Chengdu Xindu Qu Pengxi Jialing Qu Guang'an Dianjiang Zhong Xian HUBEI
Shuangliu Longquanyi Qu Daying Yuechi Huaying Shizhu Xuan'en
Suining Wusheng Linshui Meiliu
Meishan Ziyang Anyue Hechuan Qu Changshou Qu Fengdu Xianfeng
Danleng Renshou Tongliang Beibei Qu Yubei Fuling Qu Qianjiang Qu Laifeng
Hongya Qingshen Dazu Bisham Chongqing Wulong Pengshui Longshan
Leshan Jiajiang Jingyan Weiyuan Shuangqiao Qu Banan Qu
Zigong Longchang Rongchang Yongchuan Qu Nanchuan Qu Youyang
Wutongqiao Qu Gongjing Qu Ziliujing Qu Fushun Jiangjin Qu Wansheng Qu Baojing
Qianwei Yantan Qu Lu Xian Qijiang Daozhen Huayuan
Muchuan Gulai Daguan Luzhou Longmatan Qu Hejiang Xiantan Zheng'an Wuchuan Xiushan Jishou
Bingshan Nanxi Naxi Qu Dongsheng Yanhe Songtao
Yibin Changning Gong Xian Chishui Dejiang Yinjiang Fenghuang
Shuifu Xingwen Xuyong Taipingdu Tongzi Suiyang Fenggang Sinan Tongren
Leibo Junlian Gulin Renhuai Zunyi Meitan Jiangkou
Yongshan Yanjin Weixin Fenshui Chishui He Jinsha Zunyi Shiqian Wanshan Tequ
Daguan Yiliang Zhenxiong Bijie GUIZHOU Yuqing Zhenyuan Cengong Xinhuang 56
Hezhang Dafang Xifeng Weng'an Shibing Tianzhu Yuping
Weining Qianxi Kaiyang Huangping Sanhui Jianhe Jinping
Nayong Zhijin Xiuwen Fuquan Taijiang Jingzhou
Liupanshui Shuicheng Guiyang Guding Kaili Leishan Liping
Xuanwei Qingzhen Pingba Huaxi Qu Longli Majiang Duyun
Dongchuan Qu Tianba Anshun Huishui Sandu GUANGXI ZHUANGZU 60
Zhenning Changshun ZIZHIQU

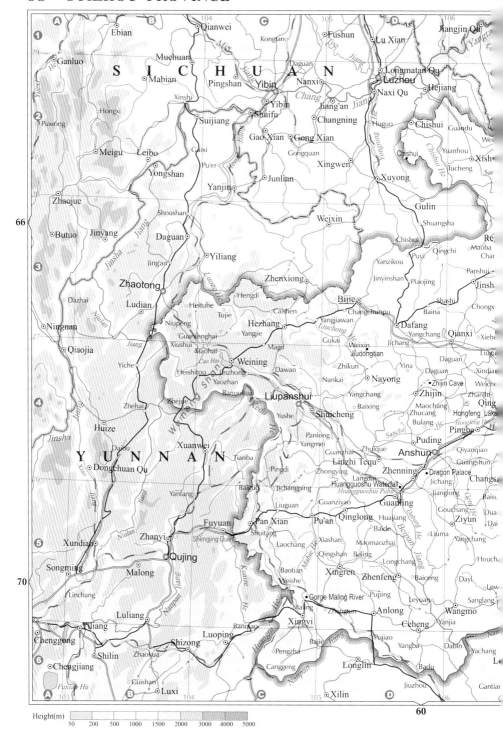

Height(m)
50 200 500 1000 1500 2000 3000 4000 5000

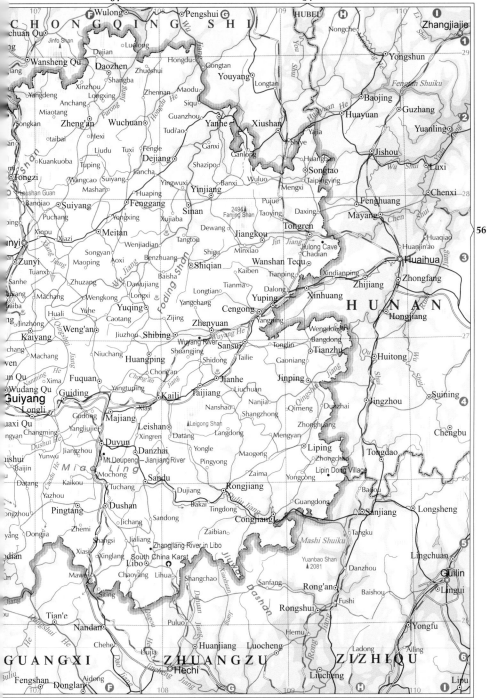

64　　　　　　54

CHONGQING SHI

107　Wulong　108　Pengshui G　109　HUBEL H　Li　110　I
Sichuan Qu　Jinfo Shan　Luolong　Nongche　Zhangjiajie　1
Wansheng Qu　Dajian　Hongdu　29　Yongshun
Jinfo Shan　Daozhen　Zhuoshui　Gongtan　Fengtan Shuiku
Yangdeng　Shangba　Zhennan　Maodu　Youyang　Longtan
Xinzhou　Longxing　Guanzhou　Siqu　Baojing　Guzhang
Miaotang　Anchang　Tudi'ao　Yanhe　Xiushan　Yajia　Huayuan
Songkan　Zheng'an　Wuchuan　Ganxi　Shiye　Yuanling
taibai　Hexi　Fengle　Shazipo　Huanghan　Wu Shui　Jishou
Liudu　Tuxi　Dejiang　Ganlong　Songtao　Luxi
Kuankuoba　Tuping　Jiancha　Yingwuxi　Banxi　Taipingying
Tongzi　Wangcao　Suiyang　Huaping　Yinjiang　Wuluo　Mengxi　Chenxi　28
Banqiao　Suiyang　Fenggang　Pujue　Fenghuang
Puchang　Yongxing　Xujiaba　Sinan　Daxing　Mayang　Chen Shui
Xinpu　Xiazi　Meitan　Dewang　Jiangkou　Tongren
Zunyi　Wenjiadian　Songyan　Tangtou　Minxiao　Jin Jiang　Julong Cave　Huaihua　3
Tuanxi　Maoping　Aoxi　Benzhuang　Shigu　Wanshan Tequ　Chadian　Zhongfang
Sanhe　Zhuzang　Baisha　Kaiben　Tianping　Xindianping　Zhijiang
Machang　Dawujiang　Tianma　Dalong　Xinhuang
Jinzhong　Wengkong　Longxi　Longtian　Yuping　HUNAN
Huali　Yuhe　Yuqing　Yangchang　Cengong　Yangying　Hongjiang
Weng'an　Caotang　Zijing　Zhenyuan　Wuyang He　Wengdong
Kaiyang　Jiuzhou　Shibing　Wuyang River　Sansui　Tonglin　Bangdong　27
Machang　Niuchang　Shuangjing　Shidong　Tailie　Gaoniang　Tianzhu　Huitong
Wudang Qu　Xima　Fuquan　Chong'an　Jinping
Guiyang　Guiding　Yangtuping　Jianhe　Liuchuan　Jingzhou　Suining
Longli　Gudong　Majiang　Kaili　Taijiang　Nanjia　Qimeng　Dunzhai
Changming　Yangliujiang　Xiasi　Nanshao　Shangzhong　Chengbu
Duyun　Leishan　Xingren　Datang　Langdong　Mengyan
Jiangzhou　Mt.Doupeng　Danzhai　Yongle　Maogong　Liping　Tongdao
Baijin　Mochong　Jianjiang River　Pingyong　Zhongchao
Datang　Kaikou　Tuchang　Sandu　Dujiang　Zaima　Yongcong　Lipin Dong Village
Yazhou　Pingtang　Dushan　Sandong　Tingdong　Guangdong　Bagou
Zhemi　Jialiang　Zaibian　Sanjiang　Longsheng
Dongjia　Shangsi　Zhangjiang River in Libo　Congjiang　Mashi Shuiku　Tangku
Fengshan　Xiasi　Xinglang　South China Karst　Yuanbao Shan　Lingchuan
Libo　Chaoyang　Lihua　Shangchao　2081　Danzhou　Guilin
Mawei　Siting　Sanfang　Rong'an　Baishou　Lingui
Tian'e　Puluo　Fushi　Rongshui　Yongfu
Nandan　Chehe　Hemu　Ladong　Ailing
Liujia　Huanjiang　Luocheng　ZIZHIQU　Lipu
GUANGXI　ZHUANGZU　Hechi　Liucheng
Fengshan　Aidong　107　108　G 109　110 I
Donglan F

56

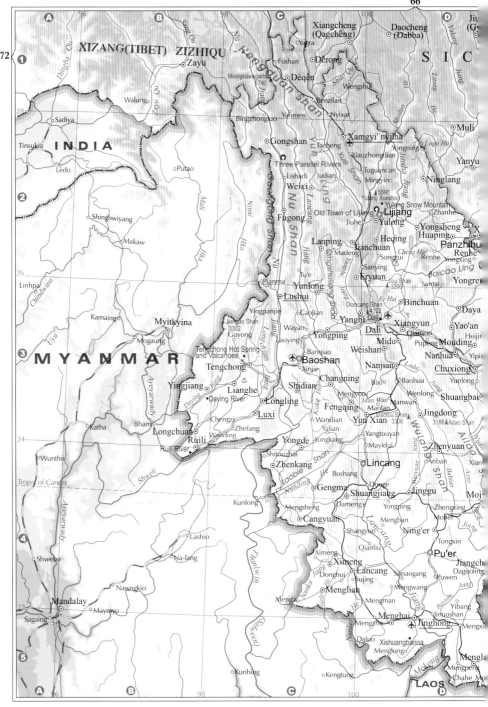

Height(m)

50 0 100 200 500 1000 1500 2000 3000 4000 5000 6000 7000

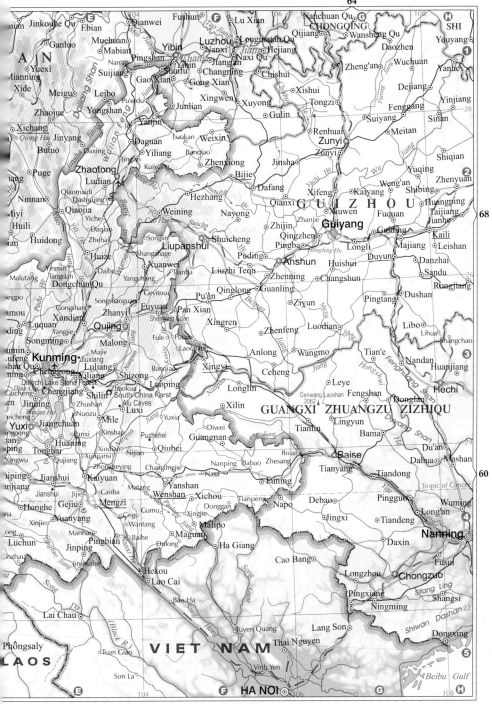

SCALE 1 : 5 000 000

0   50   100   150   200km

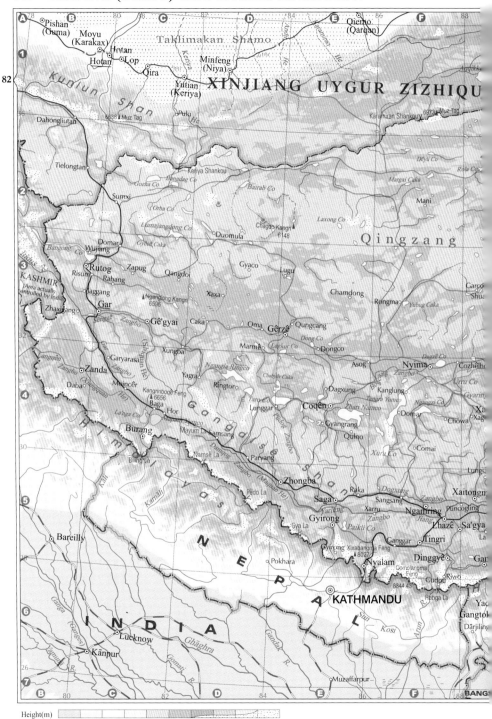

Height(m)

0   200   500   1000   2000   3000   4000   5000   6000   7000

78

Qilian Tag
Qaidam
Dong Dabsan Hu
Delhi
Fianjun
Qinghai Hu
Ulan
Caka
Toson Hu
Golmud
Dulan
Rendi
Qaidam
He
Kunlun
Shan
Buka Daban Feng
5860
Naij Tal
Hoh Sai Hu
Budongquan
QINGHAI
Donggi Conag
Hoh Xil Hu
Xijir Ulan Hu
Madoi
Yoigilangleb Qu
Kar
Gyaring Hu Ngoring Hu
Huang He
Darlag
Ulan Ul Hu
Serwolungwa
Do Qu Yellow
Tognin
Tongtian
Gaoyuan
Tanggulashan
Qumarleb
He
Zhidoi
Geladaindong Feng
6621
Tanggula Shan
6005
Zadoi
Chindu
Yushu
Serxu
SICHUAN
Tumain
Tanggula Shankou
Gangru
Qu
Ji Qu
Nangqen
Qu
Sinda
Dege
Bungona'og
Amdo
Nyainrong
Bagen
Yan'gamdo
Chido
Riwoqe Samka
Jomda
Qu'nyido
Baiyu
Qangma Co Nag
Sog
Ya'ngamdo
Rongbo
Dengqen
Riwoqe
Qamdo
Namarqe
Nagqu
Biru
Sadeng
Rayu
Morri
Gyitang
Zhag'yab
Gonjo
Langmai
Qinglung
Lhoma
Banbar
Sogdoi
Lhorong
Qamdun
Batang
Nam Co
Xarma
Lhari
Chongyu
Nagjog
Bangda
Co'nga
Deqen
Damxung
Yi'ong Tangmai
Baxoi
Markam
Nyainqentanglha Feng
7162
Pondo
Mamba
Dongjug
Bomi(Bowo)
Jidar
Zogang
Yangbajain
Lhunzhub
Gongbo'gyamda
Sumzom
Qizhong
Potala Palace
Maizhokunggar
Nyingchi
Namjagbarwa Feng
Rawu
Deqen
Doilungdeqen
Dagze
7782
Goyic
Nyemo
Quxu
Lhasa
Nyingchi
Qabnag
Medog
Rinbung
Gonggar
Nedong
Sangri
Gyaca
Medog
Zhanang
Mainling
Zayu
Nagatze
Qonggyai Qusum
Nang Xian
Gyangze
Comai
Lhunze
Qayu
Xia Zayu
Walung
Gongshan
Yamzho Yumco
Puma Yumco
Yalong River
Rigao
Lhozhag
Cona
Sadiya
Fugong
Punakha Dzong
Maindawang
Tinsukia
Putao
THIMBU
Dirangzong
Mai Hka
BHUTAN
Tashigang
Kameng
Lushui
Tezpuro
INDIA
MYANMAR
Brahmaputra
Guwahati
Lushui

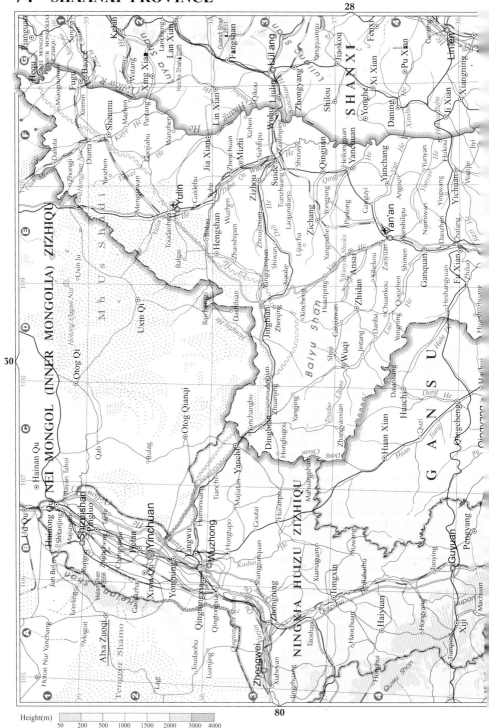

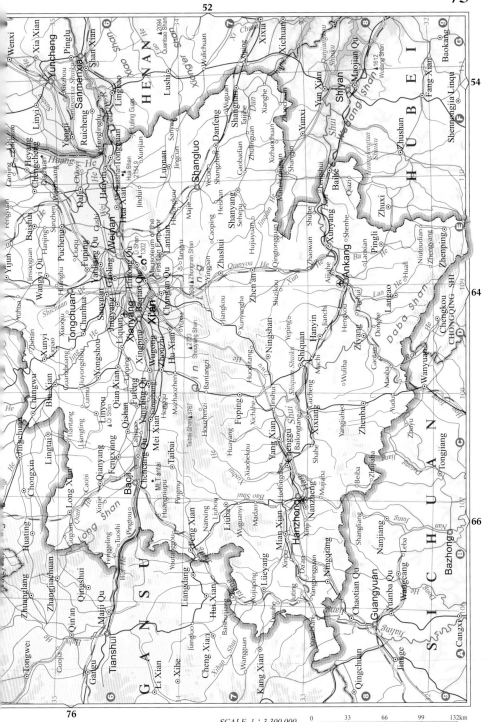

54

64

66

HENAN

HUBEI

SHANXI

GANSU

SICHUAN

CHONGQING SHI

Wenxi
Xia Xian
Pinglu
Yuncheng
Sanmenxia
Shan Xian
Lingbao
Baokang
Fang Xian
Shennongjia Linqu
Shiyan
Maojian Qu
Yun Xian
Xichuan
Xixia
Wulichuan
Danfeng
Shangnan
Shangzhou
Shangluo
Luonan
Chushan
Yunxi
Zhuxi
Baihe
Xunyang
Pingli
Zhenping
Langao
Ankang
Zhashui
Zhen'an
Ningshan
Hanyin
Shiquan
Ziyang
Wanyuan
Chengkou
Liuba
Foping
Yang Xian
Chenggu
Xixiang
Zhenba
Tongjiang
Nanjiang
Bazhong
Hanzhong
Mian Xian
Nanzheng
Ningqiang
Lüeyang
Guangyuan
Chaotian Qu
Yuanba Qu
Wangcang
Cangxi
Jiange
Qingchuan
Mei Xian
Baoji
Qishan
Fengxiang
Qianyang
Long Xian
Huating
Zhangjiachuan
Maiji Qu
Qin'an
Tianshui
Gangu
Tongwei
Qingshui
Zhuanglang
Li Xian
Xihe
Cheng Xian
Kang Xian
Hui Xian
Liangdang
Feng Xian
Taibai
Zhouzhi
Hu Xian
Chang'an Qu
Xi'an
Baqiao Qu
Lantian Qu
Weinan
Huayin
Tongguan
Ruicheng
Linyi
Heyang
Chengcheng
Baishui
Pucheng
Fuping
Sanyuan
Jingyang
Liquan
Xingping
Xianyang
Qian Xian
Yongshou
Binzhou
Changwu
Ba Xian
Linyou
Qianyang
Chunhua
Yaozhou Qu
Yijun
Tongchuan
Xunyi
Zhengning
Heshui
Zhengzhou
Yanliang Qu
Gaoling

SCALE 1 : 3 300 000

0   33   66   99   132km

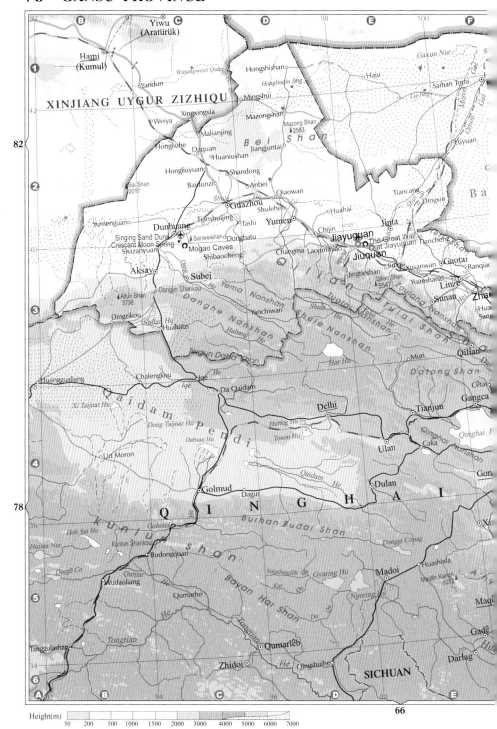

Height(m)
50 200 500 1000 1500 2000 3000 4000 5000 6000 7000

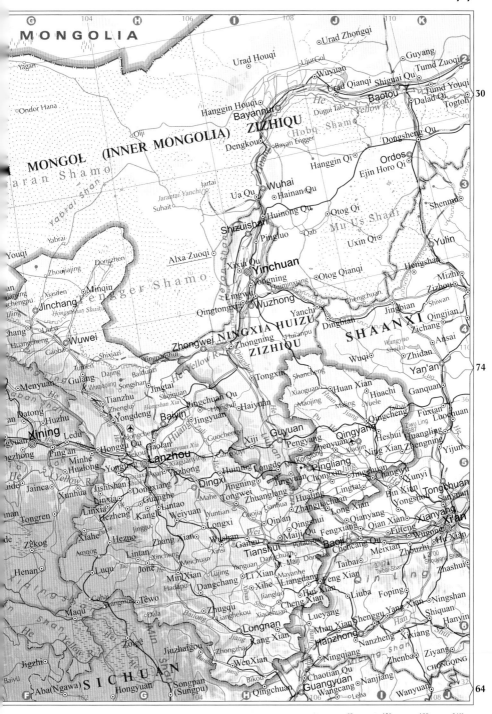

SCALE 1 : 6 000 000   0 60 120 180 240km

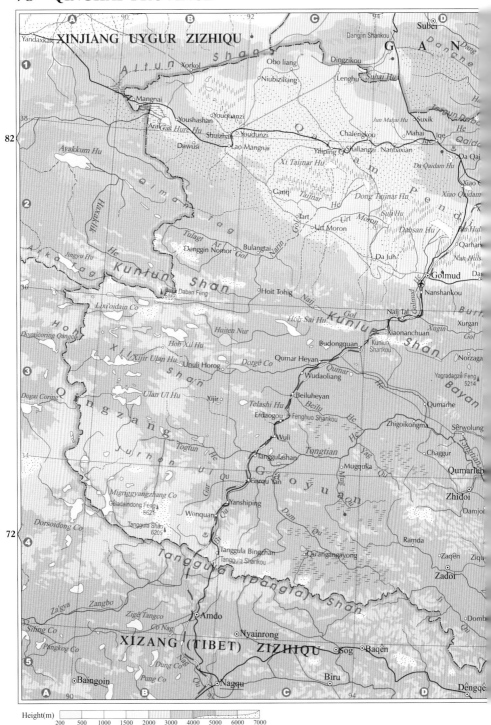

Height(m)
200 500 1000 1500 2000 3000 4000 5000 6000 7000

NEI MONGOL (INNER MONGOLIA)
ZIZHIQU

Gaotai
Jingtieshan
Qilian Shan
△5547
Linze
Zhangye
Sunan
Shandan
Alxa Youqi
Zhoujiajing
Minqin
Jiling
Jinchang
Wuwei
Minle
Yongchang
Gulang
Anyuan
Gezidong
Qilian
Oba
Qingshizui
Menyuan
Tianzhu
Yongdeng
Muri
Daliang
Muri
Cêtar
Reshui
Daban Shankou
Gangca
Hairag
Beichuan
Datong
Huzhu
Ledu
Haiyan
Haixin Shan 3266
Qinghai Lake
Haiyan
Huangyuan
Xining
Ping'an
Minhe
Heimahe
Jiangxigou
Huangzhong
Zawa
Hualong
Maying
Yongjing
Dongxiang
Linxia
Gonghe
Daotanghe
Nangdo
Guide
Jainca
Xunhua
Jishishan
Longyangxia Shuiku
Gomangxung
Tongren
Xiahe
Hezuo
Lintan
Luqu
Madoi
Maqên
Henan
Sêrlung
Maqu
Têwo
Zoigê
Jigzhi
Aba(Ngawa)
Hongyuan
Darlag
Baima
Sêrtar
Zamtang
Heishui
Barkam
Dêgê
Garzê
Luhuo (Zhaggo)
Jinchuan (Quqên)

SCALE 1 : 5 000 000   0   50   100   150   200km

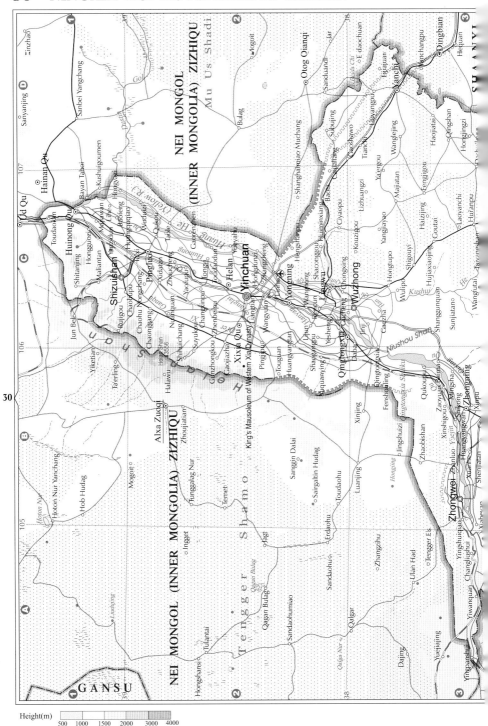

Height(m)

| 500 | 1000 | 1500 | 2000 | 3000 | 4000 |

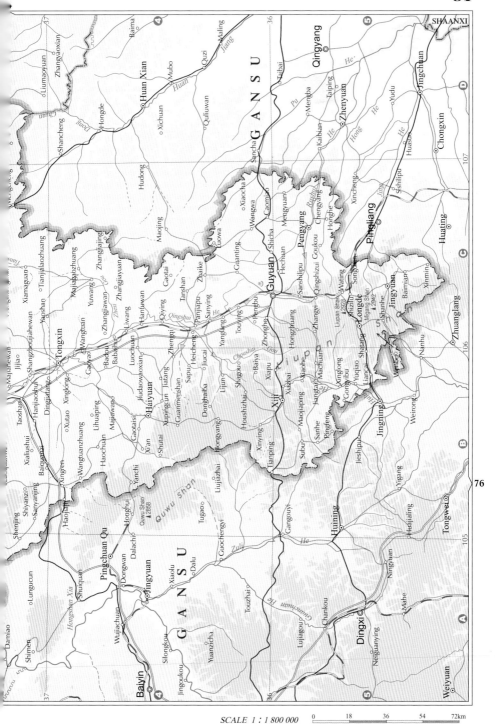

SHAANXI

GANSU

SCALE 1 : 1 800 000

| 0 | 18 | 36 | 54 | 72km |

76

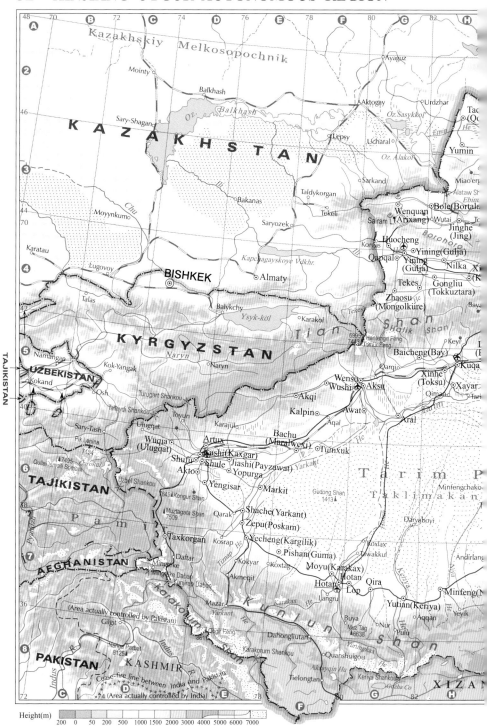

Height(m)
200 0 50 200 500 1000 1500 2000 3000 4000 5000 6000 7000

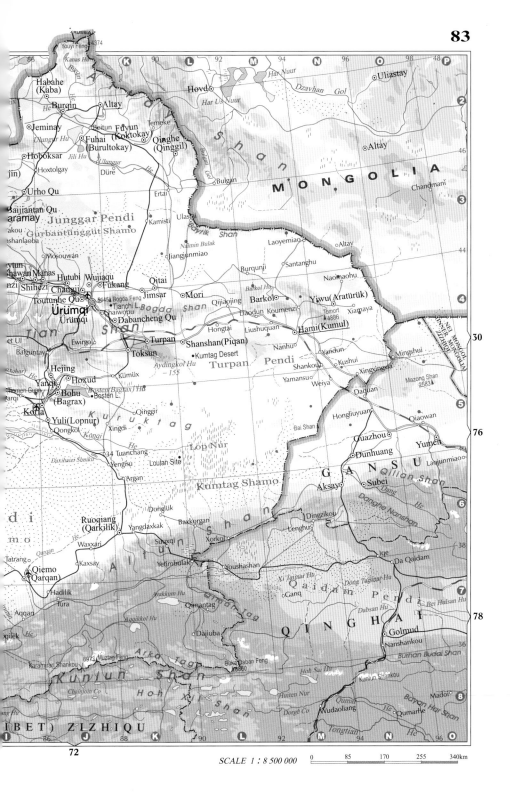

RUSSIA
Youyi Feng 4374
Kanas Hu
Bulgin
He
Habahe (Kaba)
Burqin
Altay
Jeminay
Beitun Fuyun (Koktokay)
Ulungur Hu
Fuhai (Burultokay)
Qinghe (Qinggil)
Hoboksar
Jili Hu
Hoxtolgay
Düre
Ullungur
He
Ertai
Urho Qu
Baijiantan Qu
aramay
Karamay
Junggar Pendi
Kamisti
Ulasqi
Gurbantünggüt Shamo
shanlaoba
Mosouwan
Naimin Bulak
Jiangjunmiao
Shawan Manas
Hutubi Wujiaqu
Fukang
Qitai
nzi Shihezi Changji
Jimsar
Mori
Toutunhe Qu
8445 Bogda Feng
Tianchi L.
Ürümqi
Ürümqi
Chaiwopu
Dabancheng Qu
Barkol Hu
Qijiaojing
Barkol
Yiwu(Aratürük)
et Ul
Ewirgol
Turpan
Shanshan(Piqan)
Hongtai
Liushuquan
Hami(Kumul)
Balguntay
Hejing
Toksun
Kumtag Desert
Aydingkol Hu
-155
Nanhu
Yandun
Yanqi
Hoxud
Klimüx
Turpan Pendi
Shankou
Kushui
Xingxingxia
Mazong Shan
2583
Bohu (Bagrax)
Bosten(Bagrax) Hu
Bosten L.
Yamansu
Weiya
Daquan
Korla
Qinggir
Bai Shan
Hongliuyuan
Qiaowan
Yuli(Lopnur)
Xingdi
Kuruktag
Kongi
He
Oongkol
Lop Nur
Guazhou
Yumen
Daxihaizi Shuiku
234 Tuanchang
Loulan Site
Dunhuang
Laojunmiao
Yengisu
Argan
Kumtag Shamo
GANSU
Qilian shan
Donglük
Aksay
Subei
Dang
He
Ruoqiang (Qarklik)
Yangdaxkak
Baxkorgan
Dingzikou
Danghe Nanshan
Waxxari
Sugxgi
Xorko
Lenghu
Ige
Da Qaidam
Qarqan
Kaxsay
Yetimbulak
Youshashan
Qiemo (Qarqan)
Hadilik
Qimantag
Ganq
Qaidam Pendi
Dabsan Hu
Bei Huisan Hu
Tura
Aqqan
Wakkum Hu
Maqikkol Hu
Dajiuba
QINGHAI
Golmud
Nanshankou
Burhan Budai Shan
6973 Muztag Feng
Arka tag
Buka Daban Feng 6860
Kunlun Shankou
Karamiran Shankou
Kunlun Shan
Hoh
Xil Shan
Hoh Sai Hu
Huiten Nur
Qumar
Madoi
Chainjoin Co
Dorge Co
Wudaoliang
He
Qumarhe
(TIBET) ZIZHIQU
Tongtian
Baron Har Shan

MONGOLIA
Uliastay
Dzavhan Gol
Hovd
Har Nuur
Har Us Nuur
Altay
Bulgan
Chandmani
Borlik Shan
Laoyemiao
Altay
Santanghu
Burqunji
Naomaohu
Tomort 4886
Xiamaya
Koumenzi
Haodun
Yandun

SCALE 1 : 8 500 000

0   85   170   255   340km

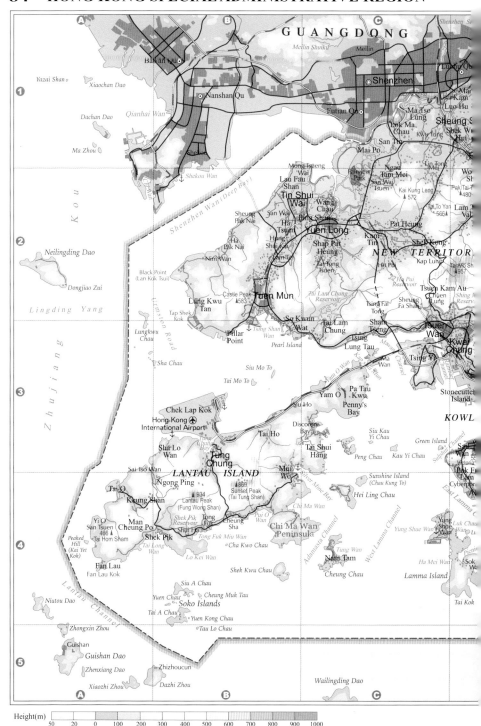

Height(m)
50 20 0 100 200 300 400 500 600 700 800 900 1000

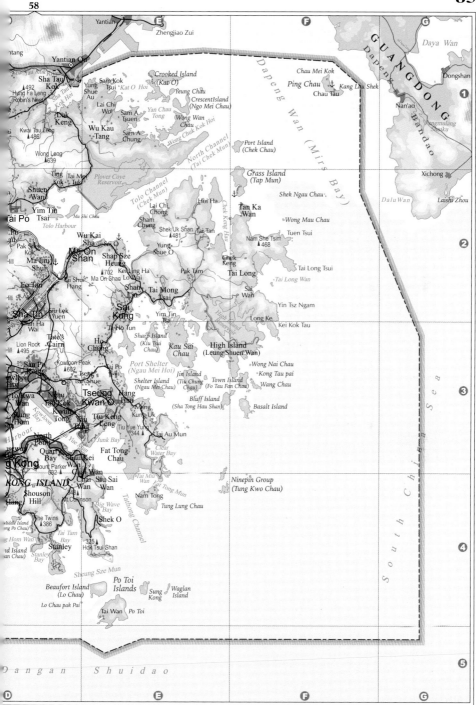

Yantian
Zhengjiao Zui
Yantian Qu

GUANGDONG

Daya Wan

Dongshan

Dapeng Bandao

①

ntang

Sha Tau
Kok ▲492
Hung Fa Leng
(Robin's Nest)
Kwai Tau Leng ▲486

Sam Kok
Yung
Shue
Au
Lai Chi
Wo
Sam A
Tsuen
Wu Kau
Tang
Sam A
Chung

Kat O Hoi

*Crooked Island
(Kat O)*
Yeung Chau
CrescentIsland
(Ngo Mei Chau)
Wong Wan
Chau
*Yan Chau
Tong*
Wong Chuk Kok Hoi

Chau Mei Kok

Ping Chau ↓ Kang Lau Shek
Chau Tau

Dapeng Wan (Mirs Bay)

Nan'ao

Fengmuliang Shuiku

Xichong

Laishi Zhou

Wong Leng ▲639

Ting
Kok
Tai Mei
Tuk
*Plover Cove
Reservoir*

Shuen
Wan
Yim Tin
Tsai
Tai Po
Tolo Harbour

Ma Shi Chau

*Tolo Channel
(Chek Mun)*

Lai Chi
Chong
Sham
Chung
Shek Uk Shan ▲481

Hoi Ha

Tan Ka
Wan

Port Island
(Chek Chau)

*Grass Island
(Tap Mun)*

Shek Ngau Chau

Daiu Wan

North Channel
(Tai Chek Mun)

Wong Mau Chau

Chek Kong Hau

②

Pak Shek
Kok
Mui Tsz
Shui
Wu Kai
Sha

Ma On
Shan
Shap Sze
Heung
▲702
Ma On Shan
Lo Wai
Kei Ling Ha

Lai O
Yung
Shue O
Tai Tan

Pak Tam

Nam She Tsim
▲468
Tuen Tsui

Tai Long Tsui

Eo Tan
Tai Shui
Hang
Sha
Tin
Tai Mong
Tsai

Chek
Keng
Tai Long
Sai
Wan

Tai Long Wan

Sha Tin
Shan Ha
Wai
Lion Rock
▲495
Tate's
Cairn
Sai
Kong
Yim Tin
Tsai
Tai Ho Tun
Ho
Chung
Long Ke
Yin Tsz Ngam
Kei Kok Tau

High Island Reservoir

San Po
Kong
Kowloon Peak
▲602
*Sharp Island
(Kiu Tsui
Chau)*
Kau Sai
Chau
High Island
(Leung Shuen Wan)

Tseng
Lan
Shue
Tai Po
Tsai
*Port Shelter
(Ngau Mei Hoi)*
Jin Island
Wong Nai Chau
Kong Tau pai

Tseung
Kwan O
Tiu Keng
Leng
*Shelter Island
(Tiu Chung
Chau)*
Town Island
(Fo Tau Fan Chau)
Wang Chau

③

To Kwa
Wan
Kwun
Tong
Yau
Tong
Tseung
Leng
Tang
Kung Uk
Tiu Yue Yung
*Bluff Island
(Sha Tong Hau Shan)*
Basalt Island

North
Point
Quarry
Bay
Mount Parker
▲582
Junk Bay
Tai Au Mun
Tai Wan Mau

g Kong
Shau Kei
Wan
Fat Tong
Chau
*Clear
Water Bay*

KONG ISLAND
Shouson
Hill
Mt Collinson
Siu Sai
Wan
*Tai Miu
Wan*
Tong Mun
Ninepin Group
(Tung Kwo Chau)

Hang
The Twins
▲386
*Big Wave
Bay*
Nam Tong
Tung Lung Chau

④

ddle Island
ng Po Chau)
*Tai Tam
Bay*
Shek O

d Island
an Chau)
Stanley
Bay
Stanley
325
Hok Tsui Shan

Shcung Sze Mun

Beaufort Island
(Lo Chau)
Po Toi
Islands
Sung
Kong
Waglan
Island

Lo Chau pak Pai
Tai Wan Po Toi

South China Sea

⑤

D a n g a n   S h u i d a o

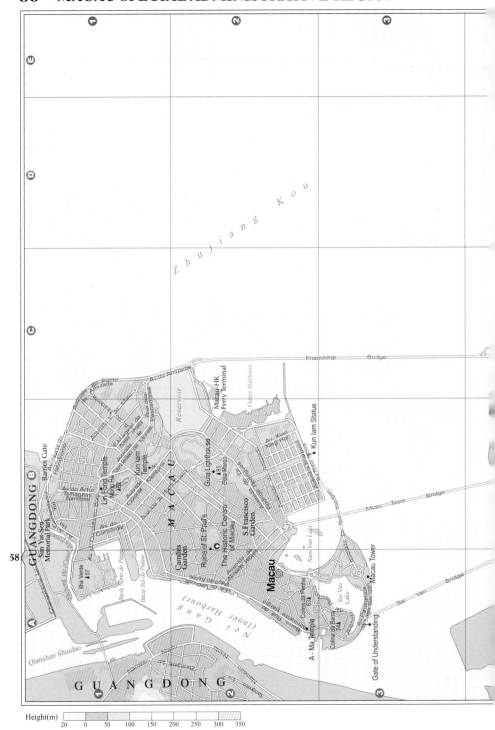

Height(m)
20 0 50 100 150 200 250 300 350

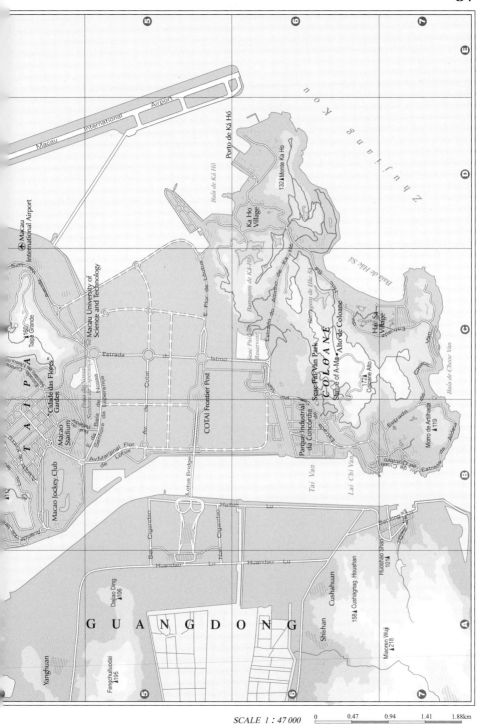

Zhujiang Kou

Macau International Airport

Airport

Macau

Porto de Ká Hó

Baía de Ká Hó

132 Monte Ka Ho

Ka Ho
Village

Barragem de Ká Hó

Barragem de Hác Sá

Baía de Hác Sá

Macau
International Airport

Macau University of
Science and Technology

T A I P A

160
Taipa Grande

"Cidade das Flores"
Garden

Estrada

do

Seac Pai Van Park

Seac Pai Van
Reservoir

C O L O A N E

Alto de Coloane

Estátue of A-Ma

Hác Sá
Village

Van

E. Flor de Lotus

Istmo

Baía de Choc Van

Macao
Stadium

Cotai

Ax

COTAI Frontier Post

Parque Industrial
da Concórdia

174
Coloane Alto

Macao Jockey Club

Av. Marginal Flor.
de Lotus

E. da Senhora da Nossa
Senhora da Esperança

Praia da Nossa
Baía de

Morro de Artilhaté
119

Estrada

Av. de Cinco

Tai Van

Lai Chi Van

Lotus Bridge

Haibin Lu

Cigandao

Cigandao

Huoshao Shan
101

Huandao Lu

Huandao Lu

Dajiao Ding
106

Shishan

Cushahuan

158 Cushagnag Houshan

Miaoren Wuj
1218

G U A N G D O N G

Yanghuan

Fengchuluodai
195

Yanghuan

Height(m)

8000	6000	4000	3000	2000	1000	200	50	0	50	200	500	1000	1500	2000	3000	4000

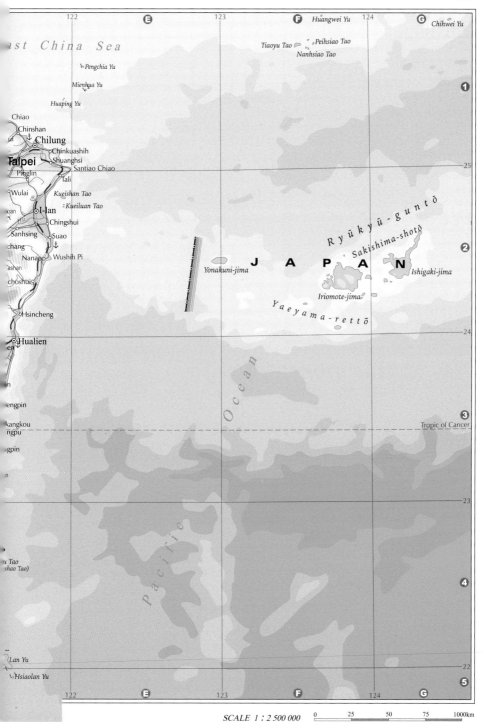

East China Sea

Chihwei Yu

Huangwei Yu

Tiaoyu Tao
Peihsiao Tao
Nanhsiao Tao

Pengchia Yu

Mienhua Yu

Huaping Yu

Chiao
Chinshan
Chilung
Chinkuashih
Shuanghsi
Taipei
Santiao Chiao
Pinglin
Tali
Wulai
Kueishan Tao
I-lan
Kueiluan Tao
Chingshui
Sanhsing
Suao
chang
Nanao
Wushih Pi
ashan
choshui

Ryūkyū-guntō

Sakishima-shotō

Ishigaki-jima

J A P A N

Yonakuni-jima

Hsincheng

Iriomote-jima

Hualien
en

Yaeyama-rettō

engpin

Ocean

kangkou
ngpu

Tropic of Cancer

gpin

Pacific

u Tao
shao Tao)

Lan Yu

Hsiaolan Yu

SCALE 1 : 2 500 000

0   25   50   75   1000km

Beijing

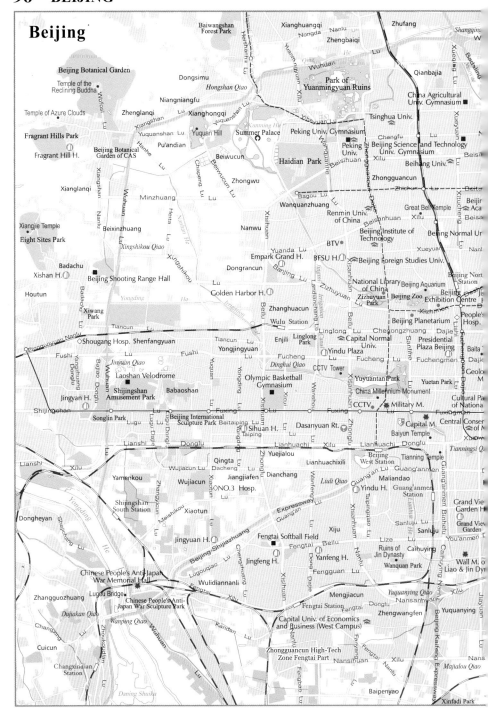

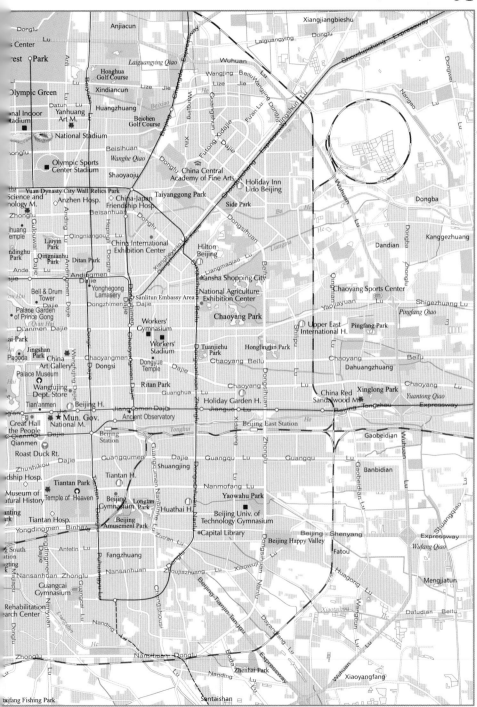

Donglu
Lu
s Center
rest Park
Anjiacun
Xiangjiangbieshu
Laiguangying
Donglu
Shoudujichang Expressway
Laiguangying Qiao
Wuhuan
Wangling Beilu
Dongwei
Honghua
Golf Course
Lize Jie
Lize Jie
Wangling Donglu
Nangao
Xindiancun
Guangshun
He
Jingshun
Olympic Green
Beixiao
Huangzhuang
Datun Lu
Xilu
Fuan Lu
Yanhuang
Art M.
Beichen
Golf Course
nal Indoor
tadium
Futong Xidajie
National Stadium
Beisihuan
Wanghe Qiao
Dongba
Olympic Sports
Center Stadium
Dongsihuan Lu
Shaoyaoju
China Central
Academy of Fine Arts
Dongba
Ba He
Dongba
Kanggezhuang
Yuan Dynasty City Wall Relics Park
Holiday Inn
Lido Beijing
Side Park
Dongba Zhonglu
Science and
nology M.
Anzhen Hosp.
China-Japan
Friendship Hosp.
Taiyanggong Park
Dandian
Zhonglu
Beisanhuan
Dongsihuan Lu
Hepingli
Qingniangou Lu
Liangma
He
Chaoyang Sports Center
huang
emple
Liuyin
Park
China International
Exhibition Center
Hilton
Beijing
Liangna
Shigezhuang Lu
ndinghu
Park
Qinglianhu
Park
Ditan Park
Liangmaqiao Lu
Beilu
Yaojiayuan
Pingfang Qiao
Ande
jie
Andingmen
Dajie
Yansha Shopping City
Shilipu
Qingnianlu
Yonghegong
Lamasery
National Agriculture
Exhibition Center
Chaoyang Park
Upper East
International H.
Pingfang Park
ou Hai
Bell & Drum
Tower
Dongzhimen Dajie
Sanlitun Embassy Area
Chaoyang
Dahuangzhuang
Palace Garden
of Prince Gong
Qian Hai
Di'anmen Dajie
Workers'
Gymnasium
Tuanjiehu
Park
Honglingjin Park
Chaoyang Beilu
Chaoyang
ai Park
Jingshan
Park
Workers'
Stadium
Dongsihuan Lu
Xinglong Park
Yuantong Qiao
Pagoda
China
Art Gallery
Chaoyangmen
Dongsi
Dongyue
Temple
Dajie
Chaoyang Beilu
China Red
Sandalwood M.
Chaoyang
Tongzhou
Expressway
Palace Museum
Ritan Park
Guanghua
Chaoyang Nanlu
Wangfujing
Dept. Store
Tian'anmen
Beijing H.
Jianguomen Dajie
Holiday Garden H.
Jianguo Lu
Gaobeidian
Great Hall
the People
Mun. Gov.
National M.
Ancient Observatory
Tonghui
He
Beijing East Station
Qianmen
Roast Duck Rt.
Beijing
Station
Zhonghuan
Guangqu Lu
Guangqu
Lu
Banbidian
Zhushikou
Dajie
Guangqumen
Dajie
Shuangjing
Guangqu Lu
Gaobeidian Lu
dship Hosp.
Tiantan Park
Tiantan H.
Nanmofang Lu
Dongsihuan Lu
Museum of
atural History
Temple of Heaven
Beijing
Gymnasium
Longtan
Park
Huatai H.
Yaowahu Park
Chengshou
anting
ark
Tiantan Hosp.
Beijing
Amusement Park
Beijing Univ. of
Technology Gymnasium
Beijing - Shenyang
Shuangqiao
Expressway
Wufang Qiao
Yongdingmen Binhe
South
ation
Anfein Lu
Zuo'an
Capital Library
Beijing Happy Valley
Fatou
Huagong Lu
Fangzhuang
Dongsihuan Lu
Xiaowuji
Nanfang
k
Nansanhuan Zhonglu
Nansanhuan
Zhoujiazhuang
Daxing
Mengjiatun
Guangcai
Gymnasium
Nanerhuan
Beijing-Tianjin-Tanggu
Davanlu
Wanghuan
Lu
Datudian Beilu
Rehabilitation
arch Center
Nanding
He
Expressway
Zhonglu
Nansihuan Donglu
Zhenhai Park
Nanding
Xiaoyangfang
aifang Fishing Park
Santaishan

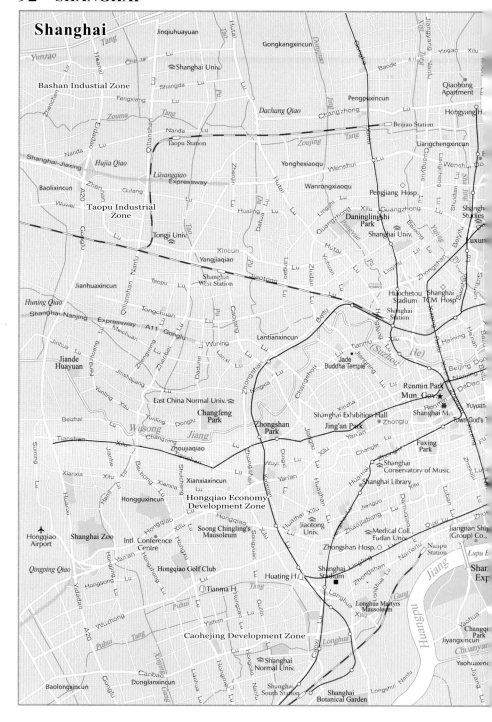

Tianji

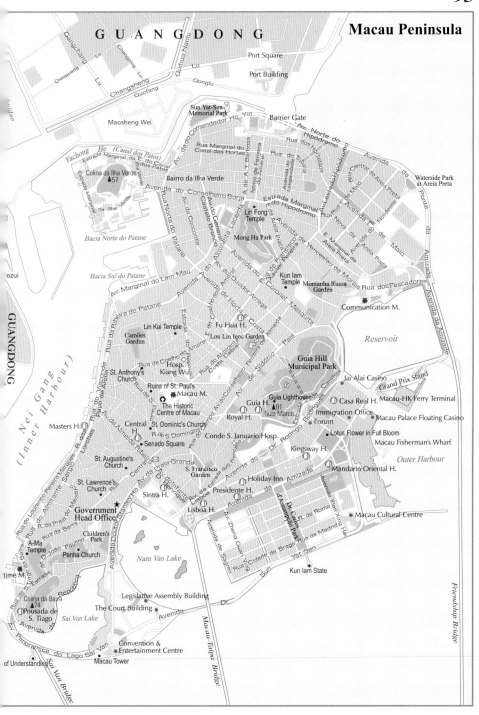

G·U·A·N·G·D·O·N·G

GUANGDONG

Port Square
Port Building

Sun Yat-Sen Memorial Park
Maosheng Wei
Ho Yin
Barrier Gate

Av. Norte do Hipodromo

Gangchang
Qiaoguang
Changsheng
Guofang
Lu
Quihua Namti
Gonglu

Yachong He (Canal dos Patos)
Estrada Marginal da E. dos Patos
Colina da Ilha Verde
57
Bairro da Ilha Verde
Estrada Marginal da Ilha Verde
Avenida do Conselheiro Borja

Rua Marginal do Canal das Hortas
Rua do Trilvra

Waterside Park at Areia Preta

Bacia Norte do Patane

Lin Fong Temple
Mong Ha Park

ozui

Bacia Sul do Patane

Av. Marginal do Lam Mau

Kun Iam Temple
Montanha Russa Garden
Rua dos Pescadores
Communication M.

Reservoir

Lin Kai Temple
Camões Garden
Fu Hua H.
Lou Lin Ioc Garden

St. Anthony's Church
Hosp. Kiang Wu
Ruins of St. Paul's
Macau M.
The Historic Centre of Macau
Royal H.
St. Dominic's Church
Central H.
Conde S. Januario Hosp.

Guia Hill Municipal Park
Jai Alai Casino
Grand Prix Stand
Guia H.
Guia Lighthouse
91
Guia Marco
Casa Real H.
Macau-HK Ferry Terminal
Immigration Office
Macau Palace Floating Casino
Forum
Lotus Flower in Full Bloom
Macau Fisherman's Wharf

Masters H.

Senado Square
St. Augustine's Church
St. Lawrence's Church
S. Francisco Garden
Kingsway H.
Outer Harbour

Government Head Office
Sintra H.
Holiday Inn
Presidente H.
Lisboa H.
Mandarin Oriental H.

Children's Park
A-Ma Temple
Penha Church
Nam Van Lake
Macau Cultural Centre

time M.

Colina da Barra
74
Pousada de S. Tiago
Sai Van Lake
Kun Iam State

The Court Building
Legislative Assembly Building

Convention & Entertainment Centre
Macau Tower

of Understanding

Nei Gang (Inner Harbour)

Friendship Bridge

Macau-Taipa Bridge

Sai Van Bridge

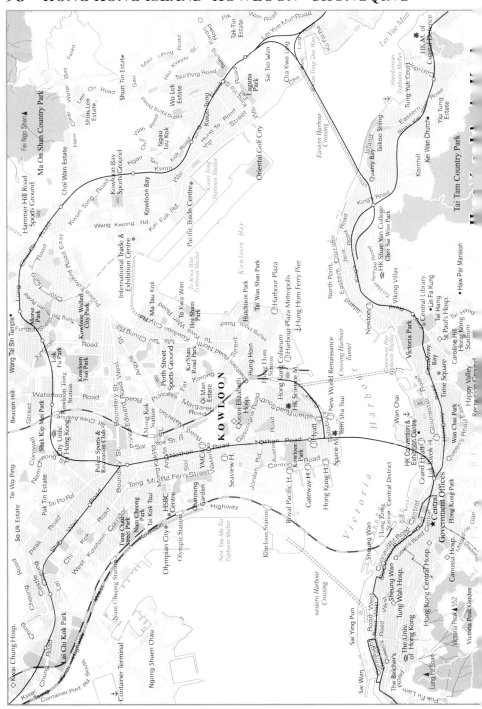

Wuhan Iron & Steel (Group) Corp.
Qingshan Park
Qingshan Gang
Yangchun Hu
Heping Park
Wuhan No.9 Hosp.
Linjiang Park
Tujiadun
Yangjiaqiqan
Xiamamiao
Yaoshangwan
Monument of the Nine Heroines
Wuhan Univ. Technology
Wuhan Children's Hosp.
Hepingxincun
Xiaotan Hu
Baima Zhou
Fei'eshan
Yaotanghu
Dong Hu
Huangjiadawan
Wuchang East Station
Dujiazui
Yanzhongzui
Xiaomachang
Ezui
Liyuan
Hubei M
East Lake Scenic Area
East Lake H.
Mo Shan
Wuhan Botanical Garden
Moshan Botanical Garden
Donghu Hosp.
Fengzheng Shan
Yujia Shan
Bijia Shan
Yujia Hu
Ma'anshan Forest Park
Huzhong Univ. of Science & Tech.
Lake View Garden
Luojia Shan
Wuhan Univ.
Huazhong Normal Univ.
The East Lake High-Tech Development Zone
Hongshan Park
Baotong Temple
Wuhan Univ. of Technology
Prov. Gov.
Caijiazui
Qingyuzui
Hubei Univ.
Sha Hu
Lijiang
Hongshan Stadium
Changchun Temple
Wuchang Station
Construction Bank
Ziyang Park
Yellow Crane Tower
Wuhan Conservatory of Music
Beigangzui
Nan Hu
Dingtaimiao
Chang Jiang
Wuhan Second Changjiang Bridge
Wuchang North Station
Yangtze R.
Jianshexincun
Xuzhouxincun
Guo Bin Grand H.
Jiefang Park
Jiang'an West Station
Mun. Gov.
HK & Macao Centre Business H.
Wuhan Port
Holiday Inn Tian'an
Golden Sanjiu H.
Shangri-La
Red Across Hosp.
Qingchuan Pavilion
Holiday Inn Riverside H.
Wuhan Changjiang Bridge
Gui Shan
Lianhuahu Park
Zhongshan Park
Union Hosp.
Wuhan No.1 Hosp.
Jinjiang
Oriental H.
Hankou Station
Asia H.
Ancient Zither Platform
Guiyuan Temple
Hanyang Station
Changqinghuayuan
Hankou West Station
Xindunxincun
Gaomiao
Han Shui
Wuhan Zoo
Moshui Hu
Taishansi
Golf Club
Macang Hu

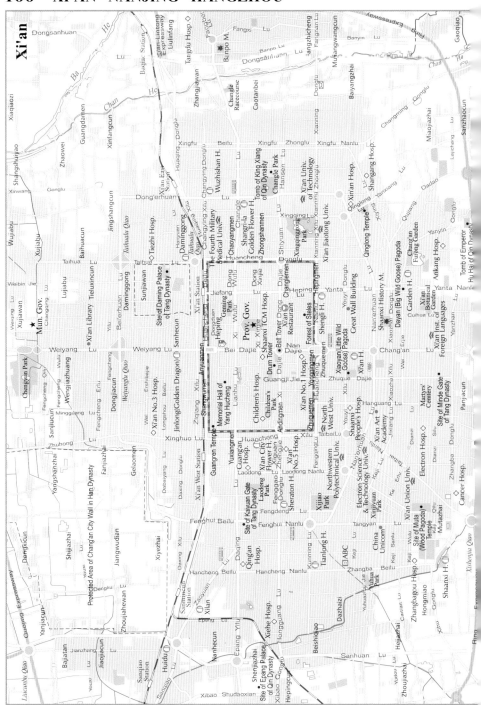

Xi'an

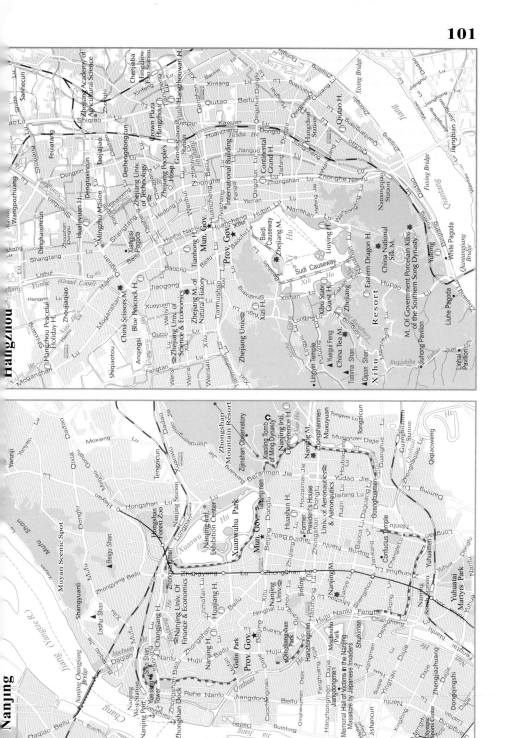

Hangzhou

Nanjing

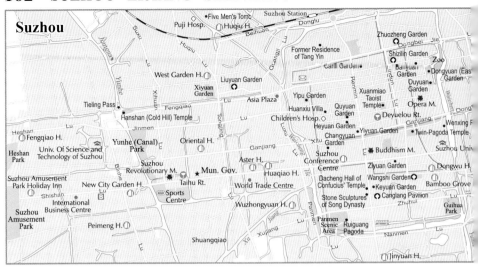

Suzhou

Five Men's Tomb
Puji Hosp.
Huqiu H.
Suzhou Station
Donglu
Beihuan
Zhuozheng Garden
Dongbei Jie
Shizilin Garden
Former Residence of Tang Yin
Caoli Garden
Zoo
Baiyuan Garden
Dongyuan (East Garden)
West Garden H.
Liuyuan Garden
Xiyuan Garden
Asia Plaza
Yipu Garden
Ouyuan Garden
Tieling Pass
Hanshan (Cold Hill) Temple
Huanxiu Villa
Xuanmiao Taoist Temple
Opera M.
Jinmen
Children's Hosp.
Quyuan Garden
Deyuelou Rt.
Wenxing
Heshan Lu
Fengqiao H.
Heyuan Garden
Changyuan Garden
Yiyuan Garden
Twin-Pagoda Temple
Heshan Park
Univ. Of Science and Technology of Suzhou
Yunhe (Canal) Park
Oriental H.
Suzhou Conference Centre
Buddhism M.
Suzhou Univ.
Suzhou Revolutionary M.
Mun. Gov.
Aster H.
Huaqiao H.
Ziyuan Garden
Dongwu H.
Suzhou Amusement Park Holiday Inn
New City Garden H.
Taihu Rt.
World Trade Centre
Dacheng Hall of Confucius' Temple
Wangshi Garden
Keyuan Garden
Bamboo Grove
International Business Centre
Sports Centre
Wuzhongyuan H.
Stone Sculptures of Song Dynasty
Canglang Pavilion
Guihua Park
Suzhou Amusement Park
Peimeng H.
Panmen Scenic Area
Ruiguang Pagoda
Nanmen
Shuangqiao
Jinyuan H.

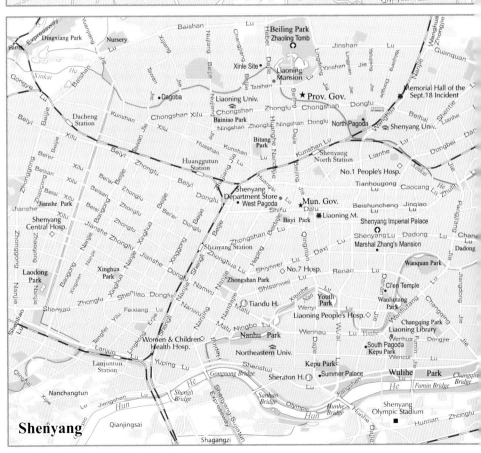

Shenyang

Expressway
Dingxiang Park
Nursery
Baishan Lu
Beiling Park
Zhaoling Tomb
Jinshan Lu
Wanghua Zhongjie
Ring
Xinkai
He
Xijiang Jie
Nujiang Jie
Changjiang Jie
Hebei Dajie
Lingdong
Guanquan
Gongye Lu
Baishan Jie
Xinle Site
Liaoning Mansion
Yinshan Jie
Yalujiang Jie
Nanjie
Dagoba
Liaoning Univ.
Taishan Jie
Prov. Gov.
Zhongshan
Donglu
Beihai
Shentie
Memorial Hall of the Sept.18 Incident
Dacheng Station
Kunshan
Chongshan Xilu
Chongshan
Bainiao Park
Ningshan Zhonglu
North Pagoda
Shenyang Univ.
Dongbei Dar
Belyi
Xilu
Xilu
Huashan
Kunshan
Bitang Park
Lianhe
Dongbei Lu
Beisan
Xilu
Bei'er Beijie
Zhonglu
Beiyi
Huanggutun Station
Shenyang North Station
No.1 People's Hosp.
Zhongguo
Jianshe Park
Beisan
Xilu
Beijie
Zhonglu
Dongbei
Huangsi
Beijing
Tianhougou Lu
Caocang Lu
He
Zhonghui
Shenyang Central Hosp.
Jianshe Zhongfu
Bei'er Dongfu
Shenyang Department Store
West Pagoda
Shifu
Mun. Gov.
Dalu
Liaoning M.
Beishuncheng Jinqiao Lu
Shenyang Imperial Palace
Chang Lu Dadong
Laodong Park
Xinghua Park
Jianshe
Xinggong
Shenyang Station
Zhongshan Lu
Heping
Bayi Park
Qingnian
Shenyang Lu Dadong
Marshal Zhang's Mansion
Wanquan Park
Zhonglu
Shenliao Donglu
Dongtu
Shengli
Zhonghua Lu
Shiyiwei
No.7 Hosp.
Renao
Ci'en Temple
Jiangdong
Feixiang Lu
Erjie
Nanwu
Zhongshan Park
Shisanwei
Xinhe
Youth Park
Wanliutang Park
Wanliutang
Changqing
Shenliao
Tiandu H.
Nan
Wenyi
Liaoning People's Hosp.
Changqing Park
Liaoning Library
Tengfei
Lanjun
Lingtou Dong
Women & Children Health Hosp.
Matu
Ningbo
Nanhu Park
Wenhua
Wai Lu
Yunhe
Dongjie
Lanjuntun Station
Yuping Lu
Northeastern Univ.
Shenshui
Kepu Park
South Pagoda
Kepu Park
Wencun
Nanchangtun
He
Gongnong Bridge
Sheraton H.
Summer Palace
Jiangnan
Wulihe Park
Changqing Bridge
Qinghai
Jiangshen
Lu
Xijie
Hun
Shengli Bridge
Sanhao Bridge
Olympic
Hunhe Bridge
Fumin Bridge
Qianjingsai
Hun
Shagangzi
Shenyang Olympic Stadium
Hunnan
Zhonglu

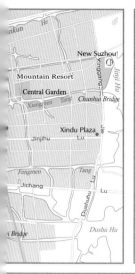

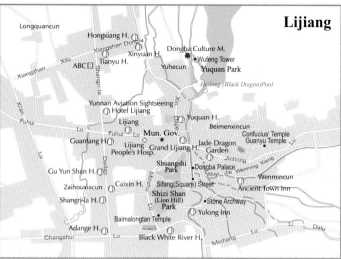

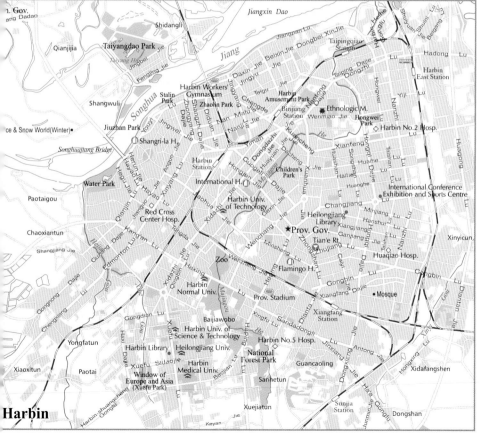

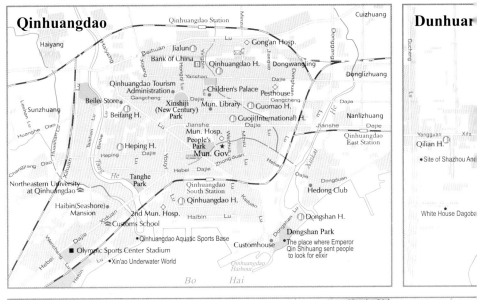

Qinhuangdao

Haiyang

Qinhuangdao Station

Cuizhuang

Gongan Hosp.

Jialun
Bank of China
Qinhuangdao H.
Dongwangling

Qinhuangdao Tourism Administration
Children's Palace
Pesthouse

Dongwangling

Donglizhuang

Beilei Store
Xinshiji (New Century) Park
Mun. Library
Guomao H.

Nanlizhuang

Beifang H.
Guoji (International) H.

Sunzhuang

Mun. Hosp.
People's Park
Mun. Gov.

Qinhuangdao East Station

Heping H.

Northeastern University at Qinhuangdao
Tanghe Park

Qinhuangdao South Station
Qinhuangdao H.

Dongduan
Hedong Club

Haibin (Seashore) Mansion
2nd Mun. Hosp.
Customs School

Dongshan H.

Qinhuangdao Aquatic Sports Base
Customhouse
Dongshan Park

Olympic Sports Center Stadium
Xin'ao Underwater World

The place where Emperor Qin Shihuang sent people to look for elixir

Qinhuangdao Harbour

Bo Hai

Dunhuan

Qilian H.

Site of Shazhou And

White House Dagoba

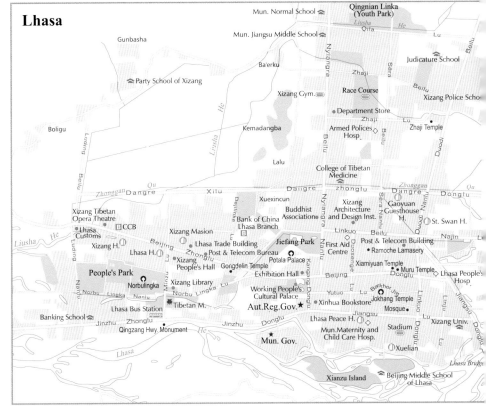

Lhasa

Mun. Normal School

Qingnian Linka (Youth Park)

Gunbasha

Mun. Jiangsu Middle School

Judicature School

Party School of Xizang

Ba'erku

Xizang Gym.
Race Course

Xizang Police Scho

Boligu

Kemadangba

Department Store
Armed Polices Hosp.

Zhaji Temple

Lalu

College of Tibetan Medicine

Dangre
Xitu
Dangre
zhonglu
Dangre
Donglu

Xuexincun
Buddhist Association
Xizang Architecture and Design Inst.
Gaoyuan Guesthouse H.
St. Swan H.

Xizang Tibetan Opera Theatre
CCB
Xizang Masion
Bank of China Lhasa Branch
First Aid Centre
Post & Telecom Building
Ramoche Lamasery

Lhasa Customs
Xizang H.
Lhasa H.
Lhasa Trade Building
Jiefang Park
Xiamiyuan Temple
Muru Temple
Lhasa People's Hosp.

People's Park
Xizang People's Hall
Gongdelin Temple
Potala Palace
Exhibition Hall

Norbulingka
Xizang Library
Working People's Cultural Palace
Xinhua Bookstore
Jokhang Temple
Mosque

Banking School
Lhasa Bus Station
Tibetan M.
Aut.Reg.Gov.
Lhasa Peace H.
Xizang Univ.

Qingzang Hwy. Monument
Mun.Maternity and Child Care Hosp.
Stadium
Xuelian

Mun. Gov.

Xianzu Island
Beijing Middle School of Lhasa

Lhasa Bridge

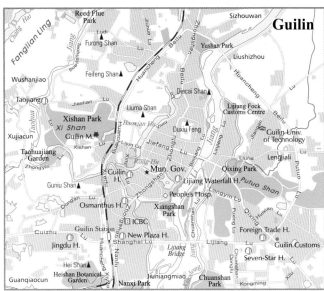

Guilin

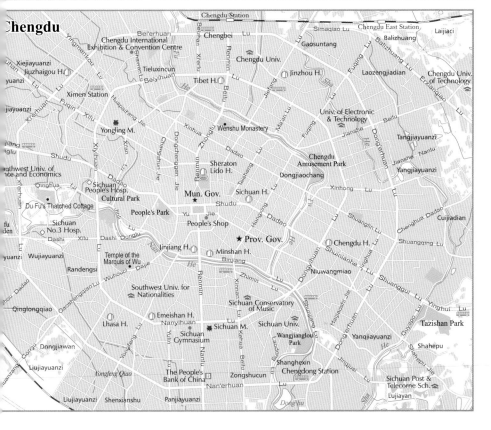

Chengdu

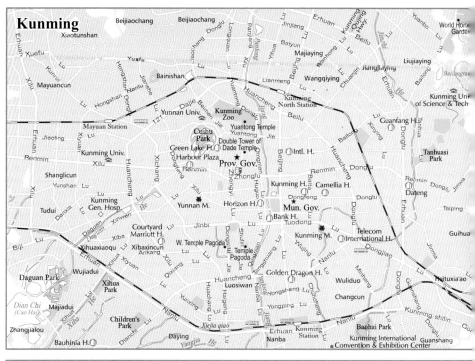

Kunming

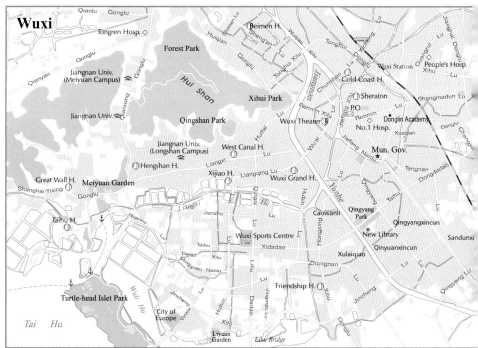

Wuxi

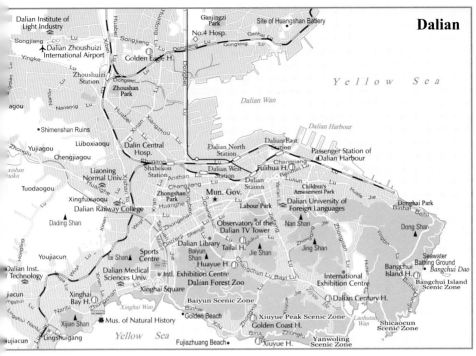

Dalian

Dalian Institute of Light Industry
Songjiang
Yingke
Dalian Zhoushuizi International Airport
Golden Eagle H.
Zhoushuizi Station
Dongwei
Zhoushan Park
Nansong
agou
Ganjingzi Park
No.4 Hosp.
Gongxing
Site of Huangshan Battery
Dongbei
Yellow Sea
Dalian Wan
Dalian Harbour
Dalian East Station
Passenger Station of Dalian Harbour
Shimenshan Ruins
Yujiacun
Chengjiagou
Lüboxiaoqu
Zhonglu
xishan
uiku
Tuodaogou
Liaoning Normal Univ.
Xingfuxiaoqu
Dalian Railway College
Dading Shan
Dalin Central Hosp.
Shahekou Station
Zhongshan Park
Changling
Dalian North Station
Anshan
Dalian West Station
Fulihua H.
Dalian Station
Mun. Gov.
Children's Amusement Park
Labour Park
Dalian University of Foreign Languages
Huale Jie
Donghai Park
Observatory of the Dalian TV Tower
Nan Shan
Dong Shan
Dalian Library
Baiyun Shan
Tailai H.
Jie Shan
Jing Shan
Youjiacun
Tai Shan
Sports Centre
Huayue H.
Intl. Exhibition Centre
Dalian Forest Zoo
International Exhibition Centre
Seawater Bathing Ground
Bangchui Dao
Bangchui Island H.
Bangchui Island Scenic Zone
Dalian Inst. Technology
Dalian Medical Sciences Univ.
Xinghai Square
Baiyun Scenic Zone
Dalian Century H.
jiacun
ngshui
Xinghai Bay H.
Xijian Shan
Lingshuigang
Mus. of Natural History
Golden Beach
Xinghai Wan
Binhai
Xiuyue Peak Scenic Zone
Golden Coast H.
Laohutan Wan
Shicaocun Scenic Zone
ujiacun
Yellow Sea
Fujiazhuang Beach
Xiuyue H.
Yanwoling Scenic Zone

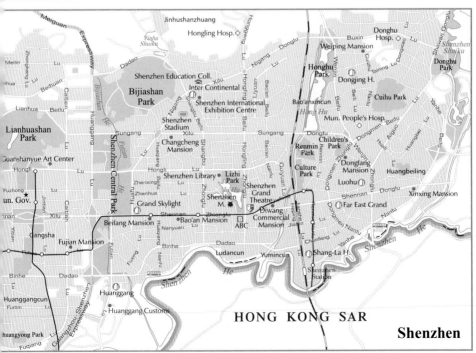

Meiguan
Jinhushanzhuang
Yinhu Shuiku
Hongling Hosp.
Buxin
Donghu Hosp.
Shawan Shuiku
Shenzhen Shuiku
Meilin
Zhongxing Lu
Dadao
Caitian
Beihuan
Weiping Mansion
Tanling
Donghu Park
ihua
Beihuan
Lianhua
Shenzhen Education Coll.
Inter Continental
Nigang
Honghu Park
Dongjing H.
Cuihu Park
Lianhuashan Park
Bijiashan Park
Shenzhen International Exhibition Centre
Shenzhen Stadium
Hong Hu
Bao'anxincun
Mun. People's Hosp.
Guanshanyue Art Center
Hongli
Sungang
Changcheng Mansion
Shangbu
Sungang
Renmin Park
Children's Park
Dongfang Mansion
Huangbeiling
Fuzhong
un. Gov.
Xitu
Shenzhen Library
Lizhi Park
Culture Park
Luohu
Xinxing Mansion
Grand Skylight
Lizhi Hu
Shenzhen M.
Shenzhen Grand Theatre
Far East Grand
Beifang Mansion
Bao'an Mansion
ABC
Diwang Commercial Mansion
Gangsha
Fujian Mansion
Binhe
Ludancun
Yumincun
Shang-La H.
Shenzhen Station
Binhe
Dadao
Huanggang
Huangganggun
Fumin
Huanggang Customs
Shenzhen He
HONG KONG SAR
huangyong Park
Fuqiang

Shenzhen

Xiamen

Ürümqi

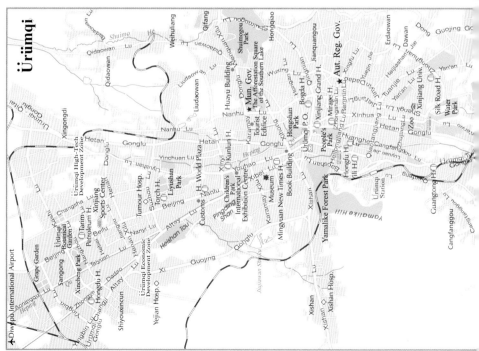

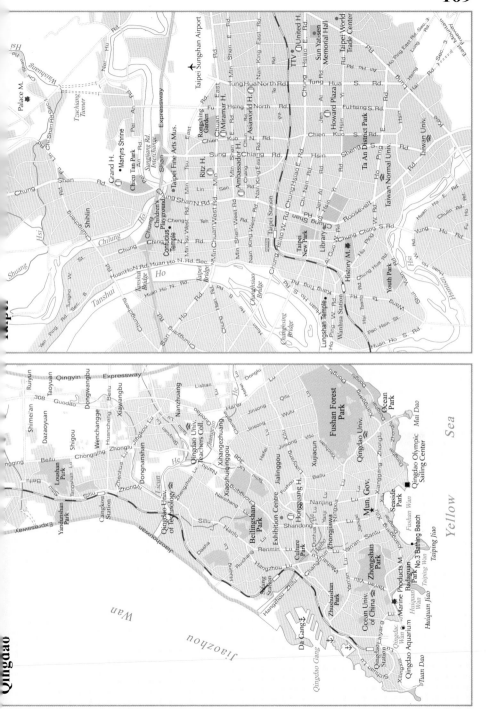

Taipei

Palace M.
Hsi Chih Shan Rd Sec. 3
Hsi
Waishuang Chi
Tsuchuang Tunnel
Taipei Sungshan Airport
TTV United H.
Sun Yat-sen Memorial Hall
Taipei World Trade Center
Hu Rd
Nai Rd
Pei An Rd
Sungkiang Rd Interchange
Shan Expressway
Min Shan E. Rd
Nan King East Rd
Chung Hsiao E. Rd Sec. 3
East Keelung Rd Sec. 3
Ping Tung East Rd Sec. 3
Tung Hua North Rd
Chung Hua
S. Rd
Grand H.
Martyrs Shrine
Chien Tan Park
Rongsing Garden
Miramar H.
Asiaworld H.
Howard Plaza
FuHsing S. Rd
Kee
Fu East
Chuan
Hsing North Rd
Jen Ai
Kuo
Taiwan Univ.
Chung
Shan
Rd
Taipei Fine Arts Mus.
Chien Kuo
Chien
Ta An District Park
Hsin
Shihlin
Children's Playground
Ritz H.
Ambassador H.
Chang
Nan King East Rd
Sheng Ping
Ta An Rd
Taiwan Normal Univ.
Hsi Chilung Ho
Chilung
Chung
Confucius Temple
Chingshan N. Rd
Chengji
Lin
Sen
Min Tsu West Rd
Nan King West Rd
Nan Shan West Rd
Taipei Station
Min Chuan West Rd
Hsin Yi
Roosevelt
Yung Ho Rd
Ho Rd
Shuang
Chung
St
HuanHoN Rd, Huan Ho N. Rd. Sec.
Taipei Bridge
Min Sheng West Rd
Nan King West Rd
Shan
Chung
PH
Buliny
Chung Ching S. Rd
Library
Taiwan Normal Univ.
Chubin
Tanshui
Tunshui Bridge
Huan Ho S. Rd
Taipei Bridge
Ho Rd
Chingshuo Bridge
Chung
Taipei New Park
Shan
History M.
Youth Park
Pao Ting
Chungking Bridge
Chunghsing Bridge
Lungshan Temple
Wanhua Station
Chung Hua Rd
Kang Ting
Huan Ho S. Rd
Wang

Qingdao

Ruiyun
Qingyin
Qingwangbu
Expressway
Donglu
Lu
Dongli
Ocean Park
Mai Dao
Yellow Sea
Shime'an
Taoyuan
Guodao
Dongwangbu
Beilu
Xiawangbu
Lishan
He
Qilu
Wulu
Fushan Forest Park
Dongli
Dazaoyuan
308
Huancheng
Nanzhuang
Qipodao
Hai'er
Jinsong
Qingdao Univ.
Shigou
Wenchangge
Zhonglu
Jin'gkou Lu
Zhangcun
Jinsong
Xujiacun
Beilu
Chongqing
Zhenhua
Zhonglu
Nanlu
Qingdao Univ. Teachers Coll.
Xihangezhuang
Jinsong H.
Qingdao Univ.
Longkou
Loushan Park
Tangานุ้ Lu
Lu
Xiaoshuijingou
308
Xiangang
Zhongliu
Qingdao Olympic Sailing Center
Bailu
Silu
Qingdao Univ. of Technology
Nanchang
Biaฺqiaoyuan
Beilingshan Park
Jialinggou
Lu
Ludao
Seaside Park
Fushan Wan
Yandushan Park
Cangkou Station
Nanfu
Exhibition Centre
Fuzhou
Hongguang H.
Nanjing
Mun. Gov.
Xiangang
Silu
Shandong
Yanta
Sanlu
Zhongshan
Expressway
Silu
Renmin
Lu
Culture Park
Minjiang
Zhongbwan
Wang
Taiping Wan
Jiaozhouwan
Huang
Ruchang
Hangzhou Lu
Wuhuashum
Chang Huan
Zhongshan Park
Badaguan
Taiping Jiao
Silu
Zhushushan Park
Ning
Yan'an
Yan'an
Marine Products M.
No.3 Bathing Beach
Huiquan Wan
Hangzhou Zhilu
Ocean Univ. of China
E
Badaguan
Taiping Jiao
Shang Station
Jiaozhou Wan
Da Cang
Qingdao Aquarium
Qingdao Station
Laiyang Lu
Qingdao Wan
Huiquan Jiao
Xinjiang
Sichuan Lu
Tuan Dao

ANHUI PROVINCE

Population   65.16 million
Area   140 000 square kilometers
Nationalities   Han, Hui, Mongol, Man, Miao, Yi, Zhuang and Buyei
Climatic features   Warm-temperate semi-humid monsoon climate north of the Huai He, and subtropical humid monsoon climate in the south
Average temperature   -1℃~2℃ north of Huai He and 0℃~3℃ south of Huai He in January, 27℃~28℃ in the north and above 28℃ in the south in July
Annual average rainfall   700 mm~800 mm north of Huai He, 800 mm~1700 mm south of the river
Mountains   Dabie Shan, Huang Shan and Jiuhua Shan
Rivers   Chang Jiang, Huai He, Xin'an Jiang
Local products   Tea, Anhui cuisine, traditional four treasures of the study-writing brush, ink stick, ink slab and paper
Capital   Hefei
Major cities   Hefei, Huainan, Huaibei, Wuhu, Tongling, Bengbu, Ma'anshan, Anqing, Huangshan, Chuzhou, Fuyang, Chaohu, Bozhou, Xuancheng
Tourist attractions   Huangshan Mountain, Ancient Villages in Southern Anhui, Jiuhua Mountain, Tianzhu Mountain, Langya Mountain
Comments   The Huizhou Culture is the most influential culture during Ming and Qing period. Hui Study, together with Tibetology, and study of Dunhuang caves, constitutes the three biggest local studies in contemporary China. Hui Opera is one of the main sources of Peking Opera

Map page: 44-45

BEIJING MUNICIPALITY

Population   11.84 million
Area   17 000 square kilometers
Nationalities   Han, Man, Hui and Mongol
Climatic features   Warm-temperate semi-humid monsoon climate
Average temperature   -10℃~-5℃ in January, 22℃~26℃ in July
Annual average rainfall   500 mm~700 mm
Mountains   Xi Shan, Jundu Shan
Rivers   Yongding He, Chaobai He, Beiyun He, Juma He and Wenyu He
Local products   Cloisonne, Chinese medicines, roast duck, ivory cavings, jade objects
Tourist attractions   Palace Museum, the Great Wall, Summer Palace, Temple of Heaven, the Ming Tombs and the Peking Man Site at Zhoukoudian, Tian'anmen Square, Yuanmingyuan Ruins, Lama Temple, Beihai Park, Lugou Bridge and Xiangshan Park
Comments   Peking Opera is a national treasure with a history of 200 years. It is a synthesis of stylized action, singing, dialogue and mime, acrobatic fighting and dancing. There are four main types of roles: sheng (male), dan (young female), jing (painted face, male), and chou (clown, male or female)

Map page: 22-23

CHONGQING MUNICIPALITY

Population   31.64 million
Area   82 000 square kilometers
Nationalities   Han, Tujia, Miao, Hui, Mongol and Yi
Climatic features   Subtropical humid monsoon climate, one of Chinese three notorious "ovens"
Average temperature   1℃~8℃ in January, 21℃~29℃ in July
Annual average rainfall   1000mm~1400mm
Mountains   Daba Shan, Wu Shan, and Dalou Shan
River   Chang Jiang (Yangtze River), Jialing Jiang, Wu Jiang, Qi Jiang, Qu Jiang and Daning He
Local products   Chongqing hotpot, pickles, beef jerk, lobster sauce, peach, orange and bamboo products

Tourist attractions Three Gorges, Dazu Rock Carvings, South China Karst, Xiaosanxia (minor three gorges) in Wushan County, Jinyun Mountain, Simian Mountain , Jinfo Mountain

Map page: 64-65

FUJIAN PROVINCE

Population 33.85 million
Area 120 000 square kilometers
Nationalities Han, She, Hui, Tujia, Miao and Zhuang
Climatic feature Subtropical humid monsoon climate, storms from summer to autumn
Average temperature 6℃～12℃ in January, 28℃～29℃ in July
Annual average rainfall 1000mm～1900mm
Mountains Wuyi Shan and Daiyun Shan
River Min Jiang, Jin Jiang, and Jiulong Jiang
Local products Wulong Tea, orange, longan, lichee, olive, loquat, banana, Zhangzhou Narcissus, Fujian cuisine, puppet making and mud sculpture
Capital Fuzhou
Major cities Fuzhou, Xiamen, Sanming, Putian, Quanzhou, Zhangzhou, Nanping, Longyan, Ningde
Tourist attractions Fujian Tulou, Wuyi Mountain, Gulangyu Island, Wanshi Mountain, Qingyuan Mountain, Taimu Mountain, Xuefeng Temple, Wanfu Temple, Guanghua Temple, Nanputuo Temple, ancient city of Chongwu and Zheng Chenggong's tomb

Map page: 46-47

GANSU PROVINCE

Population 26.00 million
Area 430 000 square kilometers
Nationalities Han, Hui, Dongxiang, Tibetan, Tu, Man, Mongol, Bonan, Yugur, Salar and Kazak
Climatic features Subtropical humid climate in the east changes to a temperate dry climate in the west, cold humid highland climate in Qilian Shan; temperatures shift greatly from day to night as well as from season to season in the central and western parts of the province
Average temperature -14℃～3℃in January, 11℃～27℃ in July
Annual average rainfall 30mm～800mm
Mountains Qilian Shan , Bei Shan , Die Shan, Min Shan, Wuqiao Ling
Rivers Huang He (Yellow River), Wei He, Tao He, Bailong Jiang, Hei He, Shule He
Local products Moonlight cups, inkstone, water pipe, lacquer carving, pebble carving and gourd carving
Capital Lanzhou
Major cities Lanzhou, Jiayuguan, Jinchang, Baiyin, Tianshui, Wuwei, Jiuquan, Zhangye
Tourist attractions Mogao Grottoes southeast to Dunhuang, Grottoes at Maiji Mountain, Labuleng Monastery, Jiayuguan Pass

Map page: 76-77

GUANGDONG PROVINCE

Population 79.00 million
Area 180 000 square kilometers
Nationalities Han, Zhuang, Yao, Tujia, Miao, Dong and She
Climatic features Subtropical-tropical humid monsoon climate
Average temperature 8℃～16℃in January, 27℃～29℃ in July
Annual average rainfall 1400mm～2000mm
Mountains Yunwu Shan, Nan Ling, Jiulian Shan and Lianhua Shan
Rivers Zhu Jiang, Han Jiang, Moyang Jiang, and Jian Jiang
Local products Banana, orange, lichee , black tea , Guangdong cuisine
Capital Guangzhou
Major cities Guangzhou, Qingyuan, Shaoguan, Heyuan, Meizhou, Chaozhou, Shantou, Shenzhen, Zhuhai, Foshan,

Zhanjiang

Tourist attractions Kaiping Diaolou, Zhaoqing Xing Hu and Dinghu Mountain, Danxia Mountain, Xiqiao Mountain, Splendid China in Shenzhen, Ancient gardens as Qinghui Garden in Shunde, Yuyin Shanfang in Panyu, Ke Garden in Dongguan, Liang Garden in Foshan

Map page: 58-59

GUANGXI ZHUANG AUT. REG.

Population 48.94 million
Area 240 000 square kilometers
Nationalities Han, Zhuang, Yao, Miao, Dong, Mulam, Maonan, Hui, Buyei, and Gin, among them Zhuang people take up 1/3 of the total population
Climatic features Subtropical humid monsoon climate
Average temperature 6℃～16℃ in January, 25℃～29℃ in July
Annual average rainfall 1000mm～2000mm
Mountains Haiyang Shan, Yuecheng Ling in the northeast; Yunkai Dashan, Liuwan Dashan and Shiwan Dashan in the south; Duyang Shan, Fenghuang Shan, and Jiuwan Dashan in the northwest; and Dayao Shan and Daming Shan in the middle
Rivers Xi Jiang, Liu Jiang, Yu Jiang and Ling Qu
Local products Chinese medicinal herbs like pseudo-ginseng, aniseed and cassia bark as well as taros, grapefruit, jackfruit
Capital Nanning
Major cities Nanning, Liuzhou, Guilin, Wuzhou, Beihai, Fangchenggang, Qinzhou, Guigang, Yulin, Chongzuo, Baise
Tourist attractions Karst hills in Guilin, Xishan Mountain in Guiping, Huashan Mountain in Ningming, Chengyang Bridge, Mapang Drum-Tower and cultural relics like Baise, Longsheng, Guihai, Zhenwu Pavilion, Liuhou Temple and Confucian Temple
Comments The Zhuang, Miao, Yao, Dong and seven other minority communities all maintain their own festivals and customs, so Guangxi is a tremendous place for a Folk Customs Tour, which highlights the music of the Zhuang nationality, the dance of the Yao nationality, the festivals of the Miao nationality and the buildings and bridges of the Dong nationality

Map page: 60-61

GUIZHOU PROVINCE

Population 38.68 million
Area 180 000 square kilometers
Nationalities Han, Miao, Buyei, Dong, Tujia, Yi, Li, Gelao, Sui, Bai, Hui and Zhuang
Climatic features Subtropical humid monsoon climate; few seasonal changes, with frequent cloudy and rainy weather
Average temperature 3℃～6℃ in January, 22℃～26℃ in July
Annual average rainfall 1100mm～1400mm
Mountains Dalou Shan and Wumeng Shan to the west and Miao Ling in the middle
Rivers Wu Jiang, Chishui He, Qingshui Jiang, Hongdu He, Nanpan Jiang, Beipan Jiang and Duliu Jiang
Local products Moutai as the so called "national liquor" of China, other well-known liquor brands like Dong Jiu, Duzhong, and Xishui
Capital Guiyang
Major cities Guiyang, Liupanshui, Zunyi, Anshun, Bijie, Tongren, Kaili, Duyun, Xingyi
Tourist attractions Huangguoshu Waterfall, South China Karst, Hongfeng Lake, Wuyang He (River), Fanjing Mountain National Nature Reserve, the site for Zunyi Meeting

Map page: 68-69

HAINAN PROVINCE

Population 8.19 million
Area 34 000 square kilometers
Nationalities Han, Li, Miao, Zhuang and Hui

Climatic features   Tropical humid monsoon climate

Average temperature   16℃~21℃ in January, 25℃~29℃ in July

Annual average rainfall   1500mm~2000mm

Mountains   Wuzhi Shan and Limu Ling

Rivers   Nandu He, Changhua Jiang and Wanquan He

Local products   Coconut, pineapple, cashew, coffee, rubber, coco, pepper, coconut shell carving, cow horn carving, shell carving, butterfly samples and pearl jewelry

Capital   Haikou

Major cities   Haikou, Sanya

Tourist attractions   Sanya tropical seashore, Wugong Temple, Tianya Haijiao, Wenchang Tower and Tropical Arboretum

Comments   With favorable climate and evergreen vegetation, Hainan exhibits unique tropical and subtropical scenery of island

Map page: 62-63

HEBEI PROVINCE

Population   68.65 million

Area   190 000 square kilometers

Nationalities   Han, Hui, Man, Mongol and Korean

Climatic features   Temperate continental climate

Average temperature   -16℃~-3℃ in January, 20℃~27℃ in July

Annual average rainfall   400mm~750mm

Mountains   Yan Shan in the north, Taihang Shan along the western border

Rivers   Hai He , Luan He

Local products   Pear, grape, peach, Chinese dates and almond, mushroom, Chinese prickly ash, herbs and Chinese wolfberry

Capital   Shijiazhuang

Major cities   Shijiazhuang, Tangshan, Handan, Xingtai, Baoding, Zhangjiakou, Chengde, Qinhuangdao, Cangzhou, Langfang

Tourist attractions   Chengde mountain resort and its outlying temples, the imperial tombs of

Qing Dynasty, Qinhuangdao-Beidaihe seaside summer resort, Shanhaiguan Pass, Zhaozhou Bridge

Map page: 26-27

HEILONGJIANG PROVINCE

Population   37.68 million

Area   460 000 square kilometers

Nationalities   Han, Man, Korean, Mongol, Hui, Daur, Xibe, Hezhen and Oroqen

Climatic features   Mild and cold temperate semi-humid continental climate; short summer and long winter; no summer in the northwest; the coldest temperature ever recorded being -52.3℃ (Mohe)

Average temperature   -30℃~-18℃ in January, 18℃~22℃ in July

Annual average rainfall   400mm~700mm

Mountains   Emur Shan, Yilehuli Shan, Xiao Hinggan Ling, Changbai Shan

Rivers   Heilong Jiang, Nen Jiang, Songhua Jiang, Wusuli Jiang

Local products   Forest products like ginseng, pilose antler, Chinese magnolia vine and other traditional Chinese medicinal herbs

Capital   Harbin

Major cities   Harbin, Qiqihar, Jixi, Daqing, Shuangyashan, Hegang, Yichun, Jiamusi, Mudanjiang, Heihe, Suihua

Tourist attractions   Jingpo Lake, Zhalong Nature Reserve as the "hometown of red-crown cranes" , the Wudalianchi Scenic Area, the Site of Longquan and the Upper Capital of Bohai Kingdom

Map page: 36-37

HENAN PROVINCE

Population   100.1 million

Area   170 000 square kilometers

Nationalities   Han, Hui, Mongol and Man

Climatic features   Between warm temperate zone and subtropical zone with humid and semi-humid continental monsoon climate

Average temperature   0℃~2℃ in the south

and -2℃～0℃ in the north in January, 26℃～28℃ in July

Annual average rainfall　700mm～1100mm

Mountains　Funiu Shan, Xiao Shan, Xiong'er Shan and Waifang Shan on the west, and Taihang Shan, Tongbai Shan and Dabie Shan on the north and south

Rivers　Huang He (Yellow River) and Huai He

Local products　Chinese dates, watermelon, pear, persimmon, paulownia, tobacco, sheep skin, green tea produced in Xinyang

Capital　Zhengzhou

Major cities　Zhengzhou，Kaifeng，Luoyang，Pingdingshan，Jiaozuo, Hebi, Xinxiang，Anyang，Puyang, Xuchang, Luohe, Sanmenxia, Nanyang, Shangqiu, Xinyang, Zhoukou, Zhumadian

Tourist attractions　Yin Xu in Anyang, Longmen Grottoes, Songshan Mountain and Shaolin Temple, Jigong Mountain, Baima Temple, Baogong Temple and Jiugong Mountain

Map page：52-53

HONG KONG SAR

Population　6.99 million

Area　1104　square kilometers

Climatic features　Sub-tropical oceanic monsoon climate, with frequent typhoons and storms

Average temperature　15℃ in January, 28℃　in July

Annual average rainfall　above 2200 mm

Local products　Textile, clothes, electronics, electric implements, watches and clocks, toys, plastic commodities, and ships

Tourist attractions　Taiping Mountain, Ocean Park, Qingshan Temple, Tian Tan Buddha, Hong Kong Disneyland, Lantau Mountain, Repulse Bay and Victorian Park

Comments　As the transportation hub of Southeast Asia, Europe, America and Oceania, Hong Kong is well developed in processing, trade and finance, and is well known as the "Oriental Pearl" and the "paradise for shoppers and tourists"

Map page：84-85

HUBEI PROVINCE

Population　59.84 million

Area　180 000 square kilometers

Nationalities　Han, Tujia, Miao, Hui, Dong and Man

Climatic features　Subtropical humid monsoon climate; adequate sunshine, hot and rainy summer

Average temperature　1℃～6℃ in January, 24℃～30℃ in July

Annual average rainfall　750mm～1600mm

Mountains　Wu Shan, Daba Shan, Wudang Shan, Jing Shan, Dahong Shan, Tongbai Shan and Dabie Shan

Rivers　Chang Jiang , Han Shui

Local products　Whitebait, Wuchang fish, orange, loquat, Chinese dates, tea, tung oil, sesame crackers

Capital　Wuhan

Major cities　Wuhan，Huangshi，Shiyan，Yichang，Jingzhou, Xiangfan，Jingmen, Ezhou, Xiaogan, Huanggang, Xianning, Suizhou

Tourist attractions　Three Georges , Wudang Mountain, Jiugong Mountain, Shennongjia National Natural Reserve, Xian Ling as a tomb of Ming Dynasty, Quyuan's hometown, Yellow Crane Tower and Chibi

Map page：54-55

HUNAN PROVINCE

Population　66.74 million

Area　210 000 square kilometers

Nationalities　Han, Tujia, Miao, Dong, Yao, Bai, Hui and Zhuang

Climatic features　Subtropical humid monsoon climate

Average temperature　3℃～8℃ in January, 27℃～30℃ in July

Annual average rainfall　1200mm～

1700mm

Mountains Wuling Shan in the northwest, Xuefeng Shan in the central west, Luoxiao Shan in the east, Nan Ling in the south

Rivers and lake Chang Jiang, Xiang Jiang, Yuan Jiang, Zi Shui, and Li Shui; Dongting Hu is the second largest fresh water lake in China

Local products Hunan style embroidery, lotus roots and seeds, tea, orange, Hunan cuisine

Capital Changsha

Major cities Changsha, Zhuzhou, Xiangtan, Hengyang, Shaoyang, Yueyang, Changde, Zhangjiajie, Chenzhou, Yiyang, Yongzhou, Huaihua, Loudi

Tourist attractions Wulingyuan Scenic Area, Hengshan Mountain, Yueyang Tower, Dongting Lake, the Han Tomb at Mawangdui

Map page: 56-57

JIANGSU PROVINCE

Population 72.53 million

Area 100 000 square kilometers

Nationalities Han, Hui, and Man

Climatic features Warm semi-humid monsoon climate in the north part, and subtropical humid monsoon climate in the south; clear-cut seasonal changes; frequent "plum rains" between spring and summer

Average temperature -1℃～3℃ in January, 27℃～28℃ in July

Annual average rainfall 800mm～1200mm

Rivers Chang Jiang (Yangtze River), Huai He, Yi He, Shu He, Qinhuai He, Xinshu He

Lakes Tai Hu, Hongze Hu, and Gaoyou Hu

Local products Silk, jade cravings, clay figures, potteries, green tea, preserved duck, crabs of Yangcheng Lake, Gaoyou duck and duck eggs

Capital Nanjing

Major cities Nanjing, Xuzhou, Lianyungang, Huai'an, Suqian, Yancheng, Yangzhou, Taizhou, Nantong, Zhenjiang, Changzhou, Wuxi, Suzhou

Tourist attractions Taihu Lake, Classical Gardens of Suzhou, Xiaoling Tomb of Ming Dynasty, Zhonghua Gate and Xuanwu Lake in Nanjing

Map page: 40-41

JIANGXI PROVINCE

Population 43.84 million

Area 170 000 square kilometers

Nationalities Han, She, Hui, Mongol, Miao, Man and Zhuang

Climatic features Subtropical humid monsoon climate; plum rains in spring, rainstorms in summer

Average temperature 4℃～9℃ in January, 28℃～30℃ in July

Annual average rainfall 1400mm～1900mm

Mountains Huaiyu Shan, Wuyi Shan, Jiuling Shan, Luoxiao Shan, Jiulian Shan, and Dayu Ling

Rivers and lake Gan Jiang, Fu He, Xin Jiang and Xiu Shui; Poyang Hu is the largest fresh water lake in China

Local products Green tea, black tea, orange, locus roots, lily bulbs, bamboo shoots, black-bone chicken, Jingdezhen porcelain, Wuyuan inkstone, brush pen, porcelain painting

Capital Nanchang

Major cities Nanchang, Jingdezhen, Pingxiang, Jiujiang, Xinyu, Yingtan, Ganzhou, Shangrao, Yichun, Fuzhou, Ji'an

Tourist attractions Lushan Mountain, Jinggang Mountain, Longhu Mountain, Sanqing Mountain, Tengwang Pavilion, Jingdezhen as the "Capital of Ceramics"

Map page: 48-49

JILIN PROVINCE

Population 26.69 million

Area 190 000 square kilometers

Nationalities Han, Korean, Man, Mongol, Hui, and Xibe

Climatic features Temperate continental monsoon climate; cold long winters; short and rainy summers

Average temperature   -18℃ in January, 20℃~23℃ in July

Annual average rainfall   400mm~800mm

Mountains   Changbai Shan

Rivers   Songhua Jiang，Yalu Jiang and Tumen Jiang, Mudan Jiang, Suifen He

Local products   Ginseng, mink, and pilous antler as the "three treasures of northeastern China", wood frog oil and wild grape

Capital   Changchun

Major cities   Changchun，Jilin，Siping，Liaoyuan，Tonghua，Baishan, Songyuan, Baicheng

Tourist attractions   Changbai Mountain, Tianchi, Songhua Lake, Jingyue Pool, Xianghai Marsh, Rime in Jilin, Capital Cities and Tombs of the Ancient Koguryo Kingdom

Map page：34-35

LIAONING PROVINCE

Population   41.89 million

Area   150 000 square kilometers

Nationalities   Han，Man，Mongol，Hui，Korean，and Xibe

Climatic features   Temperate humid monsoon climate in the coastal region, substropical semi-humid monsoon climate in the north

Average temperature   -15℃~-5℃ in January, 24℃ in July

Annual average rainfall   500mm~1000mm

Mountains   Qian Shan, Nulu'erhu Shan, Longgang Shan, Song Ling and Yiwulu Shan

Rivers   Liao He, Yalu Jiang

Local products   Apple, pear, peach, tussor silk

Capital   Shenyang

Major cities   Shenyang，Dalian，Anshan，Fushun，Benxi，Dandong，Jinzhou，Huludao, Yingkou, Fuxin, Liaoyang, Tieling, Chaoyang, Panjin

Tourist attractions   Imperial Palace and tombs of Qing Dynasty in Shenyang, the capital city of the Ancient Koguryo Kingdom, Qianshan Mountain, Shedao Island, the Water-

Cave in Benxi County, the beach in Xingcheng, the Jinshi Beach National Holiday Resort, Tiger Beach, Bangchui Island, Laotie Mountain, historical sites of war field in Sino-Japan and Japan-Russia Wars

Map page：32-33

MACAU SAR

Population   0.488 million

Area   27.5 square kilometers

Climatic features   Subtropical oceanic monsoon climate, with frequent typhoons

Average temperature   14.5℃ in January, 29℃ in July

Annual average rainfall   2000mm

Tourist attractions   The Historic Centre of Macau, the Ruins of St. Paul's Catholic Church, the Leal Senado Building, Na Tcha Temple, Casa Garden and A- Ma Temple

Comments   Macau is well known for its gambling industry and is called the "Far East Monte Carlo" , Tourism is another source of gaining foreign currency and pillar of Macau's economy

Map page：86-87

NEI MONGOL (INNER MONGOLIA) AUT. REG.

Population   23.52 million

Area   1 180 000 square kilometers

Nationalities   Han, Mongol, Man, Hui, Daur, Ewenki and Korean

Climatic features   Temperate arid and semi-arid continental climate, sharp difference between winter and summer as well as between different localities, cool and pleasant summer, long and cold winter

Average temperature   -26℃~-10℃ in January, 18℃~24℃ in July

Annual average rainfall   50mm~450mm.

Mountains   Da Hinggan Ling, Yin Shan and Helan Shan

Rivers   Huang He (Yellow River)

Local products   Leathers and wool products including thick caddice, carpet

117

Capital Hohhot

Major cities Hohhot, Baotou, Wuhai, Chifeng, Tongliao, Ordos, Hulun Buir, Ulan Qab, Bayannur

Tourist attractions Da Hinggan Ling, the tomb of Genghis Khan, the tomb of Princess Wang Zhaojun, Wudangzhao, Xiangshawan, Five Pagoda Monastery, Dazhao Monastery, Mt. Arxan Hot Spring, Hulun (Dalai) Lake, Xiritala Grassland Scenic Spot and Xilamuren Grassland Scenic Spot

Map page: 30-31

NINGXIA HUI AUT. REG.

Population 5.89 million

Area 66 000 square kilometers

Nationalities Hui, Han and Man

Climatic features Temperate semi-humid and semi-arid continental climate

Average temperature -10℃~-7℃ in January, 17℃~24℃ in July

Annual average rainfall 200mm~600mm; precipitation increases from north to south and varies greatly from year to year

Mountains Liupan Shan, Helan Shan and Niushou Shan.

Rivers Huang He (Yellow River) and its branches Qingshui He, Kushui He and Hulu He

Local products Argali sheep hide and wool, wolfberry fruit and Helan stone

Capital Yinchuan

Major cities Yinchuan, Shizuishan, Wuzhong, Guyuan, Zhongwei

Tourist attractions Royal Mausoleums of the Western Xia State, Helan Mountain, the Pagoda 108 in Qingtongxia City, Chengtiansi Pagoda, Mt. Xumi Grottoes, the Sand Lake, Nanguan Mosque, Gaomiao, Western China Film City and remains of Great Wall

Map page: 80-81

QINGHAI PROVINCE

Population 5.04 million

Area 720 000 square kilometers

Nationalities Han, Tibetan, Hui, Tu, Salar, Mongol and Man

Climatic features Typical continental highland climate, sharp change in daily temperature

Average temperature -18℃~-7℃ in January, 5℃~21℃ in July

Annual average rainfall 50mm~400mm

Mountains Qilian Shan in the north, Kunlun Shan in the middle and Tanggula (Dangla) Shan in the south

Rivers China's three major rivers — Chang Jiang (Yangtze River), Huang He (Yellow River) and Lancang Jiang all starts here. Other major rivers are Huang Shui, Datong He, Za Qu, Tongtian He, and Shule He

Local products Wool, cashmere, lamb skin, thick caddice, carpet, yak hide and marmot skin

Capital Xining

Major cities Xining, Golmud, Delhi

Tourist attraction Qinghai Lake and Bird Island, Mengda Heavenly Pond, Kumbum Monastery, Dongguan Mosque, the Salt Bridge, Temple of Princess Wencheng

Map page: 78-79

SHAANXI PROVINCE

Population 37.04 million

Area 210 000 square kilometers

Nationalities Han, Hui, Man, Mongol, Tibetan

Climatic features Temperate semi-arid monsoon climate in the north to warm temperate semi-arid and semi-humid monsoon climate in the middle till subtropical humid monsoon climate in the south

Average temperature -11℃~3.5℃ in January, 21℃~28℃ in July

Annual average rainfall 500mm~1000mm

Mountains Qin Ling, Daba Shan

Rivers Huang He (Yellow River), Luo He, Jing He and Wei He

Local products Pomegranate, persimmon,

walnut, chestnut, kiwi fruit, Jade carving, clay sculpture, fake Tang tri-colour, embroidery, pyrographed chopsticks, green porcelain bowl and shadow play figure

Capital   Xi'an

Major cities   Xi'an，Yan'an，Tongchuan，Weinan, Xianyang，Baoji, Hanzhong, Yulin

Tourist attractions   Huashan Mountain, Mausoleum of the First Qin Emperor and the grand terracotta army, Forest of Stone Steles, Shaanxi Museum, Lishan Mountain and Huaqing Hot Spring, Banpo Museum, Big Wild Goose Pagoda and Small Wild Goose Pagoda, remains of imperial palaces and tombs from Qin, Han and Tang Dynasties

Comments   Shaanxi Province is absolutely loaded with extraordinary archaeological sights and famed as an underground museum. It's one of top tourist destinations in China. But history didn't stop with ancient dynasties. Yan'an is the cradle of the People's Republic of China, and became the broadcast center for revolutionary thought for a decade from 1937

Map page：74-75

SHANDONG PROVINCE

Population   92.12 million

Area   160 000 square kilometers

Nationalities   Han，Hui and Man

Climatic features   Warm-temperate semi-humid monsoon climate influenced by the ocean, rainy summer, dry winter

Average temperature   -5℃～1℃ in January, 24℃～28℃ in July

Annual average rainfall   550mm～950mm

Mountains   Tai Shan, Lu Shan, Meng Shan and Qi Shan

Rivers   Huang He (Yellow River)，Jinghang Yunhe (Grand Canal)

Local products   Yantai apples，Leling jujubes，Laiyang pears，Pingdu grapes，Dezhou watermelons

Capital   Jinan

Major cities   Jinan，Qingdao，Zibo，Zaozhuang，Dongying，Weifang，Yantai，

Jining，Tai'an，Dezhou, Liaocheng, Heze, Rizhao

Tourist attractions   Taishan Mountain, Confucius' Temple, Old homes and family cemetery of the Confucius' off springs, Qingdao as a summer resort city, Penglai Pavilion

Map page：50-51

SHANGHAI MUNICIPALITY

Population   13.60 million

Area   6 340 square kilometers

Nationalities   Han, Hui and Man

Climatic features   Subtropical maritime monsoon climate, four distinct seasons, plum rains around June, typhoons in summer

Average temperature   3℃ in January, 28℃ in July

Annual average rainfall   1000 mm

Rivers   Huangpu Jiang, Wusong Jiang

Local products   Jewelry, jade carving, artificial flower, costumes, clothes, woolen cloth, silk, tie, leather shoes, cosmetics

Tourist attractions   Yuyuan Garden, Guyi Garden, Yufo Temple, Oriental Pearl TV Tower, Waitan, Dianshan Lake, Shanghai Museum

Comments   As a tourist city，it attracts travelers from both home and abroad by its commercial activity rather than scenic beauty. Shanghai is the largest center of commerce and finance in China. With Pudong as the renowned special economic zone, Shanghai has been developing steadily in finance, and is playing a more and more important role in international financial conduct

Map page：38-39

SHANXI PROVINCE

Population   32.94 million

Area   160 000 square kilometers

Nationalities   Han，Hui，Mongol and Man

Climatic features   Temperate continental monsoon climate

Average temperature -16℃~-2℃ in January, 19℃~28℃ in July
Annual average rainfall 400mm~600mm
Mountains Taihang Shan, Wutai Shan, Heng Shan, Luliang Shan
Rivers Huang He (Yellow River), Fen He
Local products Jishan dates, Fen Chiew, Yuanping pears, Qingxu grapes
Capital Taiyuan
Major cities Taiyuan, Datong, Yangquan, Changzhi, Jincheng, Xinzhou, Yuncheng, Linfen
Tourist attractions Wutai Mountain, Hengshan Mountain, Hukou Waterfall, Ancient City of Pingyao, Yungang Grottoes, Jinci Temple, wooden pagoda in Yingxian County.
Comments Known as "the land of coal", Shanxi ranks the first in China in the total reserve, output and cross-province transfer volume of coal

Map page: 28-29

SICHUAN PROVINCE

Population 86.42 million
Area 490 000 square kilometers
Nationalities Han, Yi, Tibetan, Qiang, Miao, Hui and Mongol
Climatic features Subtropical humid monsoon climate in the eastern lowlands with frequent fog, temperate subtropical highland climate in the west, with intense sunlight but low temperatures
Average temperature In January, 3℃~8℃ in the lowlands, -9℃~-3℃ on the plateau, and 8℃~13℃ in the south; in July, 25℃~29℃ in the lowlands, 11℃~17℃ on the plateau, and 22℃~26℃ in the south
Annual average rainfall 1000mm in the lowlands, 500mm~700mm on the plateau and 800mm~1200mm in the south
Mountains Min Shan, Qionglai Shan, Daxue Shan, Shaluli Shan, and Xiaoxiang Ling
Rivers Chang Jiang and its branches like Yalong Jiang, Min Jiang, Dadu He, Tuo Jiang, Jialing Jiang, Pu Jiang and Qu Jiang

Local products Bristle, tung oil, insect wax, raw lacquer, orange, longan, pear, apple, Sichuan cuisine, bamboo ware, fan and bamboo painting
Capital Chengdu
Major cities Chengdu, Zigong, Panzhihua, Deyang, Luzhou, Mianyang, Neijiang, Guangyuan, Suining, Leshan, Nanchong, Yibin, Guang'an, Dazhou, Bazhong, Ya'an, Meishan, Ziyang
Tourist attractions Jiuzhaigou, Huanglong, Mt. Emei-Leshan Giant Buddha, Mt. Qingcheng-Dujiangyan, Sichuan Giant Panda Sanctuaries, Gongga Mountain, Xiling Xueshan

Map page: 66-67

TAIWAN PROVINCE

Population 22.28 million
Area 36 000 square kilometers
Nationalities Han and Gaoshan
Climatic features Subtropical humid monsoon climate
Average temperature 13℃~20℃ in January, 24℃~29℃ in July
Annual average rainfall Above 2000mm
Mountains Hai'an Shan, Chungyang Shan, Yu Shan, Ali Shan and Xue Shan
Rivers Choshui Hsi, Kaoping Hsi and Tsengwen Hsi
Local products Corals, local teas, butterfly samples, camphors and spices
Capital Taipei
Major cities Taipei, Chilung, Kaohsiung, Tainan, Taichung, Hsinchu, Taitung
Tourist attractions Jihyueh Tan (Lake), Ali Mountain, Yangming Mountain, Yushan Mountain, Bagua Mountain, Palace Museum, and Mazu Temple
Comments Taiwan is traditionally an indivisible part of China. The province is made up by over 80 islands including Taiwan Tao, Penghu Liehtao, Lan Yu, Tiaoyu Tao, and Chihwei Yu. Taiwan Tao is the largest island of China

Map page: 88-89

TIANJIN MUNICIPALITY

Population 9.43 million
Area 12 000 square kilometers
Nationalities Han, Hui, Man, Mongol and Korean.
Climatic features Warm-temperate semi-humid monsoon climate
Average temperature -6℃～-4℃ in January, 26℃ in July.
Annual average rainfall 550mm～680mm
Rivers Hai He, Ziya Xinhe, Yongding Xinhe, Chaobai He, and Ji Yunhe
Local products Steamed stuffed bun, fried dough twist and deep-fried cake, New-year painting, colored clay sculpture and kite are traditional local handicrafts
Tourist attractions Panshan Mountain, Dule Temple, the Great Wall at Huangyaguan, Dagukou Fort Barbette, Tianjin TV Tower, Tianhou Temple, Confucian Temple, Street of Ancient Culture
Comments Tianjin is a port city

Map page: 24-25

XINJIANG UYGUR AUT. REG.

Population 19.62 million
Area 1 660 000 square kilometers
Nationalities Uygur, Han, Kazak, Hui, Kirgiz, Mongol, Dongxiang, Tajik, Xibe, Man, Tujia, Uzbek and Russ
Climatic features Temperate continental climate, warmer in the south, extreme temperature changes, little precipitation, frequent gales in spring and autumn
Average temperature -10℃ in January and 25℃ in July in the south, -20℃ in January and 20℃ in July in the north
Annual average rainfall 50mm～150mm
Mountains Tian Shan, Altay Shan, Karakorum Shan, Kunlun Shan, Altun Shan
Rivers Tarim He, China's longest inland river; Ili He and Ertix He
Lakes Lop Nur, a famous salt lake; Bosten Lake, the largest fresh water lake of the region; Aydingkol Lake, with the lowest altitude in China
Local products Turpan grapes, Hami melons, apple, pear, apricot, snow lotus, carpet, embroidered hat, ethnic musical instruments, knife and jade
Capital Ürümqi
Major cities Ürümqi, Karamay, Kashi, Yining, Hami, Aksu, Shihezi, Hotan, Korla
Tourist attractions Tianchi (Heavenly Lake), Heavenly Mountain range (Tianshan), Kanas Lake, Flaming Mountains, "Ghost Town", Kirzil's Thousand Buddha Cave, the ancient cities at Jiaohe and Gaochang, Loulan Site, Tomb of Xiangfei and the Idgar Mosque
Comments Largest in area in all the province-level administrative regions of China, the Xinjiang Uygur Autonomous Region covers one sixth of Chinese territory. In history, Xinjiang served as the key controlling section of the well-known Silk Road, while now it is an unavoidable part of the railway leading to the second Eurasia Continental Bridge

Map page: 82-83

XIZANG (TIBET) AUT. REG.

Population 2.68 million
Area 1 230 000 square kilometers
Nationalities Tibetan, Han, Hui, Monba, Lhoba and Naxi.
Climatic features Arid highland climate with sharp vertical change in temperature; climates as tropical, subtropical, temperate highland, sub-freezing highland, frigid highland from southeast to northwest as altitude goes up; long hours of sun shine, low temperature, sparse rainfall, low oxygen and low air pressure
Average temperature -10℃～-4℃ in January, 15℃ in July.
Annual average rainfall 50mm～500mm
Mountains Himalayas, Gangdise Shan, Kunlun Shan, Hoh Xil Shan, Tanggula (Dangla) Shan, Hengduan Shan
Rivers Yarlung Zangbo Jiang, Nu Jiang,

Lancang Jiang and Jinsha Jiang

Lakes   Nam Co, Siling Co, Tangra Yumco and Yamzho Co

Local products   Rare medicinal materials like angelica, glossy ganoderma, aweto, caladium, saffron, ginseng; ghee tea, highland barley cake, and highland barley liquor; carpets, boots, clothes, aprons in Tibetan style

Capital   Lhasa

Major towns   Lhasa，Xigaze, Nyingchi, Gar, Qamdo, Nagqu

Tourist attraction   Potala Palace, Jokhang Temple, Bharkor Street, Norbulingka as the summer palace of past Dalai Lamas, Tashilumpo Monastery, Yarlung Zangbo Valley, Qomolangma Feng (Mount Everest)

Comments   Qomolangma Feng (Mt. Everest) on the Sino-Nepal border is 8844.43m in altitude, the highest peak in the world

Map page：72-73

YUNNAN PROVINCE

Population   42.70 million

Area   390 000 square kilometers

Nationalities   Han, Yi, Bai, Hani, Zhuang, Dai, Deang, Miao, Hui, Lisu, Lahu, Va, Naxi, Yao, Jingpo, Tibetan, Blang, Buyei, Achang, Pumi, Mongol, Nu and Jino.

Climatic features   Subtropical and tropical highland humid monsoon climate

Average temperature $8\,°C \sim 12\,°C$ in January, $18\,°C \sim 24\,°C$ in July

Annual average rainfall   1000mm $\sim$ 1500mm.

Mountains   Gaoligong Shan, Nu Shan and Yun Ling in the west and Wulian Feng, Wumeng Shan in the northeast

Rivers   Jinsha Jiang, Lancang Jiang, Yuan Jiang, and Nu Jiang

Local products   Quality cigarettes, teas, herbal medicines and flowers

Capital   Kunming

Major cities   Kunming，Qujing, Yuxi, Baoshan, Zhaotong, Lijiang, Pu'er, Lincang

Tourist attractions   Dianchi (Lake), the Stone Forest, Xishuangbanna National Nature Reserve, Old Town of Lijiang, Three Parallel Rivers

Comments   Yunnan is the province with the largest number of nationalities in China, so the festivals of the ethnic minorities are varied and colorful. The famous festivals are the Torch Festival of the Yi, the Third Month Fair of the Bai, the Sanduo Festival of the Naxi, the Munao-Zongge Festival of the Jingpo and the Sword-Pole Festival of the Lisu

Map page：70-71

ZHEJIANG PROVINCE

Population   46.02 million

Area   100 000 square kilometers

Nationalities   Han, She, Tujia, Miao, Buyei, Hui, Zhuang, Dong, Li and Man

Climatic features   Subtropical monsoon climate, plum rains from early June to early July, typhoons from late August to late September

Average temperature $3\,°C \sim 8\,°C$ in January, $28\,°C$ in July; high tempretures in the central basin

Annual average rainfall   1200mm $\sim$ 1500mm

Mountains   Xianxia Ling, Yandang Shan, Kuocang Shan, Tiantai Shan, Tianmu Shan, and Huiji Shan

Rivers   Qiantang Jiang in the north, Ou Jiang in the south

Local products   Jinhua ham，Longjing tea, silk, embroidery, lace, wood carving, stone carving, shell carving, scissors, Fuchunjiang shad, Zhejiang cuisine, sea products

Capital   Hangzhou

Major cities   Hangzhou，Ningbo，Wenzhou, Jiaxing，Huzhou，Shaoxing，Jinhua, Quzhou, Zhongshan, Taizhou, Lishui

Tourist attractions   West Lake in Hangzhou, Yandang Mountain, Putuo Mountain, Shengsi Island, Tianyi Ge, Mogan Mountain and Qiandao Lake

Map page：42-43

GLOSSARY in *Pinyin* (Chinese phonetic alphabet) and English

Pinyin	English	Pinyin	English
Ansha	Shoal, Reef	Pendi	Basin (Bsn.)
Arxan	Hot spring	Pingyuan	Plain (Pln.)
Bandao	Peninsula (Pen.)	Po	Lake (L.)
Bei	North	Pubu	Waterfall
Bulag	Spring	Qi	Banner (B.)
Chuan	River (R.)	Qian	Front
Co	Lake (L.)	Qiao	Bridge
Chi	Lake (L.)	Qiuling	Hills
Da	Greater, Grand	Qu	River (R.)
Daban	Ridge, Pass	Qu	Irrigation canal
Dalai	Sea, Lake	Quan	Spring
Dao	Island (I.)	Qundao	Islands (Is.)
Dian	Shallow lake	Qunjiao	Reefs
Ding	Peak, Top	Shadi	Sandy land, Desert
Dong	East	Shamo	Desert (Des.)
Feng	Peak, Mount	Shan	Mountain (Mt.), Mountains (Mts.)
Fenhongqu	Flood diversion area	Shandi	Mountain land
Gang	Harbour, Port	Shang	Upper
Gaoyuan	Plateau (Plt.)	Shankou	Pass
Gobi	Gobi, Semidesert	Shanmai	Mountains (Mts.)
Gol	River (R.)	Shi	City
Gonglu	Highway	Shui	River (R.)
Gou	River (R.), Ditch	Shuidao	Channel (Chan.)
Guan	Pass	Shuiku	Reservoir (Res.)
Hai	Sea	Tag	Mountain
Haixia	Strait (Str.), Channel (Chan.)	Tan	Beach
He	River (R.)	Tan	Pool
Hou	Back	Ul	Mountain
Hu	Lake (L.)	Wai	Outer
Hudag	Well	Wan	Gulf (G.), Bay
Jiang	River (R.)	Xi	West
Jiao	Reef	Xi	Stream, Brook
Jie	Street (St.), Avenue (Av.)	Xia	Gorge, Valley
Jing	Well	Xia	Lower
Kou	Mouth	Xian	County (Co.)
Liedao	Islands (Is.)	Xueshan	Snowberg
Ling	Mountains (Mts.), Ridge	Yan	Rock, Crag
Linqu	Forest region	Yanhu	Salt lake
Lu	Road (Rd.)	You	Right
Moron	River	Yu	Island (I.)
Muchang	Pasture	Yunhe	Canal
Nan	South	Zangbo	River
Nei	Inner	Zhaoze	Swamp, Marsh
Nongchang	Farm	Zhong	Central, Middle
Nur	Lake (L.)	Zuo	Left
Pao	Lake (L.)		

INTRODUCTION TO THE INDEX

The index includes about 12,400 place names shown on the 34 maps of provinces, autonomous regions, municipalities and special administrative regions in China. For the romanization of place names in this Atlas, the *Pinyin* system has been adopted.

Each entry includes the name, the abbreviation of administrative division, a page number and a grid reference:

Yanqing [BJ]	36	B3
Hangzhou [ZJ]	84	E2

Names are referenced by alphanumeric grid, which indicates the location of symbol centre for point elements such as city and peak, and the location of the first alphabet for linear or area elements such as sea, river, and mountains. For each place in the Atlas, only one entry has been included in the index.

Names in the index are arranged in alphabetical order.

ABBREVIATIONS

AH	Anhui	JX	Jiangxi
BJ	Beijing	LN	Liaoning
CQ	Chongqing	MC	Macau
FJ	Fujian	NM	Nei Mongol
GD	Guangdong	NX	Ningxia
GS	Gansu	QH	Qinghai
GX	Guangxi	SC	Sichuan
GZ	Guizhou	SD	Shandong
HB	Hubei	SH	Shanghai
HEB	Hebei	SN	Shaanxi
HEN	Henan	SX	Shanxi
HK	Hong Kong	TJ	Tianjin
HI	Hainan	TW	Taiwan
HL	Heilongjiang	XJ	Xinjiang
HN	Hunan	XZ	Xizang
JL	Jilin	YN	Yunnan
JS	Jiangsu	ZJ	Zhejiang

34 Tuanchang [XJ]　82　J5

A

Aba(Ngawa) [SC]　66　D2
Abag Qi [NM]　30　F3
Aberdeen [HK]　84　D4
Acheng Qu [HL]　36　D5
Adamasta Channel [HK]　84　C4
Agan [GS]　76　G5
A'gyi [SC]　66　E2
Ahu [JS]　40　D1
Ai Shan [SD]　50　G2
Aicheng [JX]　48　C2
Aidong [GX]　60　E3
Aihui [HL]　36　D3
Aijiahe [SN]　74　E8
Ailao Shan [YN]　70　D3
Ailao Shan [YN]　70　D3
Ailing [GX]　60　G3
Aimen Guan [AH]　44　B4
Aimen Guan [HB]　54　H3
Aiting [AH]　44　B3
Aiwan Wan [ZJ]　42　E4
Akmeqit [XJ]　82　E7
Akqi [XJ]　82　F5
Aksay [GS]　76　C3
Aksayqin Hu [XJ]　82　F8
Aksu [XJ]　82　G5
Akto [XJ]　82　D6
Alag Hu [QH]　78　E3
Alataw Shankou [XJ]　82　H3
Alaying [HN]　56　B4
Ali Shan [TW]　88　C3
Alishan [TW]　88　C3
Altan Obo [NM]　30　D4
Altay Shan [XJ]　82　J1
Altay [XJ]　82　K2
Altun Shan [GS]　76　B3
Altun Shan [QH]　78　B1
Altun Shan [XJ]　82　J6
Alun He [HL]　36　B3
Alxa Youqi [NM]　30　C5
Alxa Zuoqi [NM]　30　D5
Amdo [XZ]　72　H3
Amo Jiang [YN]　70　D4
Amqog [GS]　76　G5
An He [JS]　40　D2
An Xian [SC]　66　F3
Anban [YN]　70　D4
Anbei [GS]　76　D2
Anbian [SN]　74　D3
An'bo [LN]　32　F5
Anchang [GZ]　68　G2
Anchang [ZJ]　42　D2
Ancheng [HB]　54　C2
Anda [HL]　36　C4
Ande [GX]　60　D4
Andi Shuiku [SD]　50　E4
Anding [BJ]　22　D4
Anding [HN]　56　F3
Anding [JL]　34　B2
Andirlangar [XJ]　82　H7

Andong [ZJ]　42　E2
Andun [GD]　58　F3
Anfengtang Shuiku [AH]　44　C3
Anfu [CQ]　64　B4
Antu [JX]　48　B4
Ang'angxi Qu [HL]　36　B4
Angou [SN]　74　F4
Anguang [JL]　34　C2
Anguli Nur [HEB]　26　B2
Anguo [HEB]　26　C5
Anhou [FJ]　46　C5
Anhua [HN]　56　D3
Anhua [ZJ]　42 · D3
Anji [ZJ]　42　C2
Anjia [HL]　36　D5
Anjiang [HEB]　26　E3
Anjiazhuang [BJ]　22　C3
Anjiazhuang [SD]　50　C4
Anju Qu [SC]　66　F3
Anju [SD]　50　C4
Ankang [SN]　74　E8
Ankou [JL]　34　E5
Ankyam [SC]　66　D2
Anle [FJ]　46　B3
Anling [AH]　44　D5
Anling [HEB]　26　D6
Anliu [GD]　58　G3
Anlong [GZ]　68　D5
Anlu [HB]　54　F3
Anning He [SC]　66　E5
Anning [SC]　66　E3
Anning [YN]　70　E3
Anping [HEB]　26　C5
Anpu Gang [GD]　58　A5
Anpu [GD]　58　B5
Anqing [AH]　44　D5
Anqiu [SD]　50　F3
Anren [HN]　56　F5
Anren [SD]　50　C3
Anren [ZJ]　42　C4
Anren [ZJ]　42　C4
Anrenxi [FJ]　46　D3
Ansai [SN]　74　E4
Ansha Shuiku [FJ]　46　C3
Anshan [LN]　32　G3
Anshi [JL]　34　E4
Anshun [GZ]　68　D4
Antu [JL]　34　H4
Anxi [FJ]　46　D4
Anxiang [HN]　56　E2
Anxin [HEB]　26　C5
Anxing [HL]　36　G5
Anyang [HEN]　52　F1
A'nyêmaqên Shan [GS]　76　F5
A'nyêmaqên Shan [QH]　78　F3
Anyi [JX]　48　C3
Anyou [HI]　62　B3
Anyuan [FJ]　46　B3
Anyuan [JX]　48　C6
Anyue [SC]　66　F3
Anze [SX]　28　D5
Anzhao Xinhe [HL]　36　C4

Anzhen [JS]　40　F4
Anzi [JL]　34　D3
Ao Jiang [ZJ]　42　D5
Aocheng [JX]　48　B5
Aohan Qi [NM]　30　G4
Aoquanxu [HN]　56　E6
Aoshang [HN]　56　F6
Aoshanwei [SD]　50　G3
Aotou [GD]　58　F4
Aoxi [GZ]　68　F3
Aozai [GD]　58　D3
Aqal [XJ]　82　F5
Aqqan [XJ]　82　G7
Aqqan [XJ]　82　I7
Aqqikkol Hu [XJ]　82　K7
Ar Horqin Qi [NM]　30　H4
Aral [QH]　78　B1
Aral [XJ]　82　G5
Argan [XJ]　82　K5
Arka Tag [XJ]　82　K7
Artux [XJ]　82　E6
Arun Qi [NM]　30　H2
Arxan [LN]　32　F2
Arxan [NM]　30　G3
Asog [XZ]　72　E4
Awat [XJ]　82　G5
Ayakkum Hu [XJ]　82　K7
Aydingkol Hu [XJ]　82　K4

B

Ba He [SC]　66　G3
Ba He [SN]　74　E8
Ba Shui [HB]　54　H4
Babai [JS]　40　D3
Babaihu [NX]　80　C4
Babao [HN]　56　E5
Babao [YN]　70　F4
Babian Jiang [YN]　70　D4
Bacha [HL]　36　G3
Bachu(Maralwexi) [XJ]　82　F6
Bacia Norte do Patane [MC]　86　A1
Bacia Sul do Patane [MC]　86　A1
Bacun [HEN]　52　F4
Bacun [HI]　62　B3
Badain Jaran Shamo [NM]　30　C3
Badaling [BJ]　22　C2
Badaling [BJ]　22　C2
Badaogou [HEB]　26　B2
Badaogu [TJ]　24　C4
Badaohao [LN]　32　E3
Badaohe [BJ]　22　D2
Badong [HB]　54　C3
Badou [AH]　44　D3
Badou [GX]　60　C2
Badou [NX]　80　B4
Badu [FJ]　46　E3
Badu [GZ]　68　D6
Badu [JX]　48　C4
Badu [ZJ]　42　B5
Baga [XZ]　72　C4
Bagoin [QH]　78　E4
Bagong Shan [AH]　44　C3

Name		
Bagong [SX]	28	D6
Bagongshan Qu [AH]	44	C3
Bahao [JL]	34	F2
Bai He [HEB]	26	C3
Bai He [BJ]	22	C2
Bai He [HEN]	52	D5
Bai He [SC]	66	E2
Bai Shan [GS]	76	B2
Bai Shan [XJ]	82	M5
Baía de Cheoc Van [MC]	86	C7
Baía de Hác Sá [MC]	86	C7
Baía de Ká Hó [MC]	86	D5
Baibei [SX]	28	D4
Baicao Ling [YN]	70	D2
Baicao [HEB]	26	D2
Baicaogou [JL]	34	I4
Baiceng [GZ]	68	D5
Baiceng(Bay) [XJ]	82	G5
Baicheng [JL]	34	B2
Baichengzi [SN]	74	D2
Baicuo [JX]	48	C2
Baidang Hu [AH]	44	D5
Baidaokou [HEN]	52	F2
Baide [GZ]	68	D5
Baidi [CQ]	64	F2
Baidian [AH]	44	F5
Baidishi [HN]	56	D5
Baidu [GD]	58	H2
Baidunzi [GS]	76	C2
Baidunzi [GS]	76	H4
Bai'e [JX]	48	C6
Baifeng [ZJ]	42	E3
Baifusi [HB]	54	B5
Baigou He [HEB]	26	D4
Baiguishan Shuiku [HEN]	52	E4
Baiguo [GZ]	68	C4
Baiguo [HB]	54	H3
Baihe [CQ]	64	E2
Baihe [SH]	38	C3
Baihe [SN]	74	F8
Baihe [YN]	70	E4
Baihebu [BJ]	22	C2
Baihedian [ZJ]	42	D3
Baihou [GD]	58	H2
Baihua Shan [BJ]	22	B4
Baihuyao [SX]	28	D5
Baiji Shan [ZJ]	42	B3
Baiji Shan [AH]	44	E6
Baijia [JX]	48	B5
Baijian [TJ]	24	B2
Baijiang [ZJ]	42	C3
Baijiantan Qu [XJ]	82	I3
Baijiaping [HN]	56	D6
Baijin [GZ]	68	E4
Baiju [JS]	40	F2
Baikalu Shan [HI]	36	B1
Baile [GX]	60	D3
Bailian [FJ]	46	C3
Bailian [HI]	62	C2
Bailianhe Shuiku [HB]	54	H4
Bailin [FJ]	46	F2
Bailin [HB]	54	C2
Bailin [HN]	56	F5
Bailing [JX]	48	B2
Bailong Gang [SH]	38	E3
Bailong Jiang [GS]	76	H6
Bailong [SX]	28	C5
Bailonggang [SH]	38	E3
Bailongtang [SN]	74	C7
Bailu He [HEN]	52	G5
Bailuo [HB]	54	F5
Bailuqiao [HN]	56	E3
Baima Hu [JS]	40	E2
Baima Jian [AH]	44	C4
Baima [NX]	80	B3
Baima [QH]	78	G4
Baimaguan [BJ]	22	E1
Baimajing [HI]	62	B2
Baimangshen [SX]	28	E2
Baimangying [HN]	56	D7
Baimaoping [HN]	56	C5
Baimasi [HN]	56	E3
Baimatan [SN]	74	F5
Baimi [JS]	40	F3
Baimian [NX]	80	C5
Baina [GZ]	68	D3
Bainang [XZ]	72	G5
Baingoin [XZ]	72	H4
Baini [HB]	54	G5
Bainiu [HEN]	52	D5
Baipu [GD]	58	F3
Baipu [JS]	40	F3
Baiqiao [AH]	44	E4
Baiquan [CQ]	64	E2
Baiquan [HL]	36	D4
Baiquanzi [NX]	80	B3
Baiqueyuan [HEN]	52	G6
Bairab Co [XZ]	72	D2
Bairin Youqi [NM]	30	G4
Bairin Zuoqi [NM]	30	G3
Baisangguan [HB]	54	C2
Baise [GX]	60	D4
Baisha [CQ]	64	C4
Baisha [CQ]	64	C4
Baisha [FJ]	46	C4
Baisha [FJ]	46	E3
Baisha [GD]	58	E2
Baisha [GZ]	68	G3
Baisha [HEN]	52	E3
Baisha [HI]	62	B2
Baisha [HI]	62	B2
Baisha [HN]	56	E5
Baisha [HN]	56	G3
Baisha [JX]	48	C5
Baishaguan [JX]	48	F2
Baishan [AH]	44	C2
Baishan [AH]	44	D4
Baishan [BJ]	22	D3
Baishan [GX]	60	G3
Baishan [JL]	34	F6
Baishan [JL]	34	G5
Baishanzu [ZJ]	42	C5
Baishatuo [CQ]	64	C4
Baishe [JX]	48	D4
Baisheng [GX]	60	C4
Baishi Feng [FJ]	46	B3
Baishi Shan [HEB]	26	B4
Baishi [CQ]	64	D3
Baishi [HL]	36	D5
Baishidu [HN]	56	F6
Baishilazi [HL]	36	D2
Baishishan [JL]	34	G4
Baishou [GX]	60	G2
Baishui Jiang [GS]	76	H6
Baishui [FJ]	46	C5
Baishui [HN]	56	D5
Baishui [JX]	48	C4
Baishui [SN]	74	E5
Baishui [ZJ]	42	C2
Baishuigang [HI]	62	B2
Baishuijiang [SN]	74	B7
Baisong Guan [FJ]	46	B5
Baisong Guan [GD]	58	H2
Baisuo [GZ]	68	E5
Baita He [JX]	48	D3
Baita [ZJ]	42	D4
Baitabu [JS]	40	D1
Baitang [QH]	78	E4
Baitangkou [TJ]	24	C5
Baitao [CQ]	64	D4
Baitu [GX]	60	F3
Baitu [JS]	40	E4
Baiwan [SC]	66	D3
Baiwen [SX]	28	C3
Baixiang [HEB]	26	B6
Baixing [GZ]	68	D4
Baiya [BJ]	22	E2
Baiya [NX]	80	B4
Baiyan Shan [FJ]	46	D3
Baiyang Dian [HEB]	26	D5
Baiyang [CQ]	64	E3
Baiyang [HB]	54	D4
Baiyangba [HB]	54	A4
Baiyin [GS]	76	H4
Baiyinna [HL]	36	C1
Baiyu Shan [SN]	74	D3
Baiyü [SC]	66	C3
Baiyun [GZ]	68	E4
Baiyun Shan [JX]	48	C5
Baiyun [FJ]	46	D3
Baiyunshan Shuiku [JX]	48	C5
Baiyutan Shuiku [HN]	56	E5
Baizao [JS]	40	E1
Baizhang [ZJ]	42	C5
Baizhong [FJ]	46	D3
Baizhuang [BJ]	22	D4
Bajia [GD]	58	C5
Bajiao [HB]	54	B4
Bajiaotou [JX]	48	C5
Bajiazi [JL]	34	I5
Bajie [GZ]	68	D6
Bakai [GZ]	68	G5
Bakeshiying [HEB]	26	E3
Bakog [QH]	78	E4
Balgas [SN]	74	E2

Name	Page	Grid
Balguntay [XJ]	82	J4
Balidianzi [LN]	32	H3
Baling [GZ]	68	D5
Balitai [TJ]	24	C5
Balougou [SX]	28	C3
Bam Co [XZ]	72	H4
Bama [GX]	60	E3
Bamao [ZJ]	42	D3
Bamencheng [TJ]	24	C3
Bamian Shan [HN]	56	F5
Bamian [JL]	34	C2
Bamiancheng [LN]	32	H1
Bamudi [BJ]	22	D2
Banan Qu [CQ]	64	C4
Banbar [XZ]	72	J4
Banbeidian [BJ]	22	D4
Banbidian [BJ]	22	D3
Banbishan [HEB]	26	E3
Bancheng [JS]	40	D2
Banchengzi shuiku [BJ]	22	E2
Banchengzi [BJ]	22	E2
Banfangzi [SN]	74	D7
Bangda [XZ]	72	K4
Bangdag Co [XZ]	72	C2
Bangdong [GZ]	68	H4
Bangjun [TJ]	24	C2
Bangong Co [XZ]	72	B3
Bangxi [HI]	62	B2
Banhu [JS]	40	E2
Banjieta [HEB]	26	E2
Banjin [JS]	40	F3
Bankengting [FJ]	46	D3
Banlamen [LN]	32	F3
Banli [GX]	60	E5
Banliao [HB]	54	B5
Banlu [GX]	60	G5
Banmian [FJ]	46	D3
Banpu [JS]	40	E1
Banqiao [BJ]	22	D3
Banqiao [GS]	76	F3
Banqiao [GZ]	68	E3
Banqiao [HI]	62	A3
Banqiao [HN]	56	E5
Banqiao [TJ]	24	D4
Banqiao [YN]	70	C3
Banqiao [YN]	70	F2
Banqiao [YN]	70	F3
Banqiao [ZJ]	42	C2
Banqiaoji [AH]	44	C2
Banquan [SD]	50	E4
Banshi [JX]	48	C6
Banshigou [JL]	34	F5
Banta [AH]	44	E3
Bantao [GX]	60	C3
Banuokuai [GZ]	68	C4
Banxi [GZ]	68	G2
Banzhuyuan [AH]	44	B4
Bao He [HEN]	52	H4
Bao Shui [SN]	74	C7
Bao'ai He [GX]	60	D3
Bao'an Qu [GD]	58	E4
Bao'an [GX]	60	E3
Bao'an [HEN]	52	E4
Baoban [HI]	62	A2
Baode [SX]	28	C2
Baodi Qu [TJ]	24	C3
Baodian [SX]	28	D5
Baoding [HEB]	26	C5
Baodugu [SD]	50	D5
Baofeng [HB]	54	C2
Baofeng [HEN]	52	E4
Baofeng [NX]	80	C1
Baogang [HI]	62	B3
Baohedi [HN]	56	E2
Baohu Jiao [HI]	62	C1
Baohua [YN]	70	D3
Baoji [JS]	40	D2
Baoji [SN]	74	C6
Baojia [CQ]	64	E4
Baojing [HN]	56	B3
Baokang [HB]	54	D3
Baoli [LN]	32	G2
Baolin [HL]	36	F5
Baolong [CQ]	64	F3
Baoluo [HI]	62	C2
Baomi [HL]	36	G5
Baoping [GX]	60	E3
Baoping [HI]	62	A2
Baoqing [HL]	36	G4
Baoshan Qu [HL]	36	F4
Baoshan Qu [SH]	38	D2
Baoshan [HL]	36	B3
Baoshan [YN]	70	C3
Baoshansi [BJ]	22	D2
Baoshou [JL]	34	F3
Baota [NX]	80	C2
Baotian [GZ]	68	C5
Baoting [HI]	62	B3
Baotou [NM]	30	E4
Baowei [GD]	58	B4
Baoxia [HB]	54	C2
Baoxin [HEN]	52	F5
Baoxing [HL]	36	F3
Baoxing [SC]	66	E3
Baoyi [AH]	44	C3
Baoying [JS]	40	E2
Baozhengang [SH]	38	D2
Baqên [XZ]	72	I3
Baqên [XZ]	72	J4
Baqiao Qu [SN]	74	E6
Baqiao [JS]	40	E3
Baqiu [JX]	48	C4
Barkam [SC]	66	E3
Barkol Hu [XJ]	82	M4
Barkol [XJ]	82	M4
Barong [SC]	66	C3
Barragem de Hác Sá [MC]	86	C6
Barragem de Ká-Hó [MC]	86	C6
Barun [QH]	78	E2
Basalt Island [HK]	84	F3
Bashan Shuiku [SD]	50	E4
Bashan [CQ]	64	D3
Bashan [CQ]	64	E1
Basuo Gang [HI]	62	A2
Batan [JS]	40	F1
Batang [SC]	66	C3
Batu [SD]	50	D3
Batuying [LN]	32	D3
Bawang [SC]	66	D3
Bawangling [HI]	62	B2
Baweigang [JS]	40	F4
Bawolung [SC]	66	D4
Baxkorgan [XJ]	82	L6
Baxoi [XZ]	72	K4
Baxu [GX]	60	E3
Bayan Bogd [NM]	30	C4
Bayan Bulag [NM]	30	F3
Bayan Gol [QH]	78	E2
Bayan Har Shan [QH]	78	D3
Bayan Har Shan [QH]	78	E3
Bayan Har Shan [QH]	78	F4
Bayan Har Shankou [QH]	78	E3
Bayan Nurun [NM]	30	D4
Bayan Obo Kuangqu [NM]	30	E4
Bayan Qagan [HI]	36	C4
Bayan Ul [NM]	30	F3
Bayan [HL]	36	D4
Bayan [NM]	30	E4
Bayanbulak [XJ]	82	I4
Bayannur [NM]	30	D4
Bayi Zongchang [HI]	62	B2
Baytik Shan [XJ]	82	L3
Bayuquan Qu [LN]	32	F4
Bazhan [HI]	36	C2
Bazhong [SC]	66	G3
Bazhou [HEB]	26	D4
Bazi [GD]	58	F2
Bazishao [HN]	56	E3
Beacon Hill [HK]	84	D3
Beaufort Island (Lo Chau) [HK]	84	D4
Bei Shan [GS]	76	D2
Bei Hulsan Hu [QH]	78	D2
Bei Inggen [NM]	30	D4
Bei Jiang [GD]	58	E2
Bei Shan [ZJ]	42	C3
Bei Xi [FJ]	46	C2
Bei'an [HL]	36	D3
Bei'anfeng [JS]	40	F2
Beiba [SN]	74	C8
Beibei Qu [CQ]	64	C4
Beibu Gulf [GX]	60	F6
Beibu Gulf [GD]	58	A6
Beibu Gulf [HI]	62	A1
Beibu [SH]	38	E2
Beicai [SH]	38	D3
Beichangshan Dao [SD]	50	G1
Beichangtan [NX]	80	A3
Beichen Qu [TJ]	24	D4
Beicheng [SX]	28	D5
Beicheng [YN]	70	E3
Beichuan He [QH]	78	G2
Beichuan He [SX]	28	C4
Beichuan [SC]	66	F3
Beida He [GS]	76	D3
Beida Shan [NM]	30	C5

Beida [HI]	62	C3	Beixing [HL]	36	F4	Bixi [YN]	70	D3
Beidagang Shuiku [TJ]	24	C6	Beixinjing [SH]	38	D3	Biyang He [HEN]	52	E5
Beidaihe Qu [HEB]	26	G4	Beiyandang Shan [ZJ]	42	E4	Biyang [HEN]	52	E5
Beidanche [SX]	28	E5	Beiyang [LN]	32	F4	Biyong [HN]	56	B4
Beidian [LN]	32	H3	Beiye [HEB]	26	A5	Bizhou [HL]	36	C2
Beidun [GD]	58	G2	Beiying [HL]	36	D3	Bizhou [JX]	48	B5
Beifei He [AH]	44	C2	Beiying [SX]	28	D4	Black Point		
Beigang [JL]	34	G5	Beizhakou [TJ]	24	C5	(Lan Kok Tsui) [HK]	84	A2
Beigong [BJ]	22	E3	Beizhangdai [BJ]	22	E3	Bluff Island		
Beiguan Dao [ZJ]	42	D5	Beizhen [LN]	32	E3	(Sha Tong Hau Shan) [HK]	84	E3
Beiguantao [SD]	50	B3	Beizheng [JL]	34	C3	Bo Hai [HEB]	26	F5
Beiguo [JS]	40	F4	Beizhouzhuang [SX]	28	D2	Bo Hai [LN]	32	C6
Beiguo [SD]	50	F4	Beizhuang [BJ]	22	E2	Bo Hai [SD]	50	F1
Beihai [GX]	60	G6	Beizijie [HEN]	52	D4	Bo'ai [HEN]	52	E2
Beihuaidian [TJ]	24	C4	Bencha [JS]	40	F3	Bo'ai [YN]	70	G4
Beihuangcheng Dao [SD]	50	G1	Beng He [LN]	32	C2	Bo'ao [HI]	62	C2
Beiji [HL]	36	B1	Bengbu [AH]	44	D3	Bobai [GX]	60	G5
Beijiao [FJ]	46	E3	Benniu [JS]	40	E4	Bobi [HEN]	52	E2
Beijie [ZJ]	42	C4	Benxi [LN]	32	G3	Bodu [JL]	34	D2
Beijin Gang [GD]	58	C5	Benxi [LN]	32	H3	Bogcang Zangbo [XZ]	72	F4
BEIJING [BJ]	22	D4	Benzhuang [GZ]	68	F3	Bogda Feng [XJ]	82	K4
Beijing [SX]	28	B6	Benzilan [YN]	70	C1	Bogda Shan [XJ]	82	K4
Beijipo [SD]	50	D3	Bi Qu [QH]	78	B4	Bohai Haixia [LN]	32	E6
Beijishan Liedao [ZJ]	42	E5	Biandanhe Kou [JS]	40	F1	Bohai Haixia [SD]	50	G1
Beikan [JL]	40	G3	Bianqiao [SD]	50	D4	Bohai Wan [HEB]	26	E5
Beiling [GD]	58	G2	Biantang [JS]	40	C1	Bohai Wan [TJ]	24	D6
Beiliu Jiang [GX]	60	H5	Bianya [GX]	60	C3	Bohai [BJ]	22	D2
Beiliu [GX]	60	H5	Bianyang [GZ]	68	E5	Bohai [HL]	36	E5
Beiliutang He [JS]	40	D2	Bianzhangzi [LN]	32	D3	Bohe [GD]	58	C5
Beilong Shan [ZJ]	42	E5	Bianzhao [JL]	34	C3	Bohou [HI]	62	B2
Beilu He [QH]	78	C3	Bianzhuang [AH]	44	E3	Bohu(Bagrax) [XJ]	82	J5
Beiluheyan [QH]	78	C3	Bieqiao [JS]	40	E4	Boiba [QH]	78	F4
Beilun He [GX]	60	E6	Bi'er [HN]	56	B3	Bole(Bortala) [XJ]	82	H3
Beilun Qu [ZJ]	42	E3	Bieshan [TJ]	24	C2	Boli [HL]	36	F5
Beima [SD]	50	G2	Big Wave Bay [HK]	84	E4	Bolian [HI]	62	B2
Beipan Jiang [GZ]	68	D5	Biguo [SD]	50	G2	Bolishan [JL]	34	C4
Beipiao [LN]	32	D3	Bihu [ZJ]	42	C4	Boluo [GD]	58	F3
Beiping [SX]	28	D5	Bijia Shan [FJ]	46	C2	Boluo [SN]	74	E2
Beipo [GD]	58	A5	Bijiaquan [HEB]	26	F4	Boluonuo [HEB]	26	E2
Beiqiao [SH]	38	D4	Bijie [GZ]	68	D3	Bomei [GD]	58	G4
Beirong [HN]	56	C3	Bikou [GS]	76	H6	Bomi(Bowo) [XZ]	72	J5
Beiru He [HEN]	52	D3	Bilian [ZJ]	42	D4	Bonihe [JL]	34	E4
Beisanjia [LN]	32	H2	Biling La [XZ]	72	C4	Boping Ling [FJ]	46	C5
Beishe [SX]	28	E5	Biliu He [LN]	32	F5	Boping [SD]	50	C3
Beishi Dao [HI]	62	D2	Bin Jiang [GD]	58	D2	Bor Ondor [JL]	34	B3
Beishi [GD]	58	D3	Bin Xian [HL]	36	D5	Borohoro Shan [XJ]	82	H3
Beishicao [BJ]	22	D3	Bin Xian [SN]	74	D5	Boshan Qu [SD]	50	D3
Beishicheng [BJ]	22	E2	Bincheng [SD]	50	D2	Boshang [YN]	70	D4
Beishidian [SD]	50	D4	Binchuan [YN]	70	D3	Bosten(Bagrax) Hu [XJ]	82	J5
Beishuang Dao [FJ]	46	F3	Bingzhongluo [YN]	70	C1	Botou [HEB]	26	D5
Beisi [SD]	50	E2	Binhai [JS]	40	E1	Botou [SD]	50	E2
Beita [LN]	32	D2	Binhaicun [TJ]	24	C6	Bowang [AH]	44	E4
Beitan [TJ]	24	C3	Binjiang Qu [ZJ]	42	D2	Boxiang [HEN]	52	D2
Beitang [TJ]	24	D5	Binjiang [JX]	48	B4	Boxing [SD]	50	E2
Beitian [SX]	28	D4	Binxi [HL]	36	D5	Boyang [HN]	56	B5
Beitun [XJ]	82	J2	Binyang [GX]	60	F4	Boye [HEB]	26	C5
Beiwei Tan [GD]	58	H5	Binzhou [SD]	50	E2	Bozhou [AH]	44	B2
Beiwu [BJ]	22	E3	Biru [XZ]	72	I4	Bucun [SD]	50	D3
Beixiaochuan [BJ]	22	D2	Bishan [CQ]	64	C4	Budongquan [QH]	78	C3
Beixiaoying [BJ]	22	C3	Bishui [HL]	36	B1	Bugt [NM]	30	H2
Beixin [JS]	40	G4	Bixi [JX]	48	B5	Bugugou [HEB]	26	E2
Beixing [HL]	36	C3				Buh He [QH]	78	F2

Buir Nur [NM]	30	G3
Bujiang [HEN]	52	E5
Buka Daban Feng [XJ]	82	L7
Bukou [HB]	54	E2
Bulang [GZ]	68	D4
Bulangtai [QH]	78	C2
Bulaotun [BJ]	22	E2
Buliu He [GX]	60	D3
Buliu [SD]	50	I2
Bulu [ZJ]	42	D4
Bungona'og [XZ]	72	H3
Burang [XZ]	72	C4
Burhan Budai Shan [QH]	78	D3
Burqin He [XJ]	82	J1
Burqin [XJ]	82	J2
Burqunji [XJ]	82	M3
Bütog [XZ]	72	L5
Butou [GX]	60	I3
Butuo [SC]	66	E5
Buya [XJ]	82	G7
Buyant [NM]	30	D4
Buyuan Jiang [YN]	70	D4
Buyun Shan [LN]	32	F4
Buze [SX]	28	E5
C		
Cai Xi [ZJ]	42	B4
Caidian Qu [HB]	54	G4
Caigongzhuang [TJ]	24	B6
Caigou [HEN]	52	F4
Caihe [HB]	54	F3
Caihe [HB]	54	H4
Caijiabu [TJ]	24	D5
Caijiagang [HN]	56	D2
Caijiagou [JL]	34	F2
Caijialiang [NX]	80	C2
Caijiapo [SN]	74	C6
Caijiaqiao [AH]	44	E5
Caijiaya [SX]	28	C3
Cailu [SH]	38	E3
Caishen [GZ]	68	C3
Caitang [SD]	50	C5
Caitun [SD]	50	C3
Caixi [FJ]	46	B4
Caiyu [BJ]	22	D4
Caizhai [SD]	50	E2
Caizi Hu [AH]	44	D5
Caka Yanhu [QH]	78	F2
Caka [QH]	78	F2
Caka [XZ]	72	D3
Caluo [SC]	66	E4
Cang'erhui [SX]	28	C4
Canggang [HN]	56	D3
Canggeng [GZ]	68	C6
Canggou [CQ]	64	D4
Cangling [CQ]	64	E4
Cangnan [ZJ]	42	D5
Cangshan [HL]	36	B2
Cangshan [SD]	50	E5
Cangshuipu [HN]	56	F3
Cangtou He [SX]	28	D1
Cangwu [GX]	60	I4
Cangxi [SC]	66	F3
Cangxian [HEB]	26	D5
Cangyuan [YN]	70	C4
Cangzhou [HEB]	26	D5
Cao Hai [GZ]	68	C4
Cao Xian [SD]	50	B5
Cao Yu [FJ]	46	E4
Cao'an [AH]	44	D3
Caoba [YN]	70	E4
Caobi [SN]	74	C6
Caodian [HB]	54	D2
Caodu He [GZ]	68	F4
Caoe'Jiang [ZJ]	42	D3
Caofang [FJ]	46	B3
Caofeidian [HEB]	26	F5
Caogoubu [HEB]	26	B4
Caohang [SH]	38	D3
Caohe [HEB]	26	C5
Caohekou [LN]	32	G4
Caohezhang [LN]	32	H3
Caohu [SX]	28	C3
Caoji [AH]	44	B3
Caojialu [BJ]	22	F2
Caojian [YN]	70	C3
Caojing [SH]	38	D4
Caolin [JX]	48	B5
Caomiao [NX]	80	C4
Caopie [JS]	40	F3
Caoping [SN]	74	E7
Caoqiao [JS]	40	E4
Caoshi [AH]	44	C2
Caoshi [HN]	56	F5
Caoshi [LN]	32	I2
Caotang [GZ]	68	F3
Caowang [SH]	38	D2
Caoxi [JX]	48	E3
Caoyan [JS]	40	F3
Caoyankou [JS]	40	E2
Caoyuan [HEB]	26	D2
Caozhuang [TJ]	24	B5
Castle Peak [HK]	84	B2
Causeway Bay [HK]	84	D3
Ceheng [GZ]	68	D5
Cen Shui [HN]	56	D2
Cengong [GZ]	68	G3
Centianhe Shuiku [HN]	56	D6
Central District [HK]	84	D3
Cenwang Laoshan [GX]	60	D3
Cenxi [GX]	60	I5
Cêtar [QH]	78	G2
Cetian Shuiku [SX]	28	E2
Cha Kwo Chau [HK]	84	B4
Cha'anpu [HN]	56	D3
Chabyêr Caka [XZ]	72	D4
Chadao [HEB]	26	C3
Chadian [GZ]	68	H3
Chadian [TJ]	24	D4
Chadianzi [HB]	54	C4
Chadong [HN]	56	B3
Cha'ensi [HN]	56	E4
Chafang [SN]	74	E4
Chagdo Kangri [XZ]	72	E2
Chaggur [QH]	78	D3
Chagugang [TJ]	24	B4
Chahe [AH]	44	E3
Chahe [HB]	54	F4
Chahe [HI]	62	A2
Chahe [JS]	40	F3
Chahe [YN]	70	D5
Chahua [AH]	44	B2
Chai He [LN]	32	H2
Chai Wan [HK]	84	E3
Chai Wan [HK]	84	E4
Chaichangtun [BJ]	22	D4
Chaigou [SD]	50	F3
Chaihe Shuiku [LN]	32	H2
Chaiwopu [XJ]	82	J4
Chajian [AH]	44	E3
Chajianling [HEB]	26	B4
Chalengkou [QH]	78	C1
Chaling [HN]	56	F5
Chalu [AH]	44	C3
Chaluhe [JL]	34	E4
Chamdong [XZ]	72	E3
Chang Hu [HB]	54	E4
Chang Jiang(Yangtze R.) [AH]	44	D4
Chang Jiang(Yangtze R.) [JS]	40	F4
Chang Jiang(Yangtze R.) [JX]	48	C2
Chang Jiang(Yangtze R.) [CQ]	64	E3
Chang Jiang(Yangtze R.) [HB]	54	E5
Chang Jiang(Yangtze R.) [HN]	56	F2
Chang Jiang(Yangtze R.) [JX]	48	C2
Chang'an Qu [SN]	74	D6
Changan [SX]	28	D4
Changan [ZJ]	42	D2
Changba [CQ]	64	D4
Changbai Shan [JL]	34	G6
Changbai Dao [ZJ]	42	E2
Changbai [JL]	34	H6
Changbaishan Tianchi (Baitoushan Tianchi) [JL]	34	G5
Changbiao Dao [FJ]	46	F3
Changbu [GD]	58	G3
Changcao [BJ]	22	B4
Changcheng [HI]	62	A2
Changcheng [HI]	62	B3
Changcheng [LN]	32	E6
Changcheng [SX]	28	E1
Changchun [JL]	34	E4
Changchunling [JL]	34	E2
Changchunpu [GZ]	68	D3
Changdang Hu [JS]	40	E4
Changdao [SD]	50	G2
Changde [HN]	56	D2
Changdian [LN]	32	H4
Changfa [GX]	60	I4
Changfeng [AH]	44	D3
Changfeng [HI]	62	C3
Changgang [AH]	44	D4
Changgang [GZ]	68	E3
Changge [HEN]	52	E3
Changgou [AH]	44	D2
Changgou [BJ]	22	C5
Changhai [LN]	32	F5

Changhao [HI]	62	B3	Changsheng [JX]	48	D5	Chaoyang [LN]	32	D3
Changhong [CQ]	64	E2	Changshou Hu [CQ]	64	D3	Chaoyang [SH]	38	E3
Changhua Jiang [HI]	62	A2	Changshou Qu [CQ]	64	D4	Chaoyangsi [HB]	54	A5
Changhua Jiang [HI]	62	B3	Changshou [HB]	54	E3	Chaoyangzhen [SX]	28	B7
Changhua [HI]	62	A2	Changshoujie [HN]	56	F3	Chaoyi [SN]	74	F6
Changhua [TW]	88	C2	Changshu [JS]	40	F4	Chaozhou [GD]	58	H3
Changji [XJ]	82	J3	Changshui [HEN]	52	C3	Chaozhuang [HEN]	52	F3
Changjia [HL]	36	E3	Changshun [GZ]	68	E4	Chating [JS]	40	E4
Changjiang Kou [SH]	38	F2	Changtai [FJ]	46	C5	Chau Mei Kok [HK]	84	F1
Changjiang Qu [JX]	48	E2	Changtaiguan [HEN]	52	F5	Chau Tau [HK]	84	F1
Changjiang [GD]	58	E1	Changtan Shuiku [ZJ]	42	D4	Chawu [BJ]	22	D3
Changjiang [HI]	62	B2	Changtan [CQ]	64	E3	Chayang [GD]	58	H2
Changjiang [SH]	38	D1	Changtan [ZJ]	42	E4	Chayuan [ZJ]	42	E3
Changjiangbu [HB]	54	F4	Changting [FJ]	46	B4	Chayuanpu [HN]	56	E4
Changkai [JX]	48	D3	Changting [HL]	36	E5	Checheng [TW]	88	C4
Changle [FJ]	46	E4	Changtu [LN]	32	H2	Chedaoyu [BJ]	22	E2
Changle [HN]	56	F3	Changwu [HL]	36	C5	Chedun [SH]	38	D4
Changle [SD]	50	E3	Changwu [SN]	74	C5	Chehe [GX]	60	E3
Changle [SX]	28	C7	Changxiao [FJ]	46	B4	Chejiang [HN]	56	E5
Changle [ZJ]	42	D3	Changxing Dao [SH]	38	E2	Chek Keng Hau [HK]	84	E2
Changli [HEB]	26	G4	Changxing Dao [LN]	32	E5	Chek Keng [HK]	84	E2
Changliang [JX]	48	D3	Changxing [ZJ]	42	C1	Chek Lap Kok [HK]	84	B3
Changliangzi [HB]	54	B4	Changxinpu [NX]	80	C2	Chelu [HL]	36	E3
Changling [AH]	44	C5	Changxuanling [HB]	54	G3	Cheluo [JS]	40	E3
Changling [BJ]	22	C3	Changyang [BJ]	22	C4	Chen Shui [HN]	56	B4
Changling [HB]	54	F3	Changyang [HB]	54	D4	Chen Barag Qi [NM]	30	G2
Changling [JL]	34	C3	Changyi [SD]	50	B3	Chencai [ZJ]	42	D3
Changling [JL]	34	E4	Changyi [SD]	50	F3	Chencang Qu [SN]	74	C6
Changling [LN]	32	F5	Changying [HEN]	52	F3	Chencheng [FJ]	46	C6
Changlingjie [YN]	70	F4	Changyuan He [SX]	28	D4	Chendong [FJ]	46	B5
Changliushui [NX]	80	A3	Changyuan [HEN]	52	F2	Chenfang [JX]	48	E3
Changlong [SX]	28	D5	Changzhen [SX]	28	C2	Cheng Hai [YN]	70	D2
Changlu [SD]	50	D4	Changzheng [HI]	62	B3	Cheng Xian [GS]	76	H6
Changma [GS]	76	D3	Changzhi [SX]	28	E5	Cheng'an [HEB]	26	B7
Changmao Shuiku [HI]	62	B3	Changzhi [SX]	28	E5	Chengbei [SH]	38	D1
Changmao [JS]	40	E1	Changzhou [JS]	40	E4	Chengbihe Shuiku [GX]	60	D3
Changmen Yan [SD]	50	G3	Changzhuang [SD]	50	C4	Chengbu [HN]	56	C5
Changming [GZ]	68	F4	Changzhuyuan [HEN]	52	G6	Chengcheng [SN]	74	E5
Changning [GD]	58	F3	Chao He [AH]	44	D4	Chengchuan [NM]	30	E5
Changning [HEB]	26	F4	Chao He [BJ]	22	E1	Chengde [HEB]	26	E3
Changning [HN]	56	E5	Chao He [HEB]	26	D2	Chengde [HEB]	26	F3
Changning [SC]	66	F4	Chao'an [GD]	58	H3	Chengdong Hu [AH]	44	C3
Changning [SX]	28	D4	Chaobai He [HEB]	26	D3	Chengdu [SC]	66	F3
Changning [YN]	70	C3	Chaobai He [BJ]	22	D3	Chenggang [JX]	48	C5
Changpin [TW]	88	D3	Chaobai Xinhe [TJ]	24	C3	Chenggong [YN]	70	E3
Changping Qu [BJ]	22	C3	Chaocheng [SD]	50	B3	Chenggu [SN]	74	C7
Changping [GD]	58	E4	Chaochou [TW]	88	C4	Chengguan [HEN]	52	F2
Changping [HB]	54	D3	Chaohu [AH]	44	D4	Chengguan [TJ]	24	A3
Changpo [HI]	62	B2	Chaohua [HEN]	52	E3	Chenghai Qu [GD]	58	H3
Changpo [HI]	62	C2	Chaohu Nongchang [NX]	80	C2	Chenghe [JS]	40	D2
Changqiao [FJ]	46	C5	Chaohupu [NX]	80	C1	Chengjia [GD]	58	D2
Changqing Qu [SD]	50	C3	Chaolian Dao [SD]	50	G4	Chengjiang [JX]	48	C6
Changsa [HI]	62	C2	Chaonan Qu [GD]	58	H3	Chengjiang [YN]	70	E3
Changsha [CQ]	64	E3	Chaonggang [NX]	80	C2	Chengkou [CQ]	64	E2
Changsha [HN]	56	F3	Chaor He [HL]	36	B4	Chengkou [GD]	58	E1
Changsha [HN]	56	F3	Chaor He [NM]	30	H3	Chengkou [SD]	50	D1
Changshabu [SD]	50	H2	Chaotian Qu [SC]	66	F2	Chengkung [TW]	88	D3
Changshan Qundao [LN]	32	F5	Chaoyang Qu [BJ]	22	D4	Chenglingji [HN]	56	F2
Changshan [FJ]	46	C6	Chaoyang Qu [GD]	58	H3	Chenglong [JX]	48	B7
Changshan [ZJ]	42	B4	Chaoyang [AH]	44	D2	Chengmai [HI]	62	C2
Changshantou [NX]	80	B3	Chaoyang [GZ]	68	F5	Chengqian [SD]	50	D4
Changshaoying [BJ]	22	D1	Chaoyang [JL]	34	F3	Chengshanjiao [SD]	50	I2

Chengshanwei [SD]	50	I2	Chilai Chushan [TW]	88	D2	Chuangye [HL]	36	G4
Chengtan [ZJ]	42	D3	Chilung [TW]	88	D1	Chuankou [SN]	74	D4
Chengtougu [TJ]	24	D5	Chimei Yu(Ta Yu) [TW]	88	B3	Chuanliao [ZJ]	42	D4
Chenguang [JX]	48	C7	Chindu [QH]	78	E4	Chuansha [SH]	38	E3
Chenguantun [TJ]	24	B6	Chingpu [TW]	88	D3	Chuanshan Qundao [GD]	58	D5
Chenguanzhuang [HEN]	52	H3	Chingshui [TW]	88	D2	Chuanshan [GX]	60	G3
Chengwu [SD]	50	B5	Chinkuashih [TW]	88	D1	Chuanshanping [HN]	56	F3
Chengxi Hu [AH]	44	C3	Chinmen Tao [FJ]	46	D5	Chuanshi [FJ]	46	D2
Chengxi [CQ]	64	D3	Chinmen [FJ]	46	D5	Chuantan [JX]	48	B2
Chengxi [SX]	38	C2	Chinqên [QH]	78	E4	Chuanyao Gang [JS]	40	G3
Chengxi [SH]	38	C4	Chinshan [TW]	88	D1	Chubalung [SC]	66	C4
Chengyang Qu [SD]	50	G3	Chipei Yu [TW]	88	B3	Chucun [AH]	44	C2
Chengyang [NX]	80	C5	Chiping [SD]	50	C3	Chucuo [JX]	48	D3
Chengyuan [FJ]	46	E2	Chishan His [TW]	88	C3	Chudian [AH]	44	C2
Chengzhuang [SX]	28	C3	Chishan [TW]	88	C4	Chuen Lung [HK]	84	C2
Chengzi Hu [JS]	40	D2	Chishui [GZ]	68	D2	Chukou [HN]	56	F6
Chengzi [HEB]	26	E2	Chishui He [GZ]	68	D2	Chukuang Liehtao [FJ]	46	E4
Chengzi [YN]	70	B3	Chishui He [SC]	66	F5	Chulan [AH]	44	D1
Chengzihe Qu [HL]	36	F5	Chishui [FJ]	46	D4	Chumda [QH]	78	E4
Chenhang [SH]	38	D3	Chishui [JX]	48	D5	Chumi [GZ]	68	E2
Cheniu Shan	40	E1	Chishui [SC]	66	F5	Chunan [TW]	88	C2
Cheniu Shan	50	F5	Chitou Shan [ZJ]	42	D5	Chun'an [ZJ]	42	C3
Chenji [HEN]	52	G5	Chitu [TJ]	24	C4	Chung Hom Wan [HK]	84	D4
Chenji [JS]	40	E2	Chixi [FJ]	46	D4	Chungyang Shan [TW]	88	C3
Chenjia [SH]	38	E2	Chixi [JX]	48	D3	Chunheji [HEN]	52	G5
Chenjiagang [JS]	40	E1	Chizhou [AH]	44	D5	Chunhu [ZJ]	42	E3
Chenjiahang [SH]	38	D3	Cho La [SC]	66	C3	Chunhua [JL]	34	K4
Chenjiatuan [SD]	50	H2	Chola Shan [SC]	66	C2	Chunhua [JS]	40	D4
Chenjiazhuang [SX]	28	E3	Cholan [TW]	88	C2	Chunhua [SD]	50	E2
Chenming [HL]	36	E4	Chong'an Jiang [GZ]	68	F4	Chunhua [SN]	74	D6
Chentang [GX]	60	H4	Chong'an [GZ]	68	F4	Chunkou [HN]	56	F3
Chentuan [SD]	50	F4	Chongfu [ZJ]	42	D2	Chunshen [SH]	38	D3
Chenxi [HN]	56	C3	Chonggou [SD]	50	E4	Chunshu [AH]	44	C4
Chenyang [JS]	40	F2	Chonggu [SH]	38	C3	Chunshui [GD]	58	D3
Chenzhai [AH]	44	C1	Chonghe [HL]	36	D5	Chunshui [HEN]	52	E4
Chenzhou [HN]	56	F6	Chongli [HEB]	26	C3	Chunwan [GD]	58	C4
Chenzhuang [SD]	50	E2	Chongling Shui [HN]	56	E5	Chunyang [JL]	34	I4
Cheqiao [JX]	48	C2	Chongming Dao [SH]	38	D1	Chutung [TW]	88	D2
Chetou [JX]	48	C6	Chongming [SH]	38	D2	Chuxiong [YN]	70	D3
Cheung Chau [HK]	84	C4	Chongpo [HI]	62	A3	Chuzhou Qu [JS]	40	E2
Cheung Muk Tau [HK]	84	B4	Chongqing [CQ]	64	C4	Chuzhou [AH]	44	E3
Cheung Sha [HK]	84	B4	Chongren He [JX]	48	D4	Ci He [AH]	44	B2
Chezhen [SD]	50	D2	Chongren [JX]	48	D4	Ci He [HEB]	26	B5
Chi He [AH]	44	D3	Chongren [ZJ]	42	D3	Ci He [HEB]	52	G4
Chi Ma Wan Peninsula [HK]	84	B4	Chongxian [JX]	48	C5	Ci Xian [HEB]	26	B7
Chi Ma Wan [HK]	84	B4	Chongxin [GS]	76	I5	Cigou [HEN]	52	E4
Chiahsien [TW]	88	C3	Chongxin [GZ]	68	E3	Cihuai Xinhe [AH]	44	C2
Chia-i [TW]	88	C3	Chongxing [HEB]	62	C2	Cijian [HEN]	52	D3
Chia-i [TW]	88	C3	Chongxing [NX]	80	C2	Cijiawu [BJ]	22	C4
Chiali [TW]	88	C3	Chongyang Xi [FJ]	46	D2	Cili [HN]	56	D2
Chiangchunao Yu [TW]	88	B3	Chongyang [HB]	54	G5	Ciping [JX]	48	B5
Chibi [HB]	54	F5	Chongyangdian [HEN]	52	C4	Cishan [HEB]	26	B7
Chicheng [HEB]	26	C3	Chongyi [JX]	48	B6	Cixi [ZJ]	42	E2
Chido [XZ]	72	J4	Chongyü [XZ]	72	I4	Ciyaopu [NX]	80	C2
Chifeng [NM]	30	G4	Chongzhou [SC]	66	E3	Ciyutuo [LN]	32	F3
Chigang [JX]	48	D3	Chongzuo [GX]	60	E5	Cizhu [CQ]	64	C4
Chihe [AH]	44	D3	Choshui Hsi [TW]	88	C3	Clear Water Bay [HK]	84	E3
Chihpen [TW]	88	D4	Choushui Gou [NX]	80	B4	Co Nag [XZ]	72	H4
Chihsing Yen [TW]	88	C5	Chowa [XZ]	72	F4	Colina da Barra [MC]	86	A3
Chihu [FJ]	46	C5	Chuanbu [GD]	58	C4	Colina da Penha [MC]	86	A2
Chihwei Yu [TW]	88	G1	Chuanchang He [JS]	40	E2	Coloane Alto [MC]	86	C6
Chijin [GS]	76	D2	Chuanfangyu [TJ]	24	C1	COLOANE [MC]	86	C6

Comai [XZ] 72 F4
Comai [XZ] 72 H5
Cona [XZ] 72 H6
Co'nga [XZ] 72 L4
Conghua [GD] 58 E3
Congjiang [GZ] 68 G5
Congziyu [SX] 28 D5
Coqên [XZ] 72 E4
Cozhelhoma [XZ] 72 F4
CrescentIsland
(Ngo Mei Chau) [HK] 84 E1
Crooked Island(Kat O) [HK] 84 E1
Cuigang [HL] 36 C1
Cuihuangkou [TJ] 24 B3
Cuiluan Qu [HL] 36 E4
Cuimu [SN] 74 C6
Cuipingshan [TJ] 24 C2
Cuiqiao [HEN] 52 F3
Culai Shan [SD] 50 D3
Cunqian [SX] 48 C3
Cuo He [BJ] 22 E3
Cuocheng [HEN] 52 H4
Cushijiang [HN] 56 C6
Cyberport [HK] 84 D4

D

Da Xi [ZJ] 42 D4
Da Hinggan Ling [HL] 36 B2
Da Hinggan Ling [NM] 30 H3
Da Juh [QH] 78 D2
Da Qaidam Hu [QH] 78 D2
Da Qaidam [QH] 78 D2
Da qu [SC] 66 C2
Da Xian [SC] 66 G3
Da'a [JX] 48 B6
Da'an [CQ] 64 C4
Da'an [GD] 58 G3
Da'an [GX] 60 H4
Da'an [HI] 62 B2
Da'an [HI] 62 B3
Da'an [JL] 34 D2
Da'an [SN] 74 B7
Da'anshan [BJ] 22 B4
Daba Shan [CQ] 64 F2
Daba Shan [SN] 74 D8
Daba Shan [HB] 54 A2
Daba [GD] 58 H2
Daba [GZ] 68 E2
Daba [NX] 80 C3
Daba [XZ] 72 B4
Dabaideng [SX] 28 E1
Dabaidi [JX] 48 D5
Dabaizhuang [TJ] 24 C4
Daban Shan [QH] 78 G2
Daban Shankou [QH] 78 G2
Daban [LN] 32 D3
Dabancheng Qu [XJ] 82 K4
Dabang He [GZ] 68 D5
Dabanzhuang [TJ] 24 C3
Dabeibu [AH] 44 D6
Dabeilou [BJ] 22 D4
Dabie Shan [AH] 44 B4

Dabie Shan [HEN] 52 F6
Dabin [GZ] 68 E6
Dabizhuang [TJ] 24 C5
Dabs Nur [JL] 34 C3
Dabsan Hu [QH] 78 D2
Dabu [GD] 58 H2
Dabu [JX] 48 C6
Dabu [SD] 50 E5
Dabugang [FJ] 46 C2
Dachang [HEB] 26 D4
Dachang [CQ] 64 F2
Dachang [SH] 38 D3
Dachangshan Dao [LN] 32 F5
Dachangtu Shan [ZJ] 42 F2
Dacheng [HEB] 62 B2
Dacheng [JX] 48 C3
Dachengzi [BJ] 22 E2
Dachi [FJ] 46 B4
Dacun [BJ] 22 C3
Dadi [HN] 56 G5
Dadian [SD] 50 E4
Dadianzi [LN] 32 H2
Dadong [GX] 60 F5
Dadu He [SC] 66 E3
Daduan [JX] 48 B3
Dadukou Qu [CQ] 64 C4
Dadukou [AH] 44 D5
Da'erhao [HEB] 26 C2
Dafang [GZ] 68 D3
Dafeng Nongchang [HI] 62 B2
Dafeng [JS] 40 F2
Dafeng [SC] 66 G3
DaFengman [JL] 34 F4
Daftar [XJ] 82 D7
Dafu Shui [HB] 54 F3
Dafu [FJ] 46 E4
Dagain [SC] 66 D3
Dagan [FJ] 46 C3
Dagang Qu [TJ] 24 C6
Dagang [JS] 40 F2
Dagang [JX] 48 D3
Dagang [SH] 38 C4
Dagangtou [ZJ] 42 C4
Dagangzi [JL] 34 C2
Dagong Dao [SD] 50 G4
Dagou He [GX] 60 E2
Dagtog [QH] 78 F4
Dagu He [SD] 50 G3
Dagu [TJ] 24 D5
Daguan Hu [AH] 44 C5
Daguan [GZ] 68 D4
Daguan [GZ] 68 E4
Daguan [SC] 66 F4
Daguan [YN] 70 E2
Daguangba Shuiku [HI] 62 B3
Daguantou [BJ] 22 C2
Dagudian [AH] 44 C4
Dagujia He [SD] 50 H2
Dagujiazi [LN] 32 G2
Daguokui Shan [HL] 36 E5
Daguoling [YN] 70 D4
Dagur [QH] 78 D2

Dagushan [JL] 34 E4
Dagxung [XZ] 72 E4
Dagzê Co [XZ] 72 F3
Dagzê [XZ] 72 H5
Dahaibei [TJ] 24 C4
Dahaituo Shan [BJ] 22 C2
Dahaituo Shan [HEB] 26 C3
Dahe [CQ] 64 C3
Daheba [QH] 78 F3
Dahei Shan [JL] 34 D4
Dahei Shan [JL] 34 E4
Daheiding Shan [HL] 36 E4
Daheishan Dao [SD] 50 G2
Dahenan [HEB] 26 C4
Daheping [HN] 56 C3
Dahetun [HEN] 52 E5
Dahong Shan [HB] 54 E3
Dahong Shan [HB] 54 E3
Dahonghe Shuiku [CQ] 64 C3
Dahongliutan [XJ] 82 F8
Dahongluo Shan [LN] 32 D4
Dahongqi [LN] 32 F3
Dahouzhuang [TJ] 24 B5
Dahua [GX] 60 E4
Dahuai [GD] 58 D4
Dahuan Jiang [GX] 60 F2
Dahuanglong Shan [ZJ] 42 F2
Dahuashan [BJ] 22 E3
Dahuichang [BJ] 22 C4
Dahulun [HEB] 26 C2
Dahuofang Shuiku [LN] 32 H3
Dai Jiang [FJ] 46 E3
Dai Xian [SX] 28 D2
Daibu [JS] 40 E4
Daibu [YN] 70 E2
Daicheng [HEB] 26 D5
Daihua [GZ] 68 E5
Dailing Qu [HL] 36 E4
Daimao Shan [FJ] 46 B4
Dainan [JS] 40 F3
Daishan Dao [ZJ] 42 E2
Daishan [ZJ] 42 E2
Daixi [ZJ] 42 D2
Daiyue Qu [SD] 50 D3
Daiyun Shan [FJ] 46 D4
Daiyun Shan [FJ] 46 D4
Dajdoi [SC] 66 C2
Daji Shan [ZJ] 42 F2
Daji Yang [SH] 38 F4
Dajian [GZ] 68 F1
Dajianchang [TJ] 24 B4
Dajiao [SX] 28 C6
Dajiawa [SD] 50 E2
Dajichang [HB] 54 B5
Dajin Chuan [SC] 66 E3
Dajin Shan [SH] 38 D5
Dajin Shan [SH] 38 D5
Dajin [CQ] 64 E2
Dajin [HB] 54 H4
Dajindian [HEN] 52 D3
Dajing [GD] 58 B4
Dajing [GS] 76 G4

Name			Name			Name		
Dajiuba [XJ]	82	K7	(Maquan He) [XZ]	72	D4	Dapu [LN]	32	H4
Dakai Shuiku [GX]	60	G4	Damu Yang [ZJ]	42	F3	Dapuchaihe [JL]	34	H5
Dakar [QH]	78	G4	Damxung [XZ]	72	H4	Dapuzi [HN]	56	B5
Dakeng [JX]	48	C5	Dan He [HEN]	52	E2	Daqiao [FJ]	46	D3
Dakengkou [GD]	58	E2	Dan He [SX]	28	D6	Daqiao [GX]	60	H5
Dakou [SX]	28	D6	Dan Jiang [SN]	74	F7	Daqiao [JL]	34	H4
Dakoutun [TJ]	24	B3	Danan [JX]	48	F3	Daqiao [JS]	40	F3
Dala [GS]	76	G6	Danba(Rongzhag) [SC]	66	D3	Daqiao [JX]	48	E3
Dalad Qi [NM]	30	E4	Danba [SN]	74	D4	Daqiao [YN]	70	E2
Dalai Nur [NM]	30	G4	Dancheng [HEN]	52	G4	Daqin Dao [SD]	50	G1
Dalai [NM]	30	G2	Dandai [JL]	34	C1	Daqing He [HEB]	26	D4
Dalan [GD]	58	F3	Dandian [HB]	54	H4	Daqing He [LN]	32	F4
Dalang [GD]	58	D2	Dandong [LN]	32	H4	Daqing He [SD]	50	C4
Dali [YN]	70	D3	Danfeng [SN]	74	F7	Daqing shan [HL]	36	D5
Dali He [SN]	74	E3	Dang He [GS]	76	C3	Daqing Shan [LN]	32	C4
Dali [GX]	60	H4	Dangan Liedao [GD]	58	F4	Daqing Shan [LN]	32	D3
Dali [HI]	62	B3	Dangba [HEB]	26	F3	Daqing [HL]	36	C4
Dali [SN]	74	E6	Dangbi [HL]	36	F5	Daqinggou [HEB]	26	B2
Dalian Wan [LN]	32	E6	Dangchang [GS]	76	H5	Daqiu [FJ]	46	E4
Dalian [LN]	32	E6	Dangcheng [TJ]	24	B5	Daqiutian [JX]	48	B7
Daliang Shan [SC]	66	E4	Dangchuan [GS]	76	I5	Daqiuzhuang [TJ]	24	B6
Daliang [GX]	60	G3	Danghe Nanshan [GS]	76	C3	Daqu Shan [ZJ]	42	F2
Daliang [QH]	78	G2	Dangjin Shankou [GS]	76	C3	Daquan [GS]	76	C2
Daliang [TJ]	24	B3	Dangshan [AH]	44	C1	Daquanyuan [JL]	34	E6
Daliao He [LN]	32	F4	Dangtu [AH]	44	E4	Darenzhuang [TJ]	24	B5
Daliji [JS]	40	C2	Dangyang [HB]	54	D4	Darhan Muminggan		
Daling He [LN]	32	D3	Daning He [CQ]	64	F2	Lianheqi [NM]	30	E4
Daling He [LN]	32	E3	Daning [GX]	60	I3	Darlag [QH]	78	F4
Daling [JL]	34	F2	Daning [SX]	28	B5	Darong Shan [GX]	60	H5
Dalinghe Kou [LN]	32	E4	Danjiangkou Shuiku [HB]	54	D2	Darongjiang [GX]	60	H2
Dalinzi [JL]	34	E2	Danjiangkou Shuiku [HEN]	52	C5	Daryaboyi [XJ]	82	G6
Daliuta [SN]	74	F1	Danjiangkou [HB]	54	D2	Dashahe [JL]	34	H5
Daliutan [TJ]	24	B5	Danleng [SC]	66	E3	Dashahe [TJ]	24	B3
Daliuzhuang [HEN]	52	F4	Dantu Qu [JS]	40	E3	Dashan Dao		
Dalizi [JL]	34	F6	Danyang [AH]	44	E4	(Danian Shan)	50	F4
Dalong [GZ]	68	H3	Danyang [FJ]	46	E3	Dashan Dao		
Dalongkou [AH]	44	E4	Danyang [JS]	40	E4	(Danian Shan)	40	E1
Dalongwan [TJ]	24	C4	Danzhai [GZ]	68	F4	Dashan [SD]	50	D1
Dalou Shan [GZ]	68	E3	Danzhou [GX]	60	G2	Dashentang [TJ]	24	D4
Dalu Dao [LN]	32	G5	Danzhou [HI]	62	B2	Dashetai [NM]	30	E4
Dalu [HI]	62	C2	Danzhu [GX]	60	H4	Dashetou [SX]	28	C3
Dalu [JL]	34	E6	Dao Xian [HN]	56	D6	Dashi [CQ]	64	C3
Dalubeikou [TJ]	24	B5	Daocheng(Dabba) [SC]	66	D4	Dashi [LN]	32	E3
Daluo [HL]	36	D4	Daodong [HL]	62	C2	Dashiqiao [LN]	32	F4
Daluo [YN]	70	D5	Daodou'ao [ZJ]	42	F2	Dashitou [JL]	34	H4
Daluomi [HL]	36	E5	Dao'erdeng [LN]	32	C4	Dashu [CQ]	64	F2
Dam Qu [QH]	78	C4	Daolazui [HEB]	26	C3	Dashuijing [YN]	70	E2
Damao Shan [JX]	48	E3	Daoshi [ZJ]	42	B2	Dashuikeng [NX]	80	C3
Damao [HI]	62	B3	Daotaiqiao [HL]	36	E4	Dashuisuo [QH]	78	F2
Damao [HI]	62	C3	Daotanghe [QH]	78	G2	Dashun [ZJ]	42	C4
Damaqun Shan [HEB]	26	C2	Daotian [SD]	50	E3	Dasi [AH]	44	B2
Damaying [HN]	56	E6	Daotiandi [HL]	36	F3	Dasi [GX]	60	F5
Damen Dao [ZJ]	42	E5	Daozhen [GZ]	68	F2	Dasuifen He [HL]	36	F6
Damenge [YN]	70	C4	Daozhen [SN]	74	E4	DaSuifen He [JL]	34	J4
Damengzhuang [TJ]	24	B3	Dapeng Wan(Mirs Bay) [HK]	84	F1	Dasuihe [JL]	34	F4
Damiao [HB]	54	B2	Dapeng [GD]	58	F4	Dasunzhuang [TJ]	24	C5
Damiao [JS]	40	C1	Dapeng [GX]	60	H4	Dasuzhuang [TJ]	24	C6
Daming Shan [GX]	60	F4	Daping [FJ]	46	E3	Data [AH]	44	D6
Daming Shan [GX]	60	F4	Daping [HN]	56	C2	Datan [HEB]	26	D2
Daming [HEB]	26	C7	Dapingfangzi [LN]	32	D3	Datang [GX]	60	F3
Damjong [QH]	78	D4	Dapingtai [HL]	36	E3	Datang [GX]	60	F5
Damqog Zangbo			Dapu [HN]	56	E5	Datang [GZ]	68	E5

Datang [GZ]	68	G4	Daxin [GX]	60	E5	Dazhuangke [BJ]	22	B2
Datang [HN]	56	F6	Daxin [HB]	54	G3	Dazhuangke [BJ]	22	C2
Datangzhuang [TJ]	24	C2	Daxindian [SD]	50	G2	Dazhuangzi [TJ]	24	B6
Datangzhuang [TJ]	24	C4	Daxing Qu [BJ]	22	D4	Dazu [CQ]	64	B4
Datian Ding [GD]	58	C4	Daxing [GZ]	68	H3	Dazuo [FJ]	46	D5
Datian [FJ]	46	C4	Daxing [JL]	34	C3	De'an [JX]	48	C2
Datian [GD]	58	D4	Daxing [YN]	70	E2	Debao [GX]	60	D4
Datian [HI]	62	A2	Daxinggou [JL]	34	I4	Dechang [SC]	66	E5
Datian [ZJ]	42	E4	Daxinzhuang [BJ]	22	D5	Degan [CQ]	64	C4
Datianji [SD]	50	C4	Daxinzhuang [TJ]	24	D3	Dêgê [SC]	66	C3
Datong He [QH]	78	H2	Daxu shan [JX]	48	D4	Dehua [FJ]	46	D4
Datong Hu [HN]	56	E2	Daxu [ZJ]	42	E3	Dehui Xinhe [SD]	50	C2
Datong Qu [HL]	36	C4	Daxue Shan [SC]	66	D3	Dehui [JL]	34	E3
Datong Shan [QH]	78	F2	Daya Wan [GD]	58	F4	Dejiang [GZ]	68	G2
Datong [AH]	44	D5	Daya [CQ]	64	D4	Delhi Nongchang [QH]	78	E2
Datong [HB]	54	H4	Dayang He [LN]	32	G4	Delhi [QH]	78	E2
Datong [HI]	62	C2	Dayang Shan [ZJ]	42	F2	Dengfeng [HEN]	52	E3
Datong [JL]	34	B2	Dayang [GX]	60	H4	Denggin Nomor [QH]	78	B2
Datong [JS]	40	G3	Dayang [SD]	50	C3	Dengjiapu [HN]	56	C5
Datong [QH]	78	G2	Dayang [ZJ]	42	D4	Dengkou [NM]	30	D4
Datong [SX]	28	E1	Dayangfang [BJ]	22	D4	Dêngqên [XZ]	72	J4
Datong [SX]	28	E1	Dayanggezhuang [TJ]	24	C2	Dengshangu [TJ]	24	C5
Datong [ZJ]	42	C3	Dayao Shan [GX]	60	H4	Dengta [GD]	58	F2
Datoushan [HL]	36	D2	Dayao [YN]	70	D3	Dengta [LN]	32	G3
Datu Dingzi [HL]	36	E5	Dayaopu [TJ]	24	A6	Dengyoufang [HEB]	26	B2
Datuan [SH]	38	E4	Daye [HB]	54	G4	Dengzhou [HEN]	52	D5
Datun [JL]	34	E4	Dayi [GZ]	68	E5	Deping [SD]	50	C2
Datun [JS]	40	B1	Dayi [SC]	66	E3	Deqên [YN]	70	C1
Datuo [HN]	56	E3	Dayi [SD]	50	C4	Dêqên [XZ]	72	H4
Datushan [JL]	34	C4	Daying Jiang [YN]	70	B3	Deqing [SC]	58	C3
Dawa [JL]	34	D2	Daying [AH]	44	C2	Deqing [ZJ]	42	C2
Dawa [LN]	32	F3	Daying [HEB]	26	C6	Dêrnang [QH]	78	G4
Dawa [LN]	32	G1	Daying [HEN]	52	D4	Dêrong [SC]	66	C4
Dawan [GD]	58	C4	Daying [SC]	66	F3	Desheng [GX]	60	F3
Dawan [GD]	58	D2	Daying [SX]	28	D3	Deshengbu [SX]	28	E1
Dawan [GZ]	68	C4	Daying [SX]	28	E2	Deshenggang [SH]	38	D4
Dawang Shan [JX]	48	D4	Dayingji [AH]	44	D2	Deshengguan [JX]	48	E4
Dawang [SD]	50	E3	Dayingzi [LN]	32	G4	Deshengtai [LN]	32	G2
Dawangguzhuang [TJ]	24	A3	Dayou [JS]	40	E1	Detuo [SC]	66	E4
Dawangjia Dao [LN]	32	G5	Dayu ling [GD]	58	F1	Dewang [GZ]	68	G3
Dawangzhuang [SD]	50	D3	Dayu Shan [FJ]	46	F3	Dexing [JX]	48	E3
Dawatou [TJ]	24	A5	Dayu [JX]	48	B6	Deyang [SC]	66	F3
Dawe [SC]	66	D2	Dayu [SX]	28	D3	Dêyü Co [XZ]	72	F2
Dawen He [SD]	50	C4	Dayuan [GD]	58	E1	Dezhou [SD]	50	C2
Dawen He [SD]	50	D3	Dayuan [SD]	50	F2	Dian Chi [YN]	70	E3
Dawenkou [SD]	50	D4	Dayuan [ZJ]	42	D4	Dianbai [GD]	58	B5
Dawu [HB]	54	G3	Dayunwu Shan [GD]	58	C4	Dianbei [JX]	48	B5
Dawu [SC]	66	D3	Dayushu [BJ]	22	C2	Diancang Shan [YN]	70	D3
Dawu [SX]	28	C4	Daze Shan [SD]	50	G3	Diancheng [GD]	58	C5
Dawujiang [GZ]	68	F3	Dazhanchang [NX]	80	B3	Dianfeng [SH]	38	C3
Dawujiazi [HL]	36	D3	Dazhang Xi [FJ]	46	D4	Dianji [SD]	50	G3
Dawusi [QH]	78	B2	Dazhang [GX]	60	G4	Dianjiang [CQ]	64	D3
Dawusu [HL]	36	C2	Dazhangtun [TJ]	24	B6	Dianjun Qu [HB]	54	D4
Daxi [CQ]	64	F4	Dazhen [GD]	58	E2	Dianmen [HN]	56	E4
Daxi [JX]	48	D3	Dazheng [LN]	32	F5	Dianqian [AH]	44	C5
Daxi [ZJ]	42	E4	Dazhipo [HI]	62	C2	Dianqlan [ZJ]	42	D4
Daxia He [GS]	76	G5	Dazhongzhuang [TJ]	24	C3	Dianshan Hu [JS]	40	F4
Daxiakou [HB]	54	C3	Dazhou Dao [HI]	62	C3	Dianshan Hu [SH]	38	B3
Daxiang Ling [SC]	66	E4	Dazhou [SC]	66	G3	Dianshang [SX]	28	E6
Daxie [CQ]	64	E3	Dazhou [ZJ]	42	C4	Dianta [SN]	74	F2
Daxihaizi Shuiku [XJ]	82	J5	Dazhu [SC]	66	G3	Dianya [HB]	54	D3
Daxijiang [HL]	36	C3	Dazhuang [AH]	44	D2	Diao He [HEN]	52	C5

Diao Jiang [GX]	60	E3
Diaobingshan [LN]	32	G2
Diaocheng [AH]	44	A2
Diaokou [SD]	50	E1
Diaoling [HL]	36	F5
Diaolou [HI]	62	B2
Diaoluoshan [HI]	62	B3
Diaoyutai [BJ]	22	E3
Dibabu [SX]	28	B3
Dicheng [AH]	44	B3
Didao Qu [HL]	36	F5
Diduo [JS]	40	F3
Diema [YN]	70	D4
Di'er Xi Ganqu [NX]	80	C2
Dikou [FJ]	46	D3
Diliubu [TJ]	24	B5
Ding'an [GX]	60	C3
Ding'an [HI]	62	C2
Dingba Qu [XZ]	72	J5
Dingbian [SN]	74	C3
Dingbujie [AH]	44	B4
Dingcheng Qu [HN]	56	D2
Dinggang [HEN]	52	D5
Dinggou [JS]	40	E3
Dinggyê [XZ]	72	F5
Dinghu Qu [GD]	58	D3
Dingjiatang [NX]	80	B3
Dingnan [JX]	48	C7
Dingsuo [JS]	40	F3
Dingtao [SD]	50	B4
Dingxi [GS]	76	H5
Dingxiang [AH]	44	D5
Dingxiang [SX]	28	D3
Dingxin [GS]	76	E2
Dingxing [HEB]	26	C4
Dingyu [SX]	28	F4
Dingyuan [AH]	44	D3
Dingzhou [HEB]	26	B5
Dingzi Gang [SD]	50	H3
Dingzikou [GS]	76	B3
Dingzikou [QH]	78	C1
Dirangzong [XZ]	72	I6
Discorery Bay [HK]	84	C3
Ditang [QH]	78	G4
Diwei [YN]	70	F3
Dizhuang [HN]	56	C3
Do Qu [QH]	78	E3
Dobdain [QH]	78	G3
Dogaicoring Qangco [XZ]	72	G2
Dogxung Zangbo [XZ]	72	F5
Doilungdêqên [XZ]	72	H5
Dokog He [QH]	78	G4
Domar [XZ]	72	C3
Domar [XZ]	72	F4
Domba [QH]	78	D4
Dong He [CQ]	64	E2
Dong Chuan [SN]	74	C4
Dong Co [XZ]	72	E3
Dong He [SC]	66	G3
Dong Jiang [GD]	58	F3
Dong Jiang [HN]	56	F6
Dong Taijnar Hu [QH]	78	C2
Dong Ujimqin Qi [NM]	30	G3
Dong Xi [FJ]	46	D4
Dong Xi [FJ]	46	C6
Dong Xi [FJ]	46	E2
Dong'an [CQ]	64	F2
Dong'an [HN]	56	D5
Dong'ao [HI]	62	C3
Dongba [BJ]	22	D4
Dongbanchuan [SX]	28	D2
Dongbatu [GS]	76	C2
Dongbei [GD]	58	D2
Dongbei [JX]	48	D4
Dongbeiwang [BJ]	22	C3
Dongcha [GS]	76	I5
Dongchen [JS]	40	F3
Dongcheng [JL]	34	I5
Dongchun Qu [YN]	70	E2
Dongco [XZ]	72	E3
Dongdadao [LN]	32	D3
Dongdalian Dao [LN]	32	F5
Dongding Tao [FJ]	46	D5
Dongdongting Shan [JS]	40	F4
Dongdu [SD]	50	D4
Dong'e [SD]	50	C3
Dong'e [SD]	50	C3
Dongfang [HI]	62	A2
Dongfang [HI]	62	A2
Dongfeng [JL]	34	E5
Dongfeng [SH]	38	D1
Dongfenggang [SD]	50	E1
Dongfu Shan [ZJ]	42	F2
Donggan [YN]	70	F4
Donggang Qu [SD]	50	F4
Donggang [LN]	32	H5
Donggaodi [BJ]	22	D4
Dongge [HI]	62	C2
Donggi Conag [QH]	78	F3
Donggong Shan [ZJ]	42	C5
Donggong Shan [FJ]	46	E2
Donggong [HB]	54	D3
Donggou [JS]	40	E2
Donggou [SH]	38	D3
Donggu [JX]	48	C5
Dongguan [AH]	44	D4
Dongguan [GD]	58	E3
Dongguan [JX]	48	D4
Dongguan [SX]	28	D4
Dongguang [HEB]	26	D6
Dongguanshang [BJ]	22	B4
Dongguanying [LN]	32	D3
Donghai Bridge [SH]	38	F4
Donghai Dao [GD]	58	B6
Donghai [JS]	40	D1
Donghai [SH]	38	E4
Donghaiba [NX]	80	B4
Donghe Qu [NM]	30	E4
Donghe [SN]	74	D8
Donghedian [HEN]	52	F4
Donghenan [SX]	28	F2
Donghu [HN]	56	F5
Donghui [YN]	70	C4
Dongji Liedao [ZJ]	42	E4
Dongji Shan [ZJ]	42	E4
Dongjia [GZ]	68	E5
Dongjia [JX]	48	C3
Dongjiao [HI]	62	C2
Dongjie [HEN]	52	D4
Dongjin Shui [JX]	48	B3
Dongjing He [HB]	54	F4
Dongjingcheng [HL]	36	E5
Dongjingji [HEB]	26	B3
Dongjituo [TJ]	24	C4
Dongjug [XZ]	72	J4
Dongkeng [JX]	48	B7
Dongkeng [ZJ]	42	C5
Dongkou [HN]	56	C4
Dongkou [SD]	50	B4
Dongkuang [GX]	60	F4
Donglan [GX]	60	E3
Dongli Qu [TJ]	24	C5
Dongli [GD]	58	B6
Dongli [GD]	58	H3
Dongli [SD]	50	E3
Dongliang [LN]	32	E3
Dongliang [SX]	28	E3
Dongliao He [JL]	34	D4
Dongliao He [LN]	32	G1
Dongliao [JL]	34	D5
Dongling Shan [BJ]	22	B3
Dongling Shan [HEB]	26	C3
Dongling [GX]	60	D4
Donglingjing [SX]	28	D3
Dongliu [AH]	44	C5
Dongliu [FJ]	46	B4
Dongliu [JX]	48	E2
Dongliuji [AH]	44	D2
Donglou [SX]	28	D3
Donglu [HI]	62	C2
Donglük [XJ]	82	K6
Dongmao [HEB]	26	D3
Dongmaquan [TJ]	24	A4
Dongming [SD]	50	B4
Dongmingji [SD]	50	B4
Dongning [HL]	36	F5
Dongping Hu [SD]	50	C3
Dongping [FJ]	46	D2
Dongping [GD]	58	D5
Dongping [SD]	50	C4
Dongpo [HI]	62	C1
Dongpo [YN]	70	E3
Dongqilihai Shuiku [TJ]	24	C4
Dongquan [GX]	60	G3
Dongsanjiazi [JL]	34	D3
Dongsanqi [BJ]	22	D3
Dongsha Qundao [GD]	58	H6
Dongsha Dao [GD]	58	H6
Dongsha He [HEN]	52	G3
Dongshan Ao [FJ]	46	C6
Dongshan Dao [FJ]	46	C6
Dongshan [FJ]	46	C6
Dongshan [GD]	58	B5
Dongshan [HN]	56	B5
Dongshao [JX]	48	D5
Dongshaoqu [BJ]	22	E3

Name	Page	Grid	Name	Page	Grid	Name	Page	Grid
Dongshe [SX]	28	E3	Dongzhong [SD]	50	F3	Duobaoshan [HL]	36	C2
Dongsheng [CQ]	64	C5	Dongzhou [TJ]	24	B4	Duodao Qu [HB]	54	E4
Dongshi [FJ]	46	D5	Dongzhuanghe [BJ]	22	E2	Duode [HI]	62	C3
Dongshi [HN]	56	D3	Dongziya [TJ]	24	A6	Duohuo [SX]	28	E6
Dongshuangtang [TJ]	24	B6	Doramarkog [QH]	78	E4	Duolun [NM]	30	G4
Dongshui [GD]	58	G2	Dorbod [HL]	36	C4	Duomula [XZ]	72	D2
Dongsi [SC]	66	D4	Dorgê Co [QH]	78	C3	Duowen [HI]	62	B2
Dongtai [BJ]	22	D2	Dorsoidong Co [XZ]	72	G3	Duozhuang [SD]	50	D3
Dongtai [HI]	62	C2	Doucun [SX]	28	E3	Dupang Ling [GX]	60	I2
Dongtai [JS]	40	F3	Doudian [BJ]	22	C4	Dupang Ling [HN]	56	D6
Dongtazhuang [TJ]	24	C2	Douge [YN]	70	D4	Dupu [HB]	54	G4
Dongtiangezhuang [BJ]	22	E2	Douhe Shuiku [HEB]	26	F4	Duqiao [ZJ]	42	E4
Dongtianmu Shan [ZJ]	42	C2	Douhutun [SD]	50	B3	Düre [XJ]	82	K2
Dongtiao Xi [ZJ]	42	D2	Doujiang [GX]	60	G2	Dushan Hu [SD]	50	C4
Dongting Hu [HN]	56	F2	Doulonggang He [JS]	40	F2	Dushan [GZ]	68	F5
Dongtou Dao [ZJ]	42	E5	Doulonggang Kou [JS]	40	F2	Dushanhe [HEN]	52	F6
Dongtou Yang [ZJ]	42	E5	Douluo [SX]	28	D3	Dushanzi Qu [XJ]	82	I3
Dongtou [GX]	60	F2	Doumen Qu [GD]	58	E4	Dushi [CQ]	64	C4
Dongtou [ZJ]	42	E5	Doumen [GD]	58	E4	Dushikou [HEB]	26	C2
Dongwang [HEB]	26	C6	Doushan Shuiku [SD]	50	E4	Dushu [HEN]	52	E4
Dongwankou [HEB]	26	D3	Doushui Shuiku [JX]	48	B6	Dushui He [GZ]	68	F4
Dongwuyang [FJ]	46	E3	Douzhangzhuang [TJ]	24	B4	Duwei [FJ]	46	D4
Dongxi Liandao [JS]	40	E1	Du He [HB]	54	C2	Duxun [FJ]	46	C6
Dongxi [CQ]	64	C5	Du Shan [HEB]	26	F3	Duyang Shan [GX]	60	E3
Dongxiang Dao [FJ]	46	E4	Du'an [GX]	60	F4	Duyang [GX]	60	E4
Dongxiang [GS]	76	G5	Duanji [HEN]	52	G6	Duyun [GZ]	68	F4
Dongxiang [JX]	48	D3	Duanshan [GZ]	68	E5	Duzhou [CQ]	64	D4
Dongxihu Qu [HB]	54	G4	Duanshi [SX]	28	D6	Duzhuang [SX]	28	E2
Dongxing [GX]	60	E6	Duanshuling [BJ]	22	D2	Duzhuang [SX]	28	E4
Dongxing [GX]	60	F2	Duchang [JX]	48	D2			
Dongxing [HL]	36	D4	Ducun [SX]	28	D5			
Dongyang He [HEB]	26	B3	Duguan [HEN]	52	C3			
Dongyang Jiang [ZJ]	42	C3	Duhu [GD]	58	D4			
Dongyang [HL]	36	C4	Duijiaogoumen [BJ]	22	D1	East China Sea [TW]	88	D1
Dongyang [SD]	50	D4	Duiyingzi [BJ]	22	D2	East China Sea [ZJ]	42	F4
Dongyang [SX]	28	D4	Duizhen [SX]	28	C4	East China Sea [FJ]	46	F4
Dongyang [ZJ]	42	D3	Duji Qu [AH]	44	C2	East China Sea [SH]	38	F4
Dongyangguan [SX]	28	E5	Duji [SD]	50	C2	East Lamma Channel [HK]	84	D4
Dongyao [SX]	28	C6	Dujiang Yan [SC]	66	E3	Ebian [SC]	66	E4
Dongye [SX]	28	D6	Dujiangyan [SC]	66	E3	Ebinur Hu [XJ]	82	H3
Dongye [SX]	28	E3	Dujiang [GZ]	68	G5	Echeng [SD]	50	C3
Dongying Qu [SD]	50	E2	Dujiangyan [SC]	66	E3	Ehu [JX]	48	E2
Dongying [HI]	62	C1	Dujiao [SX]	28	C3	Ehu [JX]	48	E3
Dongying [SD]	50	E2	Dujiazhuang [BJ]	22	B4	Ejin Horo Qi [NM]	30	E5
Dongyinzhuang [TJ]	24	D4	Dujiazhuang [SX]	28	D3	Ejin Qi [NM]	30	C4
Dongyou [FJ]	46	D2	Dukong He [SC]	66	D2	Ekou [SX]	28	E2
Dongyu [SX]	28	D5	Dukou [GX]	60	D2	Eljet Ul [XJ]	82	I4
Dongyuan [GD]	58	F3	Dukou [HEB]	26	B7	Eman [HI]	62	B2
Dongyuan [GD]	58	H3	Dulan [QH]	78	F2	Emei Shan [SC]	66	E4
Dongyueguan [HN]	56	D2	Dulansi [QH]	78	F2	Emeishan [SC]	66	E4
Dongyuemiao [HB]	54	D5	Dulin [HEB]	26	D5	Emin He [XJ]	82	H2
Dongyulin [SX]	28	D2	Duliu Jiang [GZ]	68	G5	Emin(Dorbilji) [XJ]	82	H2
Dongyusi [BJ]	22	B5	Duliu Jianhe [TJ]	24	B5	Emu [JL]	34	H4
Dongzhai [SX]	28	D3	Duliu [TJ]	24	B5	Emur He [HL]	36	B1
Dongzhang Shuiku [FJ]	46	E4	Dulong [YN]	70	F4	Emur Shan [HL]	36	B1
Dongzhaobao [HEN]	52	D3	Dumo [GX]	60	H3	En Jiang [JX]	48	C4
Dongzhaogezhuang [TJ]	24	C2	Dumuhe [HL]	36	G4	Encheng [SD]	50	C2
Dongzhen Shuiku [FJ]	46	D4	Dunhou [SX]	28	C3	Engh Had [NM]	30	H1
Dongzhen [GS]	76	G3	Dunhua [JL]	34	H4	Enping [GD]	58	D4
Dongzhen [SX]	28	C6	Dunhuang [GS]	76	C2	Enshi [HB]	54	B4
Dongzhi [AH]	44	D5	Dunzhai [GZ]	68	H4	Enyang [SC]	66	G3
Dongzhong [GX]	60	E6	Duobao [HB]	54	E4	Er Hai [YN]	70	D3
						Erba [AH]	44	E4
						Erdao Baihe [JL]	34	H5

E

Erdao Jiang [JL]	34	G5	Fangli [HEN]	52	F2	Fengchuan [GD]	58	C3
Erdaobaihe [JL]	34	H5	Fangliao [TW]	88	C4	Fengdu [CQ]	64	D4
Erdaodianzi [JL]	34	G4	Fanglou [JX]	48	A4	Fengdu [FJ]	46	D3
Erdaogou [QH]	78	C3	Fangmu [LN]	32	H2	Fengfeng Kuangqu [HEB]	26	B7
Erdaohezi [HL]	36	E5	Fangqian [SD]	50	E4	Fenggang [GZ]	68	F3
Erdaojiang Qu [JL]	34	F6	Fangqian [ZJ]	42	D3	Fenggeling [SN]	74	B6
Eren Gobi [NM]	30	G3	Fangshan Qu [BJ]	22	C4	Fengheying [BJ]	22	D5
Erenhot [NM]	30	F4	Fangshan [BJ]	22	C4	Fenghua [ZJ]	42	E3
Erfengshan [SX]	28	C6	Fangshan [SX]	28	C4	Fenghuang Shan [GX]	60	E2
Ergun He [NM]	30	G2	Fangshan [TW]	88	C4	Fenghuang [CQ]	64	F2
Ergun [NM]	30	H2	Fangtai [SH]	38	C3	Fenghuang [GD]	58	H3
Erhlin [TW]	88	C3	Fangtou [JX]	48	E3	Fenghuang [HN]	56	B4
Erhshui [TW]	88	C3	Fangxi [JX]	48	B3	Fenghuang [SH]	38	E2
Erlang Shan [SC]	66	E4	Fangxia [SD]	50	D3	Fenghuo Shankou [QH]	78	C3
Erlang [AH]	44	C5	Fangzheng [HL]	36	E5	Fengjia [LN]	32	F2
Erlangkou [AH]	44	E4	Fangzi Qu [SD]	50	F3	Fengjia [SD]	50	H2
Erling [JS]	40	E4	Fanjia [HI]	62	B2	Fengjiaba [CQ]	64	E4
Erlong Shan [JL]	34	H4	Fanjiashan [HN]	56	D4	Fengjiabu [HEB]	26	E5
Erlongshan Shuiku [LN]	32	H1	Fanjiatun [JL]	34	E4	Fengjiang [ZJ]	42	E4
Erlongshan [HL]	36	G4	Fanjiazhuang [TJ]	24	C5	Fengjiangkou Shuiku [HB]	54	F2
Erlongshantun [HL]	36	D3	Fanjing Shan [GZ]	68	G3	Fengjiapu [ZJ]	42	D3
Ermi [JL]	34	E6	Fankou [GD]	58	E1	Fengjie [CQ]	64	F2
Ershijiazi [LN]	32	D3	Fankou [HB]	54	G4	Fengjigou [NX]	80	C3
Ershiyizhan [HL]	36	C1	Fankuan [SC]	66	H3	Fengjing [SH]	38	C4
Ertai [HEB]	26	B2	Fanling [HK]	84	D1	Fengkai [GD]	58	C3
Ertai [XJ]	82	L3	Fanshan [ZJ]	42	D5	Fengkang [TW]	88	C4
Ertan [SC]	66	D5	Fanshi [SX]	28	E2	Fengkou [HB]	54	F4
Ertix He [XJ]	82	I2	Fanshi [ZJ]	42	E2	Fengku [JL]	34	C3
Erwangzhuang [TJ]	24	C4	Fanshui [JS]	40	E2	Fengle He [AH]	44	C4
Eryuan [YN]	70	C2	Fantong [HI]	62	B3	Fengle [AH]	44	D4
Erzhan [HL]	36	D3	Fanyang [HI]	62	B3	Fengle [FJ]	46	D2
Eshan [YN]	70	E3	Fanzhen [SD]	50	D3	Fengle [GZ]	68	F2
Ewenkizu Zizhiqi [NM]	30	G2	Fanzipai [BJ]	22	E1	Fengle [HL]	36	C5
Ewirgol [XJ]	82	J4	Fat Tong Chau [HK]	84	E3	Fengle [SH]	38	E3
Eyang [FJ]	46	D3	Fat Tong Mun [HK]	84	E4	Fenglin [HB]	54	H5
Ezhou [HB]	54	G4	Fate [JL]	34	F3	Fenglin [TW]	88	D3
Ezhuang [SD]	50	E4	Fazhong [SX]	28	D5	Fengling Guan [FJ]	46	D1
			Feihuang He [JS]	40	C1	Fengling Guan [ZJ]	42	B4
F			Fei Xian [SD]	50	D4	Fengling [HI]	62	C3
			Feicheng [SD]	50	C3	Fenglingdu [SX]	28	B7
Facheng [SD]	50	G2	Feidong [AH]	44	D4	Fengming dao [LN]	32	E5
Fairview Park [HK]	84	C2	Feihe [AH]	44	B2	Fengmu [HI]	62	C2
Faku [LN]	32	G2	Feihuanghe kou [JS]	40	F1	Fengnan Qu [HEB]	26	F4
Fan Lau Kok [HK]	84	A4	Feijiantan Shuiku [JX]	48	B4	Fengning [HEB]	26	D2
Fan Lau [HK]	84	A4	Feiluan [FJ]	46	E3	Fengpin [TW]	88	D3
Fan Xian [HEN]	52	G2	Feixi [AH]	44	D4	Fengpo [HI]	62	C2
Fanchang [AH]	44	E4	Feixian [HN]	56	E6	Fengqiao [ZJ]	42	D3
Fandi [SX]	28	C6	Feixiang [HEB]	26	B7	Fengqing [YN]	70	C3
Fang He [SD]	50	E4	Feiyun Ding [GD]	58	F3	Fengqiu [HEN]	52	F2
Fang Xian [HB]	54	C2	Feiyun Jiang [ZJ]	42	D5	Fengquan Qu [HEN]	52	E2
Fangcheng Qu [GX]	60	F6	Fen He [HEN]	52	F4	Fengrun Qu [HEB]	26	F4
Fangcheng [HEN]	52	D4	Fen He [SX]	28	C3	Fengrun [SX]	28	C3
Fangchenggang [GX]	60	F6	Fencheng [SX]	28	C6	Fengshan [GX]	60	E3
Fangchuan [JL]	34	J5	Feng He [BJ]	22	D4	Fengshan [HEB]	26	E2
Fangcun [FJ]	46	D3	Feng Xian [JS]	40	B1	Fengshan [HL]	36	E4
Fangcun [JS]	40	C1	Feng Xian [SN]	74	B7	Fengshanlinchang [HL]	36	E4
Fangcun [ZJ]	42	B3	Fengbang [SH]	38	D3	Fengshi [FJ]	46	B5
Fangdao [FJ]	46	D2	Fengcheng [JX]	48	C3	Fengshuba Shuiku [GD]	58	G2
Fangdou Shan [CQ]	64	E3	Fengcheng [LN]	32	H4	Fengshun [GD]	58	H3
Fangdou Shan [CQ]	64	E3	Fengcheng [SD]	50	H3	Fengtai Qu [BJ]	22	C4
Fangfan [HB]	54	G3	Fengcheng [SH]	38	E4	Fengtai [AH]	44	C3
Fangjiatun [LN]	32	G2	Fengchengpu [GS]	76	F3	Fengtai [TJ]	24	D3
Fangjiayao [SH]	38	C3						

Fengtan Shuiku [HN]	56	B3
Fengting [FJ]	46	D4
Fengwu [GX]	60	E4
Fengxi [HB]	54	B3
Fengxi [SH]	38	C3
Fengxian Qu [SH]	38	D4
Fengxiang [SN]	74	C6
Fengxin [JX]	48	C3
Fengxin [SH]	38	D4
Fengyang [AH]	44	D3
Fengyang [GD]	58	D1
Fengyuan [SN]	74	E5
Fengzhen [NM]	30	F4
Fengzhou [JX]	48	A6
Fenhe Shuiku [SX]	28	C3
Fenkou [ZJ]	42	B3
Fenqing He [HB]	54	C3
Fenshouling [NX]	80	B3
Fenshui Guan [FJ]	46	C2
Fenshui Guan [FJ]	46	C6
Fenshui Guan [JX]	48	E4
Fenshui [CQ]	64	E3
Fenshui [HB]	54	F4
Fenshui [JX]	48	E3
Fenshui [SC]	66	F5
Fenshuiguan [ZJ]	42	D5
Fenxi [SX]	28	C5
Fenxiang [HB]	54	D4
Fenyang [SX]	28	C4
Fenyi [JX]	48	B4
Fo Tan [HK]	84	D2
Foding Shan [GZ]	68	G3
Fogang [GD]	58	E3
Foluo [HI]	62	A3
Foping [SN]	74	C7
Foshan [GD]	58	E3
Foshan [YN]	70	C1
Fotan [FJ]	46	C5
Foziling Shuiku [AH]	44	C4
Fu He [JX]	48	D3
Fu Jiang [SC]	66	F3
Fu Jiang [CQ]	64	B3
Fu Shui [HB]	54	G5
Fu Xian [SN]	74	E4
Fu'an [FJ]	46	E2
Fu'an [JS]	40	F3
Fubao [HI]	62	B3
Fucheng [HEB]	26	D6
Fucheng [SX]	28	E6
Fuchikou [HB]	54	H5
Fuchuan [GX]	60	I3
Fuchun Jiang [ZJ]	42	C3
Fuchunjiang Shuiku [ZJ]	42	C3
Fuchunjiang [ZJ]	42	C3
Fucun [YN]	70	F3
Fuda [GX]	60	C3
Fude [FJ]	46	C4
Fudian [HEN]	52	D4
Fuding [FJ]	46	F2
Fu'er He [JL]	34	G5
Fufeng [SN]	74	C6
Fugong [YN]	70	C2
Fugou [HEN]	52	F3
Fugu [SN]	74	G1
Fuhai(Burultokay) [XJ]	82	J2
Fuhai [HL]	36	C4
Fuji [HEN]	52	F3
Fujia [LN]	32	G1
Fujiang [CQ]	64	B3
Fujiaqiao [HN]	56	D5
Fujiatan [SX]	28	C5
Fujin [HL]	36	G4
Fujunmiao [TJ]	24	B5
Fukang [XJ]	82	J3
Fuke [HI]	62	B2
Fukeshan [HL]	36	A1
Fukou [HN]	56	D4
Fukuei Chiao [TW]	88	D1
Fule [HL]	36	C1
Fule [YN]	70	F3
Fuli [AH]	44	C2
Fuli [TW]	88	D3
Fuliang [JX]	48	E2
Fuliangpeng [YN]	70	E3
Fuling Qu [CQ]	64	D4
Fulong [HI]	62	B2
Fulongquan [JL]	34	D3
Fulu [CQ]	64	D3
Fulu [GX]	60	G2
Fulu [HL]	36	C4
Fuluo [GX]	60	I3
Fumeng Xinhe [AH]	44	C2
Fumin [SH]	38	E2
Fumin [YN]	70	E3
Funan [AH]	44	B3
Funing Wan [FJ]	46	F3
Funing [HEB]	26	G4
Funing [JS]	40	E2
Funing [YN]	70	F4
Funiu Shan [HEN]	52	C4
Fuping [HEB]	26	B5
Fuping [JS]	74	E6
Fuqiao [JS]	40	G4
Fuqing [FJ]	46	E4
Fuqingpu [HN]	56	D3
Fuquan [GZ]	68	F4
Furao [HL]	36	C4
Furao [HL]	36	E3
Furong Jiang [GZ]	68	F2
Fushan Qu [SD]	50	H2
Fushan [HI]	62	B2
Fushan [SX]	28	C6
Fushi [FJ]	46	B5
Fushi [GX]	60	G2
Fushui Shuiku [HB]	54	G5
Fushui [HB]	54	F3
Fushui [HB]	54	G5
Fushuling [JX]	48	E1
Fushun [LN]	32	G3
Fushun [LN]	32	G3
Fushun [SC]	66	F4
Fusong [JL]	34	G5
Fusui [GX]	60	E5
Futian [JX]	48	C5
Futianhe [HB]	54	H3
Futou Wan [FJ]	46	C6
Futu [HB]	54	H5
Futu [HI]	62	B2
Futun Xi [FJ]	46	C2
Fuwen [HI]	62	C2
Fuxian Hu [YN]	70	E3
Fuxian [JL]	34	C4
Fuxin [LN]	32	E2
Fuxin [LN]	32	E2
Fuxing [AH]	44	C6
Fuxing [HN]	56	B3
Fuxing [JL]	34	J4
Fuxingdi [LN]	32	E2
Fuxingpo [NX]	80	B3
Fuyang He [HEB]	26	B7
Fuyang He [HEB]	26	C6
Fuyang [AH]	44	B3
Fuyang [AH]	44	B3
Fuyang [SC]	66	G2
Fuyang [ZJ]	42	C2
Fuyi Shui [HN]	56	C5
Fuying Dao [FJ]	46	F3
Fuyu [HL]	36	C4
Fuyu [JL]	34	E3
Fuyuan [HL]	36	H3
Fuyuan [LN]	32	H2
Fuyuan [TW]	88	D3
Fuyuan [YN]	70	F3
Fuyun(Koktokay) [XJ]	82	K2
Fuzhen [HEB]	26	D5
Fuzhou He [LN]	32	E5
Fuzhou Wan [LN]	32	E5
Fuzhou [FJ]	46	E3
Fuzhou [JX]	48	D4
Fuzhoucheng [LN]	32	E5
Fuzhuang [TJ]	24	D4

G

Ga Hai [QH]	78	G2
Gadê [QH]	78	F4
Gahai [GS]	76	G5
Gaiyang [FJ]	46	C3
Gaizhou [LN]	32	F4
Gala [XZ]	72	G5
Gamba [XZ]	72	G5
Gan He [NM]	30	I2
Gan Jiang [JX]	48	C3
Gan Xian [JX]	48	C6
Gana [SC]	66	D2
Gancheng [HI]	62	A3
Ganfang [JX]	48	B3
Gangbei Gang [HI]	62	C3
Gangbei [HI]	62	C3
Gangca [QH]	78	G2
Gangchangping [HB]	54	C3
Gangcheng Qu [SD]	50	D3
Gangdisê Shan [XZ]	72	D4
Ganggar [XZ]	72	F5
Ganggou He [BJ]	22	D4
Ganggou He [TJ]	24	A3
Gangji [AH]	44	D4

Name	Page	Grid
Gangkou [AH]	44	E5
Gangmei [GD]	58	C4
Gangnan Qu [GX]	60	G4
Gangnan Shuiku [HEB]	26	A5
Gangou [JL]	34	E6
Gangoumen [HEB]	26	D2
Gangouyi [GS]	76	H5
Gangru [XZ]	72	J3
Gangshangji [JX]	48	D3
Gangtun [LN]	32	D4
Gangu [GS]	76	H5
Ganguyi [SN]	74	E4
Gangwei [FJ]	46	D5
Gangyao [JL]	34	F3
Ganhe [NM]	30	H2
Ganjia'ai [FJ]	46	B3
Ganjia'ai [JX]	48	D5
Ganjing [SN]	74	F5
Ganjingzi Qu [LN]	32	E6
Ganlin [ZJ]	42	D3
Ganlong [GZ]	68	G2
Ganluo [SC]	66	E4
Gannan [HL]	36	B4
Ganq Ger [JL]	34	C1
Ganq Mod [NM]	30	D4
Ganq [QH]	78	C2
Ganquan [SN]	74	E4
Gantang [BJ]	22	E4
Gantang [FJ]	46	D3
Gantang [GX]	60	F5
Gantang [HN]	56	B5
Gantao He [HEB]	26	B6
Gantian [GX]	60	D3
Gantian [HN]	56	F4
Ganting [SX]	28	C5
Ganxi [GZ]	68	G2
Ganxi [JX]	48	F3
Ganxiang [SH]	38	C4
Ganxitan [HN]	56	D2
Ganxitang [HN]	56	B6
Ganyu [JS]	40	E1
Ganzhao [LN]	32	C3
Ganzhou [JX]	48	B6
Ganzhou [JX]	48	C3
Ganzhu [JX]	48	D5
Ganziyuan [HN]	56	D6
Gao Dao [ZJ]	42	E4
Gao Xian [SC]	66	F4
Gao'an [FJ]	46	C5
Gao'an [JX]	48	C3
Gaoba [GS]	76	G4
Gaobadian [SN]	74	F7
Gaobei [GD]	58	H2
Gaobeidian [HEB]	26	C4
Gaocheng [HEB]	26	B5
Gaochun [JS]	40	D4
Gaodong [SH]	38	D3
Gaofeng [HI]	62	B3
Gaofu [JX]	48	E4
Gaogang Qu [JS]	40	E3
Gaogou [JS]	40	E1
Gaohe [SX]	28	E5
Gaojia [CQ]	64	D3
Gaojiabu [SN]	74	F2
Gaojiadian [JL]	34	E3
Gaojiadian [LN]	32	H2
Gaojian [ZJ]	42	E3
Gaojiawan [SN]	74	D4
Gaojiazha [NX]	80	C2
Gaojiazhuang [TJ]	24	C3
Gaokan [LN]	32	F4
Gaolan Dao [GD]	58	E5
Gaolan [GS]	76	G4
Gaolan [JX]	48	B3
Gaoliang [GD]	58	C3
Gaoligong Shan [YN]	70	C2
Gaoling [BJ]	22	E2
Gaoling [GX]	60	F3
Gaoling [SN]	74	E6
Gaoliu [JS]	40	D1
Gaoliying [BJ]	22	D3
Gaolou [CQ]	64	F2
Gaoluo [SX]	28	E4
Gaomi [SD]	50	F3
Gaoming Qu [GD]	58	D4
Gaomutang [HN]	56	D5
Gaoniang [GZ]	68	H4
Gaopai [JX]	48	C6
Gaoping Qu [SC]	66	G3
Gaoping [GZ]	68	E3
Gaoping [HB]	54	C4
Gaoping [SX]	28	D6
Gaopoling Shuiku [HI]	62	A2
Gaoqiao [CQ]	64	E2
Gaoqiao [FJ]	46	C3
Gaoqiao [LN]	32	D4
Gaoqiao [SD]	50	E4
Gaoqiao [SH]	38	D2
Gaoqing [SD]	50	D2
Gaorenzhen [NX]	80	C2
Gaosha [FJ]	46	C3
Gaoshaling [TJ]	24	C6
Gaoshan [FJ]	46	E4
Gaoshanzi [LN]	32	F3
Gaoshawo [NX]	80	D3
Gaositai [HEB]	26	E2
Gaotai [GS]	76	E3
Gaotai [NX]	80	C4
Gaotaishan [LN]	32	F2
Gaotaisi [NX]	80	B4
Gaotan He [CQ]	64	D3
Gaotan [SN]	74	D8
Gaotang [AH]	44	D3
Gaotang [FJ]	46	C3
Gaotang [SD]	50	C3
Gaotingsi [HN]	56	E5
Gaowan [HEB]	26	E5
Gaoxian [SX]	28	C6
Gaoxing [JX]	48	C5
Gaoxing [SD]	50	F4
Gaoxishi [HN]	56	D5
Gaoya [NX]	80	B4
Gaoya [SD]	50	E3
Gaoyakou [BJ]	22	C3
Gaoyan [JS]	40	D2
Gaoyang [HB]	54	C3
Gaoyang [HEB]	26	C5
Gaoyang [SX]	28	C4
Gaoyao [GD]	58	D3
Gaoyi [HEB]	26	B6
Gaoyi [HEN]	52	E5
Gaoyou Hu [JS]	40	E3
Gaoyou [JS]	40	E3
Gaoze [SD]	50	F4
Gaozha [NX]	80	C3
Gaozhou [GD]	58	B5
Gaozhuang [TJ]	24	D4
Gaqag [SC]	66	D4
Gar Qu [QH]	78	B4
Gar Zangbo [XZ]	72	C4
Gar [XZ]	72	C3
Garco [XZ]	72	G3
Garqu Yan [QH]	78	C4
Garyarasa [XZ]	72	C4
Gariyi [SC]	66	C3
Garzê [SC]	66	C3
Gas Hure Hu [QH]	78	B1
Gaxun Nur [NM]	30	C4
Gaya He [JL]	34	I4
Gazê'gyablung [QH]	78	E3
Ge Hu [JS]	40	E4
Gebu [GX]	60	C3
Gedi [SX]	28	B5
Gegen Gol [NM]	30	H2
Gegong [AH]	44	D5
Gegu [TJ]	24	C4
Gegu [YN]	70	E4
Gê'gyai [XZ]	72	C3
Gejiu [YN]	70	E4
Geka [SC]	66	D3
Gekeng [FJ]	46	D4
Gêladaindong Feng [QH]	78	B4
Gelan [CQ]	64	D3
Gelong [SH]	38	C2
Gêmang [SC]	66	C2
Gen He [NM]	30	H2
Genglou [GD]	58	D4
Gengma [YN]	70	C4
Gengxin [GX]	60	D3
Gerze [XZ]	72	E3
Geshan [ZJ]	42	D3
Getai [SN]	74	F5
Getu He [GZ]	68	E5
Geyitou [YN]	70	F3
Geyuan [JX]	48	E3
Gezhou Ba [HB]	54	D4
Gezidong [QH]	78	G1
Golmud He [QH]	78	D2
Golmud [QH]	78	D2
Gomang Co [XZ]	72	G4
Gomangxung [QH]	78	G3
Gong Shui [JX]	48	C6
Gong Xian [SC]	66	F4
Gong'ai [HI]	62	A3
Gong'an [HB]	54	E4
Gongbo'gyamda [XZ]	72	I5

Gongchangling Qu [LN]	32	G3	
Gongcheng [GX]	60	H3	
Gongchuan [FJ]	46	C3	
Gongfang [JX]	48	C4	
Gongga Shan [SC]	66	D4	
Gonggar [XZ]	72	H5	
Gongguan [GX]	60	G6	
Gonghe [HL]	36	D4	
Gonghe [QH]	78	G2	
Gonghui [GX]	60	I3	
Gonghui [HEB]	26	B2	
Gongjiapeng [HEN]	52	F6	
Gongjing Qu [SC]	66	F4	
Gongliu(Tokkuztara) [XJ]	82	H4	
Gongpeng [JL]	34	F3	
Gongpingxu [HN]	56	E5	
Gongpo [HI]	62	C2	
Gongqian [HEN]	52	C3	
Gongshan [YN]	70	C2	
Gongshan [YN]	70	E3	
Gongyi [HEN]	52	D3	
Gongyibu [NX]	80	B5	
Gongyingzi [LN]	32	C3	
Gongzhuling [JL]	34	D4	
Gongzhutun [LN]	32	F2	
Gonjo [XZ]	72	L4	
Gora [SC]	66	D3	
Gosu [SC]	66	C2	
Goubangzi [LN]	32	E3	
Gouchang [GZ]	68	E5	
Goudun [JS]	40	E2	
Goujiaya [HB]	54	D3	
Goukou [NX]	80	C5	
Goulin [HEN]	52	D5	
Gouqi Dao [ZJ]	42	F2	
Goutai [NX]	80	C3	
Gouyadong [HN]	56	E6	
Goyü [XZ]	72	K5	
Gozha Co [XZ]	72	C2	
Grass Island(Tap Mun) [HK]	84	F2	
Grassy Hill [HK]	84	D2	
Green Island [HK]	84	C3	
Gu Shan [FJ]	46	E3	
Gu Xian [SX]	28	C5	
Guabu [JS]	40	D3	
Guaihe [HEN]	52	E4	
Guaimozi [LN]	32	I3	
Guan He [JS]	40	E1	
Guan He [HEN]	52	G5	
Guan Jiang [GX]	60	I2	
Guan Xian [SD]	50	B3	
Gu'an [HEB]	26	D4	
Guanbei [FJ]	46	C5	
Guancen Shan [SX]	28	D2	
Guanchang [GD]	58	B6	
Guanchao [JX]	48	B5	
Guancheng [SD]	50	B4	
Guancheng [ZJ]	42	E2	
Guandang [HN]	56	E2	
Guandi Shan [SX]	28	C4	
Guandi [JL]	34	H4	
Guandian [AH]	44	E3	
Guandian [HB]	54	C4	
Guandiping [HN]	56	C2	
Guandu He [HB]	54	C2	
Guandu [CQ]	64	F3	
Guandu [GZ]	68	E2	
Guandu [HB]	54	C3	
Guandu [HN]	56	F3	
Guan'er [SX]	28	E2	
Guanfangpu [HB]	54	B1	
Guanfenghai [GZ]	68	B3	
Guang'an [SC]	66	G3	
Guangang [AH]	44	C6	
Guangang [SH]	38	D3	
Guangba [HI]	62	A2	
Guangchang [JX]	48	D5	
Guangcun [HI]	62	B2	
Guangde [AH]	44	F5	
Guangdong [GZ]	68	H5	
Guangfeng [JX]	48	F3	
Guangfulin [SH]	38	C3	
Guanghai [GD]	58	D5	
Guanghan [SC]	66	F3	
Guanghanzhai [JX]	48	A4	
Guanghe [GS]	76	G5	
Guanghua [JL]	34	E6	
Guanghua [SX]	28	B6	
Guanghua [SX]	28	C5	
Guangling [JS]	40	F3	
Guangling [SX]	28	F2	
Guanglu Dao [LN]	32	F5	
Guangming [SH]	38	D4	
Guangnan [YN]	70	F3	
Guangning [GD]	58	D3	
Guangping [FJ]	46	C3	
Guangping [GX]	60	I4	
Guangping [HEB]	26	B7	
Guangping [JL]	34	H5	
Guangpo [HI]	62	B3	
Guangrao [SD]	50	E2	
Guangshan [HEN]	52	F5	
Guangshui [HB]	54	F3	
Guangshun [GZ]	68	E4	
Guangya [HI]	62	B2	
Guangyuan [SC]	66	F2	
Guangze [FJ]	46	C2	
Guangzhou [GD]	58	E3	
Guangzong [HEB]	26	C6	
Guanhu [JS]	40	C1	
Guanji [AH]	44	B2	
Guanjian He [CQ]	64	B3	
Guanjiazhuang [TJ]	24	C5	
Guanjiazui [HN]	56	D5	
Guanling [GZ]	68	D5	
Guanlu [ZJ]	42	D4	
Guanmenshan [NX]	80	B4	
Guanmian Shan [CQ]	64	E2	
Guanmian [CQ]	64	E2	
Guannan [JS]	40	E1	
Guanpo [HEN]	52	B4	
Guanqian [FJ]	46	B4	
Guanqian [FJ]	46	C3	
Guanqian [FJ]	46	D2	
Guanqian [JX]	48	B3	
Guanqiao [AH]	44	D5	
Guanqiao [FJ]	46	D4	
Guanqiao [FJ]	46	D5	
Guanqiao [SD]	50	D5	
Guanshan Dao [ZJ]	42	D5	
Guanshang [BJ]	22	E2	
Guanshang [SX]	28	C4	
Guanshi [HN]	56	E5	
Guanshui [LN]	32	H4	
Guantao [HEB]	26	C7	
Guantian [JX]	48	B6	
Guanting Shuiku [HEB]	26	C3	
Guanting [AH]	44	C4	
Guanting [NX]	80	C4	
Guantou [FJ]	46	E3	
Guantou [SX]	28	B5	
Guanwang [HN]	56	F5	
Guanxing [CQ]	64	C4	
Guanyang [FJ]	46	F2	
Guanyang [GX]	60	I2	
Guanyin [HB]	54	C2	
Guanyinqiao [SC]	66	D3	
Guanyinsi [HEN]	52	E3	
Guanyintan [HN]	56	D5	
Guanyintang [HEN]	52	C3	
Guanyun Shan [HEN]	52	B3	
Guanyun [JS]	40	E1	
Guanzhai [GZ]	68	D4	
Guanzhen [JS]	40	D2	
Guanzhou [GZ]	68	G2	
Guanzhuang [HEN]	52	D5	
Guanzhuang [HN]	56	C3	
Guanzhuang [SD]	50	F3	
Guanzhuang [SN]	74	D6	
Guanziyao [GZ]	68	C5	
Guazhou [GS]	76	C2	
Gubai [SC]	66	F4	
Gubei [JX]	48	C6	
Gubeikou [BJ]	22	E2	
Gucheng Hu [JS]	40	D4	
Gucheng [AH]	44	B2	
Gucheng [AH]	44	D3	
Gucheng [BJ]	22	C2	
Gucheng [HB]	54	D2	
Gucheng [HEB]	26	C4	
Gucheng [HEB]	26	C6	
Gucheng [HL]	36	C3	
Gucheng [HL]	36	F5	
Gucheng [JX]	48	D4	
Gucheng [NX]	80	C2	
Gucheng [SC]	66	F2	
Gucheng [SD]	50	B4	
Gucheng [SD]	50	D2	
Gucheng [SN]	74	C7	
Gucheng [SX]	28	C6	
Gucheng [SX]	28	C6	
Gucheng [SX]	28	D2	
Gucheng [SX]	28	E1	
Gucheng [YN]	70	E3	
Gucun [JX]	48	C4	
Gucun [JX]	48	D5	

Name	Page	Grid
Gucun [SH]	38	D2
Gudingqiao [SX]	28	E2
Gudong Shan [XJ]	82	F6
Gudong [GZ]	68	F4
Gudong [SD]	50	F2
Gudonggou [BJ]	22	E1
Gudou [XZ]	72	F6
Guguan [SN]	74	B6
Gui Jiang [GX]	60	H3
Guia Marco [MC]	86	B2
Guide [QH]	78	G2
Guide [SD]	50	C3
Guidebu [SN]	74	E2
Guiding [GZ]	68	F4
Guidong [HN]	56	F5
Guigang [GX]	60	G4
Guiji [AH]	44	C3
Guijiaba [AH]	44	D5
Guilin [GX]	60	H2
Guimeng Ding [SD]	50	D4
Guinan [QH]	78	G3
Guiping [GX]	60	H4
Guiren [JS]	40	D2
Guishi Shuiku [GX]	60	I3
Guitou [GD]	58	E2
Guiwu [JS]	40	D3
Guixi [JX]	48	E3
Guiyang [GZ]	68	E4
Guiyang [HN]	56	E5
Guiyang [HN]	56	E6
Gujiang [JX]	48	B4
Gujiao [SX]	28	C6
Gujiao [SX]	28	D4
Gujiazi [JL]	34	D4
Gukai [GZ]	68	D3
Gula [GX]	60	F4
Gulang [GS]	76	G4
Gulei [FJ]	46	C6
Guleitou [FJ]	46	C6
Guli [SD]	50	D4
Gulianhe [HL]	36	B1
Gulin [SC]	66	F4
Guling [CQ]	64	F3
Guling [GX]	60	F4
Guliya Shan [NM]	30	H2
Gulong [GX]	60	H4
Gulong [HL]	36	C5
Gulu [SH]	38	E3
Gumiao [HEN]	52	E5
Gumu [YN]	70	F4
Gun He [HB]	54	E2
Gunzhongkou [NX]	80	B2
Guo He [AH]	44	C2
Guo He [HEN]	52	F3
Guochengyi [GS]	76	H4
Guocun [AH]	44	D5
Guodao [SX]	28	D5
Guohua [GX]	60	E4
Guoji [HEN]	52	E5
Guoji [JS]	40	E1
Guojia [GS]	76	H5
Guojia [JL]	34	E3
Guojiadian [SD]	50	G2
Guojiatun [HEB]	26	E2
Guojiawan [BJ]	22	D2
Guojie [HI]	62	A3
Guokeng [FJ]	46	C5
Guotan [HEN]	52	D5
Guotun [SD]	50	B3
Guoyang [AH]	44	C2
Guoyang [SX]	28	D3
Guozhuang [BJ]	22	C3
Guozhuang [JS]	40	E4
Gupei [AH]	44	D3
Gupeng [GX]	60	F4
Gupi [JS]	40	C1
Guqiao [AH]	44	C3
Gurbantünggüt Shamo [XJ]	82	J3
Gurgan Obo [NM]	30	F4
Gurnai [NM]	30	C4
Gushan [LN]	32	F4
Gushan [LN]	32	G5
Gushan [SD]	50	C3
Gushan [SX]	28	E1
Gushan [ZJ]	42	D4
Gushankou [BJ]	22	C4
Gushi [HEN]	52	G5
Gushi [SN]	74	E6
Gushi [ZJ]	42	C4
Gutian Shuiku [FJ]	46	D3
Gutian [FJ]	46	B4
Gutian [FJ]	46	B4
Gutian [FJ]	46	D3
Guxi [CQ]	64	B3
Guxian [HEN]	52	B3
Guxian [HEN]	52	C3
Guxian [JX]	48	C3
Guxian [JX]	48	C4
Guxian [SD]	50	G3
Guyang [HEN]	52	F3
Guyang [NM]	30	E4
Guyang [SX]	28	D5
Guye Qu [HEB]	26	F4
Guyong [YN]	70	C3
Guyuan [HEB]	26	C2
Guyuan [NX]	80	C4
Guyushu [LN]	32	G1
Guzhai [GX]	60	G3
Guzhang [GX]	60	B3
Guzhang [HN]	56	B3
Guzhen [AH]	44	D2
Guzhu [GD]	58	F3
Gya La [XZ]	72	E5
Gyaca [XZ]	72	I5
Gyaco [XZ]	72	D3
Gyairong [QH]	78	E4
Gyangrang [XZ]	72	E4
Gyangzê [XZ]	72	G5
Gyaring Co [XZ]	72	G4
Gyaring Hu [QH]	78	E3
Gyawa [SC]	66	D4
Gyêcê Caka [XZ]	72	C3
Gyirong [XZ]	72	E5
Gyirong [XZ]	72	E5
Gyitang [XZ]	72	K4
Gyumgo [QH]	78	G3

H

Name	Page	Grid
Ha Mei Wan [HK]	84	C4
Ha Pak Nai [HK]	84	B2
Ha Tsuen [HK]	84	B2
Habahe(Kaba) [XJ]	82	J1
Hac Sa Village [MC]	86	C6
Hadamen [JL]	34	J5
Hadapu [GS]	76	H5
Hadat [NM]	30	G2
Hadilik [XJ]	82	J7
Hafu [JL]	34	D4
Hai He [TJ]	24	C5
Hai Jiao [ZJ]	42	G2
Haian Shan [TW]	88	D3
Hai'an [GD]	58	B6
Hai'an [JS]	40	F3
Haibei [HL]	36	D4
Haicang Qu [FJ]	46	D5
Haicheng [LN]	32	F4
Haidian Qu [BJ]	22	C4
Haifeng [GD]	58	G4
Haifu [JS]	40	G4
Haihe kou [TJ]	24	D5
Haikou [AH]	44	C5
Haikou [HI]	62	C1
Haikou [JX]	48	E2
Haikou [ZJ]	42	D4
Hailar He [NM]	30	G2
Hailin [HL]	36	E5
Hailing Dao [GD]	58	C5
Hailong [JL]	34	E5
Hailun [HL]	36	D4
Haimen Wan [GD]	58	H3
Haimen [JS]	40	G4
Hainan Dao [HI]	62	B2
Hainan Jiao [HI]	62	C1
Hainan Qu [NM]	30	D5
Haining [ZJ]	42	D2
Haiqiao [SH]	38	D1
Haiqing [HL]	36	H4
Haiqing [SD]	50	F4
Hairag [QH]	78	G2
Haitan Dao [FJ]	46	E4
Haitan Haixia [FJ]	46	E4
Haitong [JS]	40	F2
Haitou [HI]	62	A2
Haitou [JS]	40	E1
Haituo [JL]	34	C2
Haiwei [HI]	62	A2
Haixin Shan [QH]	78	G2
Haixing [HEB]	26	E5
Haixiu [HI]	62	C1
Haiyan [GD]	58	D5
Haiyan [QH]	78	G2
Haiyan [ZJ]	42	D2
Haiyang Shan [GX]	60	H2
Haiyang Dao [LN]	32	G5

Haiyang [GX]	60	H2	Hao Xi [ZJ]	42	D4	Heishan [SN]	74	E7
Haiyang [SD]	50	H3	Haobei [SX]	28	D5	Heishanke [LN]	32	C4
Haiyuan [NX]	80	B4	Haochuan [NX]	80	B4	Heishantou [NM]	30	G2
Haizhou Qu [JS]	40	E1	Haohe [HN]	56	E3	Heishanzhai [BJ]	22	C2
Haizhou Wan [JS]	40	E1	Haojiaji [NX]	80	B4	Heishanzui [HEB]	26	D2
Haizicun [BJ]	22	D3	Haojiang Qu [GD]	58	H3	Heishanzui [HEB]	26	D2
Haizijing [NX]	80	C3	Haojiatai [NX]	80	D3	Heishi [JL]	34	F5
Haju [NM]	30	B4	Haokou [HB]	54	E4	Heishi [JL]	34	H4
Halahai [JL]	34	E3	Haolianghe [HL]	36	E4	Heishitou [GZ]	68	C4
Halhiyn Gol [NM]	30	G3	Haozigang [HN]	56	E2	Heishui He [SC]	66	E5
Halik Shan [XJ]	82	G4	Har Hu [QH]	78	E1	Heishui [JL]	34	B2
Haltang He [GS]	76	C3	Harba Ling [JL]	34	I4	Heishui [LN]	32	C2
Hami(Kumul) [XJ]	82	M4	Harbin [HL]	36	D5	Heishui [SC]	66	E2
Han Jiang [GD]	58	H3	Harqin Qi [NM]	30	G4	Heita [AH]	44	E2
Han Qu [NX]	80	C3	Harqin Zuoyi [LN]	32	C3	Heitai [HL]	36	F5
Han Shui [HB]	54	B2	Hartao [LN]	32	F2	Heituhe [GZ]	68	B3
Han Shui [HB]	54	E4	He Jiang [GD]	58	C3	Heituo Shan [SX]	28	D2
Han Shui [SN]	74	C7	He Jiang [GX]	60	I4	Hejia [JX]	48	D3
Hanbei He [HB]	54	F4	He Shui [JX]	48	B5	Hejian [HEB]	26	D5
Hancheng [SN]	74	F5	He Xian [AH]	44	E4	Hejiang [SC]	66	F4
Hancheng [HEN]	52	C3	Hebei [BJ]	22	C4	Hejiaping [HB]	54	C4
Hanchuan [HB]	54	F4	Hebei [HL]	36	F4	Hejin [SX]	28	B6
Hanconggou [HL]	36	H4	Hebeizhuang [BJ]	22	D2	Hejing [XJ]	82	J4
Handan [HEB]	26	B7	Hebi [HEN]	52	F2	Hekou Qu [SD]	50	E2
Handan [HEB]	26	B7	Hebian [SX]	28	E3	Hekou [AH]	44	C3
Handian [HL]	36	C5	Hechi [GX]	60	E3	Hekou [BJ]	22	C2
Hanfang [JX]	48	C6	Hechi [GX]	60	F3	Hekou [GD]	58	D3
Hanfuwan [NX]	80	C4	Hechuan [CQ]	64	C3	Hekou [GD]	58	G3
Hang Hau [HK]	84	E3	Hechuan [NX]	80	C5	Hekou [GS]	76	G4
Hangbu He [AH]	44	C4	Hechun [GD]	58	B5	Hekou [GX]	60	G2
Hanggai [ZJ]	42	C2	Hecun [ZJ]	42	B4	Hekou [HB]	54	G3
Hanggin Houqi [NM]	30	D4	Hedi Shuiku [GD]	58	B5	Hekou [HI]	62	B3
Hanggin [NM]	30	E5	Hedi [ZJ]	42	C5	Hekou [HN]	56	C5
Hangkou [JX]	48	B2	Hedong Qu [SD]	50	E4	Hekou [HN]	56	D2
Hangou [TJ]	24	B4	Hedong [HEB]	26	C4	Hekou [JS]	40	E3
Hangtou [SH]	38	D4	Hedongdian [SN]	74	B7	Hekou [SC]	66	G3
Hangu Qu [TJ]	24	D4	Hefei [AH]	44	D4	Hekou [SX]	28	C3
Hangzhou Wan [ZJ]	42	D2	Hefeng [HB]	54	C5	Hekou [YN]	70	E4
Hangzhou [ZJ]	42	D2	Hefu [HN]	56	D2	Helan Shan [NM]	30	D5
Hanhong [SX]	28	D5	Hegang [HL]	36	F4	Helan Shan [NX]	80	B2
Hanjiacun [HEB]	26	B2	Hegeng [CQ]	64	B4	Helan Shan [NX]	80	B2
Hanjialou [SX]	28	C2	Hei He [GS]	76	F3	Helan [LN]	32	G3
Hanjiang Qu [FJ]	46	E4	Hei He [QH]	78	F1	Helan [NX]	80	C2
Hanjiang Qu [JS]	40	E3	Hei He [SC]	66	E2	Heli Shan [GS]	76	E3
Hanjiaoshui [NX]	80	B3	Hei Ling Chau [HK]	84	C4	Heli Shan [NM]	30	B5
Hanjiashu [TJ]	24	B5	Hei Shan [LN]	32	C4	Heli [GX]	60	F4
Hanjiayuanzi [HL]	36	C1	Hei Shan [LN]	32	G4	Heli [HL]	36	F4
Hanjing [SN]	74	E5	Heicha Shan [SX]	28	C3	Heliu [AH]	44	C2
Hanlin [HI]	62	C2	Heicheng [NX]	80	C4	Heliu [SC]	66	G3
Hannan Qu [HB]	54	G4	Heichengzi [LN]	32	D2	Helong [JL]	34	E3
Hanshan [AH]	44	E4	Heihanling [BJ]	22	D2	Helong [JL]	34	I5
Hanshou [HN]	56	D3	Heihe [HL]	36	D2	Helong [LN]	32	H2
Hantengri Feng [XJ]	82	G4	Heijing [YN]	70	D3	Hemianshi Shuiku [GX]	60	I3
Hanting Qu [SD]	50	F3	Heilangkou [TJ]	24	C3	Hemu [GX]	60	G3
Hanting [AH]	44	E5	Heilin [JS]	40	D1	Henan [QH]	78	G3
Hanwang [SX]	28	E4	Heilong Jiang [HL]	36	C1	Henancun [BJ]	22	D3
Hanyan Qu [NX]	80	C2	Heilonggang He [TJ]	24	A6	Henanzhai [BJ]	22	E3
Hanyang Feng [JX]	48	C2	Heilongguan [SN]	74	F4	Heng Jiang [YN]	70	F1
Hanyin [SN]	74	D8	Heilongguan [SX]	28	C5	Heng Shan [SX]	28	E2
Hanyuan [SC]	66	E4	Heilongkou [SN]	74	E6	Heng Xian [GX]	60	G5
Hanzhong [SN]	74	C7	Heimahe [QH]	78	F2	Hengbu [AH]	44	D5
Hanzhuang [SD]	50	D5	Heishan [LN]	32	F3	Hengche [HB]	54	H4

Hengdao He [LN]	32	F4	Heshan [HL]	36	C3	Hong He [AH]	44	B3
Hengdaohezi [HL]	36	E5	Heshang [ZJ]	42	D3	Hong He [HEN]	52	E4
Hengdaohezi [LN]	32	G2	Heshangyuan [SN]	74	D4	Hong He [HEN]	52	F4
Hengdi [GZ]	68	C3	Heshe [HI]	62	B2	Hong Hu [HB]	54	F5
Hengdong [HN]	56	E4	Heshengqiao [HB]	54	C4	HONG KONG ISLAND [HK]	84	D4
Hengduan Shan [XZ]	72	K5	Heshi [HN]	56	F5	Hong Kong [HK]	84	D3
Hengduan Shan [YN]	70	C1	Heshi [JX]	48	B5	Hong Kong		
Hengfeng [JX]	48	E3	Heshui [GD]	58	C4	International Airport [HK]	84	B3
Henggang [AH]	44	D5	Heshui [GD]	58	C4	Hong Lok Yuen [HK]	84	D2
Henggang [JX]	48	C2	Heshui [GS]	76	J5	Hong'an [HB]	54	G3
Henggouqiao [HB]	54	G5	Heshui [GX]	60	G2	Hongchang [HEN]	52	E3
Henghe [CQ]	64	E3	Heshun [FJ]	46	C2	Hongcheng [GS]	76	G4
Hengjian [HEN]	52	B4	Heshun [HEN]	52	E1	Hongchengshui [NX]	80	C3
Hengjian [SX]	28	E4	Heshun [SX]	28	E4	Hongcun [AH]	44	D5
Hengjiang [JX]	48	B5	Hetanbu [JX]	48	E3	Hongda [HL]	36	D4
Hengjiangqiao [HN]	56	B5	Hetang [FJ]	46	E3	Hongdao [HI]	62	B2
Hengjin Shuiku [ZJ]	42	D3	Hetian [FJ]	46	B4	Hongdao [SX]	28	E3
Hengkou [SN]	74	D8	Hetou [TJ]	24	C5	Hongdu He [GZ]	68	F2
Hengli [SH]	38	C2	Hetu [AH]	44	C5	Hongdu [GX]	60	F4
Hengling Hu [HN]	56	E3	Hexi [CQ]	64	D5	Hongdu [GX]	60	F4
Hengling [SX]	28	E4	Hexi [FJ]	46	C5	Hongdu [GZ]	68	G2
Henglongqiao [HN]	56	E3	Hexi [GZ]	68	F2	Hongdunzi [NX]	80	C2
Hengmian [SH]	38	E3	Hexi [HN]	56	B3	Hongfeng Hu [GZ]	68	E4
Hengnan [HN]	56	E5	Hexi [SX]	28	D6	Honggang Qu [HL]	36	C4
Hengqu [SN]	74	C6	Hexigten Qi [NM]	30	G4	Honggor [NM]	30	F3
Hengsha Dao [SH]	38	E2	Hexing [SH]	38	E2	Honggu Qu [GS]	76	G4
Hengshan Qu [HL]	36	F5	Hexiwu [TJ]	24	B3	Hongguan [JX]	48	E2
Hengshan [AH]	44	E4	Heyan [CQ]	64	E2	Hongguozi [NX]	80	C1
Hengshan [GD]	58	D5	Heyang [SN]	74	F5	Honghai Wan [GD]	58	G4
Hengshan [HN]	56	E4	Heye Ping [SX]	28	C3	Honghe [NX]	80	C5
Hengshan [HN]	56	E4	Heyu [HEN]	52	C4	Honghe [YN]	70	E4
Hengshan [LN]	32	E5	Heyuan [GD]	58	F3	Honghu [CQ]	64	C4
Hengshan [SN]	74	E3	Heze [SD]	50	B4	Honghu [HB]	54	F5
Hengshanpu [NX]	80	C2	Hezhang [GZ]	68	C3	Honghuabu [SD]	50	E5
Hengshitan [HB]	54	G5	Hezheng [GS]	76	G5	Honghui [GS]	76	H4
Hengshui [HEB]	26	C6	Hezhi [SX]	28	C2	Hongjiaguan [HN]	56	C2
Hengshui [HEN]	52	D3	Hezhou [GX]	60	I3	Hongjian Nur [SN]	74	E1
Hengshui [SX]	28	C6	Hezi [JX]	48	C7	Hongjiang [HN]	56	B4
Hengxi [ZJ]	42	C3	Hezijian [BJ]	22	C3	Hongjingzi [NX]	80	D3
Hengxi [ZJ]	42	D4	Hezuo [GS]	76	G5	Hongkeli [HL]	36	E4
Hengxi [ZJ]	42	E3	High Island Reservoir [HK]	84	E2	Honglin [AH]	44	E5
Hengyang [HN]	56	E5	High Island			Hongliugou [SN]	74	C3
Hengyang [HN]	56	E5	(Leung Shuen Wan) [HK]	84	E3	Hongliuhe [GS]	76	C2
Hepeng [HN]	56	C3	Himalayas [XZ]	72	C4	Hongliuqiu Jing [GS]	76	D1
Heping [FJ]	46	C4	Ho Chung [HK]	84	E3	Hongliuyuan [GS]	76	C2
Heping [GD]	58	F2	Ho Pui Reservoir [HK]	84	C2	Honglong [SC]	66	D3
Heping [HI]	62	C3	Ho Pui [HK]	84	C2	Honglu [FJ]	46	E4
Heping [ZJ]	42	C2	Hoboksar [XJ]	82	I2	Hongmao [HI]	62	B2
Hepu [GX]	60	G6	Hoh Sai Hu [QH]	78	C3	Hongmen Shuiku [JX]	48	D4
Hepu [ZJ]	42	E3	Hoh Xil Shan [QH]	78	A3	Hongmen [ZJ]	42	D3
Heqiao [JS]	40	D3	Hoh Xil Hu [QH]	78	B3	Hongqi Qu [HEN]	52	E1
Heqiao [JS]	40	E4	Hohhot [NM]	30	E4	Hongqi [HI]	62	C2
Heqing [HI]	62	B2	Hohxil Shan [XZ]	72	G2	Hongquan [NX]	80	B3
Heqing [SH]	38	E3	Hoi Ha [HK]	84	E2	Hongshan Shuiku [NM]	30	G4
Heqing [YN]	70	D2	Hoika [QH]	78	F3	Hongshan Xia [GS]	76	H4
Hequ [SX]	28	C2	Hoit Taria [QH]	78	E2	Hongshan [HB]	54	E3
Herlen He [NM]	30	G2	Hoit Tohig [QH]	78	C2	Hongshan [HI]	62	B3
Herlen [NM]	30	F2	Hok Tsui Shan [HK]	84	E4	Hongshan [SD]	50	D3
Heshan Qu [HEN]	52	F2	Holin He [JL]	34	C2	Hongshantou [HN]	56	E2
Heshan [GD]	58	D4	Holin He [NM]	30	H3	Hongshila [HEB]	26	D2
Heshan [GD]	58	D5	Holingol [NM]	30	G3	Hongshilazi [JL]	34	G5
Heshan [GX]	60	F4	Holt Gol [NM]	30	G3	Hongshishan [GS]	76	D1

Hongshui He [GX]	60	E3
Hongshui [SX]	28	E5
Hongshuikou [BJ]	22	B3
Hongshuizhuang [TJ]	24	C1
Hongsipu [NX]	80	C3
Hongtai [XJ]	82	L4
Hongtang [ZJ]	42	E3
Hongtao Shan [SX]	28	D2
Hongtian [FJ]	46	C4
Hongtong [SX]	28	C5
Hongtumiao [LN]	32	H2
Hongtupo [NX]	80	C3
Hongwei He [SD]	50	B5
Hongwei Qu [LN]	32	G3
Hongwei [HL]	36	F4
Hongweihe Beizhi [SD]	50	B4
Hongxi [SC]	66	E4
Hongxing Qu [HL]	36	E3
Hongxing [JL]	34	C3
Hongya [SC]	66	E4
Hongyan [NM]	30	I2
Hongyang [GD]	58	H3
Hongyang [NX]	80	B4
Hongyansi [HB]	54	B4
Hongyashan Shuiku [GS]	76	G3
Hongyazi [NX]	80	C1
Hongyuan [SC]	66	E2
Hongze Hu [JS]	40	D2
Hongze [JS]	40	D2
Hongzhuang [NX]	80	C5
Hor [XZ]	72	C4
Horinger [NM]	30	E4
Horqin Youyi Qianqi [NM]	30	H3
Horqin Youyi Zhongqi [NM]	30	H3
Horqin Zuoyi Houqi [NM]	30	H4
Horqin Zuoyi Zhongqi [NM]	30	H3
Hotan He [XJ]	82	G6
Hotan [XJ]	82	F7
Hotan [XJ]	82	F7
Hou Jiang [SC]	66	G3
Hou'an [HI]	62	C3
Hou'an [LN]	32	H3
Hou'anling [BJ]	22	D2
Houbai [JS]	40	E4
Houchang [GZ]	68	E5
Houcheng [HEB]	26	D3
Houdaying [BJ]	22	D4
Hougang [HB]	54	E4
Hougang [SH]	38	C4
Hougou [SX]	28	D2
Houheyu [TJ]	24	B4
Houji [HEN]	52	D5
Houjia [SH]	38	D2
Houjiaying [TJ]	24	C2
Houlung [TW]	88	C2
Houma [SX]	28	C6
Houri [QH]	78	F2
Houshayu [BJ]	22	D3
Houshizhai [NX]	80	B4
Houshui Wan [HI]	62	B2
Housuo [SX]	28	D2
Houwan [HB]	54	D1
Houxi [ZJ]	42	B4
Houxian Ling [HI]	62	B3
Houxinqiu [LN]	32	F2
Houzhen [SD]	50	E2
Houzhenzi [SN]	74	C7
Hoxtolgay [XJ]	82	J2
Hoxud [XJ]	82	J4
Hsiaolan Yu [TW]	88	D5
Hsichi Yu [TW]	88	B3
Hsichuan Tao [FJ]	46	E4
Hsienhsi [TW]	88	C2
Hsilo [TW]	88	C3
Hsincheng [TW]	88	D2
Hsinchu [TW]	88	C2
Hsinchu [TW]	88	D2
Hsinhua [TW]	88	C3
Hsin-i [TW]	88	C3
Hsink ang Shan [TW]	88	D3
Hsinpi [TW]	88	C4
Hsiukuluan His [TW]	88	D3
Hsiukuluan Shan [TW]	88	D3
Hsiyin Tao [FJ]	46	F3
Hsiyu [TW]	88	B3
Hsueh Shan [TW]	88	D2
Hsueh Shan [TW]	88	D2
Hu Men [GD]	58	E4
Hu Xian [SN]	74	D6
Hua Shan [SN]	74	F6
Hua Xian [HEN]	52	F4
Hua Xian [SN]	74	E6
Hua Yu [TW]	88	B3
Hua'an [FJ]	46	C5
Huabu [ZJ]	42	B3
Huacheng [GD]	58	G2
Huachi [GS]	76	J4
Huachong [JS]	40	D1
Huachuan [HL]	36	F4
Huade [NM]	30	F4
Huadian [JL]	34	F5
Huading Shan [ZJ]	42	E3
Huadu Qu [GD]	58	E3
Huafang [JX]	48	C2
Huafeng [SD]	50	D4
Huagang [AH]	44	D4
Huahai [GS]	76	D2
Huahaizi [GS]	76	C3
Huai He [BJ]	22	D3
Huai He [AH]	44	D3
Huai He [HEN]	52	F5
Huai'an [HEB]	26	B3
Huai'an [JS]	40	E2
Huai'ancheng [HEB]	26	B3
Huaibei [AH]	44	C2
Huaibei [BJ]	22	D2
Huaibin [HEN]	52	G5
Huaide [JL]	34	D4
Huaihua [HN]	56	B4
Huaiji [GD]	58	D3
Huailai [HEB]	26	C3
Huailin [AH]	44	D4
Huainan [AH]	44	D3
Huaining [AH]	44	C5
Huairen [SX]	28	E2
Huairou Shuiku [BJ]	22	D3
Huairou Qu [BJ]	22	D3
Huaisha He [HEB]	26	B6
Huaishu Xinhe [JS]	40	D2
Huaishuzhuang [SN]	74	D5
Huaiyang [HEN]	52	F4
Huaiyin Qu [JS]	40	E2
Huaiyu Shan [JX]	48	E3
Huaiyuan [AH]	44	D3
Huaiyuan [GX]	60	F3
Huaizhen [HEB]	26	D5
Huaji [AH]	44	B3
Huajia [JL]	34	E3
Huajiang [GX]	60	H2
Huajiang [GZ]	68	D5
Huajiaoping [HB]	54	B4
Hualandian [SD]	50	C3
Huali [GZ]	68	F3
Huali [SN]	74	E8
Hualiangting Shuiku [AH]	44	C5
Hualien Hsi [TW]	88	D3
Hualien [TW]	88	D3
Hualikan [BJ]	22	D3
Hualong [QH]	78	H2
Hualongyan [HB]	54	C2
Huama [HL]	36	F4
Huamenlou [HN]	56	E4
Huaminglou [HN]	56	E3
Huamucun [BJ]	22	D2
Huan Jiang [GS]	76	I4
Huan Shui [HB]	54	F3
Huan Xian [GS]	76	I4
Huanan [HL]	36	F4
Huancheng [SD]	50	D5
Huancheng [SH]	38	C3
Huang Shan [AH]	44	D5
Huang He(Yellow R.) [GS]	76	H4
Huang He(Yellow R.) [HEN]	52	D2
Huang He(Yellow R.) [NX]	80	C2
Huang He(Yellow R.) [QH]	78	G3
Huang He(Yellow R.) [SD]	50	D2
Huang He(Yellow R.) [SX]	28	B3
Huang He(Yellow R.) [NM]	30	D4
Huang He(Yellow R.) [SN]	74	E3
Huang He [HEN]	52	G5
Huang Hu [AH]	44	C6
Huang Shui [QH]	78	H2
Huang'an [SD]	50	B4
Huangang [JS]	40	G3
Huang'ao [JX]	48	B5
Huangbai He [HB]	54	D3
Huangbai [JX]	48	E3
Huangban [GZ]	68	H2
Huangbao [HB]	54	D3
Huangbei [JX]	40	C5
Huangbei [JX]	48	D4
Huangbizhuang Shuiku [HEB]	26	B5
Huangbu [SN]	74	E5
Huangcai [HN]	56	E3
Huangcheng [GS]	76	F4

Huangchengji [SD]	50	G2
Huangchuan [HEN]	52	G5
Huangcun [GX]	60	H3
Huangda Yang [ZJ]	42	F2
Huangdao Qu [SD]	50	G4
Huangdi [LN]	32	D4
Huangdu [SH]	38	C3
Huanggai Hu [HN]	56	F2
Huanggang Shan [FJ]	46	C2
Huanggang Shan [JX]	48	E4
Huanggang [HB]	54	G4
Huanggang [JX]	48	B3
Huanggang [JX]	48	B3
Huanggang [JX]	48	E2
Huanggang [SD]	50	C5
Huanggangmiao [HB]	54	H4
Huangguoshui Pubu [GZ]	68	D5
Huangguzha [AH]	44	D4
Huanghe Kou [SD]	50	F2
Huangheya [SD]	50	C2
Huanghezhuang [TJ]	24	D3
Huanghu [ZJ]	42	C2
Huanghua [HEB]	26	E5
Huanghua [SD]	50	F4
Huanghuacheng [BJ]	22	D2
Huanghuadian [LN]	32	G4
Huanghuadian [TJ]	24	B4
Huangji [HB]	54	E2
Huangji [JS]	40	D2
Huangjia [SD]	50	D2
Huangjian [JS]	40	F2
Huangjiao Shan [ZJ]	42	E4
Huangjin [CQ]	64	D3
Huangjin'ao [HN]	56	B4
Huangjinbu [JX]	48	D3
Huangjinjing [HN]	56	C4
Huangkan [BJ]	22	D2
Huangkeng [GD]	58	F1
Huangkou [AH]	44	C1
Huanglaomen [JX]	48	C2
Huangli [JS]	40	E4
Huangli [JS]	40	F4
Huangling [HEN]	52	F2
Huangling [HI]	62	C2
Huangling [SN]	74	E5
Huangliu [HI]	62	A3
Huanglong [SN]	74	E5
Huanglongtan Shuiku [HB]	54	C2
Huanglu [AH]	44	D4
Huanglu [SH]	38	E4
Huangmao Jian [ZJ]	42	C5
Huangmao [GX]	60	G4
Huangmao [JX]	48	B3
Huangmaoyuan [HN]	56	C4
Huangmaozhou [HN]	56	E3
Huangmu [AH]	44	E4
Huangni He [GZ]	68	C6
Huangni He [YN]	70	F3
Huangnian [SX]	28	E5
Huangnihe [JL]	34	H4
Huangnitang [HN]	56	E5
Huangniupu [SN]	74	B6
Huangpi Qu [HB]	54	G4
Huangping [GZ]	68	F4
Huangpo [GD]	58	B5
Huangpu Jiang [SH]	38	D2
Huangpu Qu [GD]	58	E3
Huangqi Wan [FJ]	46	E3
Huangqiao [HN]	56	C4
Huangqiao [JS]	40	F3
Huangquqiao [NX]	80	C1
Huangsha [HN]	56	E6
Huangshagang [JS]	40	F2
Huangshajie [HN]	56	F2
Huangshan Qu [AH]	44	E5
Huangshan [AH]	44	E6
Huangshan [ZJ]	42	D3
Huangshanguan [SD]	50	G2
Huangshantou [HB]	54	E5
Huangshatuo [LN]	32	F3
Huangshi [HB]	54	H4
Huangshi [JX]	48	D4
Huangshikou [HEB]	26	B4
Huangsongdian [JL]	34	G4
Huangta [BJ]	22	B4
Huangtan [FJ]	46	C3
Huangtan [ZJ]	42	E3
Huangtankou Shuiku [ZJ]	42	B4
Huangtian [FJ]	46	D3
Huangtianpu [HN]	56	D5
Huangtong [HI]	62	B2
Huangtu [FJ]	46	D2
Huangtu [SX]	28	C5
Huangtuanyao [AH]	44	D3
Huangtudian [HN]	56	D3
Huangtugang [HB]	54	H3
Huangtugang [JX]	48	C4
Huangtujing [GX]	60	I1
Huangtukan [LN]	32	G5
Huangtuliangzi [HEB]	26	F2
Huangtuling [HN]	56	F4
Huangtupo [BJ]	22	C4
Huangwan [ZJ]	42	D2
Huangwei Yu [TW]	88	F1
Huangxi [CQ]	64	E4
Huangxi [JX]	48	C3
Huangxiekou [HB]	54	E4
Huangxikou [FJ]	46	C2
Huangyaguan [TJ]	24	C1
Huangyan Qu [ZJ]	42	E4
Huangyangjie [JX]	48	B5
Huangyangtan [NX]	80	C2
Huangyangwan [NX]	80	B3
Huangying [CQ]	64	D4
Huangyuan [QH]	78	G2
Huangyukou [BJ]	22	C2
Huangze Shan [ZJ]	42	F2
Huangze Yang [ZJ]	42	F2
Huangzhai [ZJ]	42	D3
Huangzhong [QH]	78	G2
Huangzhu [HI]	62	C2
Huangzhuang [HEN]	52	C5
Huangzhuang [TJ]	24	B4
Huangzhuang [TJ]	24	C4
Huaniao Shan [ZJ]	42	F2
Huaning [YN]	70	E3
Huaniushan [GS]	76	C2
Huanjiang [GX]	60	F3
Huankou [JS]	10	B1
Huanren Shuiku [LN]	32	I3
Huanren Shuiku [JL]	34	E6
Huanren [LN]	32	I3
Huantai [SD]	50	E3
Huantan [HB]	54	F3
Huanxi [HN]	56	F5
Huanxizhuang [TJ]	24	C3
Huapen [BJ]	22	D1
Huapi Ling [HEB]	26	C2
Huaping Yu [TW]	88	D1
Huaping [GZ]	68	F2
Huaping [YN]	70	D2
Huaqiao [FJ]	46	C2
Huaqiao [HN]	56	C4
Huaqiao [HN]	56	D4
Huaqiao [HN]	56	D5
Huaqiao [JX]	48	E4
Huarong Qu [HB]	54	G4
Huarong [HN]	56	E2
Huashan [JS]	40	B1
Huashan [SD]	50	G3
Huashaoying [HEB]	26	B3
Huashi Shan [GD]	58	E2
Huashixia [QH]	78	F3
Huatang [HN]	56	E6
Huating [GS]	76	I5
Huating [SH]	38	C2
Huaxi Qu [GZ]	68	E4
Huayang [SN]	74	C7
Huayin [SN]	74	F6
Huaying [SC]	66	G3
Huaying Shan [SC]	66	G3
Huayuan He [HN]	56	B3
Huayuan [HN]	56	B3
Huayuan [HN]	56	C5
Huayuanzui [JS]	40	D3
Huazhaizi [GS]	76	F3
Huazhou [GD]	58	B5
Huaziping [SN]	74	E3
Hubei kou [HB]	54	B1
Huchao [GZ]	68	E4
Hucun [SX]	28	D4
Hufang [JX]	48	E3
Hufang [JX]	48	E4
Hufeng [CQ]	64	C4
Hugezhuang [BJ]	22	D4
Hugezhuang [HEB]	26	F4
Huguan [SX]	28	E5
Huhe [AH]	44	E4
Hui He [AH]	44	C2
Hui He [SX]	28	D2
Hui Xian [GS]	76	I6
Hui'an [FJ]	46	D4
Hui'anpu [NX]	80	C3
Huibie Yang [ZJ]	42	E2
Huichang [JX]	48	C6
Huidong [GD]	58	F4

Huidong [SC]	66	E5	Hulushan [FJ]	46	D3	Huyu [BJ]	22	C3
Huifa He [JL]	34	F5	Huma He [HL]	36	B1	Huzhang [SX]	28	C6
Huifa [HL]	36	E5	Huma [HL]	36	D2	Huzhen [CQ]	64	E3
Huihe [SD]	50	D3	Humen [GD]	58	E4	Huzhen [ZJ]	42	C3
Huiji He [HEN]	52	F3	Hun He [SX]	28	E2	Huzhen [ZJ]	42	D4
Huiji Qu [HEN]	52	E3	Hun He [LN]	32	F3	Huzhong [HL]	36	B1
Huiji Shan [ZJ]	42	D3	Hun He [LN]	32	H3	Huzhou [ZJ]	42	D2
Huilai [GD]	58	H3	Hun Jiang [JL]	34	E6	Huzhu [QH]	78	H2
Huili [SC]	66	E5	Hunagmei [HB]	54	H4			
Huili [SD]	50	H2	Hunan [ZJ]	42	B4	**I**		
Huili [SX]	28	C4	Hunanzhen Shuiku [ZJ]	42	B4			
Huilong [CQ]	64	D3	Hunchun He [JL]	34	J5	I-lan [TW]	88	D2
Huilong [FJ]	46	D2	Hunchun [JL]	34	J5	Ilha Verde [MC]	86	A1
Huilong [HEB]	26	B7	Hunei [TW]	88	C4	Ili He [XJ]	82	G4
Huilongshan Shuiku [LN]	32	I3	Hung Fa Leng			Inggen [NM]	30	D4
Huimin [SD]	50	D2	(Robin's Nest) [HK]	84	D1	Iqe He [QH]	78	D1
Huiminxiang [NX]	80	C2	Hung Hom [HK]	84	D3	Iqe [QH]	78	D1
Huinan [JL]	34	F5	Hung Shui Kiu [HK]	84	B2			
Huinan [JL]	34	F5	Hunjiang [LN]	32	I4	**J**		
Huining [GS]	76	H5	Hunyuan [SX]	28	E2			
Huinong Qu [NX]	80	C1	Huo Shan [SX]	28	C5	Jagdaqi [NM]	30	I2
Huinong Qu [NX]	80	C2	Huocheng [XJ]	82	G3	Jaggang [XZ]	72	B3
Huishan Qu [JS]	40	F4	Huodifangzi [HL]	36	C4	Jainca [QH]	78	H3
Huishan [HI]	62	C2	Huoditang [SN]	74	D7	Jalaid Qi [NM]	30	H3
Huishangang [HN]	56	E3	Huojia [HEN]	52	E2	Jamati [XJ]	82	H3
Huishui [GZ]	68	E4	Huolongmen [HL]	36	C3	Jargal Saihan [NM]	30	D5
Huiten Nur [QH]	78	B3	Huolongping [HB]	54	A5	Jargalangt [NM]	30	F3
Huiting [HEN]	52	H3	Huoqiu [AH]	44	C3	Jartai yanchi [NM]	30	D5
Huitong [HN]	56	B5	Huoshan [AH]	44	C4	Jartai [NM]	30	D5
Huiwan He [HB]	54	B2	Huoshaoping [HB]	54	C4	Jarud Qi [NM]	30	H3
Huiwen [HI]	62	C2	Huoshi [CQ]	64	E4	Jeminay [XJ]	82	I2
Huixian [HEN]	52	E2	Huotian [HN]	56	F5	Ji Qu [QH]	78	D4
Huiyang Qu [GD]	58	F4	Huotian [FJ]	46	C5	Ji Xian [SX]	28	B5
Huize [YN]	70	E2	Huotong Xi [FJ]	46	E3	Ji Xian [TJ]	24	C2
Huizhou Qu [AH]	44	E6	Huotong [FJ]	46	E3	Jia Xian [HEN]	52	E4
Huizhou [GD]	58	F3	Huoxian [BJ]	22	D4	Jia Xian [SN]	74	F2
Huji [HB]	54	E3	Huoyan Shan [SX]	28	B6	Jiabi [CQ]	64	E4
Huji [JS]	40	D2	Huozhou [SX]	28	C5	Jiading Qu [SH]	38	C2
Hujiang [JX]	48	B5	Huozhuangzi [TJ]	24	C4	Jiafeng [SX]	28	D6
Hujiaxiaojing [NX]	80	C3	Huqiao [SH]	38	D4	Jiafu [FJ]	46	C4
Hujiayu [SX]	28	C6	Hure Qi [NM]	30	H4	Jiagou [AH]	44	D2
Hujiayuan [SN]	74	E7	Hurleg Hu [QH]	78	E2	Jiagui [GX]	60	F3
Hukou Pubu [SN]	74	F4	Hurun [GX]	60	D5	Jiahe [HB]	54	C2
Hukou Pubu [SX]	28	B5	Hushan [FJ]	46	B5	Jiahe [HN]	56	E6
Hukou [JX]	48	D2	Hushan [HI]	62	C2	Jiahui [GX]	60	H3
Hukou [SN]	74	F4	Hushan [HL]	36	F5	Jiajiang [SC]	66	E4
Hukou [TW]	88	D2	Hushan [JX]	48	B3	Jiajiatun [SX]	28	F1
Hulan Erge Qu [HL]	36	B4	Hushan [ZJ]	42	B4	Jiajin Shan [SC]	66	E3
Hulan He [HL]	36	D4	Hushi He [CQ]	64	B4	Jialai [HI]	62	B2
Hulan He [JL]	34	G3	Hushiha [HEB]	26	D3	Jialiang [GZ]	68	F5
Hulan Qu [HL]	36	D5	Hutian [HN]	56	E4	Jialing Jiang [CQ]	64	C3
Hulan [JL]	34	F4	Hutong [HL]	36	D2	Jialing Jiang [SC]	66	F2
Hule [AH]	44	E5	Hutou [FJ]	46	D4	Jialing Jiang [SN]	74	B7
Hulianzhuang [TJ]	24	B6	Hutou [HL]	36	G5	Jialing Qu [SC]	66	G3
Hulin [HL]	36	G5	Hutubi [XJ]	82	J3	Jialou [HEN]	52	E5
Huliu He [HEB]	26	B4	Hutun [SD]	50	C3	Jialu He [HEN]	52	F3
Hulu He [NX]	80	B5	Hutuo He [HEB]	26	C5	Jialu [AH]	44	E5
Hulu [HN]	56	B3	Hutuo He [SX]	28	D3	Jiamusi [HL]	36	F4
Huludao [LN]	32	D4	Huwan [HEN]	52	F6	Jian Jiang [GD]	58	B5
Hulufa [BJ]	22	C4	Huwan [JX]	48	D4	Jian Xi [FJ]	46	D3
Hulun Buir [NM]	30	G2	Huxin [HI]	62	C2	Ji'an [JX]	48	B4
Hulun Nur [NM]	30	G2	Huyang [HEN]	52	D5	Ji'an [JX]	48	B4
						Jiancaoping Qu [SX]	28	D4

Jiancha [GZ]	68	F2	Jiangshan [ZJ]	42	B4	Jiaomiao [SD]	50	C3
Jianchang [LN]	32	C4	Jiangshuihe [BJ]	22	B3	Jiaonan [SD]	50	F4
Jianchangying [HEB]	26	F3	Jiangtai [NX]	80	B5	Jiaoshi [CQ]	64	D4
Jiancheng [GD]	58	C3	Jiangtang [SX]	28	E4	Jiaotan [JX]	48	E2
Jianchi [SN]	74	D8	Jiangtian [FJ]	46	E4	Jiaotang [JX]	48	C2
Jianchuan [YN]	70	C2	Jianguo [HEB]	26	C6	Jiaowei [FJ]	46	D4
Jiande [ZJ]	42	C3	Jiangwan [JX]	48	F2	Jiaoxi [FJ]	46	C2
Jiandou [FJ]	46	C4	Jiangwan [SH]	38	D3	Jiaoyang [FJ]	46	B4
Jianfeng [HI]	62	A3	Jiangxia Qu [HB]	54	G4	Jiaoyuan [SD]	50	B4
Jiang Xian [SX]	28	C6	Jiangxigou [QH]	78	G2	Jiaozhou Wan [SD]	50	G3
Jiangan He [TJ]	24	C3	Jiangxikou [FJ]	46	D2	Jiaozhou [SD]	50	G3
Jiang'an [SC]	66	F4	Jiangya [HN]	56	C2	Jiaozhuang [HEN]	52	F4
Jiangao Shan [YN]	70	C3	Jiangyan [JS]	40	F3	Jiaozhuanghu [BJ]	22	E3
Jiangba [JS]	40	D2	Jiangyi [JX]	48	C2	Jiaozuo [HEN]	52	E2
Jiangbei Qu [CQ]	64	C4	Jiangyin [JS]	40	F4	Jiapeng Liedao [GD]	58	F5
Jiangbei [HN]	56	F3	Jiangyong [HN]	56	D6	Jiapigou [JL]	34	G5
Jiangbei [JX]	48	C5	Jiangyou [SC]	66	F3	Jiapu [ZJ]	42	C1
Jiangbian [HI]	62	A3	Jiangyu [SD]	50	E3	Jiashan [ZJ]	42	D2
Jiangbiancun [JX]	48	C4	Jiangyuan Qu [JL]	34	F5	Jiashi(Payzawat) [XJ]	82	E6
Jiangcheng [YN]	70	D4	Jiangyuan [JL]	34	H4	Jiasi [CQ]	64	C4
Jiangchuan [YN]	70	E3	Jiangzhang [SN]	74	C6	Jiatang [NX]	80	B4
Jiangcun [HEN]	52	F3	Jiangzhou [GZ]	68	F4	Jiawang Qu [JS]	40	C1
Jiangcun [HN]	56	D6	Jiangzhou [SC]	66	E5	Jiaxiang [SD]	50	C4
Jiangdian [AH]	44	C4	Jiangzhuang [SD]	50	F3	Jiaxing [ZJ]	42	D2
Jiangdu [JS]	40	E3	Jiangzhuang [SH]	38	D4	Jiayi [HN]	56	F3
Jiange [SC]	66	F2	Jianhe [GZ]	68	G4	Jiayin [HL]	36	F3
Jianggang [JS]	40	F3	Jianhu [JS]	40	E2	Jiayou [GX]	60	D3
Jianggezhuang [HEB]	26	G4	Jianjia [HEB]	26	C7	Jiayu [HB]	54	F5
Jianghong [GD]	58	A5	Jianli [HB]	54	E5	Jiayuguan [GS]	76	E3
Jianghua [HN]	56	D6	Jianling [HI]	62	C3	Jiazhen [SD]	50	B3
Jiangji [AH]	44	C2	Jiannan [HB]	54	A4	Jiazhuan [GX]	60	E3
Jiangjia [ZJ]	42	B3	Jianning [FJ]	46	B3	Jiazi Gang [GD]	58	G4
Jiangjiadian [HEB]	26	E1	Jian'ou [FJ]	46	D2	Jiazi [GD]	58	H4
Jiangjiadian [JL]	34	F5	Jianping [LN]	32	C3	Jiazi [HI]	62	C2
Jiangjiajie [JL]	34	E5	Jianping [LN]	32	C3	Jichang [GZ]	68	D3
Jiangjin Qu [CQ]	64	C4	Jiansanjiang [HL]	36	G4	Jichang [GZ]	68	E4
Jiangjumu [HEB]	26	B6	Jianshan [CQ]	64	E2	Jichang [GZ]	68	F5
Jiangjunguan [BJ]	22	F3	Jianshan [JX]	48	C3	Jichangping [GZ]	68	C5
Jiangjunmiao [XJ]	82	K3	Jianshanzi [HL]	36	G4	Jicun [SX]	28	C4
Jiangjuntai [GS]	76	D2	Jianshe [FJ]	46	C4	Jidar [XZ]	72	K5
Jiangkou Shuiku [JX]	48	B4	Jianshi [HB]	54	B4	Jidong [HL]	36	F5
Jiangkou [CQ]	64	D4	Jianshui [YN]	70	E4	Jiebu [JX]	48	C3
Jiangkou [CQ]	64	E2	Jiantiao [ZJ]	42	E3	Jiebu [JX]	48	C4
Jiangkou [FJ]	46	D2	Jiantouji [SD]	50	D5	Jiedi Jianhe [HEB]	26	E5
Jiangkou [FJ]	46	E4	Jianxing [SC]	66	F3	Jiedong [GD]	58	H3
Jiangkou [GZ]	68	G3	Jianyang [SC]	66	F3	Jieguan [HEB]	26	C6
Jiangkou [HN]	56	B4	Jianyang [FJ]	46	D2	Jiehe [SD]	50	D4
Jiangkou [HN]	56	C4	Jianyi [YN]	70	D2	Jiehekou [SX]	28	C3
Jiangkou [JX]	48	C6	Jiao He [BJ]	50	F3	Jiehualong [JX]	48	A4
Jiangkou [SH]	38	D1	Jiao Qu [SX]	28	E4	Jieji [HL]	36	B4
Jiangkou [SN]	74	D7	Jiao Xi [FJ]	46	E2	Jieji [JS]	40	D2
Jiangkou [ZJ]	42	E3	Jiaochang [SC]	66	E2	Jiejinkou [HL]	36	G4
Jiangle [FJ]	46	C3	Jiaocheng [SX]	28	D4	Jiekou [AH]	44	E6
Jiangling [HB]	54	E4	Jiaodao [BJ]	22	C4	Jielong [CQ]	64	C4
Jianglong [GZ]	68	D5	Jiaodi [SX]	28	C6	Jiepai [AH]	44	F5
Jiangluo [GS]	76	H6	Jiaohe [JL]	34	G4	Jiepai [SD]	50	E4
Jiangmen [GD]	58	E4	Jiaokou [SX]	28	C5	Jiepaidian [HB]	54	F3
Jiangnan [HN]	56	D3	Jiaokou [SX]	28	D5	Jieshi Shan [HEB]	26	G4
Jiangning Qu [JS]	40	D4	Jiaolai He [NM]	30	H4	Jieshi Wan [GD]	58	G4
Jiangning [GX]	60	G5	Jiaolai He [SD]	50	F3	Jieshi [GD]	58	G4
Jiangou [BJ]	22	C3	Jiaoling [GD]	58	H2	Jieshou [AH]	44	B2
Jiangqiao [HL]	36	B4	Jiaoliu He [JL]	34	A2	Jieshou [JS]	40	E2

Jietou [JX]	48	D3
Jietou [ZJ]	42	D3
Jiexi [GD]	58	G3
Jiexiu [SX]	28	C4
Jieyang [GD]	58	H3
Jiezi He [SN]	74	E5
Jigong Shan [HB]	54	G3
Jigong Shan [HEN]	52	F6
Jiguan [JL]	34	I4
Jigzhi [QH]	78	G4
Jihyueh Tan [TW]	88	C3
Jijia [GD]	58	A6
Jijia [NX]	80	B3
Jijiazhuang [HEB]	26	B3
Jijie [YN]	70	E4
Jilatu [JL]	34	D2
Jili Hu [XJ]	82	J2
Jili Qu [HEN]	52	D3
Jili [YN]	70	E2
Jilin Hada Ling [JL]	34	E5
Jilin Hada Ling [LN]	32	I2
Jilin [JL]	34	F4
Jiling [GS]	76	F3
Jiliu He [NM]	30	H1
Jilong [GD]	58	F4
Jilong [HN]	56	E5
Jimei Qu [FJ]	46	D5
Jimo [SD]	50	G3
Jimsar [XJ]	82	K4
Jin Island (Tiu Chung Chau) [HK]	84	E3
Jin Jiang [FJ]	46	D5
Jin Jiang [GZ]	68	G3
Jin Jiang [JX]	48	B3
Jin Xi [FJ]	46	C3
Jinan [SD]	50	D3
Jinayang [JS]	40	E2
Jinchai [GX]	60	F3
Jinchang [GS]	76	G3
Jincheng Jiang [GX]	60	E3
Jincheng [LN]	32	E3
Jincheng [SC]	66	G3
Jincheng [SX]	28	D6
Jinchuan(Quqên) [SC]	66	E3
Jindi He [HEN]	52	G2
Jinding [JX]	48	B4
Jindui [SN]	74	E6
Jinfo Shan [CQ]	64	D4
Jinfosi [GS]	76	E3
Jing He [GS]	76	I5
Jing He [SN]	74	D6
Jing Shan [HB]	54	D3
Jing Xian [AH]	44	E5
Jing Xian [HEB]	26	D6
Jing'an [JS]	40	B1
Jing'an [JX]	48	C3
Jing'an [YN]	70	E2
Jingang [HN]	56	F4
Jingbian [SN]	74	D3
Jingchuan [GS]	76	I5
Jingcun [SN]	74	F6
Jingde [AH]	44	E5
Jingdezhen [JX]	48	E2
Jingdian [HEN]	52	F2
Jingdong [YN]	70	D3
Jing'ergou [BJ]	22	C2
Jinggang [HN]	56	E3
Jinggangshan [JX]	48	B5
Jinggongqiao [JX]	48	E2
Jinggu [GS]	76	G5
Jinggu [YN]	70	D4
Jinghai [GD]	58	H3
Jinghai [TJ]	24	B5
Jinghang Yunhe (Grand Canal) [ZJ]	42	D2
Jinghang Yunhe (Grand Canal) [SD]	50	B3
Jinghang Yunhe (Grand Canal) [JS]	40	C1
Jinghang Yunhe (GrandCanal) [HEB]	26	C7
Jinghang Yunhe (Grand Canal) [TJ]	24	B3
Jinghe(Jing) [XJ]	82	H3
Jinghe [HEB]	26	D5
Jinghe [JS]	40	E2
Jinghong [YN]	70	D4
Jinghua Shan [CQ]	64	D3
Jingjia [SD]	50	D2
Jingjiang [JS]	40	F3
Jingle [SX]	28	C3
Jingmen [HB]	54	E3
Jingmi Yinshuiqu [BJ]	22	D3
Jingning [GS]	76	H5
Jingning [ZJ]	42	C5
Jingpo Hu [HL]	36	E5
Jingpo [HL]	36	E6
Jingshan [HB]	54	F3
Jingsheng [SX]	28	C5
Jingtai [GS]	76	H4
Jingtieshan [GS]	76	D3
Jingtou [JS]	40	D1
Jingtouxu [HN]	56	D5
Jingxi [GX]	60	D4
Jingxin [JL]	34	J5
Jingxing Kuangqu [HEB]	26	B5
Jingxing [HEB]	26	B5
Jingyan [SC]	66	F4
Jingyang [SN]	74	D6
Jingyou [SX]	28	C3
Jingyu [JL]	34	F5
Jingyuan [GS]	76	H4
Jingyuan [NX]	80	C5
Jingzhi [SD]	50	F3
Jingzhou Qu [HB]	54	E4
Jingzhou [HB]	54	E4
Jingzhou [HN]	56	B5
Jingzhuang [NX]	80	A3
Jingzhupu [HN]	56	C5
Jingziguan [HEN]	52	C4
Jinhai Hu [BJ]	22	F3
Jinhe [NM]	30	H2
Jinhu [JS]	40	E2
Jinhua [JL]	34	E5
Jinhua [ZJ]	42	C3
Jinhuiqiao [SH]	38	D4
Jining [SD]	50	C4
Jinji [GX]	60	H4
Jinji [NX]	80	C3
Jinjia [HN]	56	E4
Jinjia [LN]	32	G2
Jinjiang [FJ]	46	D5
Jinjiang [JX]	48	D3
Jinjiapu [HB]	54	H4
Jinjie [GX]	60	E4
Jinjing [HN]	56	F3
Jinkeng [FJ]	46	C2
Jinkouhe Qu [SC]	66	E4
Jinlansi [HN]	56	E4
Jinling [HN]	56	E5
Jinmiaopu [SX]	28	D6
Jinnan Qu [TJ]	24	C5
Jinning [YN]	70	E3
Jinping [GZ]	68	H4
Jinping [YN]	70	E4
Jinqian He [HB]	54	C1
Jinqian He [SN]	74	E7
Jinqiao [AH]	44	C4
Jinqing [ZJ]	42	E4
Jinsha Jiang [SC]	66	C3
Jinsha Jiang [XZ]	72	L4
Jinsha Jiang [YN]	70	D2
Jinsha Xi [JX]	48	F3
Jinsha [AH]	44	E5
Jinsha [FJ]	46	D4
Jinsha [GZ]	68	E3
Jinsha [JL]	34	F4
Jinshan Qu [SH]	38	D5
Jinshan [HI]	62	C2
Jinshan [HL]	36	D2
Jinshantun Qu [HL]	36	E4
Jinshanzui [SH]	38	D5
Jinshatan [SX]	28	D2
Jinshi [HN]	56	D2
Jinshiqiao [HN]	56	C4
Jinshui [SN]	74	C7
Jinshuihe [YN]	70	E4
Jinsiniangqiao [ZJ]	42	E2
Jinsuoguan [SN]	74	E5
Jinta [GS]	76	E3
Jintan [GD]	58	D2
Jintan [HEB]	26	C7
Jintan [JS]	40	E4
Jintang Shan [ZJ]	42	E2
Jintang [HB]	54	G5
Jintang [SC]	66	F3
Jintang [SN]	74	D4
Jintian [GX]	60	H4
Jintian [JX]	48	B4
Jinuoshan [YN]	70	D4
Jinwan Qu [GD]	58	E4
Jinxi [FJ]	46	C3
Jinxi [JX]	48	D4
Jinxian [JX]	48	D3
Jinxiang [SD]	50	C4
Jinxiang [ZJ]	42	D5

Jinxiu [GX]	60	H3
Jinyang [SC]	66	E5
Jinyinshan [GZ]	68	D3
Jinyuan Qu [SX]	28	D4
Jinyun [ZJ]	42	D4
Jinze [SH]	38	B4
Jinzhai [AH]	44	B4
Jinzhong He [TJ]	24	C4
Jinzhong [GZ]	68	C4
Jinzhong [GZ]	68	E3
Jinzhong [SX]	28	D4
Jinzhou Qu [LN]	32	E5
Jinzhou Wan [LN]	32	E4
Jinzhou Wan [LN]	32	E5
Jinzhou [HEB]	26	C5
Jinzhou [LN]	32	E3
Jinzhu [GX]	60	I5
Jinzhushan [HN]	56	D4
Jinzipai [AH]	44	D6
Jiqing [HN]	56	D4
Jirin Gol [NM]	30	G3
Jishan [SX]	28	B6
Jishi [SX]	28	D5
Jishishan [GS]	76	G5
Jishixia [QH]	78	H3
Jishou [HN]	56	B3
Jishu [JL]	34	F3
Jishui [JX]	48	C4
Jitan [JX]	48	C7
Jiubujiang Shuiku [HN]	56	F4
Jiubujiang [HN]	56	F4
Jiucai Ling [HN]	56	D6
Jiucai [NX]	80	B4
Jiuchang [GZ]	68	E4
Jiucheng [GX]	60	E5
Jiucheng [HEB]	26	E5
Jiucheng [SD]	50	B4
Jiuchong [HEN]	52	C5
Jiudaowaoxian [NX]	80	B4
Jiuduhe [BJ]	22	D2
Jiufeng Shan [FJ]	46	D3
Jiufeng [GD]	58	E1
Jiugong Shan [HB]	54	G5
Jiugong Shan [JX]	48	B2
Jiugongqiao [HN]	56	D4
Jiuguan [ZJ]	42	D2
Jiuhe [YN]	70	D2
Jiuhua Shan [AH]	44	D5
Jiujiang [JX]	48	C2
Jiujiang [JX]	48	C2
Jiujing [YN]	70	C4
Jiulian Shan [GD]	58	F3
Jiulian Shan [GD]	58	F2
Jiuliancheng [HEB]	26	B2
Jiuling Shan [JX]	48	B3
Jiuliwan [SX]	28	C4
Jiulong Jiang [FJ]	46	C5
Jiulong Shan [ZJ]	42	B4
Jiulong Xi [FJ]	46	B3
Jiulong(Gyaisi) [SC]	66	D4
Jiulong [HEB]	26	C4
Jiulongpo Qu [CQ]	64	C4

Jiumiao [LN]	32	E2
Jiupu [JS]	40	D3
Jiuqihe [SD]	50	C3
Jiuquan [GS]	76	E3
Jiuqujiang [HI]	62	C2
Jiushan Liedao [ZJ]	42	F3
Jiushan [SD]	50	E3
Jiusuo [HI]	62	A3
Jiutai [JL]	34	E3
Jiuting [SH]	38	D3
Jiuwan Dashan [GX]	60	F2
Jiuwan Dashan [GZ]	68	G5
Jiuxi [HN]	56	D2
Jiuxian [BJ]	22	C2
Jiuxian [HB]	54	D3
Jiuxian [HEN]	52	C3
Jiuxian [HEN]	52	E4
Jiuxian [SX]	28	C2
Jiuxian [SX]	28	D5
Jiuxiantang [JX]	48	B3
Jiuxu [GX]	60	E3
Jiuyi Shan [HN]	56	D6
Jiuyi [HN]	56	D6
Jiuyongshou [SN]	74	D6
Jiuzhaigou [SC]	66	F2
Jiuzhan [HL]	36	C2
Jiuzhen [FJ]	46	C5
Jiuzhou [GX]	60	C3
Jiuzhou [GZ]	68	F3
Jiuzhou [HI]	62	C2
Jiwang Shan [SX]	28	B6
Jiwang [SH]	38	C3
Jixi [AH]	44	E5
Jixi [HL]	36	F5
Jixian [HL]	36	F4
Jixian [HL]	36	F4
Jixian [HL]	36	F4
Jixin [HN]	56	B3
Jiyang [SD]	50	D3
Jiyi [SN]	74	F5
Jiyuan [HEN]	52	D2
Jiyun He [TJ]	24	D3
Jize [HEB]	26	B7
Jizhou [HEB]	26	C6
Jizu Shan [YN]	70	D2
Jomda [XZ]	72	L4
Jonê [GS]	76	G5
Ju He [BJ]	22	E3
Ju He [HEB]	26	E3
Ju He [SN]	74	D5
Ju Shui [HB]	54	D3
Ju Xian [SD]	50	E4
Juan Shui [HN]	56	E4
Juancheng [SD]	50	B4
Judian [YN]	70	C2
Jugezhuang [BJ]	22	E2
Jugezhuang [TJ]	24	C5
Juhongtu [QH]	78	E2
Juhua Dao [LN]	32	D4
Jukoupu [HN]	56	D4
Julebu [SX]	28	E1
Julong Shan [HB]	54	D3

Julu [HEB]	26	C6
Juma He [HEB]	26	C4
Juma He [BJ]	22	B4
Jun Jahin Us [NM]	30	C4
Jun Mahai Hu [QH]	78	D1
Jun Shan [HN]	56	E2
Junan [SD]	50	E4
Juncheng [HEB]	26	B5
Jundu Shan [BJ]	22	C2
Jungar Qi [NM]	30	E5
Junggar Pendi [XJ]	82	J3
Junji Guan [HEB]	26	A6
Junjiguan [SX]	28	E4
Junk Bay [HK]	84	E3
Junkou [FJ]	46	B3
Junlian [SC]	66	F4
Junliangcheng [TJ]	24	C5
Junshan Hu [JX]	48	D3
Junshan Qu [HN]	56	E2
Junshanpu [HN]	56	E3
Junzhuang [BJ]	22	C3
Jurh [NM]	30	H3
Jurhen Ui [QH]	78	B3
Jurong [JS]	40	E4
Jushi [GX]	60	G4
Jushui [ZJ]	42	C5
Juting [SN]	74	B7
Juye [SD]	50	C4
Juyongguan [BJ]	22	C3
Juzhang He [HB]	54	D4
Juzhen [JS]	40	G3

K

Ka Ho Village [MC]	86	D6
Kai Kung Leng [HK]	84	C2
Kai Xian [CQ]	64	E2
Kai'an [JL]	34	E3
Kaiben [GZ]	68	G3
Kaidu(Karaxahar) He [XJ]	82	I4
Kaifeng [HEB]	54	D3
Kaifeng [HEN]	52	F3
Kaifeng [HEN]	52	F3
Kaihe [SD]	50	C4
Kaihua [ZJ]	42	B3
Kaihui [HN]	56	F3
Kaijiang [SC]	66	G3
Kaikou [GZ]	68	F4
Kaikukang [HL]	36	C1
Kaili [GZ]	68	F4
Kailu [NM]	30	H4
Kaiping Qu [HEB]	26	F4
Kaiping [GD]	58	D4
Kaishantun [JL]	34	I5
Kaiyang [GZ]	68	E3
Kaiyang [JL]	34	G3
Kaiyuan [LN]	32	H2
Kaiyuan [YN]	70	E4
Kaizhang [SX]	28	B7
Kalpin [XJ]	82	F5
Kalun [JL]	34	E3
Kam Tin [HK]	84	C2
Kamen He [XZ]	72	I6

Kamisti [XJ]	82	K3
Kanas Hu [XJ]	82	J1
Kang Lau Shek [HK]	84	F1
Kang Xian [GS]	76	H6
Kangbao [HEB]	26	B2
Kangcheng [SX]	28	C5
Kangding(Dardo) [SC]	66	D3
Kanghsicun [TW]	88	C3
Kangjiahui [SX]	28	D3
Kangjin [HL]	36	D4
Kangle [CQ]	64	F2
Kangle [GS]	76	G5
Kanglung [XZ]	72	F4
Kangmar [XZ]	72	G5
Kangning [SX]	28	C3
Kangping [LN]	32	G2
Kangrinboqê Feng [XZ]	72	C4
Kangshan [TW]	88	C4
Kangxi [ZJ]	42	E4
Kangzhuang [BJ]	22	C2
Kangzhuang [SD]	50	B3
Kanmen [ZJ]	42	E4
Kanshi [FJ]	46	B5
Kantuan [AH]	44	C2
Kaohsiung [TW]	88	C4
Kaohsiung [TW]	88	C4
Kaolao [SX]	28	B7
Kaoping Hsi [TW]	88	C4
Kaoshan [JL]	34	E3
Kaoshan [JL]	34	E4
Kaoshanji [BJ]	22	F3
Kap Lung [HK]	84	C2
Kap shui Mun [HK]	84	C3
Kar Qu [QH]	78	E3
Karajül [XJ]	82	E5
Karakax He [XJ]	82	F7
Karakorum Shan [XJ]	82	D7
Karakorum Shankou [XJ]	82	E8
Karamay [XJ]	82	I3
Karamiran He [XJ]	82	I7
Karamiran Shankou [XJ]	82	J7
Karamiran Shankou [XZ]	72	F1
Kashi(Kaxgar) [XJ]	82	D6
Kat O Hoi [HK]	84	E1
Kata [XZ]	72	J4
Kau Sai Chau [HK]	84	E3
Kau Yi Chau [HK]	84	C3
Kaxsay [XJ]	82	J6
Kecheng [SX]	28	C5
Kecun [AH]	44	D5
Kedian [HB]	54	E3
Kedong [HL]	36	D3
Kedu He [GZ]	68	C4
Kêgor [SC]	66	C2
Kehuzhai [SX]	28	B3
Kei Kok Tau [HK]	84	F3
Kei Ling Ha Lo Wai [HK]	84	E2
Kelan [XJ]	28	C3
Kelegou [HEB]	26	F2
Kelu [GD]	58	A5
Keluo He [HL]	36	C3
Keluo [HL]	36	C3
Kenli [SD]	50	E2
Keriya He [XJ]	82	G7
Keriya Shankou [XJ]	82	G8
Keriya Shankou [XZ]	72	C2
Kesha [HN]	56	B2
Keshan [HL]	36	C3
Keung Shan [HK]	84	A4
Keyi [XJ]	82	H4
Kokyar [XJ]	82	E7
Kong Tau pai [HK]	84	F3
Kongcheng [AH]	44	D4
Konglong [HB]	54	H5
Kongtong Dao [SD]	50	H2
Kongtong Shan [GS]	76	I5
Kongur Shan [XJ]	82	D6
Kongwan [HB]	54	E3
Konqi He [XJ]	82	J5
Korgas [XJ]	82	G3
Korla [XJ]	82	J5
Korlondo [SC]	66	C2
Kosrap [XJ]	82	E7
Kou He [LN]	32	H2
Koubu [SD]	50	E3
Koudong [TJ]	24	C3
Koumenzi [XJ]	82	M4
Kouzhen [SD]	50	D3
Kouzi [AH]	44	C3
Kouzigou [NX]	80	C3
Kowloon Bay [HK]	84	D3
Kowloon City [HK]	84	D3
Kowloon Peak [HK]	84	D3
Kowloon Reservoirs [HK]	84	D3
KOWLOON [HK]	84	D3
Koxlax [XJ]	82	G7
Koxtag [XJ]	82	F7
Kuai He [SX]	28	C6
Kuaize He [YN]	70	F3
Kuanao [FJ]	46	D5
Kuancheng [HEB]	26	F3
Kuandian [LN]	32	H4
Kuang Qu [SX]	28	E1
Kuangshan [HEB]	26	B7
Kuankuoba [GZ]	68	F2
Kuanmiao [TW]	88	C4
Kuanshan [TW]	88	D3
Kuanyin [TW]	88	D1
Kueiluan Tao [TW]	88	D2
Kueishan Tao [TW]	88	D2
Kuerbin He [HL]	36	E3
Kuidou [FJ]	46	D4
Kuishan Ding [GX]	60	G5
Kuitan [GD]	58	G3
Kuixi [HN]	56	C3
Kuixiang [YN]	70	F2
Kuixu [GX]	60	D4
Kuke He [YN]	70	C3
Kumtag Shamo [XJ]	82	L6
Kümüx [XJ]	82	K4
Kunjirap Daban [XJ]	82	D7
Kunlun Shan [QH]	78	B2
Kunlun Shan [XJ]	82	E7
Kunlun Shankou [QH]	78	D3
Kunlun [GX]	60	F4
Kunlunqi [HL]	36	E4
Kunming Hu [BJ]	22	C4
Kunming [YN]	70	E3
Kunshan [JS]	40	F4
Kunyu Shan [SD]	50	H2
Kuocang Shan [ZJ]	42	D4
Kuocang Shan [ZJ]	42	D4
Kuqa [XJ]	82	H5
Kuqiao [JX]	48	E3
Kuruktag [XJ]	82	J5
Kushui He [NX]	80	C3
Kushui [XJ]	82	N4
Kuye He [SN]	74	F2
Kuytun [XJ]	82	I3
Kwai Chung [HK]	84	D3
Kwai Tau Leng [HK]	84	D1
Kwan Tei [HK]	84	D1
Kwu Tung [HK]	84	C1
Kwun Tong [HK]	84	D3
Kyêbxang Co [XZ]	72	G3
Kyinzhi [QH]	78	G3

L

Labagoumen [BJ]	22	D1
Ladong [GX]	60	G3
Lafa [JL]	34	G4
Lagkor Co [XZ]	72	E3
Laha [HL]	36	C3
Lai Chi Van [MC]	86	B6
Lai Chi Chong [HK]	84	E2
Lai Chi Wo [HK]	84	E1
Lai'an [AH]	44	E3
Laibang [AH]	44	C5
Laibin [GX]	60	G4
Laicun [JX]	48	C5
Laifeng [CQ]	64	C4
Laifeng [HB]	54	B5
Laiguangying [BJ]	22	D3
Laishui [HEB]	26	C4
Laiwu [SD]	50	D3
Laixi [SD]	50	G3
Laiyang [SD]	50	G3
Laiyang [SD]	50	G3
Laiyuan [HEB]	26	B4
Laiyuan [SX]	28	D4
Laizhou Wan [SD]	50	F2
Laizhou [SD]	50	F2
Laji Shan [QH]	78	G2
Lalang [GX]	60	F3
Lalho [XZ]	72	G5
Lalin He [HL]	36	D5
Lalin He [JL]	34	E2
Lalin [HL]	36	D5
Lam Tei [HK]	84	B2
Lam Tsuen Valley [HK]	84	D2
Lamadian [JL]	34	D4
Lamadong [LN]	32	G4
Lamdo [SC]	66	C2
Lamma Island [HK]	84	C4
Lan He [SN]	74	D8
Lan Xian [SX]	28	C3

Name	Page	Grid
Lan Yu [TW]	88	D4
Lanbazi [CQ]	64	D4
Lancang Jiang [YN]	70	C2
Lancang Jiang [XZ]	72	K4
Lancang Jiang [YN]	70	D4
Lancang [YN]	70	C4
Lancheng [SX]	28	C3
Lancun [SD]	50	G3
Lang Shan [NM]	30	D4
Lang Shan [JS]	40	F4
La'nga Co [XZ]	72	C4
Langao [SN]	74	D8
Langdai [GZ]	68	D4
Langdong [GZ]	68	G4
Langfang [HEB]	26	D4
Langgangshan Liedao [ZJ]	42	F2
Langmai [XZ]	72	L4
Langmusi [GS]	76	G5
Langnuankou [SD]	50	H3
Langping [HB]	54	C4
Langqên Zangbo (Xiangquan He) [XZ]	72	B4
Langqi [FJ]	46	E3
Langqiao [AH]	44	E5
Langru [XJ]	82	F7
Langshan [HN]	56	C5
Langtang [HN]	56	D3
Langu [FJ]	46	D2
Langwogou [HEB]	26	B2
Langxi [AH]	44	F4
Langxia [SH]	38	C4
Langya Shan [AH]	44	E3
Langya Shan [HEB]	26	C4
Langya Shan [SD]	50	F4
Langzhong [SC]	66	F3
Lanhepu [HB]	54	B2
Lankao [HEN]	52	F3
Lankou [GD]	58	G3
Lanli [HN]	56	B4
Lanling [HL]	36	D5
Lanling [SD]	50	D5
Lanlu Gang [SH]	38	C3
Lanping [YN]	70	C2
Lanshan Qu [SD]	50	F4
Lanshan [HN]	56	E6
Lantang [GD]	58	F3
LANTAU ISLAND [HK]	84	B3
Lantau Peak (Fung Wong Shan) [HK]	84	B4
Lantian [SN]	74	E6
Lanting [ZJ]	42	D3
Lanxi [FJ]	46	B5
Lanxi [HL]	36	D4
Lanxi [ZJ]	42	C3
Lanxun [HI]	62	B2
Lanyang Hsi [TW]	88	D2
Lanyang [HI]	62	B2
Lanyi He [SX]	28	C3
Lanzhou [GS]	76	G4
Lanzi [JL]	34	C3
Lao Ling [JL]	34	F6
Lao He [JX]	48	C3
Lao Mangnai [QH]	78	B2
Lao Shan [SD]	50	G3
Laobian Qu [LN]	32	F4
Laobie Shan [YN]	70	C4
Laochang [GZ]	60	C5
Laochang [YN]	70	F3
Laocheng [HEN]	52	C4
Laocheng [HI]	62	C2
Laocheng [SD]	50	B2
Laodao He [HN]	56	F3
Laodaodian [HL]	36	D2
Laodaohe [HN]	56	E3
Laoge [JS]	40	E3
Laoguanxia [JX]	48	A4
Laoha He [LN]	32	C3
Laoheishan [HL]	36	F6
Laohekou [HB]	54	D2
Laohuanghe Kou [SD]	50	E1
Laohuanghe Kou [SD]	50	F2
Laohutun [LN]	32	E5
Laoji [AH]	44	B3
Laojun Shan [HEN]	52	C4
Laojundian [SN]	74	E3
Laojundong [SX]	28	D3
Laojunmiao [GS]	76	D3
Laolai [HL]	36	C3
Laoling [JL]	34	F6
Laonung His [TW]	88	C3
Laoshan Qu [SD]	50	G3
Laoshan Shuiku [SD]	50	G3
Laoshan Wan [SD]	50	G3
Laoshan [AH]	44	D4
Laotouding shan [LN]	32	H3
Laotougou [JL]	34	I5
Laoxian [SN]	74	E8
Laoyanchi [NX]	80	C3
Laoyatai [TJ]	24	C3
Laoye Ling [HL]	36	E6
Laoye Ling [JL]	34	G4
Laoye Ling [JL]	34	G4
Laoye Ling [JL]	34	I4
Laoyemiao [JX]	48	D2
Laoyemiao [XJ]	82	N3
Laoying [SX]	28	C2
Laoying [YN]	70	C3
Laoyingpan [JX]	48	C5
Laoyugou [BJ]	22	C3
Laozhong [HEN]	52	F4
Laozishan [JS]	40	D2
Laren [GX]	60	F3
Lasengmiao [NM]	30	D5
Lau Fau Shan [HK]	84	B2
Laxong Co [XZ]	72	E2
Le'an Jiang [JX]	48	E3
Le'an [JX]	48	C4
Le'anpu [HN]	56	B5
Lechang [GD]	58	E1
Lecheng [SD]	58	D3
Ledong [HI]	62	B3
Ledu [QH]	78	H2
Leguang Nongchang [HI]	62	B3
Lehua [JX]	48	C3
Lei Shui [HN]	56	E5
Lei Yue Mun [HK]	84	D3
Leibo [SC]	66	E4
Leifeng [FJ]	46	D4
Loigong Shan [GZ]	68	G4
Leihe [HB]	54	E3
Leiming [HI]	62	C2
Leiping [GX]	60	E5
Leishan [GZ]	68	G4
Leiyang [HN]	56	E5
Leizhou Bandao [GD]	58	A5
Leizhou Wan [GD]	58	B6
Leizhou [GD]	58	B6
Lelai [HI]	62	C3
Leli He [GX]	60	D3
Leling [SD]	50	D2
Lemin [GX]	60	G5
Lenghu [QH]	78	C1
Lenglong Ling [GS]	76	F4
Lenglong Ling [QH]	78	G2
Lengshui [HB]	54	E3
Lengshui [HN]	56	E6
Lengshui [SN]	74	E8
Lengshuijiang [HN]	56	D4
Lengzipu [LN]	32	F3
Leping [JX]	48	E3
Lepingpu [SD]	50	C3
Leshan [SC]	66	E4
Leshanzhuang [TJ]	24	C4
Leshi [HN]	56	C5
Lesuhe [SN]	74	B7
Leting [HEB]	26	F4
Letu [AH]	44	C2
Lewang [GZ]	68	E5
Leye [GX]	60	D3
Leyuan [GZ]	68	D5
Lezhengwu [BJ]	22	E3
Lezhi [SC]	66	F3
Lhabo [SC]	66	D4
Lhari [XZ]	72	I4
Lhasa He [XZ]	72	H5
Lhasa [XZ]	72	H5
Lhazê [XZ]	72	F5
Lhoma [XZ]	72	H4
Lhorong [XZ]	72	J4
Lhozhag [XZ]	72	H5
Lhünzê [XZ]	72	I5
Lhünzhub [XZ]	72	H4
Li Jiang [GX]	60	H2
Li Shan [SN]	74	E6
Li Shan [SX]	28	C6
Li Shui [HEN]	52	E4
Li Shui [HN]	56	C2
Li Shui [HN]	56	D2
Li Xian [GS]	76	H5
Li Xian [HEB]	26	C5
Li Xian [HN]	56	D2
Li Xian [SC]	66	E3
Lian Jiang [GD]	58	D2
Lian Jiang [GX]	60	G6
Lian Jiang [GZ]	68	E5
Lian Jiang [JX]	48	C6

Lian Shui [HN]	56	E4	Lianjiang [FJ]	46	E3	Lichuan [JX]	48	D4
Li'an [HI]	62	C3	Lianjiang [GD]	58	B5	Lichuan [SX]	28	D6
Liancai [NX]	80	B5	Lianjiangkou [GD]	58	E2	Licun [GX]	60	H5
Liancheng [FJ]	46	B4	Lianjingkou [HL]	36	F4	Licun [JX]	48	C6
Liang Shan [SD]	50	C4	Liannan [GD]	58	D2	Lidian [LN]	32	E5
Liangbingtai [JL]	34	H4	Lianping [GD]	58	F2	Lidu [CQ]	64	D4
Liangcha [JS]	40	E2	Lianping [SX]	28	E4	Lidu [JX]	48	D3
Liangcheng [NM]	30	F4	Lianpu [AH]	44	D3	Lieshan Qu [AH]	44	C2
Liangcheng [SD]	50	F4	Lianqiao [HN]	56	D4	Lifuta [HN]	56	C2
Liangchenhui [SX]	28	C3	Lianshan Qu [LN]	32	D4	Ligao [GX]	60	G3
Liangcun [GD]	58	D3	Lianshan [GD]	58	D2	Ligeta [SX]	28	D6
Liangcun [HEB]	26	C5	Lianshan [HN]	56	B5	Ligezhuang [SD]	50	G3
Liangcun [JX]	48	C5	Lianshan [LN]	32	F5	Ligou [HEB]	26	B3
Liangdang [GS]	76	I6	Lianshanguan [LN]	32	G4	Liguo [JS]	40	C1
Liangditou [SD]	50	B5	Lianshanshi [BJ]	22	D3	Lihai [ZJ]	42	D2
Liangdu [SX]	28	C5	Liansheng [SH]	38	C4	Lihe [NX]	80	C1
Liangduo [JS]	40	F3	Lianshi [ZJ]	42	D2	Lihu [GD]	58	H3
Lianggezhuang [BJ]	22	C4	Lianshui [JS]	40	E2	Lihua [GZ]	68	G5
Lianghe [CQ]	64	E4	Liantan [GD]	58	C4	Lihuaping [NX]	80	B4
Lianghe [YN]	70	C3	Liantang [GX]	60	G5	Liji [HEN]	52	G6
Lianghekou [GS]	76	H6	Liantang [HN]	56	E5	Liji [HI]	62	C3
Lianghekou [SC]	66	E3	Liantang [SH]	38	C4	Liji [JS]	40	E1
Liangji Shan [ZJ]	42	E4	Liantuo [HB]	54	D4	Lijia [LN]	32	F3
Liangjiadian [LN]	32	E5	Lianxi [SH]	38	D3	Lijia [SD]	50	E2
Liangjiang [GX]	60	G4	Lianxing [HL]	36	C3	Lijiacha [SN]	74	E3
Liangjiangkou [JL]	34	H5	Lianyin [HL]	36	B1	Lijiahe [HB]	54	B5
Liangjiazi [JL]	34	C2	Lianyuan [HN]	56	D4	Lijiajuan [NX]	80	D3
Liangkou [GD]	58	E3	Lianyun Qu [JS]	40	E1	Lijiang [YN]	70	D2
Liangkou [GX]	60	G2	Lianyun Shan [HN]	56	F3	Lijiaping [HN]	56	D5
Liangkou [JX]	48	B5	Lianyungang [JS]	40	E1	Lijiaxiang [FJ]	46	E2
Liangma [SX]	28	D5	Lianyungangdongzhan [JS]	40	E1	Lijin [LN]	32	E3
Liangnong [ZJ]	42	E3	Lianzhen [HEB]	26	D6	Lijin [SD]	50	E2
Liangping [CQ]	64	D3	Lianzhou [GD]	58	D2	Lijun [NX]	80	B4
Liangqing Qu [GX]	60	F5	Lianzhuang [TJ]	24	D4	Lijun [NX]	80	C2
Liangqiu [SD]	50	D4	Liao He [LN]	32	F3	Likang [TW]	88	C4
Liangsan [HN]	56	A4	Liao He [LN]	32	G2	Likou [JS]	40	D2
Liangshan [JX]	48	B4	Liaocheng [SD]	50	B3	Liling [HN]	56	F4
Liangshan [SD]	50	C4	Liaodong Bandao [LN]	32	E5	Limin [HEN]	52	G3
Liangshui He [BJ]	22	D4	Liaodong Wan [LN]	32	E4	Liming [GX]	60	E4
Liangshui [JL]	34	I4	Liaodun [XJ]	82	M4	Limu Ling [HI]	62	B3
Liangshuihezi [JL]	34	F5	Liaogou [JS]	40	E3	Limu Ling [HI]	62	B2
Liangshuikou [HN]	56	C2	Liaohe Kou [LN]	32	E4	Limu [GX]	60	H2
Liangshuiyuanzi [NX]	80	A3	Liaohe [HEN]	52	D5	Limu [GX]	60	H3
Liangtian [HN]	56	F6	Liaolan [SD]	50	F3	Limushan [HI]	62	B2
Liangtian [NX]	80	C2	Liaotun [LN]	32	E3	Lin Tong Mei [HK]	84	C1
Liangting [SN]	74	C6	Liaoyang [LN]	32	G3	Lin Xian [SX]	28	B4
Liangwangzhuang [TJ]	24	B5	Liaoyang [LN]	32	G3	Lin'an [ZJ]	42	C2
Liangxiongdi Dao [ZJ]	42	F2	Liaoyuan [JL]	34	E5	Lincang [YN]	70	D4
Liangyaping [HN]	56	C4	Liaoyuan [SH]	38	E4	Linchang Jiao [HI]	62	B2
Liangyuan [AH]	44	D4	Liaozhong [LN]	32	F3	Lincheng [HEB]	26	B6
Liangzhu [ZJ]	42	D2	Liaozikou [CQ]	64	E2	Lindian [HB]	54	G3
Liangzi Hu [HB]	54	G4	Libao [JS]	40	F3	Lindian [HL]	36	C4
Liangzihu Qu [HB]	54	G4	Libazhuang [SX]	28	E2	Linfen [SX]	28	C5
Lianhua Shan [GD]	58	G3	Libei [JX]	48	D4	Ling Jiang [ZJ]	42	E4
Lianhua Feng [AH]	44	E5	Libo [GZ]	68	F5	Ling Xian [SD]	50	C2
Lianhua Shan [GD]	58	G3	Libu [GD]	58	D2	Lingang [JX]	40	E2
Lianhua [GS]	76	H5	Libu [GX]	60	I4	Lingao [HI]	62	B2
Lianhua [GX]	60	H3	Licang Qu [SD]	50	G3	Lingaojiao [HI]	62	B1
Lianhua [HL]	36	C5	Licang [LN]	44	C2	Lingbao [HEN]	52	B3
Lianhua [JX]	48	A4	Licheng Qu [SD]	50	D3	Lingbei [GD]	58	D2
Lianhua [LN]	32	H2	Licheng [SX]	28	E5	Lingbei [ZJ]	42	D3
Lianjiang [AH]	44	D3	Lichuan [HB]	54	A4	Lingbi [AH]	44	D2

Lingchuan [GX]	60	H2	Lintang [JX]	48	B7	Liubao [GX]	60	I4
Lingchuan [SX]	28	E6	Lintao [GS]	76	G5	Liubinbu [BJ]	22	C2
Lingdi [JX]	48	F3	Lintingkou [TJ]	24	C3	Liubu [SD]	50	D3
Lingdong Qu [HL]	36	F4	Lintong Qu [SN]	74	E6	Liuchen [GX]	60	H4
Lingguan [HN]	56	F5	Lintou [AH]	44	D4	Liucheng [GX]	60	G3
Linghai [LN]	32	E3	Linwang [HI]	62	B3	Liuchiu Yu [TW]	88	C4
Linghe [SD]	50	F3	Linwu [HN]	56	E6	Liuchiu [TW]	88	C4
Lingjiang [SC]	66	G3	Linxi [HEB]	26	C7	Liuchong He [GZ]	68	D3
Lingjing [HEN]	52	E3	Linxi [NM]	30	G4	Liuchuan [GZ]	68	G4
Lingkou [HI]	62	C2	Linxia [GS]	76	G5	Liucun [SX]	28	C5
Lingling Qu [HN]	56	D5	Linxia [GS]	76	G5	Liudaogou [JL]	34	G6
Linglongta [LN]	32	C4	Linxiang [HN]	56	F2	Liudaohezi [HEB]	26	E3
Lingma [GX]	60	E4	Linyi [SD]	50	C2	Liudaokou [TJ]	24	B4
Lingqiao [SH]	38	D2	Linyi [SD]	50	E4	Liudaoweizi [JL]	34	J4
Lingqiao [ZJ]	42	D2	Linyi [SX]	28	B6	Liudian [BJ]	22	E3
Lingqiu [SX]	28	F2	Linying [HEN]	52	E4	Liudu [GZ]	68	F2
Lingqu [GX]	60	H2	Linyou [SN]	74	C6	Liuduo [JS]	40	F1
Lingshan Dao [SD]	50	G4	Linyuan [TW]	88	C4	Liuduzhai [HN]	56	C4
Lingshan Wan [SD]	50	G4	Linze [GS]	76	F3	Liufang [HB]	54	G4
Lingshan [GX]	60	G5	Linze [JS]	40	E2	Liufen [SD]	50	D4
Lingshan [HI]	62	C1	Linzhang [HEB]	26	B7	Liufeng [HN]	56	E6
Lingshan [SD]	50	G3	Linzheyu [SX]	28	C3	Liufu [AH]	44	D3
Lingshi [SX]	28	C5	Linzhou [HEN]	52	E1	Liugezhuang [HEB]	26	D5
Lingshou [HEB]	26	B5	Linzhuang [SD]	50	C2	Liugong Dao [SD]	50	I2
Lingshui Wan [HI]	62	B3	Linzi Qu [SD]	50	E3	Liugong [HI]	62	B3
Lingshui [HI]	62	C3	Linzijie [SD]	50	C2	Liugu He [LN]	32	D4
Lingtai [GS]	76	I5	Lion Rock [HK]	84	D3	Liuguan [GZ]	68	C5
Lingui [GX]	60	H2	Liping [GZ]	68	H4	Liuguang [GZ]	68	E4
Lingwu [NX]	80	C2	Lipu [GX]	60	H3	Liuhang [SH]	38	D2
Lingxi [HEB]	26	C4	Liqiao [AH]	44	E4	Liuhe [HEN]	52	G3
Lingxi [JX]	48	F3	Liqiao [BJ]	22	D3	Liuhe [HL]	36	E5
Lingxiang [HB]	54	G4	Liqizhuang [TJ]	24	B5	Liuhe [JL]	34	E5
Lingyuan [LN]	32	C3	Liquan [SN]	74	D6	Liuhe [JS]	40	G4
Lingyun [GX]	60	D3	Lirenpo [SX]	28	B5	Liuheng Dao [ZJ]	42	F3
Lingzhi [SX]	28	E4	Lishadi [YN]	70	C2	Liuhou [SN]	74	B7
Linhai [HL]	36	C2	Lishan [HB]	54	F3	Liuhouji [HB]	54	E3
Linhai [JS]	40	F2	Lishan [TW]	88	D2	Liuhuang [GD]	58	H3
Linhai [ZJ]	42	E4	Lishe Jiang [YN]	70	D3	Liuji [HB]	54	D3
Linhe [NX]	80	C2	Lishi [CQ]	64	C4	Liujia [GX]	60	E3
Linhong Kou [JS]	40	E1	Lishi [GD]	58	E2	Liujia [JX]	48	D3
Linhuai [AH]	44	D3	Lishi [HB]	54	E4	Liujiachang [HB]	54	D4
Linjiang [CQ]	64	E2	Lishu Qu [HL]	36	F5	Liujiagou [SD]	50	G2
Linjiang [FJ]	46	D2	Lishu [JL]	34	D4	Liujiang [GX]	60	G3
Linjiang [JL]	34	F6	Lishugoumen [BJ]	22	E3	Liujiata [SX]	28	C2
Linjiang [JX]	48	C3	Lishui [JS]	40	E4	Liujiaxia Shuiku [GS]	76	G5
Linjin [SX]	28	B6	Lishui [ZJ]	42	C4	Liujiazi [LN]	32	D3
Linkou [HL]	36	F5	Lisui [BJ]	22	D3	Liujing [GX]	60	F5
Linkou [HN]	56	B5	Lita [JX]	48	D4	Liuke [SX]	28	F2
Linli [HN]	56	D2	Litahui [SH]	38	C4	Liukesong [HL]	36	D4
Linnan [SD]	50	C2	Litan He [JX]	48	D4	Liukou [AH]	44	D6
Linnancang [HEB]	26	E4	Litan [HEB]	26	D5	Liukuei [TW]	88	C3
Linpa [HEN]	52	C5	Litang He [SC]	66	D4	Liulihe [BJ]	22	C5
Linping [SN]	74	D6	Litang [CQ]	64	E4	Liulimiao [BJ]	22	D2
Linpu [ZJ]	42	D2	Litang [GX]	60	G4	Liulin [HEN]	52	F6
Linqi [ZJ]	42	C3	Litang [SC]	66	D3	Liulin [SX]	28	B4
Linqing [SD]	50	B3	Liu He [SH]	38	C2	Liulinshui [BJ]	22	B4
Linqu [SD]	50	E3	Liu He [JL]	34	E5	Liulisi [SD]	50	C3
Linquan [AH]	44	B2	Liu He [LN]	32	F2	Liulou [SD]	50	B4
Linru [HEN]	52	D3	Liu Jiang [GX]	60	G4	Liuma [GX]	60	H5
Linshu [SD]	50	E5	Liu'ao [FJ]	46	C6	Liuma [GZ]	68	D5
Linshui [SC]	66	G3	Liuba [GS]	76	G3	Liupan Shan [GS]	76	I5
Lintan [GS]	76	G5	Liuba [SN]	74	B7	Liupan Shan [NX]	80	B5

Liupan Shan [NX]	80	C5	Lizigu [TJ]	24	C4	Longjiang [HI]	62	C2
Liupanshui [GZ]	68	C4	Lizui [GD]	58	G2	Longjiang [HL]	36	B4
Liuqu [SN]	74	E6	Lo Chau pak Pai [HK]	84	D4	Longjiao [CQ]	64	E3
Liuquan [HEN]	52	D3	Lo Kei Wan [HK]	84	B4	Longjiapu [JL]	34	E3
Liusha Gang [GD]	58	A6	Lok Ma Chau [HK]	84	C1	Longjie [GD]	58	F2
Liushahe [HN]	56	E4	Long Shan [SN]	74	B6	Longjing [JL]	34	I5
Liushan [GX]	60	G3	Long He [TJ]	24	A4	Longju [CQ]	64	E3
Liushi [HEB]	26	C5	Long Jiang [GX]	60	F3	Longju [JS]	40	E1
Liushi [JX]	48	A4	Long Jiang [JX]	48	C4	Longkang [AH]	44	C2
Liushi [ZJ]	42	D3	Long Ke [HK]	84	F2	Longkou Gang [SD]	50	G2
Liushi [ZJ]	42	D4	Long Xian [SN]	74	B6	Longkou [HB]	54	F5
Liushipu [AH]	44	B3	Long'an [GX]	60	E4	Longkou [HEN]	52	F5
Liushuhe [JL]	34	G4	Long'an [JX]	48	D4	Longkou [JX]	48	C5
Liushui [JL]	34	D3	Longbang [GX]	60	D5	Longkou [SD]	50	G2
Liushui [SN]	74	D8	Longbo [HI]	62	B2	Longli [GZ]	68	E4
Liushukou [SX]	28	E6	Longbu [JX]	48	C6	Longlin [GX]	60	C3
Liushuquan [XJ]	82	M4	Longchang [SC]	66	F4	Longling [YN]	70	C3
Liusi [JX]	48	D2	Longchang [GZ]	68	D5	Longma [HI]	62	C2
Liutaizhuang [HEB]	26	G4	Longchang [LN]	32	G4	Longmatan Qu [SC]	66	F4
Liutao [JS]	40	E1	Longcheng [HN]	56	B5	Longmen Shan [SC]	66	F2
Liutuan [HL]	36	E5	Longchi [CQ]	64	F5	Longmen Shan [SX]	28	B6
Liuwan Dashan [GX]	60	G5	Longchuan Jiang [YN]	70	C3	Longmen [FJ]	46	D5
Liuxi He [GD]	58	F3	Longchuan [GD]	58	G2	Longmen [GD]	58	A6
Liuyang He [HN]	56	F3	Longchuan [YN]	70	B3	Longmen [GD]	58	F3
Liuyang [HN]	56	F3	Longde [NX]	80	C5	Longmen [GX]	60	G5
Liuyangpu [NX]	80	D3	Longdong [CQ]	64	F3	Longmen [HEN]	52	D3
Liuyuan [SX]	28	E3	Longdu He [HI]	62	C2	Longmen [HI]	62	C2
Liuyuankou [HEN]	52	F3	Longfang [SN]	74	E5	Longmen [HL]	36	D3
Liuzao [SH]	38	E3	Longfeng Qu [HL]	36	C4	Longmen [SC]	66	G3
Liuzhai [AH]	44	B3	Longfeng [HB]	54	B4	Longmen [SN]	74	F5
Liuzhai [GX]	60	E2	Longgan Hu [AH]	44	C6	Longmen [ZJ]	42	C3
Liuzhan [HL]	36	C2	Longgang Shan [JL]	34	E6	Longmengang [GX]	60	F6
Liuzhangzi [LN]	32	B4	Longgang Qu [GD]	58	F4	Longmensuo [HEB]	26	C3
Liuzhao Shan [GX]	60	C4	Longgang Qu [LN]	32	D4	Longmentai [BJ]	22	B4
Liuzhi Tequ [GZ]	68	D4	Longgang [HB]	54	G5	Longming [GX]	60	E5
Liuzhou [GX]	60	G3	Longgang [JL]	34	H6	Longnan [GS]	76	H6
Liuzhuang [SD]	50	C4	Longgang [JX]	48	D5	Longnan [JX]	48	B7
Liwan [HI]	62	B2	Longgang [SD]	50	G2	Longqiao [HI]	62	C2
Liwang [NX]	80	C4	Longgang [ZJ]	42	C2	Longquan Xi [ZJ]	42	C4
Lixi [CQ]	64	E5	Longgu [JS]	40	B1	Longquan [JL]	34	F5
Lixi [HB]	54	E3	Longgu [SD]	50	B4	Longquan [ZJ]	42	C4
Lixi [JX]	48	B2	Longguan [HEB]	26	C3	Longquanguan [HEB]	26	A5
Lixian Jiang [YN]	70	D4	Longguang [HI]	62	B3	Longquanyi Qu [SC]	66	F3
Lixian [BJ]	22	D5	Longgun [HI]	62	C2	Longriba [SC]	66	E2
Lixin [AH]	44	C2	Longhai [FJ]	46	C5	Longsang [GX]	60	D4
Lixin [FJ]	46	B3	Longhe [AH]	44	C4	Longsha [CQ]	64	E3
Lixing [AH]	44	B2	Longhe [CQ]	64	D4	Longshan [AH]	44	C2
Lixi'oidain Co [QH]	78	B3	Longhe [HI]	62	C2	Longshan [FJ]	46	C5
Liyang [JS]	40	E4	Longhe [HL]	36	B1	Longshan [GD]	58	E3
Liyang [SX]	28	E4	Longhekou Shuiku [AH]	44	C4	Longshan [HN]	56	B2
Liyang [ZJ]	42	E3	Longhu [HI]	62	C2	Longshan [SD]	50	D3
Liye [HN]	56	B3	Longhu [JX]	48	D4	Longsheng [GD]	58	D4
Liyi [SX]	28	E6	Longhua [GD]	58	F3	Longsheng [GX]	60	H2
Liyuan [HN]	56	E6	Longhua [HEB]	26	C6	Longsheng [GX]	60	H5
Liyuan [SX]	28	C6	Longhua [HEB]	26	E2	Longshi [CQ]	64	C3
Liyutang [HN]	56	F5	Longhua [SX]	28	C6	Longshi [JX]	48	A5
Lize [SD]	50	D2	Longhui [HN]	56	D4	Longshou Shan [GS]	76	F3
Lizhigou [HI]	62	B3	Longhui [JX]	48	B6	Longshou Shan [NM]	30	C5
Lizhou [SC]	66	E4	Longhuo [GX]	60	C3	Longtan [AH]	44	C3
Lizhuang [AH]	44	C1	Longji [JS]	40	D1	Longtan [CQ]	64	E5
Lizhuang [SD]	50	B4	Longjiang [GD]	58	E4	Longtan [JS]	40	E3
Lizhuangzi [NX]	80	C3	Longjiang [GD]	58	H3	Longtang [HN]	56	D3

Longtang [JX]	48	C7	Luancheng [HEB]	26	B6	Luma [HI]	62	C3
Longtanhe [HN]	56	D2	Luanchuan [HEN]	52	C4	Lumajangdong Co [XZ]	72	C2
Longtanxu [HN]	56	E6	Luannan [HEB]	26	F4	Lunan Shan [SC]	66	E5
Longtian [FJ]	46	E4	Luanping [HEB]	26	E3	Lung Kwu Tan [HK]	84	B2
Longtian [GD]	58	G2	Lubao [GD]	58	D3	Lunggar [XZ]	77	F4
Longtian [GZ]	68	G3	Luchaogang [SH]	38	E4	Lungkwu Chau [HK]	84	A3
Longtou [GX]	60	F3	Lücheng [JS]	40	E4	Lungsang [XZ]	72	G5
Longtou [JX]	48	C7	Lucheng [BJ]	22	C4	Lunhe [HL]	36	D4
Longwan Qu [ZJ]	42	D5	Lucheng [GX]	60	D3	Luntai(Bügür) [XJ]	82	I5
Longwan [AH]	44	C5	Lucheng [SX]	28	E5	Lunzhen [SD]	50	C3
Longwan [GX]	60	F4	Luchu [TW]	88	C4	Luo He [HEN]	52	C3
Longwang [JL]	34	D3	Luchuan [GX]	60	H5	Luo He [SN]	74	D4
Longwangmiao [AH]	44	D2	Lüchun [YN]	70	E4	Luo Hu [HK]	84	D1
Longwangmiao [HL]	36	G5	Lücongpo [HB]	54	C4	Luobei [HL]	36	F4
Longwangmiao [LN]	32	G4	Lucun [SD]	50	E3	Luocheng [GX]	60	F3
Longwen Qu [FJ]	46	C5	Ludao [HL]	36	E6	Luochuan [NX]	80	C4
Longwo [GD]	58	G3	Ludian [HEN]	52	E3	Luochuan [SN]	74	E5
Longxi Shan [FJ]	46	C3	Ludian [YN]	70	E2	Luocun [SD]	50	E3
Longxi [GS]	76	H5	Luding [SC]	66	E4	Luocun [SX]	28	B5
Longxi [GZ]	68	F3	Luen Wo Hui [HK]	84	D1	Luodai [HI]	62	A2
Longxi [JX]	48	D4	Lüeyang [SN]	74	B7	Luodian [GZ]	68	E5
Longxing [GZ]	68	F2	Lufeng [FJ]	46	B5	Luodian [SH]	38	D2
Longxu He [GX]	60	D4	Lufeng [GD]	58	G4	Luoding Jiang [GD]	58	C4
Longyan [FJ]	46	C4	Lufeng [YN]	70	E3	Luoding [GD]	58	C4
Longyan [GX]	60	G4	Lugang [AH]	44	E4	Luodou Sha [GD]	58	B6
Longyangxia Shuiku [QH]	78	G2	Lugouqiao [BJ]	22	C4	Luodou [HI]	62	C2
Longyao [HEB]	26	B6	Lugu Hu [SC]	66	D5	Luofang [FJ]	46	B4
Longyin [CQ]	64	C5	Lugu Hu [YN]	70	D2	Luofang [FJ]	46	C4
Longyou [ZJ]	42	C3	Lugu [SC]	66	E4	Luofang [JX]	48	C4
Longyuanba [JX]	48	B7	Lugu [XZ]	72	E3	Luofu Shan [GD]	58	F3
Longzhai [HN]	56	B2	Luguhu [SC]	66	D5	Luogang Qu [GD]	58	E3
Longzhen [HL]	36	D3	Luguo [JL]	34	I5	Luoguhe [HL]	36	A1
Longzhen [SX]	28	E5	Luhang [SH]	38	E3	Luohe [HEN]	52	F4
Longzhou [GX]	60	D5	Luhe Qu [JS]	40	D3	Luoheya [SD]	50	E4
Longzhou [HI]	62	C2	Luhe [GD]	58	G3	Luoji [AH]	44	C2
Lop Nur [XJ]	82	L5	Luhe [HL]	36	D4	Luoji [AH]	44	D3
Lop [XJ]	82	G7	Luhongshi [HN]	56	D5	Luoji [HB]	54	E3
Loqung [SC]	66	B2	Luhui [SH]	38	D4	Luoji [HI]	62	B2
Lou Shui [HN]	56	C2	Luhuo(Zhaggo) [SC]	66	D3	Luojiang Qu [FJ]	46	D5
Loude [SD]	50	D4	Lüjiacun [BJ]	22	B4	Luojiang [SC]	66	F3
Loudi [HN]	56	D4	Lujiahe [BJ]	22	C2	Luojiawa [HEB]	26	B3
Loufan [SX]	28	C3	Lujiang [AH]	44	D4	Luojing [GD]	58	C4
Lougou [SX]	28	C2	Lujiao [CQ]	64	E4	Luojing [SH]	38	D2
Loushan Guan [GZ]	68	E2	Lujiawan [SX]	28	F1	Luojiu [HN]	56	B4
Loutang [SH]	38	C2	Lujiazhuang [SX]	28	E4	Luokan [YN]	70	F2
Louwang [JS]	40	E2	Lüjing [GS]	76	H5	Luokeng [GD]	58	E2
Louzhuang [AH]	44	D2	Lujing [GX]	60	H5	Luokou [JX]	48	D5
Lower Shing			Lüjuhe [TJ]	24	D6	Luokun [GZ]	68	E5
Mun Reservoir [HK]	84	D3	Luk Chau Wan [HK]	84	D4	Luolong Qu [HEN]	52	D3
Lu He [SN]	74	E3	Luk Chau [HK]	84	D4	Luolong [GZ]	68	F1
Lu Shui [HN]	56	F4	Luk Keng [HK]	84	D1	Luolou [GX]	60	D3
Lu Jing [NM]	30	B4	Lukang [TW]	88	C2	Luolou [SD]	50	B4
Lu Shan [SD]	50	E3	Lukou [JX]	48	B4	Luoma Hu [JS]	40	D1
Lu Shan [SD]	50	E3	Lukoupu [HN]	56	F2	Luonan [SN]	38	D2
Lu Shui [HB]	54	F5	Lukoushe [HN]	56	F3	Luonan [SN]	74	F6
Lu Shui [JX]	48	B4	Lüliang Shan [SX]	28	C5	Luoning [HEN]	52	C3
Lu Tao(Huoshao Tao) [TW]	88	D4	Lüliang [SX]	28	C4	Luoping [CQ]	64	G2
Lu Xian [SC]	66	F4	Luliang [YN]	70	E3	Luoping [YN]	70	F3
Luan He [HEB]	26	E2	Luling Guan [HEN]	52	B3	Luoqiao [FJ]	46	E3
Luan He [HEB]	26	F4	Luling Guan [SN]	74	F6	Luoqing Jiang [GX]	60	G3
Luan Xian [HEB]	26	F4	Lulong [HEB]	26	F4	Luoquanwan [NX]	80	B3
Lu'an [AH]	44	C4	Luluo [HEB]	26	A6	Luorong [GX]	60	G3

Name	Page	Grid
Luoshan [HB]	54	F5
Luoshan [HEN]	52	F5
Luoshe [JS]	40	F4
Luoshi [JX]	48	C4
Luoshuihe [SX]	28	F2
Luotang [JX]	48	B5
Luotian [CQ]	64	E3
Luotian [HB]	54	H4
Luotuo [ZJ]	42	E3
Luotuofangzi [TJ]	24	C5
Luotuoying [LN]	32	D3
Luowa [NX]	80	C4
Luowen [SC]	66	G3
Luowenzao [SX]	28	E1
Luoxi [JX]	48	B2
Luoxiao Shan [HN]	56	F5
Luoxiao Shan [JX]	48	A5
Luoxiu [GX]	60	G3
Luoxu [GX]	60	F4
Luoyan [FJ]	46	C5
Luoyang [GD]	58	E2
Luoyang [HEN]	52	D3
Luoyixi [HN]	56	B3
Luoyuan Wan [FJ]	46	E3
Luoyuan [FJ]	46	E3
Luoyukou [SX]	28	B3
Luoyun [GX]	60	H4
Luoze He [GZ]	68	C3
Luozhuang Qu [SD]	50	E5
Luozhuangzi [TJ]	24	C1
Luozigou [JL]	34	J4
Lüqiao [HEB]	26	E5
Luqiao Qu [ZJ]	42	E4
Luqiao [SD]	50	C4
Luqu [GS]	76	G5
Luquan [HEB]	26	B5
Luquan [YN]	70	E3
Lushan Qu [JX]	48	C2
Lushan [CQ]	64	C3
Lushan [HEN]	52	D4
Lushan [SC]	66	E3
Lushan [TW]	88	D2
Lushi [HEN]	52	C3
Lushui Shuiku [HB]	54	G5
Lushui [HN]	56	F5
Lushui [YN]	70	C3
Lushuihe [JL]	34	G5
Lüshunkou Qu [LN]	32	E6
Lusi Yu [FJ]	46	E4
Lüsigang [JS]	40	G3
Lutao [TW]	88	D4
Lütian [GD]	58	E3
Lutian [JX]	48	D3
Lutun [LN]	32	F4
Lüwang [HB]	54	G3
Luwu [GX]	60	F5
Luxi [YN]	70	C3
Luxi Dao [ZJ]	42	E5
Luxi [HN]	56	C3
Luxi [JX]	48	B4
Luxi [YN]	70	E3
Lüxia [FJ]	46	F3
Luxiang [SH]	38	C4
Luya Shan [SX]	28	C3
Lüyang [LN]	32	E3
Luyang [HN]	56	C4
Lüyangqiao [SH]	38	D3
Luyeh [TW]	88	D4
Luyi [HEN]	52	G4
Luzhai [GX]	60	G3
Luzhen [AH]	44	C4
Lüzhi Jiang [YN]	70	E3
Luzhi [JS]	40	F4
Luzhou [SC]	66	F4
Luzhuangzi [TJ]	24	C2

M

Name	Page	Grid
Ma Liu Shui [HK]	84	D2
Ma On Shan [HK]	84	D2
Ma On Shan [HK]	84	E2
Ma Shi Chau [HK]	84	D2
Ma Tso Lung [HK]	84	C1
Ma Wan [HK]	84	C3
Ma'an [BJ]	22	B4
Ma'anshan [AH]	44	E4
Ma'anshan [JL]	34	E4
Maba [JS]	40	D3
Mabi [SX]	28	D6
Mabian [SC]	66	E4
Mabie He [GZ]	68	C5
Mabu [JX]	48	C4
Mabu [ZJ]	42	D5
Macau [MC]	86	A2
MACAU [MC]	86	B2
Machang Jianhe [TJ]	24	B6
Machang [AH]	44	E3
Machang [GZ]	68	E3
Machang [GZ]	68	E4
Machang [HEB]	26	D5
Machang [SH]	38	E4
Machang [SH]	28	E5
Machangying [BJ]	22	E3
Machebu [ZJ]	42	C2
Macheng [AH]	44	D3
Macheng [HB]	54	H3
Machi [SN]	74	D8
Machuan [NX]	80	B5
Macongzhuang [TJ]	24	D4
Macun Qu [HEN]	52	E2
Macun [HI]	62	C2
Madao [SN]	74	B7
Madaotou [SX]	28	D2
Madeng [YN]	70	C2
Madian [SD]	50	G3
Madian [SD]	50	G3
Madihui [SX]	28	C4
Madiyi [HN]	56	C3
Madoi [QH]	78	E3
Madoi [QH]	78	F3
Madong [GX]	60	H4
Mafang [BJ]	22	E3
Mafang [SX]	28	C3
Mafang [SX]	28	E4
Magang [HB]	54	F5
Magezhuang [SD]	50	F3
Magezhuang [SD]	50	G3
Magu [GZ]	68	C4
Maguan [YN]	70	F4
Magui [GD]	58	C4
Mahai [QH]	78	D1
Mahe [GS]	76	H5
Mahuangshan [NX]	80	D3
Mai Po [HK]	84	C1
Maichen [GD]	58	A6
Maihao [HI]	62	C2
Maiji Qu [GS]	76	H5
Mailing [GX]	60	I2
Mainling [XZ]	72	J5
Maiwang [HB]	54	F4
Maiyuan [FJ]	46	C4
Maizhokunggar [XZ]	72	H5
Maji Shan [JS]	40	F4
Maji [HEN]	52	G5
Maji [JS]	40	D3
Majia He [SD]	50	B3
Majia He [SD]	50	C2
Majiadian [TJ]	24	C3
Majiagang [HL]	36	G5
Majiagang [SH]	38	E2
Majiagaozhuang [NX]	80	C4
Majiahewan [NX]	80	B3
Majian [ZJ]	42	C3
Majiang [GX]	60	I4
Majiang [GZ]	68	F4
Majiang [HN]	56	F5
Majiaqu [NX]	80	C3
Majiatan [NX]	80	C3
Majiawan [NX]	80	B4
Majiawan [NX]	80	C1
Majiazi [LN]	32	C2
Majie [SN]	74	E7
Majie [YN]	70	E3
Majin Xi [ZJ]	42	B3
Majin [ZJ]	42	B3
Majing'ao [HN]	56	B3
Majitang [HN]	56	D3
Majuqiao [BJ]	22	D4
Maliang [HB]	54	D3
Maliangji [AH]	44	C1
Malianjing [GS]	76	C2
Malianjing [GS]	76	F3
Maliantan [NX]	80	C1
Maling Guan [HEB]	26	A6
Maling [GS]	76	I4
Maling [GZ]	68	C5
Maling [JX]	48	C6
Malingguan [SX]	28	E4
Malipo [YN]	70	F4
Malong [YN]	70	E3
Malu [GX]	60	E6
Malu [HN]	56	D3
Malu [SH]	38	C3
Malutang [YN]	70	E2
Mamba [XZ]	72	I4
Man Cheung Po [HK]	84	A4
Man He [HB]	54	E3

Man Kam To [HK]	84	D1
Man Wan [YN]	70	D3
Manas [XJ]	82	J3
Mancheng [HEB]	26	C5
Manchou [TW]	88	C4
Manchuanguan [SN]	74	F7
Manduhu [LN]	32	F3
Mang Kung Uk [HK]	84	E3
Mangdang Shan [HEN]	52	H3
Mangkam Shan [XZ]	72	K4
Mangnai [QH]	78	B1
Mangniu He [LN]	32	E2
Mangshan [HEN]	52	H3
Mangui [NM]	30	H1
Mangzhang [HEN]	52	F5
Manhao [YN]	70	E4
Mani [XZ]	72	F2
Maniao [HI]	62	B2
Maniganggo [SC]	66	C3
Manjiang [JL]	34	G6
Manshuihe [AH]	44	C4
Mantou Shan [SX]	28	D2
Manwan [YN]	70	D3
Manzhouli [NM]	30	G2
Mao Xian [SC]	66	E3
Mao'an [HI]	62	B3
Maoba Gai [CQ]	64	E5
Maoba [GZ]	68	E3
Maoba [HB]	54	B4
Maoba [SN]	74	D8
Maocaojie [HN]	56	E2
Maochang [GZ]	68	E4
Maochengzi [JL]	34	D4
Maocun [FJ]	46	B4
Maocun [JS]	40	C1
Maodao [HI]	62	B3
Maodian [JX]	48	C6
Maodianzi [LN]	32	H4
Maodu [GZ]	68	G2
Mao'er Shan [GX]	60	H2
Maogan [HI]	62	B3
Maogang Qu [GD]	58	C5
Maogang [HN]	56	C2
Maogang [SH]	38	C4
Maogong [GZ]	68	G4
Maoji [HEN]	52	E5
Maojian Qu [HB]	54	C2
Maojiaping [NX]	80	B5
Maojiazao [SX]	28	E2
Maojing [GS]	76	I4
Maokui Shan [LN]	32	G4
Maolan [YN]	70	D3
Maolin [JL]	34	C4
Maomaozhai [GZ]	68	D5
Maoming [GD]	58	B5
Maoniushan [QH]	78	E2
Maoping [GZ]	68	F3
Maoping [HN]	56	B2
Maoping [JX]	48	B4
Maoping [JX]	48	C7
Maopitou [TW]	88	C5
Maoshan [HEB]	26	E3
Maoshan [JX]	48	B7
Maoshi [HN]	56	E5
Maotai [GZ]	68	E3
Maotian [HB]	54	B4
Maotou Yang [ZJ]	42	E4
Maotou Shan [YN]	70	D3
Maoxing [HL]	36	C5
Maoyang [HI]	62	B3
Maoyangtou [FJ]	46	D1
Maozhushan [ZJ]	42	C2
Mapam Yumco [XZ]	72	C4
Mapaochang [CQ]	64	B4
Mapengkou [TJ]	24	C6
Mapengwan [JS]	40	E3
Mapo [BJ]	22	D3
Maqên [QH]	78	G3
Maqên Kangri [QH]	78	F3
Maqiao [HEN]	52	H4
Maqiao [SH]	38	E2
Maqu [GS]	76	G5
Margai Caka [XZ]	72	F2
Margyang [XZ]	72	G5
Markam [XZ]	72	L5
Markit [XJ]	82	E6
Markog He [SC]	66	D2
Marme [XZ]	72	D3
Masha [FJ]	46	C2
Mashan Qu [HL]	36	F5
Mashan [GX]	60	F4
Mashan [GZ]	68	F2
Mashankou [HEN]	52	D4
Mashenqiao [TJ]	24	C1
Mashi [JX]	48	B5
Mashikou [HEB]	26	B3
Matang [HN]	56	F2
Matang [YN]	70	F4
Matian [HN]	56	E5
Matian [SX]	28	E5
Matou [AH]	44	C3
Matou [BJ]	22	E4
Matou [HEB]	26	D6
Matou [SD]	50	E5
Matouying [HEB]	26	F4
Matsu Liehtao [FJ]	46	F3
Matsu Tao [FJ]	46	E3
Mawan Channel [HK]	84	C3
Mawang [CQ]	64	E5
Mawei Qu [FJ]	46	E3
Mawei [GZ]	68	F5
Mawu [CQ]	64	E4
Maxiang [HEN]	52	F5
Maxipu [HN]	56	C3
Mayang [HN]	56	B4
Mayanhe [GS]	76	H5
Mayi He [HL]	36	E5
Mayidui [YN]	70	D3
Maying [QH]	78	H2
Mayouying [LN]	32	E3
Mayum La [XZ]	72	D4
Mazar [XJ]	82	E7
Mazhan [SD]	50	E3
Mazhang Qu [GD]	58	B5
Mazhaozhen [SN]	74	D6
Mazhen [SN]	74	F2
Mazhonghe [LN]	32	H2
Mazhou [JX]	48	C6
Mazhuang [GX]	60	D3
Mazhuang [HEN]	52	F5
Mazong Shan [GS]	76	D2
Mazongshan [GS]	76	D2
Mazongshan [NM]	30	B4
Mêdog [XZ]	72	J5
Mei Jiang [CQ]	64	E5
Mei Jiang [JX]	48	C5
Mei Xian [GD]	58	H2
Mei Xian [SN]	74	C6
Mei'an [HI]	62	C2
Meichang [TJ]	24	B4
Meicheng [HN]	56	D3
Meichi [ZJ]	42	D3
Meichuan [GS]	76	H5
Meichuan [HB]	54	H4
Meigu [SC]	66	E4
Meihekou [JL]	34	E5
Meihua [FJ]	46	E3
Meihua [HN]	56	D6
Meijiang [CQ]	64	F5
Meijie [AH]	44	D5
Meikeng [GD]	58	F2
Meilan [HI]	62	C2
Meilin [AH]	44	F5
Meilin [FJ]	46	C5
Meilin [ZJ]	42	E3
Meilisi Daurzu Qu [HL]	36	B4
Meilong [GD]	58	G4
Meilong [SH]	38	D3
Meiqiao [AH]	44	D2
Meishan Shuiku [AH]	44	B4
Meishan [FJ]	46	D4
Meishan [HN]	62	B3
Meishan [SC]	66	E3
Meishan [ZJ]	42	C1
Meitai [HI]	62	B2
Meitan [GZ]	68	F3
Meitanba [HN]	56	E3
Meitian [HN]	56	E6
Meiting [HI]	62	C2
Meixi He [CQ]	64	F2
Meixi Qu [HL]	36	E4
Meixi [GX]	60	H1
Meixia [HI]	62	B2
Meixian [HN]	56	F3
Meiyu Yang [ZJ]	42	F3
Meiyu [SC]	66	D5
Meiyuan [ZJ]	42	C4
Meizhou Dao [FJ]	46	E4
Meizhou Wan [FJ]	46	E4
Meizhou [FJ]	46	C6
Meizhou [GD]	58	H2
Meizhu [AH]	44	F4
Meizhuang [JX]	48	D3
Melmeg [JL]	34	C2
Meng Shan [SD]	50	D4
Meng Jiang [GX]	60	H3

Meng Jiang [GZ]	68	E5	Miaogoumen [SN]	74	F1	Miyi [SC]	66	E5
Meng'a [YN]	70	C4	Miaoli [TW]	88	C2	Miyun Shuiku [BJ]	22	E2
Mengban [YN]	70	D4	Miaoping [GX]	60	H2	Miyun [BJ]	22	E2
Mengcheng [AH]	44	C2	Miaoqian [SX]	28	C6	Mizhi [SN]	74	F3
Mengcheng [NX]	80	C3	Miaoshou [AH]	44	E5	Mizidian [BJ]	22	E4
Mengcun [HEB]	26	E5	Miaotan [HB]	54	D2	Mochong [GZ]	68	F4
Mengdong He [HN]	56	B2	Miaotang [GZ]	68	F2	Mocun [GD]	58	D3
Menggong [HN]	56	D4	Miaotou [JS]	40	D1	Modao Men [GD]	58	E4
Mengguying [HEB]	26	B2	Miaowan [CQ]	64	F3	Modao Xi [CQ]	64	E3
Menghai [YN]	70	D5	Miaoxi [CQ]	64	E4	Mogan Shan [ZJ]	42	C2
Mengjialou [HB]	54	D2	Miaoxia [HEN]	52	D3	Moguqi [NM]	30	H3
Mengjialou [TJ]	24	C2	Miaoyu [CQ]	64	F3	Mohan [YN]	70	D5
Mengjiang [GX]	60	H4	Miaozhen [SH]	38	D1	Mohe [HL]	36	B1
Mengjiawan [SN]	74	E2	Miaozhuang [TJ]	24	D4	Mohei [YN]	70	D4
Mengjiaxi [HB]	54	E5	Miaozi [HEN]	52	C4	Mohuan [ZJ]	42	C3
Mengjin [HEN]	52	D3	Miaozihu Dao [ZJ]	42	F2	Moincêr [XZ]	72	C4
Mengla [YN]	70	D5	Middle Island			Moindawang [XZ]	72	H6
Menglian [YN]	70	C4	(Tong Po Chau) [HK]	84	D4	Moirigkawagarbo [YN]	70	C1
Menglianggu [SD]	50	E4	Midu [YN]	70	D3	Mojiang [YN]	70	D4
Menglong [YN]	70	D5	Mienhua Yu [TW]	88	E1	Moli Feng [JS]	40	F4
Mengman [YN]	70	D4	Migang Shan [NX]	80	C5	Moling [HEN]	52	F4
Mengmengxi [CQ]	64	E2	Migriggyangzhang Co [QH]	78	B4	Moling [JS]	40	D4
Mengmiao [HEN]	52	F4	Mile [YN]	70	E3	Monan [SX]	28	B7
Mengpeng [YN]	70	D5	Miluo Jiang [HN]	56	F3	Mong Ha [MC]	86	B1
Mengquan [TJ]	24	C2	Miluo [HN]	56	F3	Mong Kok [HK]	84	D3
Mengshan [GX]	60	H3	Min Jiang [SC]	66	F4	Mong Tseung Wai [HK]	84	B1
Mengshantou [ZJ]	42	C4	Min Shan [SC]	66	E2	Monggon Bulag [NM]	30	C5
Mengsheng [YN]	70	C4	Min Jiang [FJ]	46	D3	Monte Ka Ho [MC]	86	D6
Mengtuan [SD]	50	F3	Min Jiang [SC]	66	E2	Mopan Yang [ZJ]	42	F3
Mengwang [YN]	70	D4	Min Xian [GS]	76	H1	Mopanzhang [AH]	44	D2
Mengxi [GZ]	68	G2	Minfeng(Niya) [XJ]	82	H7	Mori [XJ]	82	L4
Mengxi [HN]	56	D2	Minfengchakou [XJ]	82	H6	Morihong Shan [LN]	32	H2
Mengxing [YN]	70	D5	Ming He [HEB]	26	B7	Morin Dawa Qi [NM]	30	I2
Mengyan [GZ]	68	G4	Ming Jiang [GX]	60	E5	Morou Gol [NM]	30	C4
Mengyin [SD]	50	D4	Mingcheng [GD]	58	D4	Morri [XZ]	72	K4
Mengyou [YN]	70	C3	Mingcheng [JL]	34	E4	Morro de Artilharia [MC]	86	B7
Mengyuan [NX]	80	C5	Minggang [HEN]	52	F5	Moshi [HN]	56	C2
Mengzhe [YN]	70	D4	Mingguang [AH]	44	D3	Mosouwan [XJ]	82	J3
Mengzhou [HEN]	52	D3	Mingqian [SX]	28	D4	Mouding [YN]	70	D3
Mengzhu Ling [GX]	60	I3	Mingsha [NX]	80	B3	Mount Parker [HK]	84	D3
Mengzhu Ling [HN]	56	D7	Mingshan [SC]	66	E3	Moxi [JX]	48	C2
Mengzi [YN]	70	E4	Mingshui [GS]	76	D1	Moyang Jiang [GD]	58	C4
Mentougou Qu [BJ]	22	C4	Mingshui [HL]	36	C4	Moye Dao [SD]	50	I3
Menyuan [QH]	78	G2	Mingteke Daban [XJ]	82	D7	Moyu(Karakax) [XJ]	82	F7
Mêwa [SC]	66	E2	Mingteke [XJ]	82	D7	Mozitan Shuiku [AH]	44	C4
Mi He [SD]	50	E3	Mingxi [FJ]	46	C3	Mozitan [AH]	44	C4
Mi Shui [HN]	56	F4	Mingxikou [HN]	56	C3	Mt.Collinson [HK]	84	D4
Miagabma [QH]	78	E4	Mingyin [YN]	70	D2	Mu Us Shadi [SN]	74	E2
Mian Shui [JX]	48	C6	Mingyu [CQ]	64	D4	Mu Us Shadi [NM]	30	D5
Mian Xian [SN]	74	B7	Minhang Qu [SH]	38	D3	Muchang [AH]	44	C4
Miancaowan [QH]	78	F3	Minhang [SH]	38	D4	Muchengjian [BJ]	22	C4
Mianchi [HEN]	52	C3	Minhe [QH]	78	H2	Muchuan [SC]	66	E4
Mianning [SC]	66	E4	Minhou [FJ]	46	E3	Mudan Ling [JL]	34	G4
Mianshan [SC]	66	E4	Minjiang Kou [FJ]	46	E3	Mudan Jiang [HL]	36	E5
Mianyang [SC]	66	F3	Minle [GS]	76	F3	Mudan Jiang [JL]	34	H4
Mianzhu [SC]	66	F3	Minqin [GS]	76	G3	Mudan Ling [JL]	34	G4
Miao Ling [GZ]	68	F4	Minqing [FJ]	46	D3	Mudanjiang [HL]	36	E5
Miao Dao [SD]	50	G2	Minquan [HEN]	52	G3	Mufu Shan [HN]	56	F3
Miaoba [CQ]	64	E2	Minxiao [GZ]	68	G3	Mufu Shan [JX]	48	B2
Miaodao Qundao [SD]	50	G2	Mishan [HL]	36	F5	Mufu [HB]	54	B4
Miao'ergou [XJ]	82	H3	Mishi [HB]	54	E4	Mug Qu [QH]	78	C4
Miaofeng Shan [BJ]	22	C3	Mishidu [SH]	38	C4	Mugquka [QH]	78	C3

Mui Wo [HK] 84 B3
Mujiaba [SN] 74 C8
Mula [SC] 66 D4
Mulan Xi [FJ] 46 D4
Mulan [HI] 62 C1
Mulan [HL] 36 E5
Mule [GX] 60 H4
Muli [SC] 66 D5
Mulin [BJ] 22 E3
Muling Guan [SD] 50 E3
Muling He [HL] 36 G5
Muling [HL] 36 F5
Muling [HL] 36 F5
Muping Qu [SD] 50 H2
Muqi [LN] 32 H3
Muri [QH] 78 F1
Muri [QH] 78 G2
Mushihe [JL] 34 F3
Mutang [HI] 62 B2
Mutoudeng [HEB] 26 G3
Muyang [FJ] 46 E2
Muyu Shuiku [SD] 50 G2
Muyu [HB] 54 C3
Muz Tag [XJ] 82 G7
Muz Tag [XZ] 72 F1
Muzhen [AH] 44 D5
Muzidian [HB] 54 H3
Muztag Feng [XJ] 82 J7
Muztagata Shan [XJ] 82 D6
Myaglo [SC] 66 E3

N

Nabi [GX] 60 C3
Nafu [GD] 58 D4
Nag Qu [XZ] 72 I4
Nagarzê [XZ] 72 H5
Nagjog [XZ] 72 K4
Nagqu [XZ] 72 I4
Nahuo [GD] 58 C5
Naij Gol [QH] 78 C2
Naij Tal [QH] 78 D3
Naiman Qi [NM] 30 H4
Naimin Bulak [XJ] 82 L3
Najin [JL] 34 B2
Nalao [GX] 60 C3
Nali [GX] 60 F6
Naling [GX] 60 E5
Nam Co [XZ] 72 H4
Nam She Tsim [HK] 84 F2
Nam Tam [HK] 84 C4
Nam Tong [HK] 84 E4
Nam Van Lake [MC] 86 A2
Namarqê [XZ] 72 H4
Namjagbarwa Feng [XZ] 72 J5
Namling [XZ] 72 G5
Namsê La [XZ] 72 D5
Nan He [CQ] 64 E2
Nan He [HB] 54 D2
Nan Hulsan Hu [QH] 78 D2
Nan Jiang [SC] 66 G2
Nan Ling [HN] 56 E6
Nan Ling [GD] 58 D1

Nan Ling [GX] 60 H2
Nan Tuo [SX] 28 E3
Nan Xian [HN] 56 E2
Nan'an Qu [CQ] 64 C4
Nan'an [FJ] 46 D5
Nanan [GX] 60 E6
Nan'an [YN] 70 E1
Nan'ao [GD] 58 I3
Nanao [TW] 88 D2
Nanbao [HI] 62 B2
Nanbao [HI] 62 B2
Nanbaxian [QH] 78 D2
Nanbeihe [HL] 36 D3
Nanbu [HEB] 26 F4
Nanbu [HEB] 26 F4
Nanbu [SC] 66 G3
Nanbu [SH] 38 D2
Nanbuzi [SX] 28 C2
Nancai [BJ] 22 D3
Nancaicun [TJ] 24 B4
Nancha Qu [HL] 36 E4
Nanchang [JX] 48 C3
Nanchang [JX] 48 C3
Nanchangshan Dao [SD] 50 G2
Nanchangtan [NX] 80 A3
Nancheng [JX] 48 D4
Nanchong [SC] 66 G3
Nanchuan Qu [CQ] 64 D4
Nancun [HEN] 52 C2
Nancun [HEN] 52 E2
Nancun [SD] 50 G3
Nandahongmen [BJ] 22 D4
Nandan [GX] 60 E3
Nandashan [HN] 56 E2
Nanding He [YN] 70 C4
Nanding Tao [FJ] 46 D5
Nanding [SD] 50 E3
Nandu Jiang [HI] 62 B2
Nandu [GX] 60 H5
Nandulehe [BJ] 22 E3
Nanfen Qu [LN] 32 G3
Nanfeng [GD] 58 C3
Nanfeng [HEN] 52 G4
Nanfeng [HI] 62 B2
Nanfeng [JX] 48 D2
Nanfeng [JX] 48 D4
Nanfengmian [JX] 48 B5
Nanfu Shuiku [HI] 62 C2
Nang Xian [XZ] 72 I5
Nangangwa [BJ] 22 C4
Nangdo [QH] 78 H2
Nangezhuang [BJ] 22 D5
Nangong [HEB] 26 C6
Nangou [JL] 34 H4
Nangou [SX] 28 C7
Nangqên [QH] 78 E4
Nanguan Dao [ZJ] 42 D5
Nanguan [HEB] 26 D2
Nanguan [SX] 28 C5
Nanguan [SX] 28 D4
Nanguancun [BJ] 22 C4
Nangunlonggou [HEB] 26 A5

Nangushanzi [LN] 32 H3
Nanguzhuang [SD] 50 E5
Nanhai Qu [GD] 58 E3
Nanhe [HEB] 26 B6
Nanhe [SD] 50 E2
Nanhedian [HEN] 52 D4
Nanheng Yinhe [SH] 38 D1
Nanhsiao Tao [TW] 88 F1
Nanhu Tashan [TW] 88 D2
Nanhu [XJ] 82 M4
Nanhua [YN] 70 D3
Nanhuangcheng Dao [SD] 50 G1
Nanhui Qu [SH] 38 E4
Nanjia [GZ] 68 G4
Nanjian [YN] 70 D3
Nanjiang [SC] 66 G2
Nanjiangkou [GD] 58 C3
Nanjiangu [TJ] 24 D4
Nanjiao Qu [SX] 28 E1
Nanjiao [BJ] 22 C4
Nanjiazhuang [TJ] 24 D2
Nanjing [FJ] 46 C5
Nanjing [JS] 40 D3
Nanjing [JX] 48 B7
Nanjishan Liedao [ZJ] 42 E5
Nanka Jiang [YN] 70 C4
Nankai [GZ] 68 C4
Nankai [HI] 62 B2
Nankang [JX] 48 B6
Nankeng [JX] 48 A4
Nankou [BJ] 22 C3
Nankouqian [LN] 32 H3
Nankun [HI] 62 B2
Nanlan He [YN] 70 C5
Nanle [HEN] 52 G1
Nanlei He [YN] 70 C4
Nanliang [SX] 28 C6
Nanlin [HI] 62 B3
Nanling [AH] 44 E5
Nanliu Jiang [GX] 60 G5
Nanlou Shan [JL] 34 F4
Nanlü [HI] 62 C2
Nanluji [SD] 50 B4
Nanluo [HI] 62 A2
Nanma [ZJ] 42 D3
Nanmiao [JX] 48 B4
Nanming He [GZ] 68 E4
Nanmujiayu [BJ] 22 E2
Nanning [GX] 60 F5
Nanniwan [SN] 74 E4
Nanpan Jiang [GX] 60 B3
Nanpan Jiang [GZ] 68 C6
Nanpan Jiang [YN] 70 E3
Nanpeng Dao [GD] 58 D5
Nanpeng Liedao [GD] 58 I3
Nanpi [HEB] 26 D5
Nanpiao Qu [LN] 32 D3
Nanping [CQ] 64 C4
Nanping [FJ] 46 D3
Nanping [HI] 62 C3
Nanping [HN] 56 C1
Nanping [YN] 70 F4

Name	Page	Grid		Name	Page	Grid		Name	Page	Grid
Nanpu Xi [FJ]	46	D2		Nanyue Qu [HN]	56	E4		Nianyuxu [HN]	56	E2
Nanqiao [HI]	62	C3		Nanzamu [LN]	32	H3		Nianzhuang [JS]	40	C1
Nanqiao [JX]	48	C7		Nanzhang [HB]	54	D3		Nianzi [BJ]	22	D1
Nanquan [SD]	50	G3		Nanzhang [SX]	28	B6		Nianzishan Qu [HL]	36	B4
Nanri Dao [FJ]	46	E4		Nanzhao [AH]	44	C3		Niao Yu [TW]	88	B3
Nanri Qundao [FJ]	46	E4		Nanzhao [HEN]	52	D4		Nicheng [SH]	38	E4
Nansan Dao [GD]	58	B5		Nanzheng [BJ]	22	C5		Nihe [AH]	44	D4
Nansha Qu [GD]	58	E4		Nanzheng [SN]	74	B7		Nijiao [YN]	70	E3
Nansha Qundao [HI]	62	F6		Nanzhuang [SX]	28	E3		Nilka [XJ]	82	H4
Nanshahe [SD]	50	D4		Naodehai Shuiku [LN]	32	F2		Nim Wan [HK]	84	B2
Nanshan Qu [GD]	58	E4		Naodehai Shuiku [NM]	30	H4		Ninepin Group		
Nanshan [HI]	62	B3		Naoli He [HL]	36	G4		(Tung Kwo Chau) [HK]	84	F4
Nanshancun [BJ]	22	E3		Naomaohu [XJ]	82	N4		Ning Xian [GS]	76	I5
Nanshangle [BJ]	22	B5		Naozhou Dao [GD]	58	B6		Ning'an [HL]	36	E5
Nanshankou [QH]	78	D2		Naozhou [GD]	58	B6		Ningbo [ZJ]	42	E3
Nanshao [GZ]	68	G4		Napo [GX]	60	C4		Ningchegu [TJ]	24	D5
Nansheng [FJ]	46	C5		Narhong [JL]	34	F5		Ningcheng [NM]	30	G4
Nanshi Dao [HI]	62	D2		Narin Bulag [NM]	30	F3		Ningde [FJ]	46	E3
Nanshi [HN]	56	E6		Narin Gol [QH]	78	C2		Ningdu [JX]	48	D5
Nanshuang Dao [FJ]	46	F3		Nasa [YN]	70	F4		Ning'er [YN]	70	D4
Nanshui [GD]	58	E4		Natong [GX]	60	E4		Ninggu [SX]	28	D4
Nantang [JX]	48	C5		Naxi Qu [SC]	66	F4		Ningguo [AH]	44	E5
Nantianmen [BJ]	22	D2		Nayong [GZ]	68	D4		Ninghai [ZJ]	42	E3
Nantong [JS]	40	F3		Nazuo [GX]	60	C3		Ninghe [TJ]	24	D4
Nantonggang [JS]	40	F3		Nêdong [XZ]	72	H5		Ninghua [FJ]	46	B3
Nantou [TW]	88	C3		Needle Hill [HK]	84	D2		Ningjin [HEB]	26	B6
Nantuo [HEB]	26	A5		Nehe [HL]	36	C3		Ningjin [SD]	50	C2
Nanwan Shuiku [HEN]	52	E5		Nei Gang				Ninglang [YN]	70	D2
Nanwan [TW]	88	C5		(Inner Harbour) [MC]	86	A2		Ningling [HEN]	52	G3
Nanwang [SD]	50	C4		Neihuang [HEN]	52	F2		Ningming [GX]	60	E5
Nanwangping [TJ]	24	B4		Neijiang [SC]	66	F4		Ningqiang [SN]	74	B8
Nanwei Tan [GD]	58	G6		Neiliang [JX]	48	B6		Ningshan [SN]	74	D7
Nanweiquan [SX]	28	E5		Neipu [TW]	88	C4		Ningwu [SX]	28	D2
Nanxi He [YN]	70	E4		Neiqiu [HEB]	26	B6		Ningxiang [HN]	56	E3
Nanxi [AH]	44	B4		Neiwan [TW]	88	D2		Ningyang [SD]	50	C4
Nanxi [CQ]	64	E2		Neixiang [HEN]	52	C4		Ningyuan He [HI]	62	B3
Nanxi [HEN]	52	F3		Nemor He [HL]	36	C3		Ningyuan [HN]	56	D6
Nanxi [SC]	66	F4		Nen Jiang [HL]	36	C3		Ninnan [SC]	66	E5
Nanxiang [GX]	60	G5		Nen Jiang [JL]	34	C1		Niqiu [AH]	44	B2
Nanxiang [GX]	60	I3		Nen Jiang [NM]	30	I2		Niubaotun [BJ]	22	D4
Nanxiang [SH]	38	D3		Nenhuangji [HEN]	52	F3		Niubiziliang [QH]	78	C1
Nanxiao [GX]	60	F5		Nenjiang [HL]	36	C3		Niuchang [GZ]	68	F4
Nanxin [SD]	50	D4		NEW TERRITORIES [HK]	84	C2		Niuchehe [HN]	56	C2
Nanxing [SN]	74	B7		Ngamring [XZ]	72	F5		Niudaokou [TJ]	24	C2
Nanxiong [GD]	58	F1		Ngangla Ringco [XZ]	72	D4		Niu'erhe [NM]	30	H2
Nanxun Qu [ZJ]	42	D2		Nganglong Kangri [XZ]	72	C3		Niujiapai [TJ]	24	C3
Nanya [FJ]	46	D3		Ngangzi Co [XZ]	72	F4		Niukong [YN]	70	E4
Nanya [HI]	62	A3		Ngau Tam Mei [HK]	84	C2		Niulou [HI]	62	C3
Nanyandang Shan [ZJ]	42	D5		Ngau Tau Kok [HK]	84	D3		Niululing Shuiku [HI]	62	C3
Nanyang He [HEB]	26	B3		Ngola Shan [QH]	78	F2		Niumaowu [LN]	32	H4
Nanyang He [SX]	28	F1		Ngola Shankou [QH]	78	F3		Niupeng [GZ]	68	B3
Nanyang Hu [SD]	50	C4		Ngom Qu [XZ]	72	K4		Niupeng [SH]	38	E2
Nanyang [FJ]	46	E2		Ngong Ping [HK]	84	B4		Niupenyu [BJ]	22	D2
Nanyang [HB]	54	C3		Ngoring Hu [QH]	78	E3		Niuqitou [FJ]	46	C5
Nanyang [HEN]	52	D4		Ngoring [QH]	78	E3		Niushan [BJ]	22	D3
Nanyang [I II]	62	C2		Ngtung River [HK]	84	D1		Niushou Shan [NX]	80	C3
Nanyang [JS]	40	F2		Ni He [HEN]	52	F4		Niutian [JX]	48	C4
Nanyi Hu [AH]	44	F4		Nianbadu [ZJ]	42	B4		Niutou Shan		
Nanyi [SD]	50	D4		Niangniangmiao [LN]	32	D4		(Nantian Dao) [ZJ]	42	F3
Nanying [HEB]	26	A5		Niangziguan [SX]	28	E4		Niutoudian [SN]	74	E8
Nanyu [FJ]	46	E4		Nianjiagang [AH]	44	D3		Niutoushan [AH]	44	D5
Nanyuan [ZJ]	42	C5		Nianyushan [JX]	48	E2		Niutoushan [AH]	44	F4

Niutun [HEN] 52 F2
Niuweizhuang [SX] 28 D3
Niuzhuang [LN] 32 F4
Niuzhuang [SD] 50 F2
Niya He [XJ] 82 H7
Niyu Shan [ZJ] 42 D5
Nomhon He [QH] 78 E2
Nomhon [QH] 78 E2
Nong'an [JL] 34 E3
Nongche [HN] 56 B2
Noqilek [XJ] 82 I7
North Channel
(Tai Chek Mun) [HK] 84 E1
North Point [HK] 84 D3
Norzagabma [QH] 78 D3
Nu Shan [YN] 70 C2
Nu Jiang [YN] 70 C2
Nu Jiang [XZ] 72 J4
Nuanquan [NX] 80 C2
Nuanshui [JX] 48 E3
Nü'er He [LN] 32 D4
Nü'erhe [LN] 32 E3
Nulan Jiang [YN] 70 E2
Nulu'erhu Shan [LN] 32 C3
Nuomin He [NM] 30 H2
Nuomin [NM] 30 H2
Nuozu [YN] 70 E3
Nur [XJ] 82 G7
Nüshan Hu [AH] 44 E3
Nyainboyuzê Feng [QH] 78 G4
Nyainlung [SC] 66 D2
Nyainqêntanglha Shan [XZ] 72 H4
Nyainqêntanglha Feng [XZ] 72 H4
Nyainrong [XZ] 72 I3
Nyalam [XZ] 72 E5
Nyêmo [XZ] 72 H5
Nyidoi [SC] 66 C2
Nyikog Qu [SC] 66 C2
Nyima [XZ] 72 F4
Nyingchi [XZ] 72 J5
Nyingchi [XZ] 72 J5
Nyixar [YN] 70 C1

O

Obo liang [QH] 78 C1
Obo [QH] 78 G2
Olji [NM] 30 D4
Oluanpi [TW] 88 C5
Oma [XZ] 72 D3
Omon Gol [NM] 30 C4
Ongniud Qi [NM] 30 G4
Ongt Gol [NM] 30 C4
Onor [NM] 30 H2
Onqin Daga Shadi [NM] 30 F4
Orba Co [XZ] 72 C2
Ordos [NM] 30 E5
Oroqen Qi [NM] 30 H2
Otog Qi [NM] 30 E5
Otog Qianqi [NM] 30 D5
Ou Jiang [ZJ] 42 D4
Ou Shui [HN] 56 F6
Ouchikou [HB] 54 E5

Oudian [HB] 54 D3
Oudong [GX] 60 F3
Ouhai Qu [ZJ] 42 D5
Oupu [HL] 36 D1
Outer Harbour [MC] 86 B2
Ouyanghai Shuiku [HN] 56 E5

P

Pa Tau Kwu [HK] 84 C3
Pagri [XZ] 72 G6
Pahsien [TW] 88 D2
Paibi [HN] 56 B3
Paibu [JX] 48 B3
Paikü Co [XZ] 72 E5
Pailou [AH] 44 D5
Pailou'ao [HN] 56 B4
Paipu [HI] 62 B2
Paisha Tao [TW] 88 B3
Paishang [JX] 48 A4
Pak Shek Kok [HK] 84 D2
Pak Tai To Yan [HK] 84 D2
Pak Tam [HK] 84 E2
Paleng [TW] 88 D2
Pali [TW] 88 D1
Pamir [XJ] 82 D7
Pan Shan [TJ] 24 C1
Pan Xian [GZ] 68 C5
Pan'an [ZJ] 42 D3
Pandian [SD] 50 C3
Panggezhuang [TJ] 24 B2
Pangjiabu [HEB] 26 C3
Pangu He [HL] 36 C1
Pangu [HL] 36 B1
Pangushan [JX] 48 C6
Panji Qu [AH] 44 C3
Panjiakou Shuiku [HEB] 26 F3
Panjiapu [NX] 80 C4
Panjiasha [SH] 38 D2
Panjin [LN] 32 F3
Panlong Jiang [YN] 70 F4
Panlong [GZ] 68 D4
Panlong [SH] 38 D2
Panlong [SN] 74 E4
Panlong [SX] 28 E5
Panshan [TJ] 32 F3
Panshi [JL] 34 F5
Panshi [SH] 38 E2
Panshui [GZ] 68 E3
Pantang [SN] 74 F2
Panxi [YN] 70 E3
Panyu Qu [GD] 58 E4
Panzhihua [SC] 66 D5
Panzhuang [TJ] 24 C4
Paozi [LN] 32 F2
Parlung Zangbo [XZ] 72 J5
Parongsi [SC] 66 B2
Paryang [XZ] 72 D4
Pat Heung [HK] 84 C2
Peaked Hill
(Kai Yet Kok) [HK] 84 A4
Pearl Island [HK] 84 B3
Pêdo La [XZ] 72 D5

Pei Xian [JS] 40 B1
Peicheng [HEN] 52 E4
Peichiang His [TW] 88 C3
Peijiachuankou [SX] 28 B3
Peikantang Tao [FJ] 46 F3
Peimen [TW] 88 C3
Peinan Chushan [TW] 88 C3
Peinan His [TW] 88 D4
Peihsiao Tao [TW] 88 F1
Peitawu Shan [TW] 88 C4
Peiwei [JS] 40 D2
Peng Chau [HK] 84 C3
Peng'an [SC] 66 G3
Pengbu [NX] 80 C4
Pengchia Yu [TW] 88 E1
Pengdian [HEN] 52 F3
Penghu Liehtao [TW] 88 B3
Penghu Shuitao [TW] 88 B3
Penghu Tao [TW] 88 B3
Penghu [FJ] 46 D4
Penghu [TW] 88 B3
Pengji [SD] 50 C4
Pengkou [FJ] 46 B4
Penglai [HI] 62 C2
Penglai [SD] 50 G2
Pengshan [SC] 66 E3
Pengshi [HN] 56 F5
Pengshui [CQ] 64 E4
Pengxi [SC] 66 F3
Pengxi [ZJ] 42 D5
Pengyang [NX] 80 C5
Pengze [JX] 48 D2
Pengzha [GZ] 68 C6
Pengzhou [SC] 66 E3
Penny's Bay [HK] 84 C3
Pi He [AH] 44 C3
Pi Shan [ZJ] 42 E4
Pi Xian [SC] 66 E3
Pianguan He [SX] 28 C2
Pianguan [SX] 28 C2
Pianliang [SX] 28 E2
Pianling [LN] 32 G3
Pianling [LN] 32 G4
Pianma [YN] 70 C2
Pianqiao [SN] 74 E5
Piaohe [JL] 34 G4
Piaojing [GZ] 68 D3
Piaoli [GX] 60 G2
Piaomiao Feng [JS] 40 F4
Picheng [JS] 40 E3
Picnic Bay [HK] 84 D4
Pihe Zongganqu [AH] 44 C4
Pihe [JL] 34 G4
Pikou [LN] 32 F5
Pillar Point [HK] 84 B3
Pin'anpu [LN] 32 H1
Ping Chau [HK] 84 F1
Ping Che [HK] 84 D1
Ping Dao (Pingshan Dao) 40 E1
Ping Dao (Pingshan Dao) 50 F4
Ping Jiang [JX] 48 C3
Ping Shan [HK] 84 C2

Ping Xi [HN]	56	C4
Ping'an [JL]	34	B2
Ping'an [JL]	34	G3
Ping'an [NM]	30	H2
Ping'an [QH]	78	H2
Ping'ancheng [HEB]	26	E3
Pingba [CQ]	64	E1
Pingba [GZ]	68	E4
Pingba [HB]	54	F3
Pingbian [YN]	70	E4
Pingchang [SC]	66	G3
Pingchao [JS]	40	F3
Pingcheng [SX]	28	E6
Pingchuan Qu [GS]	76	H4
Pingchuan [SC]	66	D5
Pingcun [ZJ]	42	B3
Pingdeng [GX]	60	G1
Pingdi [GZ]	68	C4
Pingdijie [SC]	66	D5
Pingding Shan [HL]	36	E4
Pingding [GD]	58	B4
Pingding [SX]	28	E4
Pingdingpu [LN]	32	G2
Pingdingshan [HEN]	52	E4
Pingdu [SD]	50	F3
Pingfang Qu [HL]	36	D5
Pingfeng [NX]	80	B5
Pingfu [GX]	60	E5
Pinggang [GD]	58	C5
Pinggang [LN]	32	H2
Pinggu Qu [BJ]	22	E3
Pingguo [GX]	60	E4
Pinghai [FJ]	46	E4
Pinghai [GD]	58	F4
Pinghe [FJ]	46	C5
Pinghu [GD]	58	F4
Pinghu [ZJ]	42	E2
Pingjiang [HN]	56	F3
Pingjiatuan [BJ]	22	D3
Pingjing Guan [HB]	54	F3
Pingjing Guan [HEN]	52	E6
Pingjipu [NX]	80	C2
Pingkai [CQ]	64	E5
Pingkou [HN]	56	D3
Pingle [GX]	60	H3
Pingli [SN]	74	E8
Pingliang [GS]	76	I5
Pinglin [TW]	88	D2
Pingling [GD]	58	F3
Pinglu Qu [SX]	28	D2
Pinglu [SX]	28	C7
Pinglucheng [SX]	28	D2
Pingluo [NX]	80	C2
Pingmeng [GX]	60	C5
Pingmu [SN]	74	C6
Pingnan [FJ]	46	D3
Pingnan [GX]	60	H4
Pingqiao Qu [HEN]	52	F5
Pingquan [HEB]	26	F2
Pingshan [GX]	60	E5
Pingshan [HEB]	26	B5
Pingshan [SC]	66	F4

Pingshe [SX]	28	D3
Pingshi [GD]	58	E1
Pingshi [JX]	48	C6
Pingshui [HB]	54	C3
Pingshui [HN]	56	F5
Pingshun [SX]	28	E5
Pingsong [SX]	28	E4
Pingtan [FJ]	46	E4
Pingtan [GD]	58	F3
Pingtang [GX]	60	G4
Pingtang [GZ]	68	F5
Pingtou [SN]	74	B6
Pingtou [SX]	28	D4
Pingtung [TW]	88	C4
Pingwang [JS]	40	F5
Pingwu [SC]	66	F2
Pingxiang [GX]	60	D5
Pingxiang [HEB]	26	C6
Pingxiang [JX]	48	A4
Pingxifu [BJ]	22	D3
Pingxing Guan [SX]	28	E2
Pingyang [HEB]	26	B5
Pingyang [HL]	36	B4
Pingyang [ZJ]	42	D5
Pingyangkeng [ZJ]	42	D5
Pingyao [SX]	28	D4
Pingyi [SD]	50	D4
Pingyin [SD]	50	C3
Pingyong [GZ]	68	G4
Pingyu [BJ]	22	B4
Pingyu [HEN]	52	F5
Pingyuan [GD]	58	G2
Pingyuan [SD]	50	C2
Pipa Dingzi [JL]	34	H4
Pishan(Guma) [XJ]	82	F7
Pizhou [JS]	40	C1
Plover Cove Reservoir [HK]	84	E2
Po Hu [AH]	44	C5
Po Toi Islands [HK]	84	E4
Po Toi [HK]	84	E4
Pohong [GX]	60	D4
Pojiao [GZ]	68	D6
Pojie [GX]	60	E2
Pok Fu Lam [HK]	84	D3
Poli [SD]	50	F4
Poliang [AH]	44	C5
Pondo [XZ]	72	H4
Port Island (Chek Chau) [HK]	84	F1
Port Shelter (Ngau Mei Hoi) [HK]	84	E3
Potou Qu [GD]	58	B5
Potou [HEN]	52	D3
Poyang Hu [JX]	48	D2
Poyang [JX]	48	D2
Pozao [GX]	60	E4
Pozhai [HI]	62	C2
Pozi [SD]	50	F3
Praia de Nossa Senhora da Esperança [MC]	86	C4
Pu He [GS]	76	I4
Pu He [HEB]	26	F3

Pu Xian [SX]	28	C5
Pu'an [GZ]	68	C5
Pubei [GX]	60	G5
Puchang [GZ]	68	F3
Pucheng [FJ]	46	D2
Pucheng [SN]	74	E6
Puding [GZ]	68	D4
Püdog Zangbo [XZ]	72	E4
Pudong Xinqu [SH]	38	D3
Pudu He [YN]	70	E3
Pu'er [YN]	70	D4
Pu'erdu [YN]	70	F1
Puge [SC]	66	E5
Puhe [CQ]	64	C5
Pui O Wan [HK]	84	B4
Puji [HB]	54	E5
Puji [HN]	56	F4
Pujiang [SC]	66	E3
Pujiang [ZJ]	42	C3
Pujue [GZ]	68	G3
Pukou Qu [JS]	40	D3
Pukou [FJ]	46	E3
Pulandian Wan [LN]	32	E5
Pulandian [LN]	32	E5
Puli [TW]	88	C3
Pulianji [SD]	50	B5
Pulu [XJ]	82	G7
Puluo [GX]	60	F2
Puma Yumco [XZ]	72	H5
Puming [SX]	28	C3
Püncogling [XZ]	72	G5
Puning [GD]	58	H3
Pupeng [YN]	70	D3
Puping [GZ]	68	D5
Puqian [HI]	62	C1
Pushang [FJ]	46	C3
Pushang [SD]	50	F3
Putai [TW]	88	C3
Putaohua [HL]	36	C5
Putaoyuan [GS]	76	I5
Putian [FJ]	46	D4
Putuo Qu [SH]	38	D3
Putuo Qu [ZJ]	42	F3
Putuo Shan [ZJ]	42	F2
Puwa [BJ]	22	B4
Puwei [SC]	66	D5
Puwen [YN]	70	D4
Puyang Jiang [ZJ]	42	D3
Puyang [HEN]	52	F2
Puyang [HEN]	52	G2
Puyang [ZJ]	42	D3
Puyi [GZ]	68	D3
Puyuan [ZJ]	42	D2
Puzhang [SX]	28	D6
Puzi [CQ]	64	D4
Puzi [GD]	58	B5
Puzijiao [HN]	56	B5

Q

Qabnag [XZ]	72	J5
Qagan Hua [JL]	34	D3
Qagan Nur [JL]	34	D2

Qagan Nur [NM]	30	F4	Qiankou [HEN]	52	G1	Qidaohe [BJ]	22	D1
Qagan Nur [NM]	30	F4	Qianli Gang [ZJ]	42	B3	Qidong [HN]	56	E5
Qagan Obo [NM]	30	E3	Qianli Yan [SD]	50	H3	Qidong [JS]	40	G4
Qagan Us He [QH]	78	F2	Qianliu [YN]	70	D4	Qidun [SX]	28	D2
Qagca [SC]	66	C2	Qianmiqiao [TJ]	24	C6	Qiemo(Qarqan) [XJ]	82	I6
Qahar Youyi Qianqi [NM]	30	F4	Qianqi [FJ]	46	F2	Qiezihe Qu [HL]	36	F5
Qahar Youyi Houqi [NM]	30	F4	Qianqiao [SH]	38	D4	Qifanggang [HB]	54	E2
Qahar Youyi Zhongqi [NM]	30	F4	Qianqihao [JL]	34	C3	Qifengcha [BJ]	22	D2
Qaidam Pendi [QH]	78	C1	Qianqiu Guan [AH]	44	F5	Qifengdu [HN]	56	F6
Qaidam Shan [QH]	78	D1	Qianqiu Guan [ZJ]	42	C2	Qigong [JX]	48	E3
Qaidam He [QH]	78	E2	Qianqiu [JS]	40	F2	Qihe [SD]	50	C3
Qamalung [QH]	78	F3	Qianshan Qu [LN]	32	F3	Qiji [HEB]	26	C6
Qamdo [XZ]	72	K4	Qianshan Shuidao [MC]	86	A1	Qijia [HEB]	26	F2
Qamdün [XZ]	72	L4	Qianshan [AH]	44	C5	Qijia [JL]	34	E4
Qammê [SC]	66	E2	Qianshanlaoba [XJ]	82	I3	Qijiahe [HN]	56	D2
Qangdoi [XZ]	72	C3	Qiansuo [LN]	32	C4	Qijiahe [SX]	28	C7
Qangma [XZ]	72	H4	Qiansuo [YN]	70	D3	Qijiang [CQ]	64	C4
Qapqal [XJ]	82	G4	Qiantang Jiang [ZJ]	42	D2	Qijiaojing [XJ]	82	L4
Qarak [XJ]	82	E6	Qianwei [LN]	32	D4	Qijiazhuang [BJ]	22	B4
Qarhan [QH]	78	D2	Qianwei [SC]	66	E4	Qikou [HEB]	26	E5
Qarqan He [XJ]	82	I6	Qianwei [SH]	38	E2	Qikou [SX]	28	B4
Qarqi [XJ]	82	G5	Qianxi [GZ]	68	E3	Qilaotu Shan [HEB]	26	F2
Qarqi [XJ]	82	I5	Qianxi [HEB]	26	F3	Qilian Shan [GS]	76	D3
Qarsan [NM]	30	H3	Qianxu [SH]	38	C5	Qilian Shan [GS]	76	E3
Qayü [XZ]	72	I5	Qianyang [FJ]	46	D2	Qilian Shan [QH]	78	F1
Qhagan Nur [HEB]	26	A2	Qianyang [SN]	74	C6	Qilian [QH]	78	G1
Qi He [HEN]	52	C4	Qianyao [JS]	40	D2	Qilihe [LN]	32	E3
Qi Jiang [CQ]	64	C4	Qianyou He [SN]	74	E7	Qiling [FJ]	46	C5
Qi Shan [SN]	74	C6	Qianzhai [SX]	28	D2	Qiliping [HB]	54	G3
Qi Shui [HB]	54	H4	Qianzhou [HN]	56	B3	Qiman Tag [QH]	78	B2
Qi Xian [HEN]	52	F2	Qiaocun [SX]	28	D2	Qiman Tag [XJ]	82	L7
Qi Xian [HEN]	52	F3	Qiaodong [JX]	48	C3	Qiman [XJ]	82	H5
Qi Xian [SX]	28	D4	Qiaoguan [SD]	50	E3	Qimantag [XJ]	82	L7
Qian Gorlos [JL]	34	D2	Qiaohe [CQ]	64	C5	Qimen [AH]	44	D6
Qian He [AH]	44	C2	Qiaojia [YN]	70	E2	Qimeng [GZ]	68	H4
Qian He [SN]	74	B6	Qiaojian [GX]	60	E4	Qin Ling [SN]	74	D7
Qian Jiang [GX]	60	G4	Qiaojiawan [SX]	28	C5	Qin He [SX]	28	D5
Qian Jiang [SC]	66	H3	Qiaoli [GX]	60	F4	Qin Jiang [GX]	60	F5
Qian Shan [LN]	32	F4	Qiaomaidi [YN]	70	E2	Qin Jiang [JX]	48	D5
Qian Shan [LN]	32	G3	Qiaoshan [GX]	60	F3	Qin Qu [NX]	80	C2
Qian Shui [AH]	44	C5	Qiaoshe [JX]	48	C3	Qin Xian [SX]	28	D5
Qian Xian [SN]	74	D6	Qiaosi [ZJ]	42	D2	Qin'an [GS]	76	H5
Qi'an [JS]	40	G3	Qiaotou [AH]	44	D3	Qincheng [BJ]	22	D3
Qian'an [HEB]	26	F3	Qiaotou [HI]	62	B2	Qinchi [SX]	28	D6
Qian'an [JL]	34	D3	Qiaotou [HN]	56	D6	Qing He [LN]	32	H2
Qianchang [HB]	54	F4	Qiaotou [JX]	48	B5	Qing Jiang [HB]	54	A4
Qiandao Hu [ZJ]	42	B3	Qiaotou [SX]	28	C3	Qing Xian [HEB]	26	D5
Qianfeng [HL]	36	D4	Qiaotoubu [AH]	44	E5	Qing'an [HL]	36	D4
Qianfeng [HL]	36	G4	Qiaotouhe [HN]	56	D4	Qingbaikou [BJ]	22	B3
Qiangwei He [JS]	40	D1	Qiaotoupu [HN]	56	D6	Qingbowa [TJ]	24	B5
Qiangzilu [BJ]	22	E2	Qiaowan [GS]	76	D2	Qingcao Sha [SH]	38	E2
Qianhe [ZJ]	42	B4	Qiaoxian [GX]	60	F4	Qingcheng [GS]	76	I4
Qianhekou [BJ]	22	B5	Qiaozhen [SH]	38	D1	Qingcheng [SD]	50	D2
Qianjia [HI]	62	B3	Qiaozhen [SN]	74	D4	Qingchengzi [LN]	32	G4
Qianjiadian [BJ]	22	D2	Qiaozhi Nongchang [HI]	62	B2	Qingchi [GZ]	68	E3
Qianjiang Qu [CQ]	64	E4	Qiazi [SN]	74	E8	Qingchuan [SC]	66	F2
Qianjiang [GX]	60	F4	Qibao [SH]	38	D3	Qingcun [SH]	38	D4
Qianjiang [HB]	54	E4	Qibu [FJ]	46	E2	Qingdao [SD]	50	G3
Qianjietou [SD]	50	F4	Qichun [HB]	54	H4	Qingdui [SX]	32	G5
Qianjin [JL]	34	G4	Qicun [SX]	28	D3	Qingduizi [LN]	32	F4
Qianjin [JL]	34	H3	Qidao [SX]	28	B4	Qingfeng [HEN]	52	G2
Qianjin [SH]	38	D1	Qidaogou [JL]	34	F6	Qingfengling Shuiku [SD]	50	E4

Name	Page	Grid	Name	Page	Grid	Name	Page	Grid
Qinggang [HL]	36	D4	Qingshila [HEB]	26	D2	Qingzu [HEN]	52	G2
Qinggir [XJ]	82	K5	Qingshitan Shuiku [GX]	60	H2	Qinhuai He [JS]	40	D4
Qingguandu [HN]	56	C2	Qingshizui [NX]	80	C5	Qinhuangdao [HEB]	26	G4
Qingguang [TJ]	24	B4	Qingshizui [QH]	78	G2	Qinjiatun [JL]	34	D4
Qingguji [SD]	50	B5	Qingshui He [BJ]	22	B4	Qinlan [AH]	44	F3
Qinghai Hu [QH]	78	G2	Qingshui He [NX]	80	B3	Qinquan [SX]	28	E5
Qinghai Nanshan [QH]	78	F2	Qingshui He [SX]	28	E3	Qinshan Dao [JS]	40	E1
Qinghe Qu [LN]	32	H2	Qingshui Jiang [GZ]	68	F3	Qinshi [HB]	54	E5
Qinghe Shuiku [LN]	32	H2	Qingshui Jiang [GZ]	68	H4	Qinshui [SX]	28	D6
Qinghe(Qinggil) [XJ]	82	L 2	Qingshui [BJ]	22	B4	Qintong [JS]	40	F3
Qinghe [HEB]	26	C6	Qingshui [GS]	76	I5	Qinuan [SN]	74	E5
Qinghe [HL]	36	C3	Qingshui [GX]	60	I2	Qinyang [HEN]	52	D2
Qinghe [HL]	36	E4	Qingshuihe [NM]	30	E5	Qinyuan [SX]	28	D5
Qinghe [JL]	34	E6	Qingshuihe [QH]	78	E4	Qinzhou Wan [GX]	60	F6
Qinghe [SD]	50	C4	Qingshuihe [SX]	28	E2	Qinzhou [GX]	60	F6
Qinghe [SD]	50	D2	Qingshuilang Shan [YN]	70	C2	Qiong Hai [SC]	66	E5
Qinghecheng [LN]	32	H3	Qingshuiwan [HB]	54	C4	Qionghai [HI]	62	C2
Qinghei Shan [HL]	36	E4	Qingshuping [HN]	56	E4	Qionglai [SC]	66	E3
Qinghemen Qu [LN]	32	E3	Qingshuzui [HN]	56	E2	Qionglai Shan [SC]	66	E2
Qinghetou [HEN]	52	G2	Qingsong [HI]	62	B2	Qiongshan Qu [HI]	62	C1
Qinghu [GX]	60	H5	Qingtai [HEN]	52	D5	Qiongzhong [HI]	62	B2
Qinghua [JX]	48	E2	Qingtang [GD]	58	E2	Qiongzhou Haixia [GD]	58	A6
Qingjian He [SN]	74	F3	Qingtangpu [HN]	56	D3	Qipan Guan [SC]	66	G2
Qingjian [SN]	74	F3	Qingtian [ZJ]	42	D4	Qipanshan [HEB]	26	E1
Qingjiang [ZJ]	42	E4	Qingtongguan [SN]	74	E7	Qiping [JX]	48	B3
Qingkou [FJ]	46	E4	Qingtongxia Shuiku [NX]	80	B3	Qiqian [NM]	30	H1
Qinglan Gang [HI]	62	C2	Qingtongxia [NX]	80	B3	Qiqiao [CQ]	64	D3
Qinglang [HN]	56	C3	Qingtongxia [NX]	80	C2	Qiqiao [JS]	40	D4
Qinglian [GD]	58	D2	Qingtuan [AH]	44	C2	Qiqihar [HL]	36	B4
Qingliangdian [HEB]	26	C6	Qingtuo [SD]	50	E4	Qiqu Liedao [ZJ]	42	E2
Qingliangsi [SX]	28	B3	Qingtuozi [TJ]	24	D5	Qira [XJ]	82	G7
Qingliu He [CQ]	64	B4	Qingxi [AH]	44	D4	Qisha [GX]	60	F6
Qingliu [FJ]	46	B3	Qingxi [HL]	36	D3	Qishan [SN]	74	C6
Qinglong He [HEB]	26	F3	Qingxiang [SX]	28	C5	Qishui [GD]	58	A6
Qinglong [GZ]	68	D5	Qingxin [GD]	58	D3	Qishuyan Qu [JS]	40	F4
Qinglong [HEB]	26	F3	Qingxiu Qu [GX]	60	F5	Qitai [XJ]	82	K3
Qinglong [JX]	48	B6	Qingxu [SX]	28	D4	Qitaihe [HL]	36	F5
Qinglongji [AH]	44	C1	Qingyan [GZ]	68	E4	Qitamu [JL]	34	F3
Qinglongqiao [BJ]	22	C2	Qingyang [AH]	44	D5	Qitian Ling [HN]	56	E6
Qinglongshan [NX]	80	C3	Qingyang [CQ]	64	D4	Qiting [HB]	54	G3
Qinglongwan He [TJ]	24	B3	Qingyang [GS]	76	I5	Qiu Xian [HEB]	26	C7
Qinglung [XZ]	72	H4	Qingyang [HL]	36	E5	Qiubei [YN]	70	F3
Qingmuguan [CQ]	64	C4	Qingyang [JL]	34	E3	Qiucheng [HEB]	26	C7
Qingnian Yunhe [GD]	58	B5	Qingyi Jiang [AH]	44	E5	Qiucun [AH]	44	F4
Qingping [CQ]	64	C4	Qingyi Jiang [SC]	66	E3	Qiujiadian [HL]	36	D4
Qingping [GD]	58	A5	Qingyi [JS]	40	D1	Qiujin [JX]	48	C2
Qingping [HB]	54	B5	Qingyuan Qu [JX]	48	C4	Qiukou [JX]	48	E2
Qingpu Qu [SH]	38	C3	Qingyuan [GD]	58	E3	Qiuligou [JL]	34	H4
Qingqu [HB]	54	C2	Qingyuan [HEB]	26	C5	Qiulu [FJ]	46	E4
Qingshan Qu [HB]	54	G4	Qingyuan [LN]	32	H2	Qiupu He [AH]	44	D5
Qingshan [AH]	44	B4	Qingyuan [ZJ]	42	C5	Qiushui He [SX]	28	B4
Qingshan [AH]	44	C4	Qingyun Shan [GD]	58	E2	Qiuzhuang Shuiku [HEB]	26	F4
Qingshan [AH]	44	C6	Qingyun [JX]	48	D3	Qixia Qu [JS]	40	D3
Qingshan [GZ]	68	C5	Qingyun [SD]	50	D2	Qixia [SD]	50	G2
Qingshan [JL]	34	B2	Qingyundian [BJ]	22	D4	Qixian [SH]	38	D4
Qingshan [JI]	34	F2	Qingzang Gaoyuan [XZ]	72	E2	Qixing Dao [ZJ]	42	D5
Qingshan [NX]	80	D3	Qingzang Gaoyuan [QH]	78	A3	Qixing He [HL]	36	G4
Qingshan [ZJ]	42	D2	Qingzhang He [HEB]	26	A7	Qixing Qu [NX]	80	B3
Qingshanshi [HN]	56	E4	Qingzhen [GZ]	68	E4	Qixingpao [HL]	36	C3
Qingshen [SC]	66	E4	Qingzheng [CQ]	64	F2	Qiyang [HN]	56	D5
Qingshi [HB]	54	H4	Qingzhou [FJ]	46	D3	Qiyanqiao [GZ]	68	E4
Qingshi [JL]	34	F6	Qingzhou [SD]	50	E3	Qiying [NX]	80	C4

Qiyunshan [AH] 44 E6
Qizhong [XZ] 72 L5
Qizhou Yang [HI] 62 D2
Qizhou Liedao [HI] 62 D2
Qizhou [HB] 54 H4
Qizi [HN] 56 E4
Qogir Feng [XJ] 82 E8
Qomolangma Feng [XZ] 72 F6
Qonggyai [XZ] 72 H5
Qongkol [XJ] 82 J5
Qonj [QH] 78 F2
Qu Jiang [ZJ] 42 C3
Qu Jiang [SC] 66 G3
Qu Shui [HN] 56 B5
Qu Xian [SC] 66 G3
Qu'ali [JX] 48 E2
Quan He [AH] 44 B2
Quanbao Shan [HEN] 52 C3
Quandian [SX] 28 D5
Quangang Qu [FJ] 46 D4
Qu'angangayong [QH] 78 C4
Quanjiao [AH] 44 E3
Quankou [JX] 48 C2
Quanming [GX] 60 E5
Quannan [JX] 48 B7
Quanshuigou [XJ] 82 F8
Quantou [LN] 32 H2
Quanxi [HB] 54 B2
Quanyang [JL] 34 G5
Quanzhou Gang [FJ] 46 D5
Quanzhou [FJ] 46 D5
Quanzhou [GX] 60 I2
Quarry Bay [HK] 84 D3
Quchaihe [JL] 34 F4
Quchan He [SX] 28 B4
Qudi [SD] 50 D2
Qu'e [SX] 28 B5
Que'er'ao [ZJ] 42 E4
Quekou [AH] 44 D4
Queshan [HEN] 52 F5
Qufu [SD] 50 C4
Qujiang Qu [GD] 58 E2
Qujiang Qu [ZJ] 42 B4
Qujiang [YN] 70 E4
Qujie [GD] 58 B6
Qujing [YN] 70 E3
Qujiu [GX] 60 E5
Qukou [NX] 80 C2
Qukoupu [NX] 80 B3
Qulan [HN] 56 E4
Quli [GX] 60 E5
Qulno [XZ] 72 E4
Qumar He [QH] 78 C3
Qumar Heyan [QH] 78 C3
Qumarhe [QH] 78 D3
Qumarlêb [QH] 78 D3
Qungcang [XZ] 72 E3
Qu'ngoin He [QH] 78 F3
Qu'nyido [XZ] 72 L4
Qunying [HI] 62 B3
Qushui [CQ] 64 E3
Qusum [XZ] 72 I5

Qutang Xia [CQ] 64 F3
Qutou [BJ] 22 D4
Quwan [HB] 54 E2
Quwo [SX] 28 C6
Quxi [ZJ] 42 D4
Qüxü [XZ] 72 H5
Quyang [HEB] 26 B5
Quyang [JX] 48 C5
Quzhou [HEB] 26 B7
Quzhou [ZJ] 42 B4

R

Rabang [XZ] 72 C3
Rabga La [XZ] 72 F6
Ra'gya [QH] 78 G3
Raka [XZ] 72 E5
Rambler Channel [HK] 84 C3
Ramda [QH] 78 D4
Rangdong [HEN] 52 D5
Rangdu [CQ] 64 E3
Ranghulu Qu [HL] 36 C4
Rao'er [JX] 48 E3
Raohe [HL] 36 H4
Raoping [GD] 58 I3
Raoyang [HEB] 26 C5
Rawu [XZ] 72 K5
Rayü [XZ] 72 J4
Rehe Qu [SC] 66 D5
Ren Shan [FJ] 46 D2
Ren Xian [SC] 26 B6
Renchaoxi [HN] 56 C2
Rencun [HEN] 52 E1
Rencun [NX] 80 C2
Rendian [HEN] 52 E5
Renfeng [SD] 50 D2
Renfengzhuang [TJ] 24 D4
Renhe [HEN] 52 G6
Renhe [JX] 48 C4
Renhe [YN] 70 D2
Renhua [GD] 58 E1
Renhuai [GZ] 68 E3
Renju [GD] 58 G2
Renmin [HL] 36 C4
Renqiao [AH] 44 D2
Renqiu [HEB] 26 D5
Renshan [GD] 58 F4
Renshi [SC] 66 G3
Renshou [FJ] 46 C2
Renshou [SC] 66 F3
Rentian [JX] 48 D6
Renxing [HI] 62 B2
Renyi [CQ] 64 B4
Reshi [HN] 56 D2
Reshui [QH] 78 G2
Riga [XZ] 72 J5
Rinbung [XZ] 72 G5
Rinda [SC] 66 D3
Rindü [XZ] 72 G4
Ringtor [XZ] 72 D4
Risum [XZ] 72 B3
Riwo [XZ] 72 F5
Riwoqê [XZ] 72 K4

Riwoqê [XZ] 72 K4
Riyue Shan [QH] 78 G2
Rizhao [SD] 50 F4
Rola Co [XZ] 72 G2
Rong Jiang [GX] 60 G2
Rong Xian [GX] 60 H5
Rong Xian [SC] 66 F4
Rong'an [GX] 60 G2
Rongbaca [SC] 66 C3
Rongbang [HI] 62 B2
Rongbo [XZ] 72 J4
Rongchang [CQ] 64 B4
Rongcheng Wan [SD] 50 I2
Rongcheng [HEB] 26 C4
Rongcheng [SD] 50 I2
Ronggezhuang [BJ] 22 E3
Ronghe [SX] 28 B6
Rongjiang [GZ] 68 G5
Rongkou [AH] 44 D6
Rongma [XZ] 72 F3
Rongshan [HI] 62 C2
Rongshui [GX] 60 G2
Rongxi [CQ] 64 E5
Round Island
  (Ngan Chau) [HK] 84 D4
Rucheng [HN] 56 F6
Rudong [JS] 40 G3
Rugao [JS] 40 F3
Rui'an [ZJ] 42 D5
Ruichang [JX] 48 C2
Ruicheng [SX] 28 B7
Ruihong [JX] 48 D3
Ruijin [JX] 48 D6
Ruili [YN] 70 B3
Ruilin [JX] 48 C5
Ruitapu [HN] 56 C2
Ruixi [HI] 62 C2
Rujigou [NX] 80 C1
Run He [AH] 44 B3
Runan [HEN] 52 F4
Runanbu [HEN] 52 F5
Runcheng [SX] 28 D6
Runhe [AH] 44 C3
Ruo Shui [GS] 76 E3
Ruoqiang(Qarkilik) [XJ] 82 K6
Rushan [SD] 50 H3
Rushankou [SD] 50 H3
Rushui He [NX] 80 C5
Rutog [XZ] 72 B3
Rutong [GD] 58 C5
Ruxi [CQ] 64 E3
Ruyang [HEN] 52 D3
Ruyuan [GD] 58 E2
Ruzhou [HEN] 52 D3

S

Sadê [SC] 66 D4
Sadêng [XZ] 72 J4
Saga [XZ] 72 E5
Sa'gya [XZ] 72 G5
Saheqiao [HEB] 26 F3

Sai Kung [HK]	84	E2	Sangruma [QH]	78	F4	Sanqu [JS]	40	F2
Sai O [HK]	84	E2	Sangsang [XZ]	72	F5	Sanquan [CQ]	64	D4
Sai Tso Wan [HK]	84	A3	Sanguandian [AH]	44	E4	Sanquan [SX]	28	C4
Sai Van Lake [MC]	86	A3	Sanguansi [HN]	56	C2	Sanrao [GD]	58	H3
Sai Wan [HK]	84	D3	Sangyuan Xia [GS]	76	H4	Sanrong [HI]	62	B3
Sai Wan [HK]	84	F2	Sangzhi [HN]	56	C2	Sansha Wan [FJ]	46	E3
Saihan Toroi [NM]	30	C4	Sangzhou [ZJ]	42	E3	Sansha [FJ]	46	F3
Saiqi [FJ]	46	E3	Sangzhuang [HEN]	52	D5	Sanshan [HEB]	26	C2
Sam A Chung [HK]	84	E1	Sangzi [TJ]	24	B2	Sanshandao [SD]	50	F2
Sam A Tsuen [HK]	84	E1	Sanhe [GD]	58	H2	Sanshengyu [JL]	34	D3
Sam Kok Tsui [HK]	84	E1	Sanhe [GZ]	68	E3	Sanshihao [JL]	34	C3
Samai [NM]	30	G3	Sanhe [HEB]	26	E4	Sanshijia [LN]	32	C3
Samka [XZ]	72	K4	Sanhe [JL]	34	I5	Sanshilipu [NX]	80	C5
Samsang [XZ]	72	D4	Sanhe [NX]	80	B5	Sanshilipu [SN]	74	E4
San He [JS]	40	D2	Sanhe [ZJ]	42	C3	Sanshui Qu [GD]	58	D3
San Po Kong [HK]	84	D3	Sanhedian [HB]	54	F2	Sansui [GZ]	68	G4
San Tin [HK]	84	C1	Sanhejian [HEN]	52	G5	Santa [AH]	44	B3
San Wai Tsuen [HK]	84	C2	Sanhezhuang [BJ]	22	B4	Santai [LN]	32	C3
San Wai [HK]	84	B2	Sanhsing [TW]	88	D2	Santai [LN]	32	G3
Sanbao [LN]	32	D3	Sanhuang [GX]	60	G3	Santai [SC]	66	F3
Sancai [HI]	62	B3	Sanhui [CQ]	64	C3	Santai [YN]	70	D2
Sancang [JS]	40	F3	Sanjia [GD]	58	C4	Santang [AH]	44	B2
Sancha He [GZ]	68	D4	Sanjia [HEB]	26	F2	Santang [HN]	56	E5
Sancha [GX]	60	F3	Sanjia [HI]	62	A2	Santang [JX]	48	D3
Sancha [SX]	28	C2	Sanjiadian [BJ]	22	C4	Santanghu [XJ]	82	M3
Sanchagang [SH]	38	D2	Sanjianfang [BJ]	22	D4	Santangjie [HN]	56	D3
Sanchahe [LN]	32	F3	Sanjiang [CQ]	64	C5	Santangpu [HN]	56	D4
Sanchakou [HEB]	26	C3	Sanjiang [GX]	60	G2	Santiao Chiao [TW]	88	E1
Sanchuan He [SX]	28	B4	Sanjiang [HI]	62	C2	Santong He [JL]	34	E5
Sanchuan [HEN]	52	C4	Sanjiang [JX]	48	C3	Santunying [HEB]	26	F3
Sandao [HI]	62	B3	Sanjiangkou [HN]	56	F6	Sanweishan [GS]	76	C2
Sandao [HL]	36	D4	Sanjiangkou [LN]	32	G1	Sanxi [AH]	44	E5
Sandaogou [LN]	32	D4	Sanjiao [SX]	28	B4	Sanxi [HB]	54	G5
Sandaohe [BJ]	22	D1	Sanjiao [SX]	28	B4	Sanxia Daba [HB]	54	C4
Sandaohezi [HL]	36	E5	Sanjiaoping [HN]	56	C3	Sanxiang [GD]	58	E4
Sandaohu [JL]	34	F5	Sanjiaotang [ZJ]	42	E4	Sanxing [HL]	36	C4
Sandong [GZ]	68	F5	Sanjiaotu [HI]	62	B3	Sanxing [JX]	48	B3
Sandu Ao [FJ]	46	E3	Sanjiazi [LN]	32	G4	Sanxing [SH]	38	C1
Sandu [GZ]	68	E4	Sanjie [AH]	44	E3	Sanxiqiao [JX]	48	C2
Sandu [GZ]	68	F4	Sanjie [ZJ]	42	D3	Sanya Gang [HI]	62	B3
Sandu [HI]	62	B2	Sanjieshou [SD]	50	E4	Sanya [HI]	62	B3
Sandu [HN]	56	F5	Sanjing [SX]	28	C3	Sanyang [HB]	54	F3
Sandu [ZJ]	42	C3	Sanjingzi [JL]	34	E2	Sanyang [JS]	40	G4
Sanduhe [BJ]	22	D2	Sankeyushu [JL]	34	E6	Sanyang [JX]	48	B4
Sandun [SH]	38	E4	Sanli [AH]	44	E5	Sanyanggang [HN]	56	D3
Sanduo [SX]	28	B5	Sanli [GX]	60	G4	Sanyangkeng [AH]	44	E5
Sanfang [GX]	60	F2	Sanli [JX]	48	D3	Sanyanjing [NX]	80	B3
Sanfengsi [HN]	56	E2	Sanlifan [HB]	54	H4	Sanyantang [HN]	56	E3
Sang Dao [SD]	50	G2	Sanlin [SH]	38	D3	Sanyao [SN]	74	F6
Sang Qu [XZ]	72	K5	Sanlong [JS]	40	F2	Sanying [NX]	80	C4
Sangang [FJ]	46	C2	Sanlou [SX]	28	E2	Sanying [YN]	70	D2
Sangengluo [HI]	62	C3	Sanmen Wan [ZJ]	42	E3	Sanyu [JS]	40	G3
Sanggan He [HEB]	26	B4	Sanmen [HN]	56	F4	Sanyuan [AH]	44	C4
Sanggin Dalai [NM]	30	F4	Sanmen [ZJ]	42	E3	Sanyuan [CQ]	64	D3
Sanggou Wan [SD]	50	I2	Sanmenpo [HI]	62	C2	Sanyuan [SN]	74	D6
Sanglang [GZ]	68	E5	Sanmenxia Shulku [HEN]	52	C3	Sanyuanpu [JL]	34	E5
Sanglin [LN]	32	F3	Sanmenxia Shuiku [SX]	28	C7	Sanzhan [HL]	36	C5
Sangluoshu [SD]	50	D2	Sanmenxia [HEN]	52	C3	Sanzhan [HL]	36	D3
Sangmu [GZ]	68	E2	Sanming [FJ]	46	C3	Sanzheng [CQ]	64	E3
Sangou [HEB]	26	F2	Sanping [HI]	62	B3	Sanzhou [GD]	58	D5
Sangping [CQ]	64	F2	Sanpu [GS]	76	F3	Saoshui [HI]	62	B3
Sangri [XZ]	72	I5	Sanqiao [AH]	44	C5	Sapu [AH]	44	D4

Name	Pg	Grid	Name	Pg	Grid	Name	Pg	Grid
Sapu [NX]	80	B4	Shakou [GD]	58	E2	Shangjiang [JX]	48	B6
Sartai [NM]	30	C5	Shalang [GD]	58	C5	Shangjiaodao [ZJ]	42	C3
Seac Pai Van Reservoir [MC]	86	C6	Shaliangzi [BJ]	22	D1	Shangjie Qu [HEN]	52	E3
Segang [HEN]	52	F6	Shaliangzi [QH]	78	C2	Shangjin [HB]	54	C1
Sehepu [SN]	74	E7	Shaling [BJ]	22	E3	Shangjing [FJ]	46	C4
Sênggê Zangbo			Shaling [LN]	32	G3	Shanglei [GX]	60	G3
(Shiquan He) [XZ]	72	C3	Shaliu [ZJ]	42	E3	Shangli [JX]	48	A4
Sengnian [SX]	28	C5	Shaluli Shan [SC]	66	C3	Shanglian [FJ]	46	D3
Senlin Shan [JL]	34	J4	Sham Chung [HK]	84	E2	Shangliang [SC]	66	G2
Serh [QH]	78	F2	Sham Shui Po [HK]	84	D3	Shanglin [GX]	60	F4
Sêrlung [QH]	78	H3	Sham Tseng [HK]	84	C3	Shanglin [HEB]	26	D5
Sêrtar [SC]	66	D2	Shan Ling [FJ]	46	C2	Shangluo [SN]	74	E7
Sêrwolungwa [QH]	78	D3	Shan Guan [FJ]	46	C2	Shangmachang [HL]	36	D2
Sêrxü [SC]	66	C2	Shan Guan [JX]	48	E4	Shangmatai [TJ]	24	C4
Seshufen [BJ]	22	C4	Shan Ha Wai [HK]	84	D3	Shangmei [FJ]	46	D2
Sha He [HEB]	26	C5	Shan Liu [HK]	84	E2	Shangnan [SN]	74	F7
Sha Chau [HK]	84	B3	Shan Xian [HEN]	52	C3	Shangpan [ZJ]	42	E4
Sha He [BJ]	22	C3	Shan Xian [SD]	50	C5	Shangping [GD]	58	G2
Sha He [HEN]	52	E4	Shancheng Qu [HEN]	52	F2	Shangpu [ZJ]	42	D3
Sha Lo Wan [HK]	84	B3	Shancheng [GS]	76	I4	Shangqing [JX]	48	E3
Sha Tau Kok Hoi [HK]	84	D1	Shancheng [JI]	34	F5	Shangqiu [HEN]	52	G3
Sha Tau Kok River [HK]	84	D1	Shandan [GS]	76	F3	Shangrao [JX]	48	E3
Sha Tau Kok [HK]	84	D1	Shandong Bandao [SD]	50	F3	Shangrao [JX]	48	E3
Sha Tin [HK]	84	D2	Shandong [GS]	76	C2	Shangsanli [TJ]	24	B5
Sha Xi [FJ]	46	C3	Shang Boingor [QH]	78	F4	Shangshe [SX]	28	D3
Sha Xian [FJ]	46	C3	Shang Kongma [QH]	78	F4	Shangshe [SX]	28	D3
Shaba [GD]	58	C5	Shang'an [HI]	62	B3	Shangshi [HB]	54	F3
Shache(Yarkant) [XJ]	82	E6	Shangba [GZ]	68	F2	Shangshui [HEN]	52	F4
Shacheng Gang [FJ]	46	F2	Shangbai [ZJ]	42	C2	Shangsi [GX]	60	E5
Shacheng Gang [ZJ]	42	D5	Shangbancheng [HEB]	26	F3	Shangsi [ZJ]	68	F5
Shacheng [FJ]	46	F2	Shangcai [HEN]	52	F4	Shangta [SH]	38	B3
Shaconggou [NX]	80	C2	Shangcang [TJ]	24	C2	Shangtang [JS]	40	D2
Shacun [JX]	48	C5	Shangchao [GX]	60	F2	Shangtang [JX]	48	C3
Shadaoguan [HB]	54	D4	Shangcheng [HEN]	52	G6	Shangwan [BJ]	22	C4
Shadi [GD]	58	D5	Shangchuan Dao [GD]	58	D5	Shangxi [JX]	48	C5
Shadi [JX]	48	B5	Shangdachen Dao [ZJ]	42	E4	Shangxi [ZJ]	42	C3
Shagou [JS]	40	E2	Shangdian [HEN]	52	E4	Shangxing [JS]	40	E4
Shagou [NX]	80	B4	Shangdianzi [BJ]	22	E2	Shangyangwu [SX]	28	D3
Shahai [l N]	32	C3	Shangdu [HEN]	56	F6	Shangyanxi [CQ]	64	E4
Shahe [AH]	44	E3	Shangdu [NM]	30	F4	Shangyao [AH]	44	D3
Shahe [BJ]	22	C3	Shange [FJ]	46	C5	Shangye [SD]	50	D4
Shahe [GX]	60	G5	Shangen [HI]	62	C3	Shangyi [HEB]	26	A2
Shahe [HEB]	26	B7	Shangfang [ZJ]	42	B3	Shangyou Jiang [JX]	48	B6
Shahe [HEB]	26	B7	Shangfu [JX]	48	C3	Shangyou Shuiku [JX]	48	C3
Shahe [HL]	36	E4	Shanggang [JS]	40	F2	Shangyou [JX]	48	B6
Shahe [JL]	34	E5	Shangganlin Qu [HL]	36	E4	Shangyou [SD]	50	D3
Shahe [JS]	40	D1	Shanggao [JX]	48	B3	Shangyu [ZJ]	42	D2
Shahe [SC]	66	G2	Shangguan [HEN]	52	F2	Shangyuan [LN]	32	D3
Shahe [SD]	50	F2	Shanggunquan [NX]	80	C3	Shangyun [YN]	70	C4
Shahe [SN]	74	C8	Shanghai [SH]	38	D3	Shangzhage [YN]	70	E2
Shahe [SX]	28	E2	Shanghai Nongchang [JS]	40	F2	Shangzhai [SX]	28	F2
Shahedian [HEN]	52	E5	Shanghang [FJ]	46	B4	Shangzhen [BJ]	22	E3
Shaheyan [JL]	34	H4	Shanghe [SD]	50	D2	Shangzhen [SN]	74	F7
Shahezi [HL]	36	D5	Shanghekou [LN]	32	H4	Shangzhenzi [SN]	74	D5
Shahousuo [LN]	32	D4	Shanghewan [JL]	34	F3	Shangzhi [HL]	36	D5
Shahu [HB]	54	F4	Shanghexi [HN]	56	B2	Shangzhong [GZ]	68	G4
Shahukou [SX]	28	D1	Shanghou [SD]	50	E4	Shangzhoujiahewan [NX]	80	B3
Shaikou [FJ]	46	C2	Shanghu [ZJ]	42	D3	Shangzhuang [BJ]	22	C3
Shaji [SN]	74	D3	Shanghuang [CQ]	64	F2	Shangzhuang [HEB]	26	B4
Shajian [FJ]	46	C5	Shanghuangqi [HEB]	26	D2	Shanhaiguan Qu [HEB]	26	G3
Shajianzi [LN]	32	I3	Shangji [HL]	36	D4	Shanhe [HL]	36	D5
Shajingzi [TJ]	24	C6	Shangjiahe [LN]	32	H3	Shanhe [NX]	80	C5

Shanhua [TW]	88	C3
Shanji [JS]	40	C1
Shankou [GX]	60	G6
Shankou [HI]	62	B2
Shankou [JX]	48	B3
Shankou [XJ]	82	N4
Shankou [ZJ]	42	D4
Shanli [AH]	44	D6
Shanlingzi [TJ]	24	C5
Shanmatang Ding [GX]	60	I3
Shanmatang Ding [HN]	56	D7
Shanmei Shuiku [FJ]	46	D4
Shanshan(Piqan) [XJ]	82	L4
Shanshi [HL]	36	E5
Shanshulun [HN]	56	E3
Shansonggang [JL]	34	F5
Shantangyi [HN]	56	C4
Shanting Qu [SD]	50	D4
Shantou [AH]	44	E2
Shantou [GD]	58	H3
Shanwanzi [HEB]	26	E1
Shanwei [GD]	58	G4
Shanxin [GX]	60	G5
Shanxu [GX]	60	E5
Shanyang [SN]	74	E7
Shanyin [SX]	28	D2
Shanzao [HN]	56	E4
Shanzhai [SX]	28	C2
Shanzhuang [JX]	48	B4
Shaobo Hu [JS]	40	E3
Shaobo [JS]	40	E3
Shaodong [HN]	56	D4
Shaogangpu [NX]	80	C2
Shaoguan [GD]	58	E2
Shaoguo [JL]	34	E4
Shaoshan [HN]	56	E4
Shaowu [FJ]	46	C2
Shaoxing [ZJ]	42	D2
Shaoxing [ZJ]	42	D2
Shaoyang [HN]	56	D4
Shaoyang [HN]	56	D4
Shaoyun [CQ]	64	B4
Shaozhuang [HEN]	52	F4
Shaozihe [LN]	32	G4
Shap Pat Heung [HK]	84	C2
Shap Sze Heung [HK]	84	E2
Shaping [GX]	60	F5
Shaping [HB]	54	F5
Shapingba Qu [CQ]	64	C4
Sharp Island		
(Kiu Tsui Chau) [HK]	84	E3
Shashi [CQ]	64	E2
Shashi [GZ]	68	E3
Shatang [NX]	80	B5
Shatian [GX]	60	I3
Shatian [HN]	56	F6
Shatian [JX]	48	B5
Shatou [GX]	60	I4
Shatu [GZ]	68	E3
Shatu [SD]	50	B4
Shau Kei Wan [HK]	84	D3
Shaunghe [JL]	34	F4
Shawan Qu [SC]	66	E4
Shawan [XJ]	82	I3
Shawan [ZJ]	42	C5
Shawo [HEN]	52	G6
Shaxi [FJ]	46	C3
Shaxi [HN]	56	B5
Shaxi [JX]	48	B6
Shaxi [JX]	48	C5
Shaxi [JX]	48	F3
Shayang [HB]	54	E4
Shayu [HEB]	26	B5
Shayu [SX]	28	E4
Shayugou [BJ]	22	E2
Shazaoyuan [GS]	76	C3
Shazhen [SD]	50	B3
Shazi [CQ]	64	E3
Shazipo [GZ]	68	G2
She Shan [SH]	38	C3
She Shan [SH]	38	F2
She Shui [HB]	54	G3
She Xian [AH]	44	E6
She Xian [HEB]	26	A7
Shebu [GX]	60	H4
Shecheng [SX]	28	D4
Shegangshi [HN]	56	F3
Shehong [SC]	66	F3
Shejiaping [HN]	56	D3
Shek Kip Mei [HK]	84	D3
Shek Kong [HK]	84	C2
Shek Kwu Chau [HK]	84	B4
Shek Ngau Chau [HK]	84	F2
Shek O [HK]	84	E4
Shek Pik Reservoir [HK]	84	B4
Shek Pik [HK]	84	A4
Shek Uk Shan [HK]	84	E2
Shek Wu Hui [HK]	84	D1
Shekou [FJ]	46	E2
Sheli [JL]	34	C2
Shelter Island		
(Ngau Mei Chau) [HK]	84	E3
Shen Shui [HN]	56	D7
Shen Xian [SD]	50	B3
Shenbei Xinqu [LN]	32	G2
Shenchi [SX]	28	D2
Shending Shan [HL]	36	G4
Sheng Shan [ZJ]	42	F2
Shengjin Hu [AH]	44	D5
Shengjing Guan [GZ]	68	C5
Shengjing Guan [YN]	70	F3
Shengli [HB]	54	H3
Shengli [HL]	36	D3
Shengli [HL]	36	E5
Shengli [HL]	36	G4
Shengping [GX]	60	E3
Shengping [HL]	36	C4
Shengqiao [AH]	44	D4
Shengqiao [AH]	44	E5
Shengqiao [SH]	38	D2
Shengshan Yang [ZJ]	42	F2
Shengshan [ZJ]	42	F2
Shengsi Liedao [ZJ]	42	F2
Shengsi [ZJ]	42	F2
Shengze [JS]	40	F5
Shengzhou [ZJ]	42	D3
Shengzimiao [SH]	38	D4
Shenhe [SN]	74	E8
Shenjia [HB]	54	E4
Shenjia [HL]	36	D4
Shenjiatai [LN]	32	D3
Shenjiatan [NX]	80	B3
Shenjiaying [BJ]	22	C2
Shenjing [GD]	58	D4
Shenjing [NX]	80	A3
Shenjingzi [JL]	34	D3
Shenli [HEN]	52	E3
Shenmu [SN]	74	F2
Shennong Ding [HB]	54	C3
Shennongjia Linqu [HB]	54	C3
Shennü Feng [CQ]	64	G2
Shenqiu [HEN]	52	G4
Shenquan Gang [GD]	58	H4
Shenshu [HL]	36	E4
Shentangbu [SX]	28	E2
Shenxiang [AH]	44	E4
Shenxiang [SH]	38	C3
Shenxiba [CQ]	64	E5
Shenxing [HEB]	26	C4
Shenyang [LN]	32	G3
Shenzao [JS]	40	F3
Shenze [HEB]	26	C5
Shenzhen He [HK]	84	C1
Shenzhen [GD]	58	F4
Shenzhen Wan		
(Deep Bay) [HK]	84	B2
Shenzhou [HEB]	26	C5
Shenzhuang [SH]	38	D3
Sheqi [HEN]	52	D4
Sheshan [SH]	38	C3
Shetan [CQ]	64	D4
Shetianqiao [HN]	56	D4
Sheung Fa Shan [HK]	84	C2
Sheung Pak Nai [HK]	84	B2
Sheung Shui [HK]	84	C1
Sheung Sze Mun [HK]	84	D4
Shewei [HEN]	52	C4
Shexi [JX]	48	B6
Sheyang He [JS]	40	E2
Sheyang [JS]	40	F2
Sheyanghe Kou [JS]	40	F2
Shezhu [JS]	40	E4
Shi He [BJ]	22	C4
Shi He [HEN]	52	F5
Shi He [HEN]	52	G5
Shibali [AH]	44	B2
Shiban Jing [NM]	30	B4
Shibaocheng [GS]	76	D3
Shibazhan [HL]	36	C1
Shibei [FJ]	46	D2
Shibi [HI]	62	C2
Shibie [GX]	60	F3
Shibing [GZ]	68	G3
Shibuqiao [HN]	56	F2
Shibuzi [SD]	50	F3
Shicha [NX]	80	C4

Shichang [HL]	36	G4	Shili [SX]	28	D6	Shisizhan [HL]	36	C2
Shicheng Dao [LN]	32	G5	Shiliang [AH]	44	E3	Shitai [AH]	44	D5
Shicheng [FJ]	46	E4	Shiliang [HEN]	52	G4	Shitan [CQ]	64	C4
Shicheng [JX]	48	D5	Shiliang [SX]	28	E5	Shitan [GD]	58	D2
Shicheng [LN]	32	F5	Shilianghe Shuiku [JS]	40	D1	Shitang [GX]	60	I2
Shicheng [LN]	32	H4	Shilibu [AH]	44	C2	Shitang [JX]	48	C4
Shicheng [SX]	28	E5	Shilin [HI]	62	B3	Shitang [ZJ]	42	E4
Shichuan He [SN]	74	D5	Shilin [YN]	70	E3	Shitanjing [NX]	80	C1
Shicun [AH]	44	D2	Shiling [HI]	62	B3	Shiti [CQ]	64	F5
Shidao Wan [SD]	50	I3	Shiling [JL]	34	D4	Shitie [SX]	28	D4
Shidao [SD]	50	I3	Shiliping [JL]	34	J4	Shitou Sha [SH]	38	D2
Shidi [HN]	56	C2	Shilipu [HB]	54	E4	Shitou Shan [NM]	30	I2
Shidian [YN]	70	C3	Shiliu [FJ]	46	C5	Shitouzhai [YN]	70	C4
Shidong [GD]	58	D3	Shilong Qu [HEN]	52	D4	Shitouzui [HB]	54	H4
Shidong [GZ]	68	G4	Shilong [GX]	60	G4	Shituo [CQ]	64	D4
Shidongzi [BJ]	22	D1	Shilong [GX]	60	G4	Shiwan Dashan [GX]	60	E6
Shidu [BJ]	22	B4	Shilou [BJ]	22	C4	Shiwan [HN]	56	E4
Shi'e [BJ]	22	E3	Shilou [SX]	28	B5	Shiwan [SN]	74	E3
Shifang [SC]	66	F3	Shilu Shuiku [HI]	62	B2	Shiwan Feng [AH]	44	D5
Shifang [FJ]	46	B4	Shimen [HEB]	26	C3	Shiwei [NM]	30	G2
Shifosi [BJ]	22	D5	Shimen [HN]	56	D2	Shiwu [JL]	34	D4
Shifu [HI]	62	C2	Shimen [SD]	50	E5	Shixia [SX]	28	E4
Shigong [AH]	44	C2	Shimen [SN]	74	E4	Shixiazi [GS]	76	G4
Shigouyi [NX]	80	C3	Shimen [ZJ]	42	D2	Shixing [GD]	58	F2
Shigu [GD]	58	B5	Shimenjie [JX]	48	D2	Shiyan [HB]	54	C2
Shigu [GZ]	68	G3	Shimenlou [JX]	48	B3	Shiyan [JL]	34	I4
Shiguai Qu [NM]	30	E4	Shimenqiao [HEB]	26	D5	Shiyanzi [NX]	80	B3
Shiguai [SX]	28	E4	Shimenqiao [HN]	56	D3	Shiye [CQ]	64	F5
Shihao [CQ]	64	C5	Shimenshan [AH]	44	D3	Shiyiwei [JS]	40	F4
Shihe [AH]	44	B2	Shimenying [BJ]	22	C4	Shiyizhan [HL]	36	C2
Shihe [LN]	32	E5	Shimian [SC]	66	E4	Shiyuetian [HI]	62	A2
Shihe [SC]	66	G3	Shimianzhuang [TJ]	24	B4	Shiyun [HI]	62	B3
Shihezi [XJ]	82	I3	Shing Mun Reservoir [HK]	84	D2	Shizhan [HL]	36	C2
Shihtan [TW]	88	C2	Shing Mun			Shizhe [SX]	28	D5
Shihua [HB]	54	D2	River Channel [HK]	84	D2	Shizhen [JX]	48	D3
Shihudang [SH]	38	C4	Shiniu Shan [FJ]	46	D4	Shizhen [SH]	38	E3
Shihui [CQ]	64	E4	Shipai [AH]	44	C5	Shizheng [GD]	58	G2
Shihuichang [NX]	80	B2	Shipai [FJ]	46	C4	Shizhong Qu [SD]	50	D5
Shiji [AH]	44	C4	Shipai [HB]	54	E4	Shizhu [CQ]	64	E4
Shiji [SD]	50	B4	Shipan [SX]	28	D4	Shizhu [HN]	56	C4
Shijiahe [CQ]	64	E4	Shipaogou [TJ]	24	C1	Shizhu [ZJ]	42	D4
Shijian [AH]	44	D4	Shiping [YN]	70	E4	Shizhuang [JS]	40	F3
Shijian [GD]	58	D3	Shipodian [AH]	44	C4	Shizi [AH]	44	F5
Shijiao [GD]	58	D3	Shipu [ZJ]	42	E3	Shizigou [HEB]	26	C2
Shijiapu [JL]	34	D4	Shiqian [GZ]	68	G3	Shizikou [SN]	74	D7
Shijiaqiao [ZJ]	42	D2	Shiqiao [AH]	44	F5	Shizilu [NX]	80	C5
Shijiaying [BJ]	22	B4	Shiqiao [HEN]	52	D4	Shizishan Qu [AH]	44	D5
Shijiazhuang [HEB]	26	B5	Shiqiao [JX]	48	D4	Shizong [YN]	70	E3
Shijiazhuang [SX]	28	C3	Shiqiao [SC]	66	G3	Shizui [SX]	28	E3
Shijiazi [LN]	32	F2	Shiqiu [BJ]	62	B2	Shizuishan [NX]	80	C1
Shijiehe [HEN]	52	C4	Shiquan Shuiku [SN]	74	D7	Shizuiyi [SN]	74	F3
Shijing [SD]	50	E4	Shiquan [SN]	74	D7	Shou Xian [AH]	44	C3
Shijingshan Qu [BJ]	22	C4	Shiren Shan [HEN]	52	D4	Shouchang [ZJ]	42	C3
Shijiu Hu [JS]	40	D4	Shiren [JL]	34	F6	Shouguang [SD]	50	E3
Shijiu [TJ]	24	C1	Shisandaogou [JL]	34	G6	Shouning [FJ]	46	E2
Shikengkong [GD]	58	D2	Shisanling Shuiku [BJ]	22	C3	Shouson Hill [HK]	84	D4
Shikengkong [HN]	56	E7	Shisanzhan [HL]	36	C2	Shouyang Shan [SN]	74	D7
Shikong [NX]	80	B3	Shishan [FJ]	46	D4	Shouyang [SX]	28	E4
Shikou [JX]	48	C4	Shishan [HI]	62	C2	Shu He [SD]	50	E4
Shikou [JX]	48	D3	Shishang [JX]	48	D5	Shu Shui [JX]	48	B5
Shikou [SX]	28	C5	Shishi [FJ]	46	D5	Shu Xi [AH]	44	E5
Shilai [SD]	50	D4	Shishou [HB]	54	E5	Shuangba [HEN]	52	G3

Shuangbai [YN]	70	D3	Shuidongdi [HN]	56	D4	Sifang Ling [GX]	60	E5
Shuangcheng [HL]	36	D5	Shuifu [YN]	70	F1	Sifangtai Qu [HL]	36	F4
Shuangchi [SX]	28	C5	Shuihou [AH]	44	C5	Sifangtai [HL]	36	D4
Shuangdian [JS]	40	D1	Shuiji [FJ]	46	D2	Sifen [HN]	56	F4
Shuangfeng [HL]	36	D4	Shuijiang [CQ]	64	D4	Sihai [BJ]	22	D2
Shuangfeng [HN]	56	E4	Shuijing [SC]	66	F2	Sihaidian [HL]	36	D4
Shuangfu [AH]	44	B2	Shuikou [AH]	44	E3	Siheyong [HEB]	26	E2
Shuangfupu [HN]	56	E3	Shuikou [FJ]	46	D4	Sihong [JS]	40	D2
Shuanggang [JL]	34	B2	Shuikou [GD]	58	D4	Sihui [GD]	58	D3
Shuanggou [AH]	44	B2	Shuikou [GX]	60	D5	Sijia [HN]	56	F5
Shuanggou [JS]	40	C1	Shuikou [HN]	56	F5	Sijia [JS]	40	G3
Shuanggou [JS]	40	D2	Shuikouwei [GD]	58	F1	Sijiao Shan [ZJ]	42	F2
Shuanggui [CQ]	64	D3	Shuiku [HN]	56	D7	Sijiao [SX]	28	C6
Shuanghe [AH]	44	C4	Shuiluo He [SC]	66	D4	Sijiazhuang [TJ]	24	D3
Shuanghe [HB]	54	E3	Shuiming [GX]	60	G5	Sijiazi [LN]	32	G2
Shuanghe [HL]	36	F5	Shuinan [JX]	48	D5	Sijing [SH]	38	C3
Shuanghe [SC]	66	G3	Shuiping [HB]	54	B2	Sijiqing [BJ]	22	C4
Shuanghsi [TW]	88	D1	Shuiquan [GS]	76	H4	Sikou [SD]	50	G2
Shuanghu [XZ]	72	G3	Shuitang [GZ]	68	C5	Silin [GX]	60	E4
Shuangji He [HEN]	52	E3	Shuitou [BJ]	22	C1	Siling Co [XZ]	72	G4
Shuangjian [AH]	44	C2	Shuitou [FJ]	46	D5	Silu [ZJ]	42	D3
Shuangjiang [CQ]	64	B3	Shuitou [SX]	28	C6	Silun [GD]	58	C4
Shuangjiang [YN]	70	C4	Shuiwen [GX]	60	H5	Silver Mine Bay [HK]	84	C4
Shuangjing [GZ]	68	G4	Shuiyang Jiang [AH]	44	E5	Simajia [JL]	34	E2
Shuangkou [TJ]	24	B4	Shuiyang [AH]	44	E4	Simaogang [YN]	70	D4
Shuangliao [JL]	34	C4	Shuiye [HEN]	52	F1	Simen [ZJ]	42	E2
Shuangliu [SC]	66	E3	Shuiyuan [GX]	60	F3	Siming Shan [ZJ]	42	E3
Shuanglu [CQ]	64	D4	Shuiyuguan [SX]	28	C4	Siming Shan [ZJ]	42	D3
Shuangluan Qu [HEB]	26	E3	Shuizhai [SD]	50	D3	Sinan [GZ]	68	G3
Shuangmiaozi [JL]	34	E5	Shuizhan [QH]	78	B1	Sinda [XZ]	72	K3
Shuangmiaozi [LN]	32	H2	Shuizi [JL]	34	C2	Siping [JL]	34	D4
Shuangpai Shuiku [HN]	56	D6	Shulan [JL]	34	F3	Sipu [AH]	44	C2
Shuangpai [HN]	56	D6	Shule He [GS]	76	C2	Siqian [FJ]	46	C2
Shuangqiao Qu [CQ]	64	B4	Shule He [QH]	78	E1	Siqian [GD]	58	F2
Shuangqiao [AH]	44	C2	Shule Nanshan [QH]	78	E1	Siqin Jiang [GX]	60	I3
Shuangqiao [AH]	44	C3	Shule [XJ]	82	E6	Siqu [GZ]	68	G2
Shuangqiao [GX]	60	F4	Shulehe [GS]	76	D2	Sishilijie [JX]	48	D2
Shuangqiao [JX]	48	B3	Shulehe [HL]	36	E4	Sishilipu [SN]	74	F3
Shuangshan [JL]	34	C4	Shunchang [FJ]	46	C3	Sishuang Liedao [FJ]	46	F3
Shuangshanzi [HEB]	26	G3	Shunde Qu [GD]	58	E4	Sishui [SD]	50	D4
Shuangtaizi He [LN]	32	E3	Shunhe [JS]	40	B1	Sishun [JX]	48	B6
Shuangtaizihe Kou [LN]	32	E4	Shunping [HEB]	26	C5	Sitang [GX]	60	D4
Shuangtang [JX]	48	D3	Shunyi Qu [BJ]	22	D3	Siting [GZ]	68	F5
Shuangxi [AH]	44	E5	Shuo [YN]	70	C1	Sitou [SX]	28	E5
Shuangxi [FJ]	46	E2	Shuoliang [GX]	60	E4	Situan [SH]	38	E4
Shuangxi [ZJ]	42	C4	Shuolong [GX]	60	D5	Siu A Chau [HK]	84	B4
Shuangxing [HL]	36	C4	Shuozhou [SX]	28	D2	Siu Ho [HK]	84	B3
Shuangyang Qu [JL]	34	E4	Shushan [AH]	44	D4	Siu Kau Yi Chau [HK]	84	C3
Shuangyashan [HL]	36	F4	Shutai [NX]	80	B4	Siu Lek Yuen [HK]	84	D2
Shuangzhongmiao [AH]	44	D2	Shuyang [JS]	40	D1	Siu Mo To [HK]	84	B3
Shucha [AH]	44	D4	Shuzhang [SX]	28	E6	Siu Sai Wan [HK]	84	E4
Shucheng [AH]	44	C4	Si He [SD]	50	C4	Siwang [GX]	60	H4
Shuen Wan [HK]	84	D2	Si Xian [AH]	44	D2	Sixia [JX]	48	B6
Shufu [XJ]	82	D6	Si'an [ZJ]	42	C2	Sixingang [HN]	56	D2
Shuguan [HEB]	26	C7	Siha [GX]	60	F3	Siyang [JS]	40	D2
Shuguang [HL]	36	F4	Sibao [GX]	60	F2	Sizhou [JX]	40	E2
Shuhe [SN]	74	E8	Sichakou [HEB]	26	D2	Sizhoutou [ZJ]	42	E3
Shuhong [ZJ]	42	D4	Sicundian [TJ]	24	B4	Sizhuang [SX]	28	D6
Shui Hau [HK]	84	B4	Sidaogou [JL]	34	G6	Siziwang Qi [NM]	30	E4
Shuiche [GD]	58	H2	Sidaoqiao [TJ]	24	C5	So Kwun Wat [HK]	84	B2
Shuicheng [GZ]	68	C4	Siding [GX]	60	G2	Sog [XZ]	72	I4
Shuidong Gang [GD]	58	C5	Sidou [FJ]	46	B4	Sogdoi [XZ]	72	J4

Sok Kwu Wan [HK]	84	D4	Songyan [SX]	28	E4	Suli Hu [QH]	78	D2
Soko Islands [HK]	84	B4	Songyang [ZJ]	42	C4	Sulin Gol [QH]	78	E2
Solon [NM]	30	H3	Songyankou [SX]	28	E3	Sulphur Channel [HK]	84	C3
Somang [SC]	66	F3	Songyin Xi [ZJ]	42	C4	Sumber [NM]	30	C4
Song Shan [HEN]	52	E3	Songyuan [JL]	34	D2	Sumdo [SC]	66	D4
Song Xi [FJ]	46	D2	Songzhan [HL]	36	C4	Sumxi [XZ]	72	C2
Song Xian [HEN]	52	D3	Songzhangzi [LN]	32	C3	Sumzom [XZ]	72	K5
Song'acha He [HL]	36	G5	Songzhuang [BJ]	22	D4	Sunan [GS]	76	E3
Song'ao [ZJ]	42	E3	Songzi Guan [AH]	44	B4	Sunbu [AH]	44	E5
Songbai [HN]	56	E5	Songzi Guan [HB]	54	H3	Sunfang [JX]	48	D4
Songbai [SD]	50	F4	Songzi [HB]	54	D4	Sung Kong [HK]	84	E4
Songbu [HB]	54	G3	Sonid Youqi [NM]	30	F4	Sungeng [SD]	50	D3
Songcun [SD]	50	I2	Sonid Zuoqi [NM]	30	F4	Suning [HEB]	26	C5
Songdian [NX]	80	C5	South China Sea [HI]	62	C3	Sunji [SX]	28	B6
Songgang [GD]	58	E4	South China Sea [GD]	58	E6	Sunjiatan [NX]	80	C3
Songgui [YN]	70	D2	South China Sea [HK]	84	G4	Sunqiao [HB]	54	F3
Songhe [HB]	54	F3	South China Sea [TW]	88	A5	Sunset Peak		
Songhu [JX]	48	C3	Stanley Bay [HK]	84	D4	(Tai Tung Shan) [HK]	84	B4
Songhua Hu [JL]	34	F4	Stanley [HK]	84	D4	Sunshine Island		
Songhua Jiang [HL]	36	D5	Stonecutters Island [HK]	84	D3	(Chau Kung To) [HK]	84	C4
Songhua Jiang [JL]	34	E3	Suao [TW]	88	D2	Suntuan [AH]	44	C2
Songhuajiang [JL]	34	E3	Sub Nur [NM]	30	C4	Sunwu [HL]	36	D3
Songjiagou [SX]	28	C3	Suban [FJ]	46	C4	Sunzhen [SD]	50	D2
Songjiang Qu [SH]	38	C4	Subao Ding [HN]	56	C4	Sunzhen [SN]	74	E5
Songjiang [JL]	34	G4	Subei [GS]	76	C3	Suohuang [SX]	28	E4
Songjiang [JL]	34	H5	Subei Guangai Zongqu [JS]	40	E2	Suqian [JS]	40	D2
Songjianghe [JL]	34	G5	Subu [NX]	80	B5	Suqiao [GX]	60	H2
Songjiaqiao [JS]	40	E3	Subujing [NX]	80	D2	Sushan Dao [SD]	50	I3
Songjiaying [HEB]	26	F4	Sucheng [SX]	28	E5	Sushui He [SX]	28	B6
Songjiazhuang [SX]	28	E2	Sugu [HB]	54	D2	Susong [AH]	44	C5
Songkan He [CQ]	64	C5	Suhai Hu [GS]	76	C3	Suuxqi [XJ]	82	K6
Songkan [GZ]	68	E2	Suhai Hu [QH]	78	C1	Suwan [AH]	44	D4
Songkou [FJ]	46	B3	Suhait [NM]	30	D5	Suxik [QH]	78	D1
Songkou [FJ]	46	D4	Suhunt [NM]	30	D4	Suyahu Shuiku [HEN]	52	F4
Songkou [GD]	58	H2	Sui He [AH]	44	D2	Suyu Qu [JS]	40	D2
Songlin [YN]	70	F2	Sui Jiang [GD]	58	D3	Suyukou [NX]	80	B2
Songlingzi [LN]	32	C4	Sui Xian [HEN]	52	G3	Suzhou [AH]	44	C2
Songlou [JS]	40	B1	Suibin [HL]	36	F4	Suzhou [JS]	40	F4
Songmen [ZJ]	42	E4	Suichang [ZJ]	42	C4	Suzhuang [ZJ]	42	B3
Songming [YN]	70	E3	Suichuan Jiang [JX]	48	B5	Suzi He [LN]	32	H3
Songpan Caodi [SC]	66	E2	Suichuan [JX]	48	B5	Suzui [JS]	40	E2
Songpan(Sungpu) [SC]	66	E2	Suide [SN]	74	F3			
Songshan Shuiku [SD]	50	E3	Suifen He [HL]	36	F5	**T**		
Songshan [GS]	76	G4	Suifenhe [HL]	36	F5			
Songshan [LN]	32	E3	Suihua [HL]	36	D4	Ta Ho Tun [HK]	84	E3
Songshanpu [LN]	32	H2	Suijiang [YN]	70	E1	Ta Kwu Ling [HK]	84	D1
Songshaoguan [YN]	70	E3	Suileng [HL]	36	D4	Taan Hsi [TW]	88	C2
Songshu [LN]	32	F5	Suining [HN]	56	C5	Tachakou [XJ]	82	I3
Songshutai [BJ]	22	D1	Suining [JS]	40	C2	Tacheng(Qoqek) [XJ]	82	H2
Songshuyu [BJ]	22	E2	Suining [SC]	66	F3	Tacheng [TW]	88	C3
Songta [SX]	28	E4	Suiping [HEN]	52	E4	Tacheng [YN]	70	C2
Songtao Ganqu [HI]	62	B2	Suixi [AH]	44	C2	Tachia His [TW]	88	C2
Songtao Shuiku [HI]	62	B2	Suixi [GD]	58	B5	Tachia [TW]	88	C2
Songtao [GZ]	68	H2	Suiyang Qu [HEN]	52	G3	Tachoshui [TW]	88	D2
Songtao [HI]	62	B2	Suiyang [GZ]	68	F2	Tahe [HL]	36	C1
Songwang [GX]	60	G6	Suiyang [GZ]	68	F3	Tahu [TW]	88	C2
Songxi He [SX]	28	E4	Suiyang [HL]	36	F5	Tai Van [MC]	86	B6
Songxi [FJ]	46	B3	Suiyangdian [HB]	54	E2	Tai A Chau [HK]	84	B4
Songxi [FJ]	46	D2	Suizhong [LN]	32	D4	Tai Au Mun [HK]	84	E3
Songxi [ZJ]	42	C2	Suizhou [HB]	54	F3	Tai Ho [HK]	84	B3
Songxia [FJ]	46	E4	Suji [AH]	44	B2	Tai Hom Sham [HK]	84	A4
Songyan [GZ]	68	F3	Sujiatun Qu [LN]	32	G3	Tai Hu [JS]	40	F4
						Tai Kok [HK]	84	D4

Tai Lam Chung Reservoir [HK]	84	C2
Tai Lam Chung [HK]	84	C3
Tai Long Tsui [HK]	84	F2
Tai Long Wan [HK]	84	A4
Tai Long Wan [HK]	84	F2
Tai Long [HK]	84	F2
Tai Mei Tuk [HK]	84	D2
Tai Miu Wan [HK]	84	E4
Tai Mo Shan [HK]	84	D2
Tai Mo To [HK]	84	B3
Tai Mong Tsai [HK]	84	E2
Tai O [HK]	84	A4
Tai Po Kau [HK]	84	D2
Tai Po Tsai [HK]	84	E3
Tai Po [HK]	84	D2
Tai Shan [SD]	50	D3
Tai Shui Hang [HK]	84	C3
Tai Shui Hang [HK]	84	D2
Tai Tam Bay [HK]	84	D4
Tai Tan [HK]	84	E2
Tai To Yan [HK]	84	C2
Tai Tong Tsuen [HK]	84	C2
Tai Wai [HK]	84	D3
Tai Wan [HK]	84	E4
Tai'an [LN]	32	F3
Tai'an [SD]	50	D3
Taibai Ding [HB]	54	F2
Taibai Ding [HEN]	52	E5
Taibai Shan [SN]	74	C7
Taibai Shan [SX]	28	F2
Taibai [GS]	76	J4
Taibai [GZ]	68	F2
Taibai [SN]	74	C6
Taibao [GD]	58	D2
Taibo Ding [SD]	50	H2
Taibus Qi [NM]	30	F4
Taicang [JS]	40	G4
Taichung [TW]	88	C2
Taichung [TW]	88	C2
Tai'erzhuang Qu [SD]	50	D5
Taigu [SX]	28	D4
Taihang Shan [SX]	28	E5
Taihang Shan [HEB]	26	B5
Taihe [AH]	44	B2
Taihe [GD]	58	E3
Taihe [HN]	56	E6
Taihe [JX]	48	B5
Taihe [JX]	48	D4
Taihezhuang [BJ]	22	D4
Taihsi [TW]	88	C3
Taihu [AH]	44	C5
Taihuai [SX]	28	E2
Taijiang [GZ]	68	G4
Taijihe [SN]	74	F7
Taijnar He [QH]	78	C2
Taikang [HEN]	52	F3
Tailai [HL]	36	B4
Tailie [GZ]	68	G4
Tailing [BJ]	22	C3
Tailong [CQ]	64	E3
Taimali [TW]	88	D4
Taimei [GD]	58	F3
Taimu Shan [FJ]	46	E3
Tainan [TW]	88	C3
Tainan [TW]	88	C4
Taining [FJ]	46	C3
Taipa Grande [MC]	86	C4
Taipa Pequena [MC]	86	B4
TAIPA [MC]	86	B4
Taipei [TW]	88	D1
Taipei [TW]	88	D1
Taiping Hu [AH]	44	E5
Taiping ling [HL]	36	F5
Taiping Ling [NM]	30	H3
Taiping [FJ]	46	C6
Taiping [FJ]	46	D3
Taiping [GD]	58	D2
Taiping [GX]	60	E3
Taiping [GX]	60	G3
Taiping [GX]	60	H4
Taiping [HB]	54	B5
Taiping [HB]	54	E2
Taiping [HEN]	52	C4
Taiping [HI]	62	C2
Taiping [HN]	56	D2
Taiping [HN]	56	E6
Taiping [SD]	50	C4
Taiping [SD]	50	E2
Taiping [TJ]	24	C6
Taipingchuan [JL]	34	C3
Taipingcun [TJ]	24	D5
Taipingdu [SC]	66	G4
Taipinggou [HL]	36	F3
Taipinggou [JL]	34	J4
Taipingling [HN]	56	F6
Taipingshan [JL]	34	D3
Taipingshan [LN]	32	F4
Taipingshao [LN]	32	I4
Taipingsi [HN]	56	E4
Taipingying [GZ]	68	H2
Taipingzhuang [TJ]	24	B4
Taipo [HI]	62	B2
Taiqian [HEN]	52	G2
Tairi [SH]	38	D4
Taishan Liedao [FJ]	46	F3
Taishan [GD]	58	D4
Taishitun [BJ]	22	E2
Taishun [ZJ]	42	C5
Taitou [SX]	28	C5
Taitou [TJ]	24	A5
Taitung [TW]	88	D4
Taiwan Haixia [TW]	88	B2
Taiwan Haixia [FJ]	46	D6
Taiwan Tao [TW]	88	C3
Taixi [NX]	80	C2
Taixing [JS]	40	F3
Taiyanghe [HB]	54	B4
Taiyangshan [NX]	80	C3
Taiyangsheng [JX]	48	B2
Taiyuan [SX]	28	D4
Taiyuansi [HN]	56	E4
Taiyue Shan [SX]	28	C5
Taizhou Liedao [ZJ]	42	E4
Taizhou Wan [ZJ]	42	E4
Taizhou [JS]	40	E3
Taizhou [ZJ]	42	E4
Taizimiao [HN]	56	D3
Takangkou [TW]	88	D3
Taklimakan Shamo [XJ]	82	G6
Talaha [HL]	36	C4
Tali [TW]	88	D2
Talin [TW]	88	C3
Taling [LN]	32	G4
Talkiydi Shankou [XJ]	82	D5
Taman Shan [TW]	88	D2
Tan Jiang [GD]	58	D4
Tan Ka Wan [HK]	84	F2
Tanbo [HN]	56	E4
Tanbu [SD]	50	E4
Tancheng [SD]	50	E5
Tanfang [JX]	48	D4
Tang He [HEB]	26	B4
Tang He [AH]	44	D2
Tang He [BJ]	22	D1
Tang He [HEN]	52	D5
Tang Xian [HEB]	26	B5
Tangba [CQ]	64	B3
Tangbu [JX]	48	C3
Tangcheng [SX]	28	D5
Tangchuan [FJ]	46	D3
Tangcun [HEN]	52	G5
Tangdan [YN]	70	E2
Tangdaohe [HEB]	26	F3
Tanggangzi [LN]	32	F3
Tanggu Qu [TJ]	24	D5
Tangguantun [TJ]	24	B6
Tanggula Bingzhan [QH]	78	B4
Tanggula Shan [QH]	78	B4
Tanggula Shankou [QH]	78	B4
Tanggula Shankou [XZ]	72	H3
Tanggula(Dangla) Shan [QH]	78	B4
Tanggula(Dangla) Shan [XZ]	72	C3
Tanggulashan [QH]	78	C3
Tanghai [HEB]	26	F4
Tanghang [SH]	38	C2
Tanghe Shuiku [LN]	32	G3
Tanghe [HEN]	52	D5
Tanghekou [BJ]	22	D1
Tangji [JS]	40	E2
Tangjiabo [SD]	50	H2
Tangjiahe [TJ]	24	C6
Tangjiahui [AH]	44	B4
Tangjiang [JX]	48	B6
Tangjiawan [HN]	56	D5
Tangkou [AH]	44	E5
Tangkou [FJ]	46	E3
Tangku [GX]	60	G2
Tanglag [QH]	78	F4
Tanglai Qu [NX]	80	C2
Tangmai [XZ]	72	J4
Tangnag [QH]	78	G3
Tangnanji [AH]	44	D2
Tangpeng [GD]	58	B5
Tangpu [JX]	48	B3
Tangqiao [JS]	40	F4

Tangqiao [SH]	38	C3	Taolin [HN]	56	E4	Tengzhuang [SD]	50	C2
Tangquan [FJ]	46	C4	Taolin [HN]	56	F2	Tergun Daba Shan [GS]	76	D2
Tangra Yumco [XZ]	72	F4	Taolin [SD]	50	F4	Tergun Daba Shan [QH]	78	D1
Tangshan Gang [HEB]	26	G4	Taolinsi [HN]	56	F3	Têwo [GS]	76	G5
Tangshan [HEB]	26	F4	Taoluo [SD]	50	F4	The Twins [HK]	84	D4
Tangshancheng [LN]	32	H4	Taonan [JL]	34	B2	Tian He [BJ]	22	D1
Tangshang [BJ]	22	B4	Taosha [JX]	48	D3	Tian He [HB]	54	C1
Tangtianshi [HN]	56	D5	Taoshan [AH]	44	D1	Tian Shan [XJ]	82	G4
Tangtou [GZ]	68	G3	Taoshan [NX]	80	B3	Tian'an [HI]	62	A2
Tangtou [SD]	50	E4	Taoshan [ZJ]	42	D5	Tianba [YN]	70	F2
Tangwai [SH]	38	E4	Taowu [JS]	40	D4	Tianbei [JL]	34	F3
Tangwan [AH]	44	C4	Taoxi [AH]	44	C4	Tiancang [GS]	76	E2
Tangwan [HN]	56	C4	Taoxi [FJ]	46	B4	Tianchang [AH]	44	F3
Tangwang He [HL]	36	E4	Taoxi [ZJ]	42	C4	Tiancheng [GS]	76	E3
Tangwanghe Qu [HL]	36	E3	Taoxing [SX]	28	D4	Tianchi [NX]	80	D3
Tangxi He [CQ]	64	E2	Taoying [GZ]	68	G3	Tiande [LN]	32	H1
Tangxi [ZJ]	42	C3	Taoyu [CQ]	64	E5	Tiandeng [GX]	60	E4
Tangxia [GD]	58	F4	Taoyuan Airport [TW]	88	D1	Tiandian [HB]	54	F3
Tangxian [HB]	54	F3	Taoyuan [FJ]	46	C4	Tiandong [GX]	60	E4
Tangyang [JS]	40	F3	Taoyuan [HN]	56	D3	Tiandu [HI]	62	B3
Tangyin [HEN]	52	F2	Taoyuan [TW]	88	C3	Tian'e [GX]	60	E2
Tangyu [SN]	74	E6	Taoyuan [TW]	88	D1	Tianfanjie [JX]	48	D2
Tangyuan [HL]	36	E4	Tap Shek Kok [HK]	84	B2	Tianfeng Ling [SX]	28	E2
Tangzha [JS]	40	F3	Tapu [TW]	88	C3	Tianfengping [SX]	28	C2
Tangzhuang [SD]	50	E5	Taqian [JX]	48	E2	Tianfu'an [SH]	38	C3
Taniantaweng Shan [XZ]	72	J3	Targan Obo [NM]	30	G3	Tiangang [JL]	34	F4
Tanjiaqiao [AH]	44	E5	Tarim Pendi [XJ]	82	G6	Tiangongmiao [SD]	50	B5
Tankou [JX]	48	B6	Tarim He [XJ]	82	H5	Tianguan [CQ]	64	E5
Tanluo [GX]	60	E5	Tarim [XJ]	82	H5	Tianheng Dao [SD]	50	G3
Tanmen [HI]	62	C2	Taro Co [XZ]	72	D4	Tianhu [HEN]	52	D3
Tanniu [HI]	62	C2	Tarqi [NM]	30	H3	Tianhua [JX]	48	C7
Tanshan [NX]	80	C4	Tart [QH]	78	C2	Tianji [AH]	44	B3
Tanshi [HN]	56	E4	Tashi [GS]	76	C2	Tianjialaozhuang [NX]	80	C3
Tanshi [ZJ]	42	B4	Tashi [HI]	62	C1	Tianjiazhen [HB]	54	H5
Tanshui [TW]	88	D1	Tatalin He [QH]	78	D2	Tianjin Xingang [TJ]	24	D5
Tantang Qu [GX]	60	G4	Tate's Cairn [HK]	84	D3	Tianjin [TJ]	24	B5
Tantou Shan [ZJ]	42	F3	Tathong Channel [HK]	84	E4	Tianjun [QH]	78	F2
Tantou [HEN]	52	C3	Tatrang [XJ]	82	I6	Tianlin [GX]	60	D3
Tantou [ZJ]	42	C3	Tatu Hsi [TW]	88	C2	Tianliu [SD]	50	E3
Tantou [ZJ]	42	E3	Tau Lo Chau [HK]	84	B5	Tianma Shan [SH]	38	C3
Tantu [JL]	34	C1	Tawakkul [XJ]	82	G7	Tianma [GZ]	68	G3
Tanwan [HN]	56	C4	Tawu [TW]	88	C4	Tianmen He [HB]	54	E4
Tanwen [HI]	62	C2	Taxkorgan [XJ]	82	D7	Tianmen [HB]	54	F4
Tanxi [GD]	58	G4	Tayang [HI]	62	C2	Tianmu Shan [ZJ]	42	C2
Tanxu Shan [ZJ]	42	E2	Tayuan [HL]	36	C2	Tianning [ZJ]	42	D2
Tanxu [GX]	60	G5	Tayuan [TW]	88	D1	Tianpeng [YN]	70	F4
Tanzhesi [BJ]	22	C4	Tayuling [TW]	88	D2	Tianping [GX]	60	H4
Tanzishan [HN]	56	E5	Tazhong [XJ]	82	I6	Tianping [GZ]	68	H3
Tao He [GS]	76	G5	Tekes He [XJ]	82	G4	Tianping [HN]	56	D4
Tao Jiang [JX]	48	B6	Tekes [XJ]	82	G4	Tianping [NX]	80	B4
Taocheng [HEN]	52	F4	Telashi Hu [QH]	78	C3	Tianqiaoling [JL]	34	I4
Taochuan [HN]	56	D6	Temeke [XJ]	82	K2	Tianquan [SC]	66	E3
Taocun [SD]	50	H2	Têmpung [QH]	78	F2	Tianshifu [LN]	32	H3
Tao'er He [JL]	34	C2	Teng Xian [GX]	60	H4	Tianshui He [NX]	80	C3
Tao'er He [NM]	30	H3	Tengchong [YN]	70	C3	Tianshui [GS]	76	H5
Taohongpo [SX]	28	C4	Tengger Shamo [GS]	76	G3	Tianshuijing [GS]	76	C2
Taohua Dao [ZJ]	42	F3	Tengger Shamo [NM]	30	C5	Tiantai Shan [ZJ]	42	E3
Taohuayu [HEN]	52	E3	Tengjia [SD]	50	I2	Tiantai [ZJ]	42	E3
Taohuayuan [HN]	56	D3	Tengqiao [HI]	62	B3	Tiantang [GD]	58	C4
Taojiang [HN]	56	E3	Tengtian [JX]	48	C4	Tiantang [HN]	56	E6
Taojiatun [LN]	32	G2	Tengtiao Jiang [YN]	70	E4	Tiantang [SN]	74	C6
Taole [NX]	80	C2	Tengzhou [SD]	50	D4	Tiantangzhai [AH]	44	B4

Tiantangzhai [HB]	54	H3	Tomortei [NM]	30	F4	Tongwan [GX]	60	G4
Tianwan [HN]	56	C3	Tomür Feng [XJ]	82	G4	Tongwei [GS]	76	H5
Tianwang [JS]	40	E4	Tong Fuk Miu Wan [HK]	84	B4	Tongxiang [ZJ]	42	D2
Tianxin [HN]	56	D4	Tong Fuk [HK]	84	B4	Tongxin [NX]	80	B4
Tianxin [HN]	56	F4	Tong Hu [GD]	58	F4	Tongxin [YN]	70	D4
Tianya [HI]	62	B3	Tong Jiang [SC]	66	G3	Tongxu [HEN]	52	F3
Tianyang [GX]	60	D4	Tong'an Qu [FJ]	46	D5	Tongyang Yunhe [JS]	40	F3
Tianzai [HI]	62	B3	Tong'an [GX]	60	H3	Tongyanggang [JS]	40	F2
Tianzhen [SX]	28	F1	Tongbai Shan [HB]	54	F2	Tongyi [NX]	80	C2
Tianzhu Shan [AH]	44	C5	Tongbai [HEN]	52	E5	Tongyu Yunhe [JS]	40	E2
Tianzhu [BJ]	22	D3	Tongban [JX]	48	F3	Tongyu [JL]	34	C3
Tianzhu [GS]	76	G4	Tongbei [HL]	36	D4	Tongyu [JS]	40	E2
Tianzhu [GZ]	68	H4	Tongcheng [AH]	44	C4	Tongyu [SX]	28	E5
Tianzhuang [BJ]	22	C3	Tongcheng [AH]	44	E3	Tongyuanpu [LN]	32	G4
Tianzhuang [HEB]	26	E4	Tongcheng [HB]	54	F5	Tongzha [AH]	44	E4
Tianzhuang [HN]	56	F6	Tongchuan Qu [SC]	66	G3	Tongzhaipu [HEN]	52	D5
Tianzhuang [SN]	74	F3	Tongchuan [SN]	74	D6	Tongzhong [HEN]	52	F5
Tianzhuangtai [LN]	32	F4	Tongdao [HN]	56	B5	Tongzhou Qu [BJ]	22	D4
Tiaoxiankou [HB]	54	E5	Tongde [QH]	78	G3	Tongzhou [GZ]	68	E5
Tiaoyu Tao [TW]	88	F1	Tonggor [SC]	66	E2	Tongzhou [JS]	40	G3
Tiechang [GD]	58	G2	Tonggu Zhang [GD]	58	H2	Tongzi [CQ]	64	D4
Tiefosi [AH]	44	C2	Tonggu Zui [HI]	62	D2	Tongzi [GZ]	68	E2
Tieli [HL]	36	E4	Tonggu [JX]	48	B3	Toson Hu [QH]	78	E2
Tieling [LN]	32	G2	Tongguan [SN]	74	F6	Tost [NM]	30	D4
Tieling [LN]	32	G2	Tongguanyi [CQ]	64	C4	Toubei [JX]	48	D5
Tielongtan [XJ]	82	F8	Tonghai [YN]	70	E3	Toudao Chuan [SN]	74	C3
Tielu [JX]	48	C4	Tonghe [GX]	60	H4	Toudao Jiang [JL]	34	G5
Tiemen Guan [XJ]	82	J5	Tonghe [HL]	36	E5	Toudao [JL]	34	I5
Tienchung [TW]	88	C3	Tonghua [JL]	34	E6	Toudaodun [NX]	80	C2
Tieniu Guan [FJ]	46	C2	Tonghua [JL]	34	E6	Toudaohezi [SN]	74	E2
Tieniu Guan [JX]	48	E4	Tonghua [SX]	28	B6	Toudaokan [NX]	80	C1
Tieqiao [CQ]	64	E2	Tongjia [HI]	62	B3	Touguan [NX]	80	B2
Tieshan Qu [HB]	54	G4	Tongjiang [HL]	36	G4	Toulin [HL]	36	G4
Tieshan [CQ]	64	B4	Tongjiang [SC]	66	G3	Toumen Shan [ZJ]	42	E4
Tieshan [FJ]	46	D2	Tongjiangkou [LN]	32	G2	Toupai [GX]	60	H3
Tieshangang Qu [GX]	60	G6	Tongjiangling [JX]	48	C2	Toupeng [ZJ]	42	D2
Tieshikou [JX]	48	B6	Tongjing [JS]	40	D4	Touqiao [SH]	38	E4
Tiexi [SC]	66	G2	Tongjing [SD]	50	E4	Toutunhe Qu [XJ]	82	J4
Tin Shui Wai [HK]	84	B2	Tongjunzhuang [BJ]	22	D3	Touying [NX]	80	C4
Ting Jiang [FJ]	46	B4	Tongken He [HL]	36	D4	Touzeng [JS]	40	F1
Ting Kok [HK]	84	D2	Tongli [JS]	40	F4	Town Island		
Tingdong [GZ]	68	G5	Tongliang [CQ]	64	C4	(Fo Tau Fan Chau) [HK]	84	E3
Tinglin [SH]	38	D4	Tongliao [NM]	30	H4	Toyun [XJ]	82	D5
Tingliuhe [HEB]	26	F4	Tonglin [GZ]	68	G4	Tsaotun [TW]	88	C3
Tingluo [SD]	50	E2	Tongling [AH]	44	D5	Tseng Lan Shue [HK]	84	E3
Tingping [HN]	56	C5	Tongling [AH]	44	D5	Tsengwen Hsi [TW]	88	C3
Tingri [XZ]	72	F5	Tongling [FJ]	46	C6	Tseung Kwan O [HK]	84	E3
Tingsiqiao [HB]	54	G5	Tongling [GX]	60	G4	Tsim Sha Tsui [HK]	84	D3
Tingxiandu [HN]	56	D2	Tonglu [ZJ]	42	C3	Tsing Fai Tong [HK]	84	C2
Tiu Keng Leng [HK]	84	E3	Tongluo [JS]	40	F5	Tsing Lung Tau [HK]	84	C3
Tiu Yue Yung [HK]	84	E3	Tongmu [GX]	60	G3	Tsing Shan Wan [HK]	84	B3
Tiznap He [XJ]	82	E7	Tongmu [JX]	48	A4	Tsing Yi [HK]	84	C3
To Kwa Wan [HK]	84	D3	Tongmuxi [HN]	56	C4	Tsuen Kam Au [HK]	84	C2
Todog [XJ]	82	H3	Tongnan [CQ]	64	B3	Tsuen Wan [HK]	84	C3
Togtoh [NM]	30	E4	Tongnan [HL]	36	C3	Tuan He [HEN]	52	C4
Togtun He [QH]	78	B3	Tongren [GZ]	68	H3	Tuanbao [HB]	54	B4
Toksun [XJ]	82	K4	Tongren [QH]	78	H3	Tuanbo [TJ]	24	B6
Toli [XJ]	82	H3	Tongshan [HB]	54	G5	Tuanbokou [HEB]	26	A5
Tolo Channel			Tongshan [JS]	40	C1	Tuanbowa Shuiku [TJ]	24	B6
(Chek Mun) [HK]	84	E2	Tongshan [SX]	28	C6	Tuancun [JX]	48	D4
Tolo Harbour [HK]	84	D2	Tongshi [SD]	50	D4	Tuanfeng [HB]	54	G4
Tomort [XJ]	82	N4	Tongtian He [QH]	78	C3	Tuanjie [HL]	36	D4

Name	Page	Grid
Tuanlinpu [HB]	54	E4
Tuanshansi [HB]	54	E5
Tuanxi [GZ]	68	F3
Tuban [SX]	28	B3
Tuchang [GZ]	68	F5
Tuchang [TW]	88	D2
Tucheng [GZ]	68	D2
Tucheng [HB]	54	C2
Tucheng [HEB]	26	D2
Tuchengzi [HEB]	26	B2
Tuchengzi [LN]	32	H4
Tudi'ao [GZ]	68	G2
Tuding [JL]	34	E4
Tu'e [YN]	70	C2
Tuen Mun [HK]	84	B2
Tuen Tsui [HK]	84	F2
Tufang [FJ]	46	B4
Tuguancun [YN]	70	C2
Tuhai He [SD]	50	D2
Tujie [GZ]	68	C3
Tukan [CQ]	64	D4
Tukan [CQ]	64	D4
Tulagt Ar Gol [QH]	78	B2
Tulai He [QH]	78	F1
Tulai Nanshan [QH]	78	F1
Tulai Shan [QH]	78	F1
Tulan [TW]	88	D4
Tuligen He [HEB]	26	D1
Tulongpu [HN]	56	G3
Tumain [XZ]	72	H3
Tumd Youqi [NM]	30	E4
Tumd Zuoqi [NM]	30	E4
Tumen Jiang [JL]	34	H5
Tumen [GS]	76	G4
Tumen [JL]	34	I5
Tumulu [HEB]	26	B2
Tumxuk [XJ]	82	F6
Tunchang [HI]	62	B3
Tung Chung Bay [HK]	84	B3
Tung Chung [HK]	84	B3
Tung Lung Chau [HK]	84	E4
Tung Wan [HK]	84	C4
Tungchi Yu [TW]	88	B3
Tungchuan Tao [FJ]	46	F4
Tungho [TW]	88	D4
Tunghsiao [TW]	88	C2
Tungkang [TW]	88	C4
Tungmen [TW]	88	D3
Tungo Wan [HK]	84	D4
Tungshih [TW]	88	C2
Tungshih [TW]	88	C3
Tungyin Lie Tao [FJ]	46	F3
Tunli [SX]	28	B5
Tunliu [SX]	28	D5
Tuo He [AH]	44	D2
Tuo Jiang [SC]	66	F3
Tuo Shui [HN]	56	D6
Tuochuanbu [JX]	48	C3
Tuoheji [AH]	44	D2
Tuoji Dao [SD]	50	G1
Tuokou [HN]	56	B4
Tuolai Nanshan [GS]	76	D3
Tuoli [BJ]	22	C4
Tuoniang Jiang [GX]	60	C3
Tuoshi [SN]	74	B6
Tuowu [SC]	66	E4
Tuoxing Shuiku [HI]	62	A3
Tuozhamin [NM]	30	H2
Tuping [GZ]	68	F2
Tupo [NX]	80	B3
Tuqiao [AH]	44	D4
Tuqiao [BJ]	22	D4
Tuqiao [HN]	56	C5
Tuqiao [JS]	40	E4
Tuqiao [SN]	74	D5
Tuquan [NM]	30	H3
Tura [XJ]	82	J7
Turpan Pendi [XJ]	82	L4
Turpan [XJ]	82	K4
Turugart Shankou [XJ]	82	D5
Tushan [JS]	40	C1
Tuwei He [SN]	74	F2
Tuxi [GZ]	68	F2

U

Ud Qu [NM]	30	D5
Ulan Buh Shamo [NM]	30	D5
Ulan Moron [SN]	74	F1
Ulan Qab [NM]	30	F4
Ulan Tug [JL]	34	D3
Ulan Ul Hu [QH]	78	B3
Ulan [QH]	78	F2
Ulanhot [NM]	30	H3
Ulastai [XJ]	82	L3
Ulgai [NM]	30	G3
Ulgain Gobi [NM]	30	G3
Ulgain Gol [NM]	30	G3
Ulugqat [XJ]	82	D6
Ulungur He [XJ]	82	K2
Ulungur Hu [XJ]	82	J2
Unuli Horog [QH]	78	B3
Urad Houqi [NM]	30	D4
Urad Qianqi [NM]	30	E4
Urad Zhongqi [NM]	30	E4
Uragxan [NM]	30	H2
Urho Qu [XJ]	82	I2
Urmston Road [HK]	84	B2
Urru Co [XZ]	72	F4
Urt Moron [QH]	78	C2
Urt Moron [QH]	78	C2
Ürümqi [XJ]	82	J4
Ürümqi [XJ]	82	J4
Usu [XJ]	82	I3
Uxin Qi [NM]	30	E5
Uyerin Gol [HL]	36	C4
Uzbel Shankou [XJ]	82	C6

V

| Victoria Harbour [HK] | 84 | D3 |
| Victoria Peak [HK] | 84 | D3 |

W

Wabu Hu [AH]	44	C3
Wabu [AH]	44	C3
Wafang [JL]	34	B2
Wafangdian [LN]	32	F5
Waglan Island [HK]	84	E4
Waichen [ZJ]	42	D3
Waifang Shan [HEN]	52	D4
Waigang [SH]	38	C2
Wailuo [GD]	58	B6
Waitoushan [LN]	32	G3
Waiyang [FJ]	46	C3
Walagan [HL]	36	C1
Walêg [SC]	66	D4
Wali [BJ]	22	D3
Walong [AH]	44	C5
Walung [XZ]	72	K5
Wan He [AH]	44	C5
Wan'an Shuiku [JX]	48	B5
Wan'an Xi [FJ]	46	B4
Wan'an [FJ]	46	C3
Wan'an [JX]	48	B5
Wanbao [JL]	34	A2
Wanbao [JL]	34	E3
Wanbu [JX]	48	C3
Wanchong [HI]	62	B3
Wanda Shan [HL]	36	G4
Wande [SD]	50	C3
Wandian [YN]	70	C3
Wandianzi [LN]	32	I3
Wanding [YN]	70	C3
Wanfu He [SD]	50	B4
Wanfu [JX]	48	B4
Wanfu [LN]	32	F4
Wang Chau [HK]	84	C2
Wang Chau [HK]	84	F3
Wangan Tao (Pachao Tao) [TW]	88	B3
Wangben [JL]	34	C4
Wangbuzhuang [TJ]	24	C3
Wangcang [SC]	66	G2
Wangcao [GZ]	68	F2
Wangcheng [HN]	56	E3
Wangcheng [SD]	50	G3
Wangcun [AH]	44	D6
Wangcun [HN]	56	B3
Wangcun [SX]	28	D5
Wangcundian [SD]	50	C2
Wangcunkou [ZJ]	42	C4
Wangdain [XZ]	72	G5
Wangdian [GX]	60	D3
Wangdu [HEB]	26	C5
Wang'er [JX]	48	E3
Wangfu [GD]	58	C5
Wangfutai [NX]	80	C3
Wanggao [GX]	60	I3
Wanggong [SX]	28	D4
Wangguo [SD]	50	E4
Wangguantun [SX]	28	E1
Wanghai Shan [LN]	32	E3
Wanghaotun [SD]	50	B4
Wanghezhuang [SD]	50	G3
Wanghong [NX]	80	C2
Wanghu [SD]	50	F4
Wanghu [SX]	28	E2

Wanghua [JX] 48 B4
Wangji [JS] 40 C2
Wangji [JS] 40 D2
Wangjia [ZJ] 42 F2
Wangjiachang Shuiku [HN] 56 D2
Wangjiachang [HN] 56 D2
Wangjiadian [LN] 32 C4
Wangjiajing [HEB] 26 C6
Wangjiang [AH] 44 C5
Wangjiapu [JX] 48 C2
Wangjiazhuang [SX] 28 D3
Wangjieliu [AH] 44 C3
Wangkou [TJ] 24 A5
Wangkuai Shuiku [HEB] 26 B5
Wangkuangtun [TJ] 24 B6
Wangkui [HL] 36 D4
Wanglejing [NX] 80 D3
Wangling [HN] 56 F4
Wangliu [HEN] 52 G5
Wangmao [GX] 60 G5
Wangmao [SX] 28 C6
Wangmo [GZ] 68 E5
Wangmudu [JX] 48 C6
Wangou [JL] 34 F5
Wangpan Shan [ZJ] 42 E2
Wangqi [JL] 34 F4
Wangqing [JL] 34 I4
Wangqingmen [LN] 32 I3
Wangqingtuo [TJ] 24 B5
Wangshi [AH] 44 C2
Wangshu [HEB] 26 E6
Wangtai [SD] 50 F3
Wangtan [ZJ] 42 D3
Wangtao [SX] 28 D5
Wangtian'e [JL] 34 G6
Wangtuan [AH] 44 C2
Wangtuan [HEB] 26 D6
Wangtuan [NX] 80 B4
Wangtuan [SD] 50 H2
Wangtuanzhuang [NX] 80 B4
Wangwa [NX] 80 C4
Wangwenzhuang [TJ] 24 C6
Wangwu Shan [SX] 28 D6
Wangwu [HI] 62 B2
Wangxia [HI] 62 B2
Wangxian [HN] 56 F4
Wangxian [JX] 48 C4
Wangyi Qu [SN] 74 E5
Wangying [HB] 54 A4
Wangyuan [NX] 80 C2
Wangzhai [AH] 44 C1
Wangzhai [SX] 28 D6
Wangzhai [ZJ] 42 C4
Wangzhuang [JS] 40 D1
Wangzizhuang [SD] 50 C3
Wanji [HB] 54 E3
Wanjia [LN] 32 C4
Wanjialing [LN] 32 F5
Wanjiazhai [SX] 28 C2
Wanjinta [JL] 34 E3
Wanli Qu [JX] 48 C3
Wanli [AH] 44 E4

Wanliang [JL] 34 G5
Wanling [HI] 62 B2
Wanmu [CQ] 64 E5
Wannian [JX] 48 E3
Wanning Shuiku [HI] 62 C3
Wanning [HI] 62 C3
Wanqingsha [GD] 58 E4
Wanquan He [HI] 62 C2
Wanquan He [HI] 62 C2
Wanquan [HEB] 26 B3
Wanquan [HEB] 26 B3
Wanquan [HI] 62 C2
Wanrong [SX] 28 B6
Wanshan Qundao [GD] 58 E5
Wanshan Tequ [GZ] 68 H3
Wansheng Qu [CQ] 64 C5
Wantan [HB] 54 C4
Wantan [HEN] 52 E3
Wantang [YN] 70 E4
Wanxiang [SH] 38 E4
Wanyang Shan [JX] 48 B5
Wanyao Shuiku [SN] 74 E4
Wanyuan [SC] 66 H2
Wanzai [JX] 48 B3
Wanzhen [SN] 74 F2
Wanzhou Qu [CQ] 64 E3
Wanzi Hu [HN] 56 E3
Waqên [SC] 66 E2
Watang [GX] 60 G5
Watang [SX] 28 B3
Wating [NX] 80 C5
Wawutang [HN] 56 C5
Waxie [SH] 38 E3
Waxing [HL] 36 D4
Waxxari [XJ] 82 J6
Wayao [JS] 40 D1
Wayao [YN] 70 C3
Wayuan [HN] 56 E5
Wazijie [SN] 74 F5
Wei He [SN] 74 B6
Wei He [GS] 76 H5
Wei He [HEB] 26 C7
Wei He [HEN] 52 F2
Wei He [SD] 50 B3
Wei He [SD] 50 F3
Wei He [SN] 74 E6
Wei Shui [HB] 54 D4
Wei Shui [HN] 56 E3
Wei Xian [HEB] 26 B7
Wei Xian [HEN] 26 C7
Weichang [HEB] 26 E2
Weicheng [GZ] 68 E4
Weifang [SD] 50 F3
Weifen He [SX] 28 C3
Weihai [SD] 50 I2
Weihu Ling [JL] 34 G4
Weihui [HEN] 52 F2
Weijiatan [SX] 28 C3
Weijin [JL] 34 E5
Weijing [NM] 30 E4
Weiling [HL] 36 E4
Weilu [SX] 28 D1

Weiluo [GX] 60 F5
Weima [SX] 28 E4
Weimin [FJ] 46 C2
Weinan [SN] 74 E6
Weining [GZ] 68 C4
Weiqiao [JS] 40 D2
Weiqiu [HEN] 52 F2
Weishan Hu [SD] 50 D5
Weishan [HL] 36 D3
Weishan [SD] 50 D5
Weishan [YN] 70 D3
Weishanzhuang [BJ] 22 D4
Weishe [GZ] 68 C5
Weishi [HEN] 52 F3
Weitian [FJ] 46 D2
Weitou Wan [FJ] 46 D5
Weitou [FJ] 46 D5
Weiwan [SD] 50 B5
Weixi [YN] 70 C2
Weixin [GZ] 68 D3
Weixin [HN] 56 D2
Weixin [YN] 70 F2
Weiya [XJ] 82 N5
Weiyuan Jiang [YN] 70 D4
Weiyuan [GS] 76 H5
Weiyuan [SC] 66 F4
Weizhou Dao [GX] 60 F6
Weizhou [GX] 60 G6
Weizhou [NX] 80 C3
Weizhuang [SN] 74 E6
Weizhuang [SX] 28 B6
Weiziyu [BJ] 22 E2
Weiziyu [LN] 32 H3
Wen He [SD] 50 E4
Wen He [SD] 50 F3
Wen Xian [HEN] 52 E3
Wen'an [HB] 54 D4
Wen'an [HEB] 26 D5
Wenbu [NX] 80 B5
Wenchang [HI] 62 C2
Wencheng [HI] 62 C2
Wencheng [ZJ] 42 D5
Wenchuan [SC] 66 E3
Wenchun [HL] 36 E5
Wendeng [SD] 50 I2
Wendi [GX] 60 H6
Wendian [SD] 50 D2
Wendou [HB] 54 A5
Wenfang [JX] 48 E3
Weng Jiang [GD] 58 E2
Weng'an [GZ] 68 F3
Wengcheng [GD] 58 E2
Wengda [SC] 66 D3
Wengdong [GZ] 68 H3
Wengjiang [HN] 56 F3
Wengkong [GZ] 68 F3
Wengshui [YN] 70 C1
Wengtian [HI] 62 C2
Wengyuan [GD] 58 F2
Wenjia [FJ] 46 E4
Wenjiadian [GZ] 68 F3
Wenjiang Qu [SC] 66 E3

Name	Page	Grid
Wenjiao [HI]	62	C2
Wenjiashi [HN]	56	F3
Wenling [ZJ]	42	E4
Wenlong [JX]	48	B7
Wenlong [YN]	70	D3
Wenluo [HI]	62	B3
Wenqiao [JX]	48	D2
Wenquan(Arixang) [XJ]	82	G3
Wenquan [AH]	44	C5
Wenquan [CQ]	64	E2
Wenquan [QH]	78	B4
Wenru [HI]	62	C2
Wenshan [YN]	70	F4
Wenshang [SD]	50	C4
Wenshi [GX]	60	I2
Wenshui [GZ]	68	E2
Wenshui [SX]	28	D4
Wensu [XJ]	82	G5
Wentang [JX]	48	B2
Wenxi [SX]	28	C6
Wenxi [ZJ]	42	D4
WenXian [GS]	76	H6
Wenyu He [BJ]	22	D3
Wenyu He [SX]	28	C4
Wenyu shuiku [SX]	28	C4
Wenzhen [JX]	48	D3
Wenzhou Wan [ZJ]	42	D5
Wenzhou [ZJ]	42	D4
Wenzhu [JX]	48	A5
Wenzu [SD]	50	D3
West Lamma Channel [HK]	84	C4
Wo Hop Shek [HK]	84	D2
Wofo [CQ]	64	B4
Woinbo [SC]	66	C2
Woken He [HL]	36	E4
Woken [HL]	36	F5
Wong Chuk Hang [HK]	84	D4
Wong Chuk Kok Hoi [HK]	84	E1
Wong Leng [HK]	84	D1
Wong Mau Chau [HK]	84	F2
Wong Nai Chau [HK]	84	F3
Wong Wan Chau [HK]	84	E1
Woyangchang [SX]	28	D3
Wu Jiang [CQ]	64	E5
Wu Shan [CQ]	64	F3
Wu Jiang [GZ]	68	F3
Wu Kai Sha [HK]	84	E2
Wu Kau Tang [HK]	84	E1
Wu Shan [HB]	54	C3
Wu Shui [HN]	56	B4
Wu Shui [HN]	56	C5
Wu Shui [GD]	58	E1
Wu Shui [HN]	56	B3
Wu Xia [CQ]	64	G2
Wu Xia [HB]	54	C3
Wu'an [HB]	54	D3
Wu'an [HEB]	26	B7
Wubaihu [TJ]	24	C2
Wubu [SN]	74	F3
Wuchang Hu [AH]	44	C5
Wuchang [HL]	36	D5
Wucheng [AH]	44	E6
Wucheng [JX]	48	C2
Wucheng [SD]	50	C2
Wucheng [SX]	28	B5
Wucheng [SX]	28	C4
Wuchi [TW]	88	C2
Wuchiu Yu [FJ]	46	E5
Wuchuan [GD]	58	B5
Wuchuan [GZ]	68	F2
Wuchuan [NM]	30	E4
Wuda Lianchi [HL]	36	C3
Wudalianchi [HL]	36	D3
Wudang Qu [GZ]	68	E4
Wudang Shan [HB]	54	C2
Wudang Shan [HB]	54	C2
Wudang [JX]	48	B7
Wudao [LN]	32	E5
Wudaogou [HL]	36	D2
Wudaogou [JL]	34	E5
Wudaogou [JL]	34	J4
Wudaoliang [QH]	78	C3
Wudaoshui [HN]	56	B2
Wudi [SD]	50	D2
Wudian [HB]	54	E3
Wudian [HEN]	52	E5
Wuding He [SN]	74	F3
Wuding [YN]	70	E3
Wudu [JX]	48	F3
Wudu [SC]	66	F3
Wudu [ZJ]	42	C5
Wuduhe [HB]	54	D3
Wuduizi [NX]	80	C2
Wufeng [HB]	54	C4
Wufeng [LN]	32	F2
Wufengpu [HN]	56	D5
Wugang [AH]	44	E3
Wugang [HEN]	52	E4
Wugang [HN]	56	C5
Wugong Shan [JX]	48	A4
Wugong [SN]	74	D6
Wugouying [HEN]	52	F4
Wuguan [SN]	74	F7
Wuguanyi [SN]	74	B7
Wuhai [NM]	30	D5
Wuhan [HB]	54	G4
Wuhe [AH]	44	D2
Wuhu [AH]	44	E4
Wuhu [AH]	44	E4
Wuhua [GD]	58	G3
Wuhuanchi [LN]	32	E2
Wuji [HEB]	26	B5
Wujia [CQ]	64	B4
Wujia [GX]	60	G6
Wujiadian [HB]	54	F3
Wujiang [XZ]	72	B3
Wujiang [AH]	44	E4
Wujiang [GX]	60	H3
Wujiang [GZ]	68	E3
Wujiang [JS]	40	F4
Wujiang [JX]	48	C4
Wujiaqu [XJ]	82	J3
Wujiatang [FJ]	46	C2
Wujiaxiang [SH]	38	D3
Wujiazhan [JL]	34	E3
Wujiazhuang [SX]	28	B4
Wujin Qu [JS]	40	F4
Wujing [GD]	58	F1
Wujing [SD]	50	E3
Wujing [SH]	38	D4
Wujingfu [GD]	58	H3
Wuke [TJ]	24	D4
Wukeshu [JL]	34	C1
Wulai [TW]	88	D2
Wulajie [JL]	34	F3
Wulang Shan [YN]	70	D3
Wuleidao Wan [SD]	50	H3
Wuli Jiang [GX]	60	G5
Wuli [GX]	60	G5
Wuli [HB]	54	C5
Wuli [QH]	78	C3
Wulian Feng [YN]	70	E2
Wulian [SC]	66	F3
Wulian [SD]	50	F4
Wuliba [SN]	74	D8
Wulichuan [HEN]	52	C4
Wulie He [HEB]	26	E2
Wulie [HI]	62	A2
Wulikou [HEN]	52	E3
Wuling Shan [HN]	56	B3
Wuling Shan [HEB]	26	E3
Wulingyuan Qu [HN]	56	C2
Wulipo [BJ]	22	C2
Wulipo [NX]	80	C3
Wulipu [HB]	54	E4
Wulong He [SD]	50	G3
Wulong [CQ]	64	D4
Wuluo [GZ]	68	G2
Wuma [CQ]	64	F3
Wumahe Qu [HL]	36	E4
Wumang Dao [LN]	32	G5
Wumei Shan [JX]	48	B3
Wumeng Shan [YN]	70	E2
Wumeng Shan [GZ]	68	B4
Wuming [GX]	60	F4
Wuning Shui [JX]	48	B3
Wuning [JX]	48	C2
Wuping [FJ]	46	B4
Wupo [HI]	62	C2
Wuqi [SN]	74	D4
Wuqia(Ulugqat) [XJ]	82	D6
Wuqiang [HEB]	26	C5
Wuqiang [HEN]	52	G3
Wuqiangxi [HN]	56	D3
Wuqiao [HEB]	26	D6
Wuqiaoling [GS]	76	G4
Wuqing Qu [TJ]	24	B4
Wurenqiao [HEB]	26	C5
Wushan [AH]	44	D3
Wushan [CQ]	64	F2
Wushan [GS]	76	H5
Wusheng Guan [HB]	54	G3
Wusheng Guan [HEN]	52	F6
Wusheng [SC]	66	G3
Wushi [GD]	58	A6
Wushi [HI]	62	B2

Wushi [XJ]	82	F5
Wushih Pi [TW]	88	D2
Wushu [JX]	48	B5
Wusi [SH]	38	E4
Wusong Jiang		
(Suzhou He) [SH]	38	C3
Wusong Kou [SH]	38	D2
Wusong [SH]	38	D2
Wusu [HL]	36	H3
Wusu [HN]	56	C3
Wusuli Jiang [HL]	36	G4
Wusuli [HL]	36	B1
Wutai Shan [SX]	28	E3
Wutai [SX]	28	E3
Wutai [XJ]	82	H3
Wutong He [HL]	36	E4
Wutong [FJ]	46	D4
Wutong [GX]	60	H2
Wutonghe [HL]	36	F4
Wutongqiao Qu [SC]	66	E4
Wuwei [AH]	44	D4
Wuwei [GS]	76	G4
Wuxi [CQ]	64	F2
Wuxi [HN]	56	C3
Wuxi [JS]	40	F4
Wuxian [AH]	44	C4
Wuxiang [SX]	28	D5
Wuxiang [ZJ]	42	E3
Wuxiqiao [AH]	44	D5
Wuxu [GX]	60	F5
Wuxuan [GX]	60	G4
Wuxue [HB]	54	H5
Wuxun [JS]	40	F2
Wuyang He [GZ]	68	G3
Wuyang [HEN]	52	E4
Wuyang [HN]	56	C5
Wuyang [JX]	48	C6
Wuyang [SX]	28	E5
Wuyi Shan [JX]	48	D5
Wuyi Jiang [ZJ]	42	C4
Wuyi Shan [FJ]	46	C2
Wuyi [AH]	44	E3
Wuyi [FJ]	46	C2
Wuyi [HEB]	26	C6
Wuyi [ZJ]	42	C4
Wuyiling Qu [HL]	36	E3
Wuying Qu [HL]	36	E3
Wuyishan [FJ]	46	D2
Wuyishan [JX]	48	E4
Wuyuan [JX]	48	E2
Wuyuan [NM]	30	E4
Wuyuancun [HEN]	52	C3
Wuyun Ding [CQ]	64	G2
Wuyun [GD]	58	G3
Wuyun [JX]	48	B6
Wuzhai [SX]	28	C3
Wuzhen [SN]	74	E3
Wuzhi Feng [JX]	48	B5
Wuzhi Shan [HEB]	26	F3
Wuzhi Shan [HI]	62	B3
Wuzhi Shan [HI]	62	B3
Wuzhi [HEN]	52	E2

Wuzhishan [HI]	62	B3
Wuzhishan [HI]	62	B3
Wuzhong Qu [JS]	40	F4
Wuzhong [NX]	80	C3
Wuzhou [GX]	60	I4

X

Xago [XZ]	72	G4
Xainza [XZ]	72	G4
Xaitongmoin [XZ]	72	G5
Xamgyi'nyilha [YN]	70	C2
Xar Gut [NM]	30	G3
Xar Obt [NM]	30	G3
Xarag [QH]	78	F2
Xarlag [NM]	30	E5
Xarma [XZ]	72	I4
Xarqu [XZ]	72	I4
Xarru [XZ]	72	F5
Xaxa [XZ]	72	D3
Xayar [XJ]	82	H5
Xi Xi [FJ]	46	D4
Xi Chuan [HEN]	52	C4
Xi He [AH]	44	D4
Xi He [JX]	48	D2
Xi He [LN]	32	E3
Xi Jiang [GD]	58	C3
Xi Qu [SC]	66	D5
Xi Shan [BJ]	22	B4
Xi Shui [HB]	54	H4
Xi Taijnar Hu [QH]	78	C2
Xi Ujimqin Qi [NM]	30	G3
Xi Xi [FJ]	46	C5
Xi Xian [HEN]	52	F5
Xi Xian [SX]	28	B5
Xia Boingor [QH]	78	F4
Xia Xian [SX]	28	C6
Xia Zayü [XZ]	72	K5
Xia'ao [GX]	60	E3
Xiabuji [JX]	48	D3
Xiacang [AH]	44	C5
Xiacengpu [HN]	56	D6
Xiachengzi [HL]	36	F5
Xiachuan Dao [GD]	58	D5
Xiachuan [SX]	28	D6
Xiacun [JX]	48	B4
Xiadachen Dao [ZJ]	42	E4
Xiadian [SX]	28	D5
Xiadong [GD]	58	D4
Xiage [AH]	44	D4
Xiagezhuang [SD]	50	G3
Xiaguan [HEN]	52	C4
Xiaguan [ZJ]	42	D5
Xiaguanying [GS]	76	H5
Xiahe [GS]	76	G5
Xiahebei [BJ]	22	D1
Xiaheyan [NX]	80	B3
Xiahuaqiao [HN]	56	D5
Xiahuayuan Qu [HEB]	26	C3
Xiajia [GX]	60	D3
Xiajiang [JX]	48	C4
Xiajiapu [LN]	32	H2
Xiajin [SD]	50	C3

Xiakeng [AH]	44	E6
Xiakou [ZJ]	42	B3
Xiakou [ZJ]	42	B4
Xialao [GX]	60	D2
Xialaxiu [QH]	78	E4
Xialiu [HN]	56	E4
Xialiushui [NX]	80	B3
Xialu Qu [HB]	54	G4
Xiamaguan [NX]	80	C3
Xiamao [FJ]	46	C3
Xiamaoshan [BJ]	22	D1
Xiamaya [XJ]	82	N4
Xiamen Gang [FJ]	46	D5
Xiamen [FJ]	46	D5
Xian Xian [HEB]	26	D5
Xi'an [NX]	80	B4
Xi'an [SN]	74	D6
Xian'an Qu [HB]	54	G5
Xiandu [FJ]	46	C4
Xianfeng [HB]	54	B5
Xi'anfeng [JS]	40	E2
Xiang Jiang [HN]	56	E4
Xiang Jiang [GX]	60	H2
Xiang Jiang [GZ]	68	F3
Xiang Shui [JX]	48	C6
Xiang Xi [HB]	54	C3
Xiang'an Qu [FJ]	46	D5
Xiang'an [AH]	44	D4
Xiangba [HB]	54	B3
Xiangbei [GX]	60	F3
Xiangchang [AH]	44	C5
Xiangcheng Qu [JS]	40	F4
Xiangcheng(Qagchêng) [SC]	66	C4
Xiangcheng [HEN]	52	E4
Xiangcheng [HEN]	52	F4
Xiangcheng [SD]	50	D5
Xiangcunying [BJ]	22	C2
Xiangdong Qu [JX]	48	A4
Xiangfan [HB]	54	E2
Xiangfen [SX]	28	C6
Xianghai [JL]	34	B2
Xianghe [HEB]	26	D4
Xianghe [SN]	74	F7
Xianghongdian Shuiku [AH]	44	C4
Xianghua Ling [HN]	56	E6
Xianghua [SH]	38	E2
Xianghuang		
(Hobot Xar) Qi [NM]	30	F4
Xianghuaqiao [SH]	38	C3
Xiangjia [ZJ]	42	B4
Xiangjiangkou [HN]	56	D6
Xianglan [HL]	36	E4
Xiangling [SX]	28	C5
Xianglinpu [HN]	56	D6
Xianglutai [SX]	28	F2
Xiangning [SX]	28	B6
Xiangou [HI]	62	C2
Xiangride [QH]	78	E3
Xiangshan Gang [ZJ]	42	E3
Xiangshan [AH]	44	E4
Xiangshan [ZJ]	42	E3
Xiangshao [HN]	56	E4

Xiangshui [HI]	62	B3
Xiangshui [JS]	40	E1
Xiangshuihe [SX]	28	C6
Xiangtan [HN]	56	E4
Xiangtan [HN]	56	E4
Xiangtandong [HN]	56	E4
Xiangtang [JX]	48	C3
Xiangxi [ZJ]	42	C4
Xiangxiang [HN]	56	E4
Xiangyang Qu [HB]	54	E2
Xiangyang [HL]	36	D5
Xiangyang [HN]	56	E5
Xiangyang [JL]	34	E5
Xiangyin [HN]	56	E3
Xiangyu [AH]	44	C5
Xiangyuan [SX]	28	E5
Xiangyun [YN]	70	D3
Xiangzhi [FJ]	46	D5
Xiangzhou [GX]	60	E4
Xiangzhou [GX]	60	G4
Xiangzhou [SD]	50	F3
Xiangzikou [HN]	56	D3
Xianhe [YN]	70	D4
Xianjiang [ZJ]	42	D5
Xianjin [HL]	36	F4
Xianju [ZJ]	42	D4
Xianlai [HI]	62	C2
Xianning [HB]	54	G5
Xianren [SX]	28	E3
Xianrendong [LN]	32	F5
Xianrendu [HB]	54	D2
Xianrenqiao [JL]	34	G5
Xianshui He [SC]	66	D3
Xianshui [GX]	60	H2
Xiantan [SC]	66	G4
Xiantang Gang [SH]	38	D3
Xiantao [HB]	54	F4
Xianxi [HN]	56	B5
Xianxi [HN]	56	D3
Xianxia Ling [ZJ]	42	B4
Xianxia [JX]	48	C5
Xianxiang [ZJ]	42	E3
Xianyan [ZJ]	42	D3
Xianyang [FJ]	46	D1
Xianyang [SN]	74	D6
Xianyou [FJ]	46	D4
Xianyuan [AH]	44	E5
Xianyuan [JX]	48	B3
Xiao He [SX]	28	C4
Xiao Hinggan Ling [HL]	36	D3
Xiao Jiang [CQ]	64	E2
Xiao Jiang [YN]	70	E2
Xiao Qaidam Hu [QH]	78	D2
Xiao Qaidam [QH]	78	D2
Xiao Shan [HEN]	52	B3
Xiao Shui [HN]	56	D5
Xiao Surmang [QH]	78	E4
Xiao Xi [ZJ]	42	C4
Xiao Xian [AH]	44	C1
Xiaoba [CQ]	64	E5
Xiaobodian [TJ]	24	B3
Xiaobole shan [HL]	36	C2

Xiaobu [JX]	48	C5
Xiaocha [NX]	80	C4
Xiaochang [GX]	60	E2
Xiaochang [HB]	54	F3
Xiaochang [HEB]	26	C2
Xiaochangshan Dao [LN]	32	F5
Xiaocheng [JL]	34	G3
Xiaochengzi [JL]	34	D4
Xiaochengzi [JL]	34	E3
Xiaochengzi [LN]	32	G2
Xiaochi [AH]	44	C5
Xiaochi [HB]	54	H5
Xiaochuan [GS]	76	H6
Xiaocuogang [FJ]	46	D4
Xiaodian Qu [SX]	28	D4
Xiaodian [BJ]	22	E3
Xiaodian [TJ]	24	B4
Xiaodong [GX]	60	F5
Xiaodong [ZJ]	42	E2
Xiaodongzhuang [TJ]	24	C5
Xiaogan [HB]	54	F4
Xiaogang [HB]	54	F3
Xiaogang [JX]	48	C3
Xiaogang [TJ]	24	C1
Xiaogu shan [JX]	48	D2
Xiaoguan [GS]	76	I4
Xiaogushanzi [LN]	32	H3
Xiaohai [GZ]	68	C4
Xiaohai [JS]	40	F2
Xiaohe [HB]	54	E3
Xiaohe [NX]	80	B5
Xiaohe [SN]	74	E3
Xiaohekou [SN]	74	C7
Xiaohenglong [HN]	56	C4
Xiaohetou [SX]	28	C2
Xiaohezi [HEB]	26	C2
Xiaohezi [NM]	30	G2
Xiaohongmen [BJ]	22	D4
Xiaohuan Jiang [GX]	60	F2
Xiaoji [HEN]	52	E2
Xiaoji [JS]	40	E3
Xiaoji [SD]	50	G3
Xiaojiafang [FJ]	46	C2
Xiaojiahe [HL]	36	G4
Xiaojiang [JX]	48	B6
Xiaojiang [ZJ]	42	D5
Xiaojiang [ZJ]	42	E3
Xiaojieling [HB]	54	H3
Xiaojin Shan [SH]	38	D5
Xiaojin(Zainlha) [SC]	66	E3
Xiaojin [GS]	76	I5
Xiaolan [GD]	58	E4
Xiaolangdiba [HEN]	52	D3
Xiaoli [SD]	50	C3
Xiaoliangqian [BJ]	22	D1
Xiaolin [HB]	54	F2
Xiaoling He [LN]	32	D3
XiaoLiuxiang [AH]	44	E2
Xiaolizhuang [HEN]	52	E3
Xiaolongshan Dao (She Dao) [LN]	32	D6
Xiaolu Dao [LN]	32	G5

Xiaoluan He [HEB]	26	D1
Xiaomei Guan [GD]	58	F1
Xiaomei Guan [JX]	48	B6
Xiaomei [ZJ]	42	B5
Xiaomian [CQ]	64	C3
Xiaomuhe [HL]	36	G4
Xiaonanchuan [QH]	78	D3
Xiaopingyang [GX]	60	G4
Xiaoqiao [FJ]	46	D3
Xiaoqin Dao [SD]	50	G1
Xiaoqing He [BJ]	22	C5
Xiaoqing He [SD]	50	E2
Xiaoqinghe [HL]	36	G4
Xiaoqiu [SN]	74	D6
Xiaosanjiang [GD]	58	D2
Xiaoshan Qu [ZJ]	42	D2
Xiaoshangqiao [HEN]	52	E4
Xiaoshuhe [SH]	38	D1
Xiaoshui [HN]	56	E5
Xiaoshun [ZJ]	42	C3
Xiaosigou [HEB]	26	F3
Xiaosong [JX]	48	D5
Xiaosunzhuang [TJ]	24	B5
Xiaotang [SH]	38	D4
Xiaotangshan [BJ]	22	D3
Xiaotashan Shuiku [JS]	40	D1
Xiaotian [AH]	44	C4
Xiaotianlong [AH]	44	E6
Xiaoting Qu [HB]	54	D4
Xiaowangzhuang [TJ]	24	B6
Xiaowei [AH]	44	D2
Xiaowu [BJ]	22	E4
Xiaowutai Shan [HEB]	26	C4
Xiaoxi [AH]	44	D2
Xiaoxi [JX]	48	C6
Xiaoxiang Ling [SC]	66	E4
Xiaoxihe [AH]	44	D3
Xiaoxingkai Hu [HL]	36	G5
Xiaoyan [HB]	54	D3
Xiaoyang Shan [ZJ]	42	F2
Xiaoyao [HEN]	52	F4
Xiaoyi [SX]	28	C4
Xiaoyuan [HN]	56	F6
Xiaozhaiba [GZ]	68	E3
Xiaozhangjiakou [BJ]	22	C2
Xiaozhongdian [YN]	70	C2
Xiaozhuang [BJ]	22	C4
Xiaozuo [FJ]	46	D5
Xiaping [HB]	54	C4
Xiapu [CQ]	64	F2
Xiapu [FJ]	46	F3
Xiapu [NX]	80	B5
Xiaqiao [AH]	44	C3
Xiaruyue [SX]	28	E2
Xiasha [SH]	38	D4
Xiashan Qu [GD]	58	B5
Xiashan Shuiku [SD]	50	F3
Xiashan [GZ]	68	D5
Xiashe [SX]	28	E2
Xiashibu [BJ]	22	B4
Xiashu [JS]	40	E3
Xiashuitou [SX]	28	D2

Xiasi [GZ]	68	F4	Xieyang Dao [GX]	60	G6	Ximayi Dao [LN]	32	E5
Xiasi [GZ]	68	F5	Xiezhou [SX]	28	B7	Ximeng [YN]	70	C4
Xiasi [HEN]	52	C5	Xifei He [AH]	44	C3	Ximeng [YN]	70	C4
Xiasifen [GS]	76	G3	Xifeng [GZ]	68	E3	Ximu [LN]	32	F4
Xiatang [CQ]	64	E4	Xifeng [LN]	32	H2	Xin Barag Youqi [NM]	30	G2
Xiatun [BJ]	22	C2	Xifengshan [BJ]	22	C3	Xin Barag Zuoqi [NM]	30	G2
Xiaweidian [BJ]	22	C3	Xifo [LN]	32	F3	Xin Bulag Jun [NM]	30	G2
Xiawotou [TJ]	24	C2	Xifuying [BJ]	22	D1	Xin Jiang [JX]	48	D3
Xiawuqi [TJ]	24	B3	Xigangzi [HL]	36	D3	Xin Jiang [JX]	48	E3
Xiayang [FJ]	46	B5	Xigazê [XZ]	72	G5	Xin Xian [HEN]	52	F6
Xiayang [FJ]	46	D3	Xihan Shui [GS]	76	H5	Xinan [FJ]	46	C4
Xiayang [FJ]	46	D4	Xihaoping [HB]	54	C3	Xinan [FJ]	46	E3
Xiayi [HEN]	52	H3	Xihe Qu [LN]	32	E2	Xin'an [GD]	58	G3
Xiaying [BJ]	22	E2	Xihe [AH]	44	E5	Xin'an [HEN]	52	D3
Xiaying [SD]	50	F2	Xihe [GS]	76	H5	Xin'an [HN]	56	D2
Xiaying [TJ]	24	C1	Xihe [HB]	54	F3	Xin'an [JL]	34	C3
Xiayunling [BJ]	22	B4	Xihekou [SN]	74	E4	Xin'an [JL]	34	G3
Xiazhai [NX]	80	B5	Xiheying [HEB]	26	B4	Xin'an [JS]	40	F4
Xiazhang [SD]	50	C3	Xihongmen [BJ]	22	D4	Xin'an [JX]	48	D5
Xiazhi Dao [ZJ]	42	F3	Xihu Qu [LN]	32	G3	Xin'an [SD]	50	E2
Xiazhuang [HEN]	52	G5	Xihu [AH]	44	B3	Xin'an [SD]	50	G3
Xiazhuang [SD]	50	E4	Xihu [HN]	56	E2	Xin'an [TJ]	24	C3
Xiazi [GZ]	68	F3	Xihu [JX]	48	E2	Xin'andian [HEN]	52	F5
Xibaipo [HEB]	26	A5	Xihua [HEN]	52	F4	Xin'ao [FJ]	46	E3
Xibaxa Qu [XZ]	72	J5	Xihuang [HEN]	52	C4	Xinba [JS]	40	E1
Xibei [FJ]	46	C4	Xiji [BJ]	22	E4	Xinbang [SH]	38	C4
Xibing [FJ]	46	E3	Xiji [HL]	36	D4	Xinbian He [AH]	44	D2
Xibu [AH]	44	E4	Xiji [NX]	80	B5	Xinbin [LN]	32	I3
Xicen [SH]	38	C3	Xiji [SD]	50	D5	Xinbo [HEB]	26	E1
Xichahe [SN]	74	C7	Xijiadian [HB]	54	D2	Xinbuhai [HI]	62	C1
Xichang [SC]	66	E5	Xijiang [JX]	48	C6	Xincai [HEN]	52	F5
Xichang [HI]	62	C2	Xijiaozi [SX]	28	C4	Xincang [ZJ]	42	D2
Xichatou [HEB]	26	B5	Xijin Shuiku [GX]	60	G5	Xinchang [HN]	56	B5
Xichehe [HN]	56	B2	Xijin [FJ]	46	D2	Xinchang [SH]	38	E4
Xicheng Shan [SX]	28	D6	Xijing [SX]	28	E5	Xinchang [ZJ]	42	D3
Xichong [SC]	66	F3	Xijir Ulan Hu [QH]	78	B3	Xincheng [GS]	76	G5
Xichou [YN]	70	F4	Xijir [QH]	78	B3	Xincheng [GX]	60	F3
Xichuan [HEN]	52	C4	Xikeng [FJ]	46	D2	Xincheng [HB]	54	F2
Xicun [JX]	48	B4	Xikeng [GD]	58	G3	Xincheng [HL]	36	F4
Xidamo [BJ]	22	B4	Xikou [AH]	44	E6	Xincheng [JX]	48	B6
Xidatan [NX]	80	C2	Xikou [FJ]	46	C4	Xincheng [SD]	50	D3
Xidawa [JL]	34	D2	Xikou [HN]	56	C2	Xincheng [SN]	74	D3
Xidayang Shuiku [HEB]	26	B5	Xikou [JX]	48	B2	Xincheng [SX]	28	D4
Xide [SC]	66	E4	Xikou [ZJ]	42	C2	Xincheng [ZJ]	42	D2
Xidian [ZJ]	42	E3	Xikou [ZJ]	42	C4	Xinchengzi [BJ]	22	F2
Xiditou [TJ]	24	C4	Xikou [ZJ]	42	E3	Xinci [FJ]	46	C5
Xidongting Shan [JS]	40	F4	Xikuangshan [HN]	56	D4	Xincun [GX]	60	G3
Xie Chi [SX]	28	B7	Xil [NM]	30	F4	Xincun [HEB]	26	E5
Xie Shan [JX]	48	D2	Xilang He [JL]	34	G3	Xincun [HI]	62	B3
Xie Shui [HN]	56	C2	Xilaotou Shan [NM]	30	H3	Xindi [GX]	60	I4
Xiefang [JX]	48	C6	Xiliao He [NM]	30	H4	Xindian [AH]	44	C3
Xiehe [GZ]	68	E3	Xilin Gol [NM]	30	G4	Xindian [GZ]	68	E4
Xieji [GD]	58	B5	Xilin Qu [HL]	36	E4	Xindian [HEN]	52	D4
Xieji [JS]	40	E3	Xilin [GX]	60	C3	Xindian [HEN]	52	E4
Xiejiaji Qu [AH]	44	C3	Xiling Xia [HB]	54	C3	Xindian [SX]	28	D5
Xiejiatan [JX]	48	D2	Xilingjing [SX]	28	D3	Xindian [YN]	70	E3
Xiejiaya [HN]	56	C3	Xilinhe [HL]	36	F5	Xindianping [HN]	56	B4
Xielai Shui [HN]	56	F5	Xilinhot [NM]	30	G4	Xindianzi [CQ]	64	F2
Xieqiao [AH]	44	C3	Xilonghuyu [TJ]	24	D2	Xindu Qu [SC]	66	F3
Xi'erdaohe [BJ]	22	C2	Xilühua Dao [ZJ]	42	F2	Xindu [AH]	44	C5
Xietan [FJ]	46	E2	Xima [GZ]	68	F4	Xindu [GX]	60	I4
Xietun [LN]	32	E3	Xima [HB]	54	H4	Xinduqiao [SC]	66	D3

Xin'e [HL]	36	D3	Xingtai [HEB]	26	B6	Xinmaqiao [AH]	44	D2
Xinfeng Jiang [GD]	58	F2	Xingtang [HEB]	26	B5	Xinmei [HI]	62	C3
Xinfeng [GD]	58	F2	Xinguangwu [SX]	28	D2	Xinmi [HEN]	52	E3
Xinfeng [GD]	58	H2	Xingwen [SC]	66	F4	Xinmiao [JL]	34	D2
Xinfeng [JS]	40	E3	Xingxingxia [XJ]	82	N5	Xinmin Cun [HI]	62	C3
Xinfeng [JX]	48	B6	Xingxiu Hai [QH]	78	E3	Xinmin [CQ]	64	D3
Xinfeng [JX]	48	D4	Xingyang [HEN]	52	E3	Xinmin [CQ]	64	F3
Xinfengjiang Shuiku [GD]	58	F3	Xingye [GX]	60	G5	Xinmin [HL]	36	D3
Xing Xian [SX]	28	C3	Xingyi [GZ]	68	C5	Xinmin [LN]	32	F3
Xing'an Qu [HL]	36	F4	Xingzhou He [HEB]	26	D2	Xinmin [NX]	80	C5
Xing'an [GX]	60	H2	Xingzi [GD]	58	D1	Xinmin [SH]	38	D2
Xingan [JX]	48	C4	Xingzi [JX]	48	D2	Xinmin [SH]	38	E3
Xingang [LN]	32	E6	Xinhai [HI]	62	C1	Xinmin [SN]	74	F1
Xing'anying [BJ]	22	D5	Xinhai [SH]	38	D1	Xinmintun [LN]	32	G3
Xingcheng [LN]	32	D4	Xinhe(Toksu) [XJ]	82	H5	Xinning [HN]	56	C5
Xingcun [SD]	50	G3	Xinhe [GX]	60	E5	Xinningpo [HI]	62	A2
Xingdi [XJ]	82	J5	Xinhe [HEB]	26	C6	Xinnong [SH]	38	C4
Xingdian [JS]	40	D3	Xinhe [JL]	34	H5	Xinping [YN]	70	E3
Xingfeng [CQ]	64	D3	Xinhe [SH]	38	D2	Xinping'an [JL]	34	C2
Xingguo [JX]	48	C5	Xinhua [HB]	54	C3	Xinpingbu [SX]	28	F1
Xinghai [QH]	78	G3	Xinhua [HN]	56	D4	Xinpo [HI]	62	C2
Xinghe [NM]	30	F4	Xinhua [JL]	34	B3	Xinpu [GZ]	68	F3
Xinghua [HL]	36	D1	Xinhuang [HN]	56	B4	Xinpu [NX]	80	B3
Xinghua Wan [FJ]	46	E4	Xinhui Qu [GD]	58	E4	Xinpu [SN]	74	B7
Xinghua [HEN]	52	C3	Xining [QH]	78	G2	Xinpu [ZJ]	42	E2
Xinghua [JS]	40	E3	Xiningpu [NX]	80	C3	Xinqiang [HN]	56	F2
Xinghuacun [SX]	28	C4	Xiniu [GD]	58	E2	Xinqiao He [FJ]	46	C4
Xingji [HEB]	26	D5	Xiniujiao [GX]	60	F6	Xinqiao [FJ]	46	C2
Xingji [HEN]	52	E5	Xinji [AH]	44	D2	Xinqiao [GX]	60	H5
Xingjiawan [HEB]	26	B6	Xinji [HB]	54	E3	Xinqiao [HEN]	52	F4
Xingjie [YN]	70	F4	Xinji [HEB]	26	C6	Xinqiao [HI]	62	C2
Xingkai Hu [HL]	36	G5	Xinji [SD]	50	B4	Xinqiao [ZJ]	42	E3
Xingkai [HL]	36	G5	Xinji [SN]	74	B7	Xinqing Qu [HL]	36	E3
Xinglang [GZ]	68	F5	Xinjian [HN]	56	C4	Xinqiu Qu [LN]	32	E2
Xingliu [AH]	44	B2	Xinjian [JX]	48	C3	Xinqizhou [JX]	48	C3
Xinglong [CQ]	64	C4	Xinjian [SH]	38	C1	Xinquan [FJ]	46	B4
Xinglong [CQ]	64	F3	Xinjian [ZJ]	42	D4	Xinrong Qu [SX]	28	E1
Xinglong [CQ]	64	F4	Xinjiang [SX]	28	C6	Xinshao [HN]	56	D4
Xinglong [HEB]	26	E3	Xinjie [HB]	54	E3	Xinshao [YN]	70	E3
Xinglong [HL]	36	C2	Xinjie [HI]	62	A2	Xinsheng [CQ]	64	D3
Xinglong [HL]	36	D4	Xinjie [JX]	48	C3	Xinshi [HI]	62	C2
Xinglong [LN]	32	G3	Xinjie [NM]	30	E5	Xinshi [HN]	56	F3
Xinglong [NX]	80	B4	Xinjie [SN]	74	B6	Xinshi [SC]	66	E4
Xinglong [NX]	80	B5	Xinjie [YN]	70	C3	Xinshi [SH]	38	E4
Xinglongchang [HN]	56	B3	Xinjie [YN]	70	E4	Xinshigou [NX]	80	B3
Xinglongshan [JL]	34	B3	Xinjieji [HL]	36	D1	Xinshu He [JS]	40	D1
Xinglongshan [JL]	34	E4	Xinjin [SC]	66	E3	Xinshui He [SX]	28	B5
Xinglongsi [SD]	50	C2	Xinkai He [TJ]	24	C4	Xinsi [GS]	76	H5
Xingning [GD]	58	G2	Xinkaikou [TJ]	24	B3	Xinsui He [AH]	44	D2
Xingning [HN]	56	F6	Xinkailu [TJ]	24	C5	Xintai [SD]	50	D4
Xingnong [HL]	36	C4	Xinkaitang [HN]	56	F2	Xintan [HB]	54	F4
Xingou [HB]	54	F4	Xinkou [SX]	28	D3	Xintang [HB]	54	B4
Xingping [SN]	74	D6	Xinle [HEB]	26	B5	Xintian [CQ]	64	E3
Xingping [GX]	60	H3	Xinli [JL]	34	F3	Xintian [HN]	56	E6
Xingren [GZ]	68	D5	Xinliao Dao [GD]	58	B6	Xintian [JX]	48	C6
Xingren [GZ]	68	F4	Xinlicheng Shuiku [JL]	34	E4	Xintongyang Yunhe [JS]	40	E3
Xingren [NX]	80	B4	Xinlitun [HL]	36	D2	Xinwei [FJ]	46	C5
Xingshan [HB]	54	C3	Xinlitun [LN]	32	F2	Xinwo [ZJ]	42	D4
Xingshan [HL]	36	B4	Xinliuji [AH]	44	C3	Xinwu [HI]	62	C2
Xingshan [HL]	36	C5	Xinlong(Nyagrong) [SC]	66	D3	Xinwushe [SH]	38	C4
Xingshutai [BJ]	22	D2	Xinlong [HI]	62	A3	Xinxiang [HEN]	52	E2
Xingta [SH]	38	C4	Xinluwan [ZJ]	42	C4	Xinxing Jiang [GD]	58	D4

Name	Page	Grid
Xinxing [GD]	58	D4
Xinxing [HI]	62	C2
Xinxing [JL]	34	B3
Xinxing [JL]	34	H5
Xinxing [JL]	34	I4
Xinxing [JS]	40	F2
Xinxing [SD]	50	F3
Xinxu [GX]	60	D4
Xinyang [HEN]	52	F5
Xinyanggang Kou [JS]	40	F2
Xinye [HEN]	52	D5
Xinyi He [JS]	40	E1
Xinyi [GD]	58	B4
Xinyi [JS]	40	D1
Xinying [HI]	62	B2
Xinying [HI]	62	B2
Xinying [JX]	48	E3
Xinying [NX]	80	B4
Xinyu [JX]	48	B4
Xinyuan(Künes) [XJ]	82	H4
Xinzhai [SD]	50	D3
Xinzhai [YN]	70	E4
Xinzhai [ZJ]	42	C4
Xinzhan [GZ]	68	E2
Xinzhan [HEN]	52	F4
Xinzhan [HL]	36	C5
Xinzhan [JL]	34	G4
Xinzhangfang [NM]	30	H2
Xinzhangzi [HEB]	26	E3
Xinzhen [HEB]	26	D4
Xinzhen [HEN]	52	F2
Xinzheng [HEN]	52	E3
Xinzheng [HI]	62	B3
Xinzhi [JX]	48	B4
Xinzhou Qu [HB]	54	G4
Xinzhou [GD]	58	D5
Xinzhou [GZ]	68	F2
Xinzhou [HN]	56	D2
Xinzhou [SX]	28	D3
Xinzhu [HI]	62	C2
Xinzhuang [HI]	62	A3
Xinzhuang [SD]	50	D4
Xinzhuang [SD]	50	D4
Xinzhuangji [NX]	80	C3
Xinzhuangzi [NX]	80	D3
Xiong Xian [HEB]	26	D5
Xiongdi Yu [FJ]	46	C6
Xiong'er Shan [HEN]	52	C4
Xiongjiang [FJ]	46	D3
Xiongkou [HB]	54	E4
Xiongyue [LN]	32	F4
Xipan [SX]	28	E3
Xipaozi [LN]	32	G2
Xiping [HEN]	52	C4
Xiping [HFN]	52	F4
Xiping [LN]	32	D4
Xiping [SX]	28	D6
Xipo [SX]	28	B6
Xiqin [FJ]	46	D3
Xiqing Shan [QH]	78	G3
Xiqing Qu [TJ]	24	B5
Xiqing Shan [GS]	76	F5
Xisadian [AH]	44	D3
Xisha Qundao [HI]	62	F5
Xishabu [JX]	48	C4
Xishan Qu [JS]	40	F4
Xishan Qu [YN]	70	E3
Xishe [SX]	28	B6
Xishe [SX]	28	C4
Xishu [HEB]	26	A7
Xishuba [SX]	28	C4
Xishui [GZ]	68	E2
Xishui [HB]	54	H4
Xishui [HI]	62	B2
Xitiangezhuang [BJ]	22	D2
Xitianmu Shan [ZJ]	42	C2
Xitianyang [BJ]	22	D4
Xitiao Xi [ZJ]	42	C2
Xitieshan [QH]	78	D2
Xitong [HL]	36	H4
Xituo [CQ]	64	E3
Xiu Shui [JX]	48	B2
Xiu Shui [JX]	48	C2
Xiuning [AH]	44	E6
Xiuqi [CQ]	64	E2
Xiuren [GX]	60	H3
Xiushan Dao [ZJ]	42	F2
Xiushan [CQ]	64	E5
Xiushui He [LN]	32	G2
Xiushui [GZ]	68	B4
Xiushui [JL]	34	F3
Xiushui [JX]	48	B2
Xiushuihezi [LN]	32	G2
Xiuwen [GZ]	68	E4
Xiuwu [HEN]	52	E2
Xiuxikou [HN]	56	C4
Xiuyan [LN]	32	G4
Xiuying Qu [HI]	62	C1
Xiuyu Qu [FJ]	46	E4
Xiwaizi [JL]	34	I4
Xiwang [AH]	44	D3
Xiwengzhuang [BJ]	22	E2
Xiwu [QH]	78	E4
Xiwu [ZJ]	42	E3
Xiwujiang [SX]	28	D6
Xiwuliying [BJ]	22	C2
Xixabangma Feng [XZ]	72	E5
Xixi He [SC]	66	E5
Xixi [AH]	44	E6
Xixi [FJ]	46	D3
Xixia Qu [NX]	80	C2
Xixia [HEN]	52	C4
Xixiang [SN]	74	C8
Xixiangdapu [LN]	32	H3
Xixiaoying [BJ]	22	C3
Xixiaozhan [TJ]	24	C6
Xiyan [HN]	56	C5
Xiyang Dao [FJ]	46	F3
Xiyang [AH]	44	C2
Xiyang [FJ]	46	C4
Xiyang [FJ]	46	D3
Xiyang [JL]	34	F4
Xiyang [SX]	28	E4
Xiyang Jiang [YN]	70	F3
Xiying [SX]	28	E5
Xize [ZJ]	42	E3
Xizhai [HB]	54	D4
Xizhaizhuang [TJ]	24	B6
Xizhaochuan [SN]	74	F7
Xizhen [SN]	74	F3
Xizhong Dao [LN]	32	E5
Xizhou Shan [SX]	28	D3
Xizhou [ZJ]	42	E3
Xizhuang [BJ]	22	D2
Xizhuang [JX]	48	D2
Xizhuangzi [BJ]	22	E2
Xorkol [XJ]	82	L6
Xu Jiang [JX]	48	D4
Xu Shui [HN]	56	C4
Xuancheng [AH]	44	E5
Xuan'en [HB]	54	B4
Xuanfeng [JX]	48	B4
Xuangang [SX]	28	D3
Xuanhan [SC]	66	G3
Xuanhe [NX]	80	B3
Xuanhua Qu [HEB]	26	C3
Xuanhua [HEB]	26	C3
Xuanhuadian [HB]	54	G3
Xuanqiao [SH]	38	E4
Xuanwei [YN]	70	F2
Xuchang [HEN]	52	E3
Xuchang [HEN]	52	E4
Xucun [AH]	44	E5
Xue Shan [YN]	70	C2
Xuebao Ding [SC]	66	E2
Xuecheng Qu [SD]	50	D5
Xuedian [HEN]	52	E3
Xuedian [HEN]	52	E3
Xuedou shan [ZJ]	42	E3
Xuefang [SD]	50	G3
Xuefeng Shan [HN]	56	C4
Xuefeng [HN]	56	C4
Xuehua Shan [SX]	28	B7
Xuejiaping [HB]	54	C3
Xuetian [ZJ]	42	D3
Xueyan [JS]	40	F4
Xueye Shuiku [SD]	50	D3
Xugin Gol [QH]	78	D3
Xugou [SX]	28	D4
Xugui [QH]	78	D3
Xuhui Qu [SH]	38	D3
Xuji [AH]	44	C4
Xujia [CQ]	64	F2
Xujiaba [GZ]	68	G3
Xujiadu [JX]	48	B3
Xujiaping [SN]	74	B7
Xujiatai [TJ]	24	C2
Xujiaya Shuiku [SD]	50	D4
Xuling [AH]	44	C5
Xuliu [JS]	40	D2
Xun He [HL]	36	D3
Xun He [SN]	74	E7
Xun Jiang [GX]	60	H2
Xun Jiang [GX]	60	H4
Xun Xian [HEN]	52	F2
Xundian [YN]	70	E3

Xungba [XZ]	72	C3	Yajiang(Nyagquka) [SC]	66	D3	Yangchang [GZ]	68	E5
Xungmai [XZ]	72	G4	Yajiang [CQ]	64	D4	Yangchang [GZ]	68	G3
Xunhe [HL]	36	E3	Yakeshi [NM]	30	H2	Yangchang [YN]	70	F2
Xunhua [QH]	78	H3	Yali [HEB]	26	B7	Yangcheng [SX]	28	D6
Xunjian [SN]	74	F6	Yalian [YN]	70	C3	Yangchu [SD]	50	G2
Xunjiansi [YN]	70	E4	Yaliang [HI]	62	B3	Yangchun [GD]	58	C4
Xunke [HL]	36	E3	Yalong Jiang [SC]	66	C2	Yangcun [GD]	58	F3
Xunle [GX]	60	F2	Yalong Jiang [SC]	66	D4	Yangcun [HEB]	26	C4
Xunqiao [ZJ]	42	E4	Yalong Wan [HI]	62	B3	Yangcun [JX]	48	B7
Xunwu Shui [JX]	48	C7	Yalu He [NM]	30	H3	Yangcunqiao [ZJ]	42	C3
Xunwu [JX]	48	C7	Yalu Jiang [JL]	34	F6	Yangdaxkak [XJ]	82	K6
Xunyang [SN]	74	E8	Yalu Jiang [JL]	34	H6	Yangdeng [GZ]	68	E2
Xunyangba [SN]	74	D7	Yalu Jiang [LN]	32	I4	Yangdi [TJ]	24	B4
Xunyi [SN]	74	D5	Yam O Wan [HK]	84	C3	Yangdong [GD]	58	D5
Xunzhen [SX]	28	C2	Yam O [HK]	84	C3	Yangfang [BJ]	22	C3
Xupingcun [NX]	80	B4	Yaman Gol [NM]	30	H1	Yangfangkou [SX]	28	D2
Xupu [HN]	56	C4	Yamansu [XJ]	82	M5	Yanggang [HL]	36	G5
Xupu [JS]	40	F4	Yamzho Yumco [XZ]	72	H5	Yanggao [SX]	28	E1
Xurgan [QH]	78	D3	Yan Chau Tong [HK]	84	E1	Yanggu [HEN]	52	F3
Xuru Co [XZ]	72	F4	Yan He [JS]	40	E2	Yanggu [SD]	50	B3
Xusanwan [GS]	76	E3	Yan He [SN]	74	E3	Yanghang [SH]	38	D2
Xushi [FJ]	46	D2	Yan Shan [BJ]	22	D1	Yanghe [JS]	40	D2
Xushi [HN]	56	E2	Yan Shan [HEB]	26	E3	Yanghe [LN]	32	G4
Xushi [JS]	40	F4	Yan'an [SN]	74	E4	Yanghu [AH]	44	D5
Xushuguan [JS]	40	F4	Yanbei [HN]	56	E4	Yangi [HEN]	52	G2
Xushui He [SN]	74	C7	Yanbian [SC]	66	D5	Yangji [JS]	40	E1
Xushui [HEB]	26	C4	Yanbodu [HN]	56	C2	Yangji [SD]	50	E5
Xutao [NX]	80	B4	Yancang [SH]	38	E3	Yangjiahe [SN]	74	C8
Xutun [LN]	32	F4	Yanchang [SN]	74	F4	Yangjiang [GD]	58	C5
Xuwei [JS]	40	E1	Yanchangbu [SN]	74	C3	Yangjiang [HB]	54	E4
Xuwen [GD]	58	B6	Yancheng Qu [HEN]	52	E4	Yangjiao [CQ]	64	D4
Xuxinzhuang [BJ]	22	D4	Yancheng [JS]	40	F2	Yangjiapu [LN]	32	G4
Xuyi [JS]	40	D2	Yanchi [AH]	44	E4	Yangjiatan [HN]	56	D4
Xuyong [SC]	66	F4	Yanchi [BJ]	22	C3	Yangjiawan [GZ]	68	C3
Xuzhen [HEN]	52	G2	Yanchi [NX]	80	B4	Yangjiawan [HEB]	26	F1
Xuzhou [JS]	40	C1	Yanchi [NX]	80	D3	Yangjiayao [NX]	80	C3
Xuzhuangzi [TJ]	24	B5	Yanchiwan [GS]	76	D3	Yangjiayuan [TJ]	24	B6
			Yanchuan [SN]	74	F4	Yangjie [GZ]	68	C3
Y			Yandang Shan [ZJ]	42	D5	Yangjie [YN]	70	E3
			Yandang [ZJ]	42	E4	Yangjing [SN]	74	C3
Ya Men [GD]	58	E4	Yandian [LN]	32	E5	Yangjinzhuang [TJ]	24	C2
Ya'an [SC]	66	E4	Yandian [SD]	50	B3	Yangjuanzi [LN]	32	E3
Yabral Shan [NM]	30	C5	Yandong [GX]	60	D4	Yangkou [FJ]	46	C3
Yabuli [HL]	36	E5	Yandong [GX]	60	E3	Yangkou [JS]	40	F3
Yachang [GX]	60	D3	Yandu Qu [JS]	40	F2	Yangkou [SD]	50	E2
Yacheng [FJ]	46	F3	Yanduhe [HB]	54	C3	Yanglang [NX]	80	C4
Yacheng [HI]	62	B3	Yandun [XJ]	82	N4	Yanglaowa [SX]	28	E1
Yachi He [GZ]	68	E3	Yandunbu [AH]	44	E5	Yanglin [HN]	56	F5
Yachong He			Yanduntou [SH]	38	D4	Yanglin [ZJ]	42	B3
(Canal dos Potos) [MC]	86	A1	Yandunxu [HI]	62	C2	Yangling Qu [SN]	74	D6
Yadian Shuiku [TJ]	24	B5	Yang He [HEB]	26	C3	Yangliu [AH]	44	E5
Yadong [XZ]	72	G6	Yang Xian [SN]	74	C7	Yangliuchi [HB]	54	C4
Ya'ergou [NX]	80	C3	Ya'ngamdo [XZ]	72	J4	Yangliudian [SD]	50	D3
Yafan [ZJ]	42	C3	Yang'an [SD]	50	D2	Yangliujie [GZ]	68	F4
Yag Qu [QH]	78	D3	Yangba [GZ]	68	D6	Yanglou [AH]	44	C1
Yagan [NM]	30	C4	Yangbajain [XZ]	72	H4	Yangloudong [HB]	54	F5
Yagkêng [QH]	78	F2	Yangbi Jiang [YN]	70	C2	Yanglousi [HN]	56	F2
Yagra [XZ]	72	D4	Yangbi [YN]	70	C3	Yangma Dao [SD]	50	H2
Yagra [YN]	70	C1	Yangbu [HEN]	52	F5	Yangmahe [SN]	74	E3
Yagradagzê Feng [QH]	78	D3	Yangce [HEN]	52	E5	Yangmei [GZ]	68	C4
Yahekou Shuiku [HEN]	52	D4	Yangchang [GZ]	68	D3	Yangmiao [AH]	44	D3
Yahekou [HEN]	52	D4	Yangchang [GZ]	68	D4	Yangmiao [HEN]	52	F3
Yajia [GZ]	68	H2						

Yangming Shan [HN]	56	D5	Yanjia [LN]	32	E4	Yaogou [SD]	50	E3
Yangmingbu [SX]	28	D2	Yanjiagou [HEB]	26	C3	Yaogu [GD]	58	D4
Yangmugang [HL]	36	G5	Yanjiang [HI]	62	C2	Yaojiaji [HB]	54	G3
Yangmulin [JL]	34	E5	Yanjiang [JL]	34	C2	Yaokou [AH]	44	C3
Yangping [GZ]	68	G3	Yanjiatai [BJ]	22	B3	Yaoli [AH]	44	C4
Yangping [HB]	54	D3	Yanjin [HEN]	52	F2	Yaoli [JX]	48	E2
Yangping [SX]	28	C3	Yanjin [YN]	70	F1	Yaoluoping [AH]	44	C4
Yangpingguan [SN]	74	B8	Yanjing [CQ]	64	C4	Yaopi [HN]	56	F5
Yangpu Gang [HI]	62	B2	Yanlan [HI]	62	B3	Yaoqianhutun [LN]	32	G3
Yangpu Qu [SH]	38	D3	Yanli [SX]	28	D6	Yaoqu [SX]	28	B5
Yangpu [HI]	62	B2	Yanliang Qu [SN]	74	E6	Yaoshan [NX]	80	C3
Yangqiao [AH]	44	B3	Yanling [HEN]	52	F3	Yaoshang [BJ]	22	C5
Yangqiao [HN]	56	E3	Yanling [HN]	56	F5	Yaoshi [HN]	56	B4
Yangqiaopan [SN]	74	E3	Yanliu [AH]	44	C3	Yaotou [SX]	28	C3
Yangqu Shan [SX]	28	E4	Yanmeidong [HEB]	26	B4	Yaotun [HL]	36	D3
Yangqu [SX]	28	D3	Yanmen [HN]	56	B4	Yaowen Nongchang [HI]	62	A3
Yangquan [SX]	28	E4	Yanmen [SC]	66	F2	Yaozhan [GZ]	68	C4
Yangshan [GD]	58	D2	Yanmen [YN]	70	C1	Yaozhan [SD]	50	C2
Yangshi [CQ]	64	F3	Yanmenguan [SX]	28	D2	Yaozhen [SN]	74	F2
Yangshudixia [BJ]	22	D2	Yanminghu [JL]	34	H4	Yaqueling [HB]	54	D4
Yangshufang [LN]	32	F5	Yanqi [XJ]	82	J4	Yaqueshui [HB]	54	B4
Yangshuo [GX]	60	H3	Yanqian [FJ]	46	B5	Yarkant He [XJ]	82	E7
Yangtan [AH]	44	F5	Yanqing [BJ]	22	C2	Yarkant He [XJ]	82	F6
Yangtouyan [YN]	70	D3	Yanqiu [HEN]	52	D3	Yarlung Zangbo Jiang [XZ]	72	E5
Yangtuan [AH]	44	D2	Yanshan [GX]	60	H2	Yatan [AH]	44	C5
Yangtun [JS]	40	B1	Yanshan [HEB]	26	E5	Yau Ma Tei [HK]	84	D3
Yangtuping [GZ]	68	F4	Yanshan [JX]	48	E3	Yau Tong [HK]	84	D3
Yanguan [GS]	76	H5	Yanshan [YN]	70	F4	Yaxing [HI]	62	B2
Yangwei [HB]	54	C2	Yanshi Xi [FJ]	46	C4	Yayuan [JL]	34	F6
Yangwei [JX]	48	C3	Yanshi [HEN]	52	D3	Yazhou [GZ]	68	F5
Yangwu [YN]	70	E4	Yanshiping [QH]	78	C4	Ye Xian [HEN]	52	E4
Yangxi [AH]	44	E5	Yanshou [HL]	36	E5	Yecheng(Kargilik) [XJ]	82	E7
Yangxi [FJ]	46	C3	Yanshou [HN]	56	F6	Yecun [SN]	74	F7
Yangxi [GD]	58	C5	Yantai [SD]	50	H2	Yeda [HB]	54	C2
Yangxi [HB]	54	D4	Yantan Qu [SC]	66	F4	Yedou Feng [SX]	28	E2
Yangxi [HN]	56	D4	Yantan [GX]	60	E3	Yehe [JL]	34	D5
Yangximu He [LN]	32	F2	Yantian Qu [GD]	58	F4	Yeji [AH]	44	B4
Yangxin [HB]	54	H5	Yantian [FJ]	46	E3	Yejituo [HEB]	26	F4
Yangxin [SD]	50	D2	Yantian [JX]	48	B4	Yellow Sea [JS]	40	G2
Yangxipu [HB]	54	C2	Yanting [SC]	66	F3	Yellow Sea [LN]	32	G6
Yangxu [GX]	60	D4	Yantongshan [JL]	34	E4	Yellow Sea [SD]	50	G4
Yangxu [GX]	60	F4	Yantongtun [HL]	36	C4	Yema Nanshan [GS]	76	C3
Yangyi [HEB]	26	A7	Yantou [JS]	40	D1	Yematan [QH]	78	F2
Yangyi [SX]	28	D4	Yantou [ZJ]	42	D4	Yematan [QH]	78	F3
Yangyuan [HEB]	26	B3	Yanwei [JS]	40	E1	Yengisar [XJ]	82	E6
Yangzhai [HB]	54	G3	Yanwodao [HL]	36	G4	Yengisar [XJ]	82	I5
Yangzhai [JS]	40	E2	Yanxi [FJ]	46	C5	Yengisu [XJ]	82	J5
Yangzhen [BJ]	22	E3	Yanxing [HL]	36	F4	Yeniugou [QH]	78	E3
Yangzhong [FJ]	46	E3	Yanyuan [SC]	66	D5	Yenshui [TW]	88	C3
Yangzhong [JS]	40	E3	Yanzhou [SD]	50	C4	Yeping [SN]	74	D7
Yangzhou [JS]	40	E3	Yanzhuang [TJ]	24	A6	Yesanguan [HB]	54	C4
Yangzhuangji [SD]	50	C4	Yanzibian [SN]	74	A8	Yesheng [NX]	80	C2
Yangzi [SD]	50	F2	Yanzidun [NX]	80	C1	Yetimbulak [XJ]	82	L6
Yangziqiao [JX]	48	C2	Yanzihe [AH]	44	B4	Yeung Chau [HK]	84	E1
Yangzishao [JL]	34	F5	Yanziji [JS]	40	D3	Yexie [SH]	38	D4
Yanhe [GZ]	68	G2	Yanzikou [GZ]	68	D3	Yeyik [XJ]	82	H7
Yanhecheng [BJ]	22	B3	Yao'an [YN]	70	D3	Yeyuan Shuiku [SD]	50	E3
Yanhulun [HEB]	26	C2	Yaocun [AH]	44	F5	Yezhuang [SX]	28	D3
Yanji [HEN]	52	G3	Yaocun [SD]	50	C4	Yi He [HEN]	52	D3
Yanji [JL]	34	I5	Yaodianzi [SD]	50	E4	Yi He [JS]	40	D1
Yanji [JS]	40	D1	Yaofupu [NX]	80	C2	Yi He [SD]	50	E3
Yanjia [GZ]	68	D5	Yaogou [AH]	44	D4	Yi O San Tsuen [HK]	84	A4

Yi Shan [SD]	50	E3
Yi Shan [SD]	50	E3
Yi Xian [AH]	44	D6
Yi Xian [HEB]	26	C4
Yi Xian [LN]	32	E3
Yi'an [HL]	36	C4
Yiban [FJ]	46	D4
Yibang [YN]	70	D4
Yibianmen [LN]	32	H4
Yibin [SC]	66	F4
Yibin [SC]	66	F4
Yichang [HB]	54	D4
Yiche [YN]	70	E2
Yicheng Qu [SD]	50	D5
Yicheng [HB]	54	E3
Yicheng [SX]	28	C6
Yichuan [HEN]	52	D3
Yichuan [SN]	74	F4
Yichun [HL]	36	E4
Yichun [JX]	48	B4
Yidan [JL]	34	E4
Yidao [SD]	50	G2
Yidie [SX]	28	B4
Yidouquan [SX]	28	F2
Yidu [FJ]	46	C4
Yidu [HB]	54	D4
Yidu [JX]	48	C3
Yidushui [HN]	56	D5
Yifeng [JX]	48	B3
Yigou [HEN]	52	F2
Yihuang Shui [JX]	48	D4
Yihuang [JX]	48	D4
Yijiadian [JL]	34	E2
Yijiangshan Dao [ZJ]	42	E4
Yijiawan [HN]	56	F4
Yijin [AH]	44	D5
Yijing [SX]	28	C2
Yijun [SN]	74	E5
Yikou [FJ]	46	C3
Yilan [HL]	36	E4
Yilehuli Shan [HL]	36	C2
Yilehuli Shan [NM]	30	H2
Yili He [YN]	70	E2
Yiliang [YN]	70	E3
Yiliang [YN]	70	F2
Yilin [JS]	40	E2
Yiling Qu [HB]	54	D4
Yiling [JS]	40	E3
Yiliping [QH]	78	C2
Yilong [HL]	36	C4
Yilong [SC]	66	G3
Yim Tin Tsai [HK]	84	D2
Yim Tin Tsai [HK]	84	E2
Yima [HEN]	52	C3
Yima [JL]	34	F4
Yimaling [HEB]	26	B4
Yimatu He [HEB]	26	E2
Yimatu [HEB]	26	C2
Yimatu [LN]	32	E3
Yimen [SC]	66	E5
Yimen [YN]	70	E3
Yimianpo [HL]	36	E5
Yimin [NM]	30	G2
Yiminhe [NM]	30	G2
Yin Shan [NM]	30	D4
Yin Tsz Ngam [HK]	84	F2
Yina [GZ]	68	D4
Yinan [SD]	50	E4
Yincha [GX]	60	E4
Yincheng [SX]	28	E6
Yinchuan [NX]	80	C2
Yindian [HB]	54	F2
Yinfang [HEB]	26	B4
Ying He [HEN]	52	E3
Ying Xian [SX]	28	E2
Yingcheng [HB]	54	F4
Yingchengzi [JL]	34	E4
Yingchun [HL]	36	G4
Yingde [GD]	58	E2
Ying'e Ling [JL]	34	H5
Ying'emen [LN]	32	I2
Yingfang [SD]	50	G3
Yingfengqiao [HN]	56	E3
Yingge Ling [HI]	62	B2
Yinggehai [HI]	62	A3
Yinghe [AH]	44	C3
Yinghua [JL]	34	C2
Yingjiakou [JX]	48	F3
Yingjiang [YN]	70	B3
Yingjing [SC]	66	E4
Yingko [TW]	88	D2
Yingkou [LN]	32	F4
Yingpan [BJ]	22	C2
Yingpan [SN]	74	E7
Yingpanjie [YN]	70	C3
Yingpanshui [GS]	76	H4
Yingpanshui [NX]	80	A3
Yingpanxu [JX]	48	B5
Yingqian [JX]	48	B6
Yingqiao [HEN]	52	E4
Yingshan [HB]	54	H4
Yingshan [SC]	66	G3
Yingshang [AH]	44	C3
Yingshouyinzi Kuangqu [HEB]	26	E3
Yingshuiqiao [NX]	80	B3
Yingtan [JX]	48	E3
Yingtian [HN]	56	E3
Yingwang [SN]	74	E4
Yingwuxi [GZ]	68	G2
Yingxian [HI]	62	A2
Yingxin [TJ]	24	C6
Yingyang Guan [GX]	60	I3
Yingyang [HEN]	52	D3
Yingzhou [HI]	62	B3
Yining(Gulja) [XJ]	82	G3
Yining(Gulja) [XJ]	82	G4
Yinji [AH]	44	D2
Yinjiafu [BJ]	22	E3
Yinjiahui [AH]	44	D5
Yinjiang [GZ]	68	G2
Yinkeng [JX]	48	C5
Yinlanshushui Mingqu [TJ]	24	C3
Yinliu [TJ]	24	C2
Yinma He [JL]	34	E3
Yinmin [YN]	70	E2
Yinshan [SD]	50	C3
Yinta [SX]	28	C2
Yintian [HN]	56	E5
Yinxian [AH]	44	C3
Yinxiang [SD]	50	D2
Yinyang [JS]	40	G4
Yinzhu [ZJ]	42	C3
Yinzu [HB]	54	G5
Yi'ong Zangbo [XZ]	72	J4
Yi'ong [XZ]	72	J4
Yipin [CQ]	64	C4
Yipinglang [YN]	70	D3
Yipingyuan [SX]	28	C5
Yiqian [JX]	48	D5
Yirshi [NM]	30	G3
Yishui [SD]	50	E4
Yitang [SD]	50	E4
Yitang [SX]	28	C4
Yiting [ZJ]	42	C3
Yitong He [JL]	34	E5
Yitong [JL]	34	E4
Yiwanquan [NX]	80	A3
Yiwu(Araturuk) [XJ]	82	N4
Yiwu [ZJ]	42	D3
Yiwulü Shan [LN]	32	E3
Yixiken [HL]	36	C1
Yixing [JS]	40	E4
Yixun He [HEB]	26	E2
Yiyang [HEN]	52	D3
Yiyang [HN]	56	E3
Yiyang [JX]	48	E3
Yiyang [SD]	50	C3
Yiyuan [SD]	50	E3
Yiyuankou [HEB]	26	G3
Yizhang [HN]	56	E6
Yizheng [JS]	40	E3
Yizhou [GX]	60	F3
Yoigilanglêb Qu [QH]	78	E3
Yong Jiang [GX]	60	F5
Yong'an Xi [ZJ]	42	D4
Yong'an [AH]	44	D2
Yong'an [FJ]	46	C4
Yong'an [HL]	36	D4
Yong'an [HN]	56	E6
Yong'an [SD]	50	E2
Yong'anguan [HN]	56	D6
Yong'anpu [LN]	32	C4
Yongchang [GS]	76	F3
Yongchang [JX]	48	B5
Yongcheng [HEN]	52	H4
Yongchuan Qu [CQ]	64	B4
Yongchun [FJ]	46	D4
Yongcong [GZ]	68	H4
Yongde [YN]	70	C3
Yongdeng [GS]	76	G4
Yongding He [BJ]	22	B3
Yongding He [HEB]	26	D4
Yongding Xinhe [TJ]	24	C4
Yongding [FJ]	46	B5
Yongfa [HI]	62	C2
Yongfeng [JX]	48	C4

Yongfu [FJ]	46	C4		Youcheng [JX]	48	D2		Yuanping [SX]	28	D3
Yongfu [GX]	60	G3		Youdunzi [QH]	78	B1		Yuanqiang [AH]	44	B2
Yonghan [GD]	58	E3		Youfanggou [SN]	74	B6		Yuanqu [SX]	28	C6
Yonghe [HN]	56	F3		Youguzhuang [TJ]	24	B2		Yuanquan [SD]	50	E3
Yonghe [SX]	28	B5		Youhao Qu [HL]	36	E4		Yuanquzhan [SX]	28	C6
Yonghecun [TJ]	24	C5		Youheji [AH]	44	B2		Yuansha [SH]	38	E3
Yongheguan [SX]	28	B5		Youji [AH]	44	D2		Yuanshanzi [GS]	76	E3
Yongji [JL]	34	F4		Youjia [HN]	56	D4		Yuanshi [HEB]	26	B6
Yongji [SX]	28	B7		Youju [JX]	48	B3		Yuantan [AH]	44	C5
Yongjia [ZJ]	42	D4		Youlan [GX]	60	G3		Yuantan [GD]	58	E3
Yongjing [GS]	76	G5		Youlan [JX]	48	D3		Yuantan [HN]	56	F2
Yongkang [AH]	44	D3		Youmakou [GX]	60	H3		Yuantou [GX]	60	H3
Yongkang [YN]	70	C3		Youquanzi [QH]	78	B1		Yuantou [HEB]	26	B6
Yongkang [ZJ]	42	D4		Youshashan [QH]	78	B1		Yuanwu [HEN]	52	E2
Yonglaxi [SC]	66	D3		Youshui [JX]	48	C6		Yuanxiang [HEN]	52	G3
Yongle Jiang [HN]	56	F5		Youtian [JX]	48	B4		Yuanyang [HEN]	52	E2
Yongle [GX]	60	G2		Youting [CQ]	64	B4		Yuanyang [YN]	70	E4
Yongle [GZ]	68	G4		Youtingxu [HN]	56	D5		Yuanyi [CQ]	64	D3
Yongledian [BJ]	22	D4		Youxi [CQ]	64	C4		Yuanzi He [SX]	28	D2
Yongnian [HEB]	26	B7		Youxi [FJ]	46	D3		Yubug Caka [XZ]	72	F3
Yongnian [HEB]	26	B7		Youxian Qu [SC]	66	F3		Yucai [HI]	62	B3
Yongning Qu [GX]	60	F5		Youxikou [FJ]	46	D3		Yucheng [HEN]	52	E2
Yongning [BJ]	22	C2		Youyang [CQ]	64	E5		Yucheng [SD]	50	C3
Yongning [GD]	58	C4		Youyang [FJ]	46	D4		Yucheng [SD]	50	C5
Yongning [JL]	34	F4		Youyi Feng [XJ]	82	J1		Yuchi [CQ]	64	E3
Yongning [LN]	32	E5		Youyi Shuiku [HEB]	26	B3		Yudao [HI]	62	A3
Yongning [NX]	80	C2		Youyi [HL]	36	F4		Yudaokou [HEB]	26	D1
Yongning [SN]	74	D4		Youyi [SC]	66	C3		Yudi Shan [HL]	36	A1
Yongning [YN]	70	D2		Youyiguan [GX]	60	D6		Yudong [JS]	40	G3
Yongping [JX]	48	E3		Youyu [SX]	28	D1		Yudouquan [BJ]	22	B4
Yongping [SN]	74	E3		Youyu [SX]	28	D1		Yudu [JX]	48	C6
Yongping [YN]	70	C3		Youzhagou [AH]	44	E4		Yudu [SN]	74	C8
Yongping [YN]	70	D4		Yu Shan [JX]	48	C5		Yuebei Qu [CQ]	64	C4
Yongqing [HEB]	26	D4		Yu Ling [ZJ]	42	B3		Yuecheng Ling [HN]	56	D5
Yongquan [ZJ]	42	E4		Yu He [SX]	28	E1		Yuecheng Ling [GX]	60	H2
Yongren [YN]	70	D2		Yu Jiang [CQ]	64	E4		Yuecheng Shuiku [HEB]	26	B7
Yongshan [JX]	48	E2		Yu Jiang [GX]	60	G5		Yuecheng [HEB]	26	B7
Yongshan [YN]	70	E1		Yu Jiang [HB]	54	A5		Yuechi [SC]	66	G3
Yongsheng [YN]	70	D2		Yu Ling [AH]	44	E6		Yuegezhuang [BJ]	22	C5
Yongshou [SN]	74	D6		Yu Shan [JS]	40	F4		Yuehe [HEN]	52	E5
Yongshun [HN]	56	B3		Yu Shan [TW]	88	C3		Yuejiashan [SC]	66	E3
Yongsui [GX]	60	I1		Yu Shan [TW]	88	C3		Yuejin Qu [NX]	80	B3
Yongtai [FJ]	46	D4		Yu Xian [HEB]	26	B4		Yuejin [HI]	62	B2
Yongtai [JX]	48	C4		Yu Xian [SX]	28	E3		Yuejin [SH]	38	C1
Yongxi [AH]	44	D5		Yu Yan [LN]	32	E6		Yuekou [HEB]	54	F4
Yongxin [JX]	48	B5		Yuan Dao [LN]	32	F6		Yuekou [JX]	48	D4
Yongxing [GZ]	68	F3		Yuan Jiang [HN]	56	C3		Yuelai [CQ]	64	E3
Yongxing [HI]	62	C2		Yuan Jiang [YN]	70	D3		Yuele [GS]	76	I4
Yongxing [HN]	56	F5		Yuan Shui [JX]	48	B4		Yueli [GX]	60	E2
Yongxing [YN]	70	D2		Yuan'an [HB]	54	D3		Yueliang Pao [JL]	34	C2
Yongxingqiao [JX]	48	D4		Yuanba Qu [SC]	66	F2		Yuelong [HN]	56	F3
Yongxiu [JX]	48	C2		Yuanbao Shan [GX]	60	G2		Yuelong [TJ]	24	D3
Yongyang [JX]	48	B5		Yuanbaoshan Qu [NM]	30	G4		Yuelu Qu [HN]	56	E3
Yongzhou [HN]	56	D5		Yuanhou [GZ]	68	D2		Yuelu Shan [HN]	56	E3
Yopurga [XJ]	82	E6		Yuanjiang [HN]	56	F3		Yuen Chau [HK]	84	B4
You Jiang [GX]	60	E4		Yuanjiang [YN]	70	E4		Yuen Kong Chau [HK]	84	B4
You Shan [GD]	58	F1		Yuanli [TW]	88	C2		Yuen Long [HK]	84	C2
You Shan [JX]	48	B6		Yuanlin [NM]	30	H2		Yuepu [SH]	38	D2
You Shui [CQ]	64	F5		Yuanlin [TW]	88	C3		Yueqing Wan [ZJ]	42	E4
You Shui [HN]	56	C3		Yuanling [HN]	56	C3		Yueqing [ZJ]	42	D4
You Xi [FJ]	46	D3		Yuanmen [HI]	62	B2		Yu'ershan [HEB]	26	D2
You Xian [HN]	56	F4		Yuanmou [YN]	70	D3		Yu'erya [HEB]	26	F3

Name			Name			Name		
Yueshan [AH]	44	C5	Yung Shue Wan [HK]	84	C4	Yuting [AH]	44	D6
Yuetian [HN]	56	F2	Yung Shue Wan [HK]	84	C4	Yutou [ZJ]	42	B4
Yuetuo [HEB]	26	F4	Yungang [SX]	28	C1	Yuwang [NX]	80	C4
Yuexi He [SC]	66	E4	Yunhe [JS]	40	E1	Yuwang [SX]	28	C6
Yuexi [AH]	44	C5	Yunhe [ZJ]	42	C4	Yuweng Tao [TW]	88	B3
Yuexi [SC]	66	E4	Yunjiang [GX]	60	G3	Yuwu [SX]	28	D5
Yueyahu [NX]	80	C2	Yunkai Dashan [GD]	58	B4	Yuxi He [AH]	44	D4
Yueyang [HN]	56	F2	Yunkai Dashan [GX]	60	H5	Yuxi [FJ]	46	E4
Yueyang [HN]	56	F2	Yunlin [TW]	88	C3	Yuxi [YN]	70	E3
Yuezhangji [AH]	44	C3	Yunlong [HI]	62	C2	Yuxia [SN]	74	D6
Yufa [BJ]	22	C5	Yunlong [YN]	70	C3	Yuxia [YN]	70	F3
Yufeng [GX]	60	E4	Yunlong [YN]	70	D3	Yuxiakou [HB]	54	C4
Yugan [JX]	48	D3	Yunmeng Shan [BJ]	22	D2	Yuxiang [SX]	28	B7
Yugou [AH]	44	D2	Yunmeng [HB]	54	F3	Yuyang [HB]	54	E4
Yuhang Qu [ZJ]	42	D2	Yunmenling [JX]	48	C6	Yuyangguan [HB]	54	D4
Yuhe [GZ]	68	F3	Yunshan [JX]	48	C2	Yuyao [ZJ]	42	E2
Yuhe [SN]	74	E3	Yunshan [JX]	48	D3	Yuzaokou [SX]	28	E3
Yuhong Qu [LN]	32	G3	Yuntai Shan [JS]	40	E1	Yuzhong [GS]	76	H5
Yuhua shan [JX]	48	C4	Yuntai [CQ]	64	D3	Yuzhou [HEN]	52	E3
Yuhua [SN]	74	D5	Yuntian [GS]	76	H5	Yuzhuang [SX]	28	D3
Yuhuan Dao [ZJ]	42	E4	Yunwu Shan [GD]	58	C4	Yuzhuangzi [TJ]	24	C5
Yuhuan [ZJ]	42	E4	Yunwu Shan [HEB]	26	D2	Yuzishan [BJ]	22	E3
Yuhuang Ding [SD]	50	D3	Yunwu [GZ]	68	F4			
Yuhuangmiao [SD]	50	D2	Yunxi Qu [HN]	56	F2	**Z**		
Yujia [JX]	48	E3	Yunxi [HB]	54	C1			
Yujiafang [LN]	32	F3	Yunxiao [FJ]	46	C6	Za Qu [QH]	78	D4
Yujiang [JX]	48	D3	Yunyan He [SH]	38	E3	Zadoi [QH]	78	D4
Yujing Feng [JX]	48	F3	Yunyan He [SN]	74	E4	Za'gya Zangbo [XZ]	72	G3
Yujing [SX]	28	D2	Yunyan [SN]	74	F4	Zaibian [GZ]	68	G5
Yuke [HEB]	26	C6	Yunyang [CQ]	64	E3	Zaima [GZ]	68	G4
Yukou [BJ]	22	E3	Yunyang [HEN]	52	D4	Zalantun [NM]	30	H2
Yuli(Lopnur) [XJ]	82	J5	Yunzhong Shan [SX]	28	D3	Zamtang [SC]	66	D2
Yuli [SD]	50	H2	Yunzhou Shuiku [HEB]	26	C2	Zanda [XZ]	72	B4
Yuli [TW]	88	D3	Yunzhou [HEB]	26	C2	Zangjiazhuang [SD]	50	G2
Yulin He [SN]	74	E2	Yuping [GZ]	68	G3	Zanhuang [HEB]	26	B6
Yulin [GX]	60	H5	Yuqian [ZJ]	42	C2	Zaohe [JS]	40	D1
Yulin [JL]	34	E7	Yuqiao Shuiku [TJ]	24	C2	Zaojiacheng [TJ]	24	C4
Yulin [SN]	74	E2	Yuqiao [NX]	80	B5	Zaojiao [CQ]	64	C4
Yuling Guan [AH]	44	E5	Yuqing [GZ]	68	F3	Zaolinping [SN]	74	F3
Yuling Guan [ZJ]	42	B2	Yuquan [CQ]	64	E2	Zaoqiang [HEB]	26	C6
Yulong Xueshan [YN]	70	D2	Yuquan [HL]	36	D5	Zaoshi [HB]	54	F4
Yulong [SC]	66	F3	Yuquanying [NX]	80	B2	Zaoyang [HB]	54	E2
Yulong [YN]	70	D2	Yurungkax He [XJ]	82	G8	Zaoyuan [NX]	80	B3
Yumen [GS]	76	D2	Yushan Liedao [ZJ]	42	F4	Zaoyuan [SN]	74	E4
Yumenguan [GS]	76	B2	Yushan [CQ]	64	E4	Zaozhuang [SD]	50	D5
Yumenkou [SX]	28	B6	Yushan [FJ]	46	D3	Zapug [XZ]	72	C3
Yumin [XJ]	82	H2	Yushan [JX]	48	F3	Zaqên [QH]	78	D4
Yun Ling [YN]	70	C2	Yushe [GZ]	68	C4	Zawa [QH]	78	G2
Yun Shui [HB]	54	F3	Yushe [SX]	28	D4	Zayü Qu [XZ]	72	K5
Yun Xian [HB]	54	C2	Yushu [JL]	34	F3	Zayü [XZ]	72	K5
Yun Xian [YN]	70	D3	Yushu [LN]	32	H3	Ze Shan [SD]	50	D4
Yun'an [CQ]	64	E2	Yushu [QH]	78	E4	Zêkog [QH]	78	G3
Yunan [GD]	58	C3	Yushuchuan [JL]	34	I5	Zênda [SC]	66	B2
Yun'an [GD]	58	D3	Yushugou [JL]	34	G3	Zeng Jiang [GD]	58	E3
Yunbiao [GX]	60	G5	Yusi [LN]	32	E2	Zengcheng [GD]	58	E3
Yuncao [AH]	44	E4	Yutai [SD]	50	C4	Zengfeng Shan [JL]	34	H5
Yuncheng [SD]	50	B4	Yutai [TJ]	24	B5	Zengmu Ansha [HI]	62	F6
Yuncheng [SX]	28	B6	Yutan [JX]	48	E2	Zengtian [GD]	58	F2
Yunfeng Shuiku [JL]	34	F6	Yutang [HN]	56	E4	Zengtian [JX]	48	C4
Yunfu [GD]	58	D4	Yutian(Keriya) [XJ]	82	G7	Zepu(Poskam) [XJ]	82	E6
Yung Shue Au [HK]	84	E1	Yutian [HEB]	26	E4	Zetouji [SD]	50	H2
Yung Shue O [HK]	84	E2	Yutian [JX]	48	B5	Zezhou [SX]	28	D6
						Zhabei Qu [SH]	38	D3

Zhag'yab [XZ]	72	K4	Zhangjiajing [NX]	80	C4	Zhanjiang [GD]	58	B5
Zhai He [HEN]	52	F5	Zhangjiakou [HEB]	26	B3	Zhanjie [GZ]	68	E4
Zhaiba [GZ]	68	E2	Zhangjialou [SD]	50	F4	Zhanluo [NX]	80	B3
Zhaidian [SX]	28	B6	Zhangjiang [SH]	38	D3	Zhanyi [YN]	70	E3
Zhaigang [GD]	58	D2	Zhangjiashan [JX]	48	C3	Zhanyu [JL]	34	B3
Zhaihao [SD]	50	E2	Zhangjiawan [BJ]	22	D4	Zhao He [HEN]	52	D5
Zhaihe [HEN]	52	F5	Zhangjiawan [NX]	80	C4	Zhao Xian [HEB]	26	B6
Zhaike [NX]	80	C4	Zhangjiawo [TJ]	24	B5	Zhao'an Wan [FJ]	46	C6
Zhaikoucun [BJ]	22	C3	Zhangjiayuan [NX]	80	C4	Zhao'an [FJ]	46	C6
Zhaili [FJ]	46	C2	Zhangjin [HB]	54	E4	Zhaoben [TJ]	24	D4
Zhaiqian [HN]	56	F6	Zhanglan [SX]	28	D4	Zhaobishan [NX]	80	B3
Zhaishi [HN]	56	C5	Zhanglao [GX]	60	E3	Zhaocheng [SX]	28	C5
Zhaitang [BJ]	22	B3	Zhangli [SX]	28	C6	Zhaochuan [HEB]	26	C3
Zhaixi [ZJ]	42	C3	Zhangliang [HEN]	52	E4	Zhaochuan [SN]	74	F7
Zhaixu [GX]	60	G5	Zhangling [HL]	36	B1	Zhaocun [BJ]	22	C5
Zhaizi [HEB]	26	D6	Zhangling [JX]	48	D2	Zhaocun [HEN]	52	D4
Zhajiang [HN]	56	E4	Zhangmu [GX]	60	I3	Zhaodong [HL]	36	C4
Zhajin [JX]	48	B2	Zhangmutou [GD]	58	F4	Zhaogezhuang [HEB]	26	C4
Zhakou [HB]	54	E5	Zhangou [AH]	44	C3	Zhaogezhuang [SD]	50	F3
Zhan He [HL]	36	D3	Zhangping [FJ]	46	C4	Zhaogezhuang [SD]	50	G2
Zhanang [XZ]	72	H5	Zhangpu [FJ]	46	C5	Zhaogezhuang [TJ]	24	B3
Zhanda [AH]	44	D5	Zhangqiang [LN]	32	F2	Zhaoguang [HL]	36	D3
Zhandian [HB]	54	G3	Zhangqiao [HEN]	52	F4	Zhaohe [HEN]	52	D4
Zhandian [HEN]	52	E2	Zhangqiu [SD]	50	D3	Zhaoji [AH]	44	C2
Zhang He [HEB]	26	B7	Zhangsanying [HEB]	26	E2	Zhaojia [CQ]	64	E2
Zhang Jiang [FJ]	46	C5	Zhangshanji [AH]	44	E3	Zhaojiabu [HEB]	26	E5
Zhang Shui [HB]	54	D3	Zhangshanying [BJ]	22	C2	Zhaojue [SC]	66	E4
Zhang Shui [JX]	48	B6	Zhangshe [SD]	50	F3	Zhaokang [SX]	28	C6
Zhang Xian [GS]	76	H5	Zhangshu [HN]	56	F5	Zhaokua [YN]	70	E3
Zhangbaling [AH]	44	E3	Zhangshu [JX]	48	C3	Zhaoling [HN]	56	F4
Zhangbei [HEB]	26	B2	Zhangtai [HEB]	26	C6	Zhaoliqiao [HB]	54	F5
Zhangcun [AH]	44	C2	Zhangtao [HEN]	52	F5	Zhaoping [GX]	60	H3
Zhangcun [HEN]	52	C5	Zhangwan [FJ]	46	E3	Zhaoqing [GD]	58	D3
Zhangcuo [FJ]	46	C2	Zhangwei Xinhe [HEB]	26	D6	Zhaoqizhuang [TJ]	24	B6
Zhangdeng [HEB]	26	C5	Zhangwei Xinhe [SD]	50	C2	Zhaoqu [SX]	28	C6
Zhangdian [AH]	44	C4	Zhangwu [LN]	32	F2	Zhaoshi [HN]	56	B2
Zhangdian [JS]	40	F3	Zhangwu [ZJ]	42	C2	Zhaoshipan [SN]	74	E3
Zhangdian [SX]	28	C7	Zhangxi [AH]	44	D5	Zhaosu(Mongolküre) [XJ]	82	G4
Zhangdian [SX]	28	D5	Zhangxi [JX]	48	D4	Zhaosutai He [LN]	32	G1
Zhangdian [SX]	28	D6	Zhangxi [ZJ]	42	D4	Zhaotan [AH]	44	C6
Zhangdiyingzi [HL]	36	D2	Zhangyan [SH]	38	C4	Zhaotong [YN]	70	E2
Zhangfang [BJ]	22	B5	Zhangyaoxian [SN]	74	C4	Zhaotun [AH]	44	C2
Zhanggezhuang [SD]	50	G3	Zhangye [GS]	76	F3	Zhaotun [SH]	38	C3
Zhanggou [HB]	54	F4	Zhangyi [NX]	80	C5	Zhaowan [SN]	74	E8
Zhangguan [AH]	44	B3	Zhangyuan [SX]	28	D5	Zhaowang He [SD]	50	C4
Zhangguan [SD]	50	C2	Zhangze [SH]	38	C4	Zhaoxian [SD]	50	E4
Zhangguang [AH]	44	D3	Zhangzhen [BJ]	22	E3	Zhaoxian [ZJ]	42	B4
Zhangguangcai Ling [HL]	36	D5	Zhangzheng [NX]	80	C2	Zhaoxie [JX]	48	C4
Zhanggutai [LN]	32	F2	Zhangzhou [FJ]	46	C5	Zhaoxing [HL]	36	F4
Zhanghe Shuiku [HB]	54	D3	Zhangzhu [JS]	40	E4	Zhaoyang Hu [SD]	50	C5
Zhanghuang [GX]	60	G5	Zhangzhuang [HEN]	52	G2	Zhaoyanghe [HEB]	26	B1
Zhangji [AH]	44	B2	Zhangzhuang [JX]	48	B4	Zhaoyuan [HEN]	52	D2
Zhangji [HB]	54	E3	Zhangzhuang [SD]	50	C2	Zhaoyuan [HL]	36	C5
Zhangji [HEB]	26	B2	Zhangzhuang [SD]	50	D4	Zhaoyuan [SD]	50	G2
Zhangji [JS]	40	D1	Zhangzhuang [SD]	50	D4	Zhaozhou [HL]	36	C5
Zhangjia [SD]	50	I2	Zhangzhuang [SD]	50	E3	Zhapo [GD]	58	C5
Zhangjiachuan [GS]	76	I5	Zhangzi Dao [LN]	32	F6	Zhapu [ZJ]	42	E2
Zhangjiadu [AH]	44	E5	Zhangzi [SX]	28	D5	Zhari Namco [XZ]	72	E4
Zhangjiafang [HN]	56	G3	Zhanhe [YN]	70	D2	Zhashui [SN]	74	E7
Zhangjiafen [BJ]	22	D2	Zhanhua [SD]	50	E2	Zhaxigang [XZ]	72	B3
Zhangjiagang [JS]	40	F4	Zhanji [HEN]	52	G3	Zhecheng [HEN]	52	G3
Zhangjiajie [HN]	56	C2	Zhanjiang Gang [GD]	58	B5	Zheduo Shan [SC]	66	D3

Zhefang [YN]	70	C3
Zhegao [AH]	44	D4
Zhehai [YN]	70	E2
Zhehor [SC]	66	D3
Zhejue [GZ]	68	B4
Zhelang [GD]	58	G4
Zhelin Hu [JX]	48	C2
Zhelin [GD]	58	I3
Zhelin [SH]	38	D4
Zhemi [GZ]	68	F5
Zhen Shui [GD]	58	E2
Zhen'an Qu [LN]	32	H4
Zhen'an [SN]	74	E7
Zhenba [SN]	74	C8
Zhenbao Ding [GX]	60	H1
Zhenbaotun [SD]	50	B3
Zhenbeipu [NX]	80	C2
Zhenchengdi [SX]	28	D4
Zhenchuan [SN]	74	F3
Zhenfeng [GZ]	68	D5
Zheng Shui [HN]	56	D4
Zheng'an [GZ]	68	F2
Zheng'an [HEN]	52	E3
Zhengang [JX]	48	C7
Zhengcheng [SD]	50	D4
Zhengdian [SD]	50	D2
Zhengdian [SH]	38	C4
Zhengding [HEB]	26	B5
Zhengfang [JX]	48	E3
Zhenghe [FJ]	46	D2
Zhengji [JS]	40	C1
Zhengjiayi [HN]	56	D3
Zhengjiazhai [SD]	50	C2
Zhenglan (Xulun Hoh) Qi [NM]	30	F4
Zhenglu [GS]	76	G4
Zhengning [GS]	76	J5
Zhengping [JX]	48	B6
Zhengqi [NX]	80	B4
Zhengtun [GZ]	68	D5
Zhengwuji [AH]	44	B3
Zhengxiangbai(Xulun Hobot Qagan) Qi [NM]	30	F4
Zhengxing [YN]	70	D4
Zhengyang [AH]	44	C3
Zhengyang [HEN]	52	F5
Zhengyang [SN]	74	E8
Zhengyi [JS]	40	F4
Zhengzhou [HEN]	52	E3
Zhengzhuang [SX]	28	D6
Zhengzhuang [ZJ]	42	C4
Zhenhai Qu [ZJ]	42	E3
Zhenhai [FJ]	46	D5
Zhenhaijiao [FJ]	46	D5
Zhenjiang [HL]	36	G4
Zhenjiang [JS]	40	E3
Zhenjiangguan [SC]	66	E2
Zhenjiazhuang [SX]	28	E2
Zhenjing [SN]	74	D3
Zhenkang [YN]	70	C4
Zhenlai [JL]	34	C2
Zhenlong [GD]	58	B4
Zhenlong [GX]	60	F5
Zhenluoying [BJ]	22	E3
Zhennan [GZ]	68	F2
Zhennan [JL]	34	C2
Zhenning [GZ]	68	D4
Zhenping [HEN]	52	D4
Zhenping [SN]	74	E9
Zhenqian [FJ]	46	E2
Zhenshang [JX]	48	E3
Zhenxi [CQ]	64	D4
Zhenxi [JL]	34	B2
Zhenxing [LN]	32	H2
Zhenxiong [YN]	70	F2
Zhenyuan [GS]	76	I5
Zhenyuan [GZ]	68	G3
Zhenyuan [YN]	70	D3
Zhenzi [HB]	54	C3
Zheqiao [HN]	56	E5
Zherong [FJ]	46	E2
Zhesang [YN]	70	F4
Zhesi Gou [NX]	80	C4
Zhewang [JS]	40	E1
Zhexi Shuiku [HN]	56	D3
Zhexi [HN]	56	D3
Zhicheng [HB]	54	D4
Zhichuan [SN]	74	F5
Zhidan [SN]	74	D4
Zhidian [HEN]	52	G4
Zhidoi [QH]	78	D4
Zhifang [SD]	50	C4
Zhifu Dao [SD]	50	H2
Zhifu Qu [SD]	50	H2
Zhigoikongma [QH]	78	D3
Zhigou [SD]	50	F4
Zhijiang [HB]	54	D4
Zhijiang [HN]	56	B4
Zhijin [GZ]	68	D4
Zhikun [GZ]	68	D4
Zhiluo [SN]	74	E5
Zhimugkamdo [QH]	78	F4
Zhinü Qu [QH]	74	E3
Zhitan [JX]	48	E2
Zhitang [JS]	40	F4
Zhitian [SN]	74	D5
Zhixia [JX]	48	C5
Zhixitou [ZJ]	42	D4
Zhizhong [HI]	62	B3
Zhong Xian [CQ]	64	E3
Zhong'ao [CQ]	64	B4
Zhongba [GD]	58	G3
Zhongba [HB]	54	C2
Zhongba [XZ]	72	E5
Zhongbao [HB]	54	B5
Zhongbu [JX]	48	E3
Zhongcang [AH]	44	D4
Zhongchao [GZ]	68	H4
Zhongcun [HN]	56	F5
Zhongcun [SD]	50	D4
Zhongcun [SX]	28	C6
Zhongdong [GX]	60	E5
Zhongfan [JX]	48	E3
Zhongfang [HN]	56	B4
Zhongfang [SD]	50	E5
Zhonggang [SH]	38	F4
Zhongguan [JX]	48	D2
Zhonghe [HI]	62	B2
Zhonghe [HL]	36	C4
Zhonghe [HL]	36	E5
Zhonghe [NX]	80	C4
Zhongheying [YN]	70	E4
Zhonghuang [GZ]	68	H4
Zhongji [SN]	74	F1
Zhongjiang [SC]	66	F3
Zhongjieshan Liedao [ZJ]	42	F2
Zhongliang [CQ]	64	F2
Zhongling [JX]	48	D3
Zhonglu [HB]	54	A4
Zhonglupu [HN]	56	E4
Zhongmiao [AH]	44	D4
Zhongmou [HEN]	52	F3
Zhongnan Shan [SN]	74	E7
Zhongning [NX]	80	B3
Zhongping [HI]	62	C2
Zhongruinongchang [HI]	62	C2
Zhongsha Qundao [HI]	62	F5
Zhongsha [FJ]	46	B3
Zhongsha [HI]	62	A3
Zhongshan [FJ]	46	B4
Zhongshan [GD]	58	E4
Zhongshan [GX]	60	I3
Zhongtiao Shan [SX]	28	B7
Zhongwang [TJ]	24	B6
Zhongwei [NX]	80	B3
Zhongxian [FJ]	46	D4
Zhongxiang [HB]	54	E3
Zhongxin [GD]	58	F2
Zhongxin [HL]	36	C4
Zhongxing [AH]	44	C3
Zhongxing [CQ]	64	E3
Zhongxing [HI]	62	B2
Zhongxing [HL]	36	B4
ZhongXingqiao [JS]	40	F2
Zhongxinzhuang [TJ]	24	C5
Zhongyang [SX]	28	C4
Zhongyaozhan [HL]	36	C2
Zhongying [GZ]	68	D4
Zhongyong [GX]	60	H2
Zhongyu [ZJ]	42	C3
Zhongyuan [HI]	62	C2
Zhongyuan [JX]	48	B3
Zhongyun [JX]	48	E2
Zhongzhai [GS]	76	H6
Zhongzhai [GX]	60	G2
Zhongzhai [HN]	56	B4
Zhongzhai [ZJ]	42	F3
Zhongzhan Qu [HEN]	52	E2
Zhongzhou [GD]	58	D2
Zhongzhuangpu [SX]	28	E2
Zhongzui [CQ]	64	D4
Zhou He [SC]	66	G3
Zhou He [TJ]	24	C2
Zhoucheng [NX]	80	C2
Zhoucheng [SD]	50	C4
Zhoucun Qu [SD]	50	D3

Zhoudang [HEN]	52	F6	Zhujia Jian [ZJ]	42	F3	Zi He [SD]	50	E3
Zhougou [HB]	54	E5	Zhujiaba [SN]	74	C8	Zi Qu [QH]	78	E4
Zhouhu [JX]	48	B4	Zhujiajiao [SH]	38	C3	Zishan [JX]	48	C6
Zhouji [AH]	44	C3	Zhujiang Kou [MC]	86	C2	Zi Shui [HN]	56	D3
Zhoujiadian [HN]	56	D2	Zhujiang Kou [MC]	86	D7	Zibo [SD]	50	E3
Zhoujiajing [GS]	76	G3	Zhujiang Kou [GD]	58	E4	Zichang [SN]	74	E3
Zhoujiatun [LN]	32	E3	Zhujiang [JX]	48	B4	Zichuan Qu [SD]	50	D3
Zhoujiaxian [SN]	74	E3	Zhujing [SH]	38	C4	Zidutai [LN]	32	E2
Zhoukou [HEN]	52	F4	Zhukeng [GD]	58	D3	Zigê Tangco [XZ]	72	H3
Zhoukoudian [BJ]	22	C4	Zhukou [FJ]	46	C3	Zigong [SC]	66	F4
Zhouliangzhuang [TJ]	24	C3	Zhulan [JX]	48	C6	Zigui [HB]	54	C4
Zhoulizhuang [TJ]	24	B5	Zhuli [HEN]	52	F4	Zihe [SD]	50	E3
Zhoulu [GX]	60	E4	Zhuliang [JX]	48	D4	Zihong [SX]	28	D4
Zhouning [FJ]	46	E2	Zhulin [JS]	40	E4	Zijiao [SD]	50	D2
Zhoupu [SH]	38	D3	Zhulinguan [SN]	74	F7	Zijin [GD]	58	G3
Zhoushan Dao [ZJ]	42	F2	Zhuliudian [SD]	50	E3	Zijin [HB]	54	D2
Zhoushan Qundao [ZJ]	42	F2	Zhulong [AH]	44	E3	Zijing [GZ]	68	G3
Zhoushan [ZJ]	42	F2	Zhuluke [LN]	32	C3	Zilaiqiao [AH]	44	E3
Zhoutian [JX]	48	C6	Zhumadian [AH]	44	C3	Ziliang [GX]	60	H4
Zhouwangpu [HN]	56	D4	Zhumadian [HEN]	52	F5	Ziliujing Qu [SC]	66	F4
Zhouxi [JX]	48	D2	Zhuo He [CQ]	64	E4	Zimenqiao [HN]	56	E4
Zhouzhi [SN]	74	D6	Zhuogang [HB]	54	H4	Ziqudukou [QH]	78	D4
Zhouzhuang [JS]	40	E3	Zhuolu [HEB]	26	C3	Zitong [SC]	66	F3
Zhouzhuang [JS]	40	F4	Zhuoshui [CQ]	64	E4	Zitong [ZJ]	42	B3
Zhouzhuang [JS]	40	F4	Zhuoshui [GZ]	68	F2	Ziwu He [SN]	74	D7
Zhu Dao [LN]	32	E5	Zhuotian [FJ]	46	B4	Ziwu Ling [GS]	76	J5
Zhu Gang [SH]	38	D3	Zhuozhang He [SX]	28	E5	Zixi [JX]	48	E3
Zhu Jiang [GD]	58	E3	Zhuozhou [HEB]	26	C4	Zixi [JX]	48	E4
Zhuaji [HL]	36	H3	Zuozi [NM]	30	F4	Zixing [HN]	56	F5
Zhuandian [HEN]	52	F5	Zhuqiao [SH]	38	C2	Zixishi [HN]	56	D5
Zhuangbian [FJ]	46	D4	Zhuqiao [SH]	38	D2	Ziya He [HEB]	26	D5
Zhuanghe [LN]	32	F5	Zhuqiao [SH]	38	E3	Ziya He [TJ]	24	A5
Zhuanglang He [GS]	76	G4	Zhuru [HB]	54	F4	Ziyang Qu [HN]	56	E3
Zhuanglang [GS]	76	I5	Zhusha [GD]	58	B4	Ziyang [AH]	44	E2
Zhuanglu [SD]	50	B3	Zhushan [HB]	54	C2	Ziyang [SC]	66	F3
Zhuangma [SX]	28	C6	Zhushan [JX]	48	C3	Ziyang [SN]	74	D8
Zhuangmu [AH]	44	D3	Zhushan [YN]	70	E3	Ziyuan [GX]	60	H1
Zhuangshi [HEN]	52	F3	Zhushi [HN]	56	C4	Ziyun [CQ]	64	C5
Zhuangxi [SD]	50	E1	Zhushui He [SD]	50	C4	Ziyun [GZ]	68	E5
Zhuangxing [SH]	38	D4	Zhutai [SD]	50	E3	Ziyundong Shan [FJ]	46	C4
Zhuangzhai [SD]	50	B4	Zhutan [JX]	48	B3	Ziyunshan Shuiku [JX]	48	C4
Zhuanjing [SN]	74	C3	Zhutian [JX]	48	E3	Zizhong [SC]	66	F4
Zhuankou [HB]	54	G4	Zhuting [HN]	56	F4	Zizhou [SN]	74	F3
Zhuanmiao [SD]	50	B5	Zhuting [SN]	48	B4	Zogang [GZ]	72	K5
Zhuatang [ZJ]	42	D2	Zhuwo [BJ]	22	B3	Zoigê [SC]	66	E2
Zhubi Jiang [HI]	62	B2	Zhuxi [HB]	54	B2	Zong'ai [SX]	28	E4
Zhubijiang Nongchang [HI]	62	B2	Zhuxi [ZJ]	42	D4	Zongpu [AH]	44	D3
Zhubu [AH]	44	C4	Zhuxiang [AH]	44	D3	Zongyang [AH]	44	D5
Zhucang [GZ]	68	D4	Zhuxianzhen [HEN]	52	F3	Zongza [SC]	66	C4
Zhucheng [SD]	50	F4	Zhuxianzhuang [AH]	44	D2	Zoucheng [SD]	50	C4
Zhugan He [HEN]	52	F6	Zhuya [SD]	50	E3	Zoulang Nanshan [GS]	76	E3
Zhuge [SD]	50	E3	Zhuyangguan [HEN]	52	C4	Zoulang Nanshan [QH]	78	F1
Zhuge [ZJ]	42	C3	Zhuyangzhen [HEN]	52	B3	Zouma [GX]	60	H3
Zhugou [HEN]	52	E5	Zhuyu [SC]	66	G2	Zouma [HB]	54	C5
Zhugou [SD]	50	G3	Zhuzang [GZ]	68	F3	Zouping [SD]	50	D3
Zhugqu [GS]	76	H6	Zhuzhai [SH]	38	D3	Zouxu [GX]	60	F4
Zhuguang Shan [HN]	56	F6	Zhuzhao Xinhe [SD]	50	B4	Zuli He [GS]	76	H4
Zhuguang Shan [JX]	48	A6	Zhuzhou [HN]	56	F4	Zunhua [HEB]	26	E3
Zhuguansi [HN]	56	E6	Zhuzhou [HN]	56	F4	Zuntan [HI]	62	C2
Zhuhai [GD]	58	E4	Zhuzhuang Shuiku [HEB]	26	B6	Zunyi [GZ]	68	E3
Zhuique [GZ]	68	D4	Zhuzhuang [SD]	50	B3	Zunyi [GZ]	68	E3
Zhuji [ZJ]	42	D3	Zi He [HN]	56	E2	Zuo Jiang [GX]	60	E5

Zuo'an [JX]	48	B5
Zuoba [AH]	44	C5
Zuodeng [GX]	60	E4
Zuohui [SX]	28	E5
Zuojia [JL]	34	F3
Zuoquan [SX]	28	E4
Zuoshan [SD]	50	F3
Zuoshi [HN]	56	D2
Zuoyun [SX]	28	D1
Zuozhou [GX]	60	E5

World Heritage and important scenic area

A—Ma Temple [MC]	86	A2
Alu Caves [YN]	70	E3
Ancient City of Pingyao [SX]	28	D4
Ancient Villages in Southern Anhui [AH]	44	D6
Badabu—Jingyue L. [JL]	34	E4
Bailong Lake [SC]	66	F2
Baiyun Cave in Mt. Kongshan [HEB]	26	B6
Baiyun Hill [GD]	58	E3
Baizhangji—Feiyun Lake [ZJ]	42	D5
Bamboo Forest in Southern Sichuan [SC]	66	F4
Benxi Water Cave [LN]	32	H3
Bosten L. [XJ]	82	J5
Caishi [AH]	44	E4
Capital Cities and Tombs of the Ancient Koguryo Kingdom [JL]	34	F6
Capital Cities and Tombs of the Ancient Koguryo Kingdom [LN]	32	I3
Chaohu Lake [AH]	44	D4
Chengde Mountain Resort [HEB]	26	F3
Chishui [GZ]	68	D2
Classical Gardens of Suzhou [JS]	40	F4
Dali [YN]	70	D3
Dalian Seashore—Lüshunkou [LN]	32	E6
Daying River [YN]	70	B3
Dazu Rock Carvings [CQ]	64	B4
Dianchi Lake [YN]	70	E3
Dianshan Hu [SH]	38	C3
Dongting Lake [HN]	56	E2
Dragon Palace [GZ]	68	D4
E. Qing Tombs [HEB]	26	E3
East Lake [HB]	54	G4
Fangchuan [JL]	34	J5
Fangyan [ZJ]	42	D4
Fuchun River—Xin'an River [ZJ]	42	C3
Furong R. [CQ]	64	D4
Gate of Understanding [MC]	86	A3

Giant Panda Sanctuaries [SC]	66	E3
Gorge Maling River [GZ]	68	C5
Guia Lighthouse [MC]	86	B2
Guiteng Peak [JX]	48	E3
Gulang Islet—Mt. Wanshi [FJ]	46	D5
Haitan Island [FJ]	46	E4
Hongfeng Lake [GZ]	68	E4
Huangguoshu Waterfall [GZ]	68	D4
Huanglong [SC]	66	E2
Huangpu Jiang [SH]	38	D3
Huanjiang R.—Wuxie [ZJ]	42	D3
Huashan Mysterious Grottoes Jianjiang River [AH]	44	E6
Huguangyan Lake [GD]	58	B5
Hukou Waterfall [SX]	28	B5
Jianmen Pass [SC]	66	F2
Jianshui [YN]	70	E4
Jiaodong Peninsula Seashore [SD]	50	H2
Jihyueh Lake [TW]	88	C3
Jingpo Lake [HL]	36	E6
Jinhu Lake [FJ]	46	C3
Jinshi Beach [LN]	32	E5
Jiudongtian [GZ]	68	D4
Jiulong Cave [GZ]	68	H3
Jiuxiang [YN]	70	E3
Jiuzhaigou [SC]	66	E2
Kaiping Diaolou and Villages [GD]	58	D4
King's Mausoleum of Western Xia Dynasty [NX]	80	B2
Kumtag Desert [XJ]	82	L4
Kun Iam Temple [MC]	86	B1
Kun Iam Statue [MC]	86	B2
Lijiang River [GX]	60	H2
Lin Fong Temple [MC]	86	B1
Lipin Dong Village [GZ]	68	H4
Longmen Grottoes [HEN]	52	D3
Longzhong [HB]	54	E3
Loulan Site [XJ]	82	K5
Lushui Lake [HB]	54	F5
Macau Tower [MC]	86	A3
Mausoleum of Emperor Huangdi [SN]	74	E5
Mausoleum of the First Qin Emperor [SN]	74	E6
Mengdong River [HN]	56	B3
Ming Tombs [BJ]	22	C3
Mogao Caves [GS]	76	C3
Mt. Ali [TW]	88	C3
Mt. Boshan [SD]	50	D3
Mt. Cangyan [HEB]	26	B6
Mt. Dahong [HB]	54	E3
Mt. Danxia [GD]	58	E1
Mt. Doupeng—Jianjiang River [GZ]	68	F4
Mt. Gongga [SC]	66	D4
Mt. Guanzhai [FJ]	46	B4
Mt. Gushan [FJ]	46	E3
Mt. Hengshan [HN]	56	E4
Mt. Huangshan [AH]	44	E5
Mt. Huashan [GX]	60	E5

Mt. Jigong [HEN]	52	F6
Mt. Jinfo [CQ]	64	D4
Mt. Jinggang [JX]	48	B5
Mt. Jinyun [CQ]	64	C4
Mt. Jiugong [HB]	54	G5
Mt. Jiuhua [AH]	44	D5
Mt. Kongtong [GS]	76	I5
Mt. Langshan [HN]	56	C5
Mt. Langya [AH]	44	E3
Mt. Laoshan [SD]	50	G3
Mt. Linlü [HEN]	52	E1
Mt. Longhu [JX]	48	D3
Mt. Luofu [GD]	58	E3
Mt. Lushan [JX]	48	C2
Mt. Maiji [GS]	76	I5
Mt. Meiling—Tengwang Tower [JX]	48	C3
Mt. Mogan [ZJ]	42	C2
Mt. Panshan [TJ]	24	C1
Mt. Putuo [ZJ]	42	F2
Mt. Qingyuan [FJ]	46	D5
Mt. Qingyun [FJ]	46	D4
Mt. Qiyun [AH]	44	E6
Mt. Sanbai [JX]	48	C6
Mt. Sanqing [JX]	48	F3
Mt. Shaoshan [HN]	56	E4
Mt. Shiren [HEN]	52	D4
Mt. Simian [CQ]	64	C5
Mt. Songshan [HEN]	52	E3
Mt. Taimu [FJ]	46	F2
Mt. Taishan [SD]	50	D3
Mt. Tiantai [ZJ]	42	E3
Mt. Tianzhu [AH]	44	C5
Mt. Wangwu [HEN]	52	D2
Mt. Wudang [HB]	54	D2
Mt. Wuyi [FJ]	46	C2
Mt. Xiqiao [GD]	58	D4
Mt. Xishan [GX]	60	G4
Mt. Xuedou [ZJ]	42	E3
Mt. Yuelu [HN]	56	E3
Mt. Yuntai [HEN]	52	E2
Mt. Yuntai [JS]	40	E1
Mt. Emei [SC]	66	E4
Mt. Fenghuang [LN]	32	H4
Mt. Guangwu—Nuoshui R. [SC]	66	G2
Mt. Hengshan [SX]	28	E2
Mt. Huashan [SN]	74	F6
Mt. Jianglang [ZJ]	42	B4
Mt. Leshan Giant Buddha [SC]	66	E4
Mt. Longmen [SC]	66	E3
Mt. Qianshan [LN]	32	G4
Mt. Qingcheng-Dujiangyan [SC]	66	E3
Mt. Siguniang [SC]	66	E3
Mt. Tiantai [SC]	66	E3
Mt. Tiantai [SN]	74	C6
Mt. Wutai [SX]	28	E2
Mt. Yandang [ZJ]	42	E4
Mt. Yiwulü [LN]	32	E3
Nanxi River [ZJ]	42	D4

North Wudang Mts. [SX]   28   C4
Old Town of Lijiang [YN]   70   D2
Olympic Rowing—
Canoeing Park [BJ]   22   D3
Palace Museum [BJ]   22   D4
Peking Man Site at
Zhoukoudian [BJ]   22   C4
Potala Palace [XZ]   72   H5
Puzhehei [YN]   70   F3
Qiachuan [SN]   74   F5
Qinghai Lake [QH]   78   G2
Qingshan valley [LN]   32   I3
Qingzhou [SD]   50   E3
Qinhuangdao—
Beidaihe [HEB]   26   G4
Qionghai Lake—
Mt. Luoji [SC]   66   E5
Ruili River [YN]   70   B4
Ruins of St. Paul's [MC]   86   B2
Sairam L. [XJ]   82   G3
Sanshan Island [JS]   40   E3
Sanya Tropical Seashore [HI]   62   B3
Shengsi Islands [ZJ]   42   F2
Shenyang
Imperial Palace [LN]   32   G3
Shibachongxi R. [FJ]   46   E4
Shihai Dongxiang karst [SC]   66   F4
Shihua Cave [BJ]   22   C4
Shuanglong [ZJ]   42   C3
Shugang Hill—Slim
West Lake [JS]   40   E3
Singing Sand Dune—
Crescent Moon Spring [GS]   76   C2

Songhua Lake [JL]   34   F4
South China Karst [CQ]   64   D4
South China Karst [GZ]   68   G5
South China Karst [YN]   70   E3
Star Lake [GD]   58   D3
Statue of A—Ma [MC]   86   C6
Stone Forest [YN]   70   E3
Summer Palace [BJ]   22   C3
Taihu Lake [JS]   40   F4
Taiji Cave [AH]   44   F4
Taohuayuan [HN]   56   D3
Taoyuan Cave—Linyin
Stone Forest [FJ]   46   C3
Temple of Heaven [BJ]   22   D4
Temple, Cemetery and
Mansion of Confucius [SD]   50   C4
Tengchong Hot Spring
and Volcanoes [YN]   70   C3
The Great Wall at
Badaling [BJ]   22   C2
The Great Wall at
Jiayuguan [GS]   76   E3
The Historic Centre
of Macau [MC]   86   B2
Three Gorges of
Yangtze R. [CQ]   64   G2
Three Parellel Rivers [YN]   70   C2
Three Tombs of
Sheng Jing Dynasty [LN]   32   G3
Tianchi L. [XJ]   82   K4
Tiankengdifeng [CQ]   64   F3
W. Qing Tombs [HEB]   26   C4
West Lake [GD]   58   F3

West Lake [ZJ]   42   D2
Wudalianchi [HL]   36   D3
Wulao Peak [SX]   28   B7
Wulingyuan [HN]   56   C2
Wuyang River [GZ]   68   G3
Xiandu [ZJ]   42   D4
Xianjingtai [JL]   34   H5
Xianju [ZJ]   42   D4
Xianling Tomb [HB]   54   E3
Xiannu Lake [JX]   48   B4
Xiaoling Tomb [JS]   40   D3
Xibaipo—Mt. Tiangui [HEB]   26   A5
Xiling Snow Mountain [SC]   66   E3
Xingcheng Seashore [LN]   32   D4
Xishuangbanna [YN]   70   D5
Yalong River [XZ]   72   H5
Yalu River [LN]   32   H4
Yesanpo [HEB]   26   C4
Yin Xu [HEN]   52   F1
Yuanyang Stream [FJ]   46   E2
Yueyang Tower [HN]   56   F2
Yuhua Cave [FJ]   46   C3
Yulong Snow Mountain [YN]   70   D2
Yungang Grottoes [SX]   28   E1
Zalantun [NM]   30   H2
Zhangjiang River in Libo [GZ]   68   F5
Zhangshiyan [HEB]   26   B6
Zhijin Cave [GZ]   68   D4

Responsible Editor: Di Xiangping

Text Editor: Liu Hongtao

Computer Mapping: Wang Hongbo, Liu Yanling, Zhao Juan, Zhang Shiqi

Proofreaders: Du Huaijing, Zhang Hong, Di Xiangping

Tai Xiangrong

Examiners: Lu Yongsen, Fan Yi